CHIPPENDALE FURNITURE

A. A lacquered and japanned 'Pagoda Cabinet'. *Mrs. R. Meade–Fetherstonhaugh,*
Uppark, Sussex.
Photograph and block courtesy of The Connoisseur.

CHIPPENDALE FURNITURE

circa 1745—1765

The Work of Thomas Chippendale
and his Contemporaries in the Rococo Taste

Vile, Cobb, Langlois, Channon, Hallett, Ince and Mayhew,

Lock, Johnson,

and others

by

ANTHONY COLERIDGE

 *Clarkson N. Potter, Inc./Publisher* **NEW YORK**

Distributed by Crown Publishers, Inc.

IN MEMORY OF
K.C.C.

Acknowledgements

The illustrations of furniture from the Royal Collections are reproduced by gracious permission of H.M. The Queen.

Grateful acknowledgement is made under the captions, accompanying each photograph, to the owners of pieces illustrated and for the use of photographs. I am deeply indebted to all of them.

So many have helped and encouraged me during the preparation of this book that it is invidious to single out so few, but I must thank Mr. John Lowe, the original editor of this Series, and Mr. Clifford Musgrave, both of whom persuaded me to write the book, Mr. Peter Thornton, the present editor of the Series, and Mr. Paul Dinnage, who both so expertly and meticulously read my typescripts and who, by doing so, vastly improved them, Mr. John Hayward, Mrs. John Hayward, Mr. Peter Ward-Jackson, Mr. John Hardy and Mr. Alex Lewis who also, so kindly, read my typescripts.

I am further deeply indebted to Mr. Ralph Edwards and the late Miss Margaret Jourdain, the authors of *Georgian Cabinet-Makers*, as, in the preparation of my book, I have found theirs to be an inestimable help. Finally, I would like to thank the Editors of *Apollo*, *The Connoisseur* and *Country Life* who have allowed me to quote so freely from articles, published by them, which I have previously written on subjects dealt with in this book. I trust that all the others who have encouraged and helped me have been thanked in the text and footnotes and, if any are not, I hope that they will forgive me.

Editor's Foreword

The name of Chippendale is one to conjure with. Indeed, many dealers and collectors have conjured with it to advantage over the past seventy years or so! His was in fact the only name of an English eighteenth-century cabinet-maker that has been handed down to us by successive generations, a name that had come to signify quality and elegance — and all the refinement of that dazzling age.

Later research has done little to reduce the stature of Thomas Chippendale. It is clear that he was one of the great cabinet-makers of his day, that he provided furniture (and furnishings of all kinds) for many of the most splendid houses in the land, and that he was an enterprising businessman as well. But more recent research has now shown that there were half-a-dozen other cabinet-makers of equal stature working in London during the middle decades of the eighteenth century. Moreover, the identity of a shoal of lesser furniture-makers has slowly begun to take shape.

During the past decade or so, no one has done so much as Mr. Coleridge to further our knowledge of this important phase in the history of English furniture. By his energetic investigations and his flair for recognising the furniture itself, he has already established himself among the foremost scholars in this field — and he has revived the memory and identified the work of several long-forgotten but important cabinet-makers of the period.

Students of English furniture are thus already indebted to Mr. Coleridge, but their debt is likely to be greatly increased with the publication of this book, in which he assembles all the information we have about the principal mid-eighteenth-century English makers. This represents a considerable feat in itself, since much of the information he produces has had to be unearthed in obscure corners. Moreover, conflicting views have had to be evaluated and the chief arguments succinctly stated. And finally, no small amount of quite fresh information is here published for the first time. Although this book will no doubt have to be revised every now and then, in the light of subsequent research, it will certainly remain one of the corner-stones of studies in this field for a very long time.

By publishing a book of furniture designs, Chippendale lent his name to a whole style. It was a style adopted by most of his contemporaries in his native country, and imitated — with varying degrees of success — all over Northern Europe, in Portugal, in Spain, and in the North American Colonies. It is a style that has been much beloved by the producer of reproduction furniture over the past century. And it is a style of furniture that, more than 'Queen Anne', more than 'Adam', more than 'Sheraton', is so very characteristically

EDITOR'S FOREWORD

English, even though it was an off-shoot of Continental Rococo and thus had most of its roots abroad. Any work that further reveals the characteristics of this style will be widely welcomed; any work that increases our understanding of this great period of English cabinet-making is likely to be appreciated all over the civilised world. Mr. Coleridge's book does just this.

PETER THORNTON

Contents

ACKNOWLEDGEMENTS   *page*   7

EDITOR'S FOREWORD   9

ILLUSTRATIONS   13

INTRODUCTION   17

CHAPTER I   VILE, COBB, LANGLOIS, CHANNON, AND HALLET   19

II   ENGLISH ROCOCO DESIGNERS (excluding Chippendale)   47

III   THOMAS CHIPPENDALE (1719–79)

Part I : His Life   73

Part II : *The Director*   80

Part III : His Clients   105

IV   SOME LEADING CABINET-MAKERS WORKING IN THE *Director* TRADITION   133

NOTES TO THE ILLUSTRATIONS   172

SELECT BIBLIOGRAPHY   216

ARTICLES QUOTED   217

INDEX   221

Illustrations

COLOUR PLATES

A   A lacquered and japanned 'Pagoda Cabinet'   *frontispiece*
B   A lacquered commode, from a set of four, at Uppark   *facing page 36*
C   The 'Chippendale' bedstead from Badminton House   *facing page 98*

MONOCHROME PLATES
at the end of the book

	Plates nos.
Pieces supplied by, or in the manner of, WILLIAM VILE	1–37
Pieces supplied by, or in the manner of, JOHN COBB	38–44
Examples of English inlaid case-furniture, *c.* 1760–65	45–49
Pieces supplied by, or in the manner of, PIERRE LANGLOIS	50–59
Pieces supplied by, or in the manner of, JOHN CHANNON	60–66
Pieces supplied by, or in the manner of, WILLIAM HALLETT	67–72
A chair inspired by a design of, GAETANO BRUNETTI	73
Designs and pieces by, or in the manner of, JOHN VARDY	74–83
Pieces supplied by, or in the manner of, WILLIAM and JOHN GORDON	82–88
A table after a design by WILLIAM JONES	89
Designs and pieces by, or in the manner of, MATTHIAS LOCK	90–98
Designs and pieces by, or in the manner of, THOMAS JOHNSON	99–114
Pieces carved by, or in the manner of, GEORGE COLE	100–102
	104
Designs and pieces by, or in the manner of, WILLIAM INCE and JOHN MAYHEW	115–126
Designs and pieces by, or in the manner of, JOHN LINNELL	127–131
Designs and pieces by, or in the manner of, ROBERT MANWARING and MATHEW DARLY	132–145
A dolls' house, *c.* 1740, at Nostell Priory	146
A contemporary map of London showing St. Martin's Lane	147
Pieces in the Gothic Taste	148–163
Examples of, and a *Director* design for, 'Dressing Tables'	164–166
Examples of seat-furniture and some *Director* designs	167–205
Examples of bedsteads	206–207

MONOCHROME PLATES

Plates nos.

Examples of, and a *Director* design for, 'Breakfast Tables' — 208–211
Examples of china and side-tables — 212–218
Examples of, and a *Director* design for, 'Shaving Tables' and 'Bason Stands' — 219–223
Examples of tripod-tables and dumb-waiters — 224–228
Examples of, and a *Director* design for, 'Buroe-Tables' — 229–232
Examples of, and a *Director* design for, 'French Commode Tables' — 233–239
Examples of, and a *Director* design for, 'Writing Tables' — 240–244
Examples of, and a *Director* design for, library-tables — 245–249
Examples of, and a *Director* design for, bookcases — 250–258
A 'Chamber Organ', and a *Director* design for it — 259–260
A 'Dressing Chest' and writing-tables — 261–263
Examples of, and a *Director* design for, 'China Cases' — 264–268
Examples of display-cabinets, etc. — 269–273
Examples of wardrobes — 274–276
Examples of, and a *Director* design for, 'Hanging Shelves', etc. — 277–284
Examples of *what-nots* in the *Director* tradition — 285–286
Examples of, and a *Director* design for, 'Candle Stands' — 287–294
Examples of lanterns and chandeliers — 295–299
Examples of fire-screens — 300–304
Examples of 'brackets for Bustos' — 305–306
A longcase-clock of *Director* design — 307
Examples of, and a *Director* design for, 'Gerandoles' — 308–315
Examples of pier-glasses, overmantles, etc. — 316–324
Examples of, and a *Director* design for, mantlepieces — 324–326
Examples of Chinese mirror pictures, etc. — 327–331
Examples of 'Chippendale' furniture from Badminton House* — 332–333
Examples of commodes faced with panels of 'coromandel' lacquer — 334–337
A stool supplied by Chippendale for Christ Church, Oxford — 338
A *bonheur-du-jour* from Coombe Abbey,* etc. — 339–340
An armchair from Corsham Court* — 341
Examples of 'Chippendale' furniture at Harewood House* — 342–344
Examples of 'Chippendale' furniture at Nostell Priory,* etc. — 345–360
Examples of 'Chippendale' furniture at Paxton House* — 361–363
A side-table from Raynham Hall* — 364
Examples of 'Chippendale' furniture at St. Giles's House* — 365–366
An armchair made by Chippendale to an Adam design for 19, Arlington Street* — 367
Pieces supplied by, or in the manner of, BENJAMIN GOODISON — 368–371 380
Pieces supplied by, or in the manner of, GILES GRENDEY — 372–377
Pieces supplied by PAUL SAUNDERS — 378–379
Pieces supplied by JAMES WHITTLE and SAMUEL NORMAN — 381–385
A settee supplied by SAMUEL FELL and WILLIAM TURTON — 386

MONOCHROME PLATES

	Plates nos.
Pieces supplied by, or in the manner of, Messrs. FRANCE and BRADBURN	387–393
A bookcase supplied by Messrs. GILLOWS of LANCASTER	394
An account and pieces presented and supplied by WILLIAM MASTERS	395–402
A portrait of, and pieces supplied by, GEORGE SANDEMAN of PERTH	403–406
Designs and pieces supplied by, or in the manner of, JAMES CULLEN	407–419
A 'pagoda cabinet' of *Director* design	420

*Other pieces from these 'Chippendale' houses are illustrated in plates 146–331.

Introduction

The aim of this book is to discuss, in some detail, the history of English furniture and its design from about 1745 to about 1765. These twenty years may be taken to cover the short period in the evolution of furniture design in this Country when the imported Rococo style, in its fully developed form, was all the rage. The gestation, birth and growth of the Rococo style on the Continent, especially in France, is discussed in Chapter II, while the peculiarly English adaptation of it is described in Chapter III. It is difficult to define what is meant by 'Rococo', but one might say it is a style in which the decoration takes the form of living amorphous organisms combined with an unnatural, and essentially assymetrical, mixture of vegetable and rock-like features. The very elusiveness of the words with which one can adequately describe Rococo ornament helps to explain why the designers were able to express themselves so freely in their interpretation of it.

The study of English furniture is, in my opinion, based on the lives and work of the men who actually designed and made the individual pieces, and this book is therefore, in the main, devoted to the discussion of such craftsmen who flourished during 'the Rococo period'. Thomas Chippendale, with some justice, has for long been the most celebrated of these, and his name has now been taken by many to epitomise the period under discussion. He was, in fact, by no means 'head and shoulders' above his contemporaries, as will become evident in this book. But because he published *The Gentleman and Cabinet-Maker's Director*, the most important book of furniture designs of the period, his name became immortalised many years before those of some of his equally important rivals were rediscovered. Posterity plays strange tricks. Had Vile, Cobb or Hallett published design-books of equal magnitude, they might well have lent their names to this period of English furniture in the place of Thomas Chippendale.

The Director may be claimed to epitomise the English interpretation of the 'Rococo' phase in the field of furniture design, but it will be seen that 'Neo-classicism' had already begun to take its place soon after the publication of its third edition in 1762. Chippendale, and many of the other cabinet-makers discussed in this book, gradually deserted the now outmoded Rococo and worked in this new style. There was obviously a period of 'Transition' between the two, as in France between the so-called 'Louis XV' and 'Louis XVI' styles. Pieces from this Transitional period are described here, but those falling into the Neo-Classical period are fully discussed by Mr. Clifford Musgrave in his companion book

INTRODUCTION

in this Series, *Adam and Hepplewhite and other Neo-Classical Furniture*. The careers of many eminent craftsmen are thus discussed in these two books, but from two very different points of view. This division was inevitable on account of the vast subject matter and the complete antithesis of the Rococo and the Neo-Classic styles. Thus Chippendale's important work in the neo-classical tradition at Harewood House and Nostell Priory, for example, are beyond the scope of the present work, but are discussed by Mr. Musgrave. All the same, the two books inevitably overlap and the same items are, in some cases, referred to. However the Dundas Suite of Seat-furniture (p. 122), which is patently Neo-Classic, is included here, as the highly significant discovery of the fact that it was made by Chippendale to Adam's design — thus finally establishing the relationship between the two — was discovered after *Adam and Hepplewhite Furniture* had been sent to press. The two books should therefore be read in conjunction with one another.

This book is divided into four chapters. The first deals with the careers and work of Thomas Chippendale's most celebrated rivals — Vile, Cobb, Langlois, Hallett, and the newly-discovered John Channon. The second is devoted to the professional designers, some of whom, were also cabinet-makers, such as Ince and Mayhew. Copland's career, however, is discussed with that of Chippendale's in Chapter 3. Lastly, some cabinet-makers, who might be described as forming 'the Second Eleven', but all men of considerable importance, are discussed in Chapter IV.

ANTHONY COLERIDGE
London 1967

CHAPTER I

Vile, Cobb, Langlois, Channon, and Hallett

In this chapter the careers and *oeuvre* of the cabinet-makers, Vile, Cobb, Langlois, Channon, and Hallett are discussed — in that order. Vile and Cobb can probably be taken to have been Chippendale's most serious rivals. The real importance of the other three has only recently become established. Much, however, still remains to be discovered about these men.

The firm of Messrs. Vile and Cobb is first recorded in the *London Directory* in 1750 and their names continue to be entered together there until 1765. From the following year, Vile's name ceases to be mentioned and the firm is merely described as *John Cobb, Upholsterer*, until 1778.[1] It thus would appear that Vile retired sometime during the year of 1765 — probably on account of ill-health — and that Cobb carried on their business by himself until his death on 24th August, 1778.[2] Throughout this period the business premises were at 72 St. Martin's Lane, which is on the corner where it joins Long Acre.

William Vile has, probably quite correctly, always been accepted as the dominant member of the partnership and, in this connection, it is interesting to note that the two partners are always referred to differently in the Lord Chamberlain's Accounts with regard to the work that they carried out for the Royal Family.[3] Vile is classified as *Cabinet-Maker* and Cobb only as *Upholsterer* — and then only in conjunction with Vile's name. The whole question of the formation of partnerships between cabinet-makers during the latter half of the eighteenth century is extremely complex, but it would generally appear that cabinet-makers tended to form partnerships with *upholsterers*. The author has discussed this relationship in his article 'Vile and Cobb, and France and Bradburn at The Vyne',[4] in which it was shown that both Cobb and France appear to have been specialist upholsterers, at any rate when they were working for the Crown. This is probably the reason why Cobb was not appointed *Cabinet-maker to the Royal Household* in Vile's place when the latter disappears from the scene in 1765. In fact John Bradburn, Vile's one-time assistant, was nominated to this prestige post, and Vile may well have pressed the former's suit when he realised that his partner, Cobb, had not got the necessary qualifications for the

---

[1] The last recorded reference to the firm is in the *1778 London Directory* in which the address is given as 73 St. Martin's Lane. It thus appears that Cobb, at this date, owned No. 73 in addition to No. 72.

[2] *Gentleman's Magazine*, 1778, p. 835.

[3] H. Clifford-Smith, *Buckingham Palace*, 1930, p. 74, note 3.

[4] Anthony Coleridge, 'Eighteenth Century Furniture at The Vyne', *Country Life*, 25 July 1963.

appointment. Cobb however took a far greater interest in the cabinet-making side of the business after Vile's retirement as will be shown later in this chapter.

The partners enjoyed the highest reputation during the mid-decades of the century — as is shown by the list of their important clients, the references to them in the contemporary literature, and the high quality of their surviving work. However, in order to remain fashionable and to retain their position at the top of the ladder in their trade, it was necessary to acquire premises in St. Martin's Lane, then the centre of the cabinet-making trade. It was for this reason that they moved to No. 72 in 1750 and found themselves next door to the famous cabinet-maker William Hallett (see below), and ten doors away from Thomas Chippendale. The business careers of the two partners are naturally bound up with one another but, as far as is possible, they will be discussed separately.

Before tracing the careers of Vile and Cobb the question of attributing furniture to them on stylistic grounds must be considered. It has now become common practice in some museums, auction houses and the antique trade alike to hang Vile and Cobb's label on any piece of high-quality furniture of the correct date that incorporates any of the decorative features which have become associated with their styles. Mr. Ralph Edwards utters a stern warning when discussing this question and claims that 'the practice of assigning furniture to this maker on inadequate evidence has increased, is increasing and ought to be diminished — to adapt a famous Parliamentary pronouncement made in his (Vile's) lifetime. . . . Vile published no designs, nor are any original drawings by him known and these important facts should be borne in mind by those who light-heartedly invoke his name.'[1] Furthermore, it will be shown below that the celebrated cabinet-maker, William Hallett, almost certainly worked in conjunction with Vile and Cobb, and that he, as is the case with France, Bradburn, Beckwith, Graham, Jenkins, Strickland and others (see below) — all of whom had links with Vile and Cobb or with one another — may easily have been responsible for many of the pieces that are so glibly attributed to the partners. It must therefore be remembered that when the pieces discussed in this chapter are ascribed to Vile, Cobb, Langlois, Channon or Hallett, they are in fact being associated with the *styles* in which these cabinet-makers are known to have worked, and not necessarily with the men themselves, or their firms. Mr. Ralph Edwards again writes pertinently in this connection when he says, 'While the stylistic test can supply reliable evidence, it calls for caution and is open to abuse. Comparisons may show parallelisms or tricks of handling that may at first sight appear conclusive, and other evidence may support the test; but if a skilled carver transferred his services, his distinctive repertory of ornament might be expected to figure in the productions of a rival firm. The apprentices of leading makers, starting business on their own account,[2] would be likely to take in some of their former master's employees and at that period partnerships were seldom of long duration. Finally, it is well to remember that furniture cannot be assigned to cabinet-makers of the eighteenth century in the same sense as pictures. For all we know Vile and Cobb may have retained a designer, a professional ornamentalist, who would have done for them what Lock and Copland did for Chippendale and to whom much of the credit for their achievement would be due.'

[1] Ralph Edwards, 'Attributions to William Vile', *Country Life*, 7 October 1954.
[2] *e.g.* Jenkins and Strickland (see below, in the text) and Bradburn, p. 145.

It is neither known where William Vile had his premises prior to his move to St. Martin's Lane in 1750, nor is it recorded whether he formed his partnership with Cobb before this date. The earliest pieces of furniture that can reasonably be attributed to Vile are in the Baroque manner associated with Lord Burlington and William Kent. In fact a mahogany library writing-table (Pl. 1) which it has been previously suggested may have been designed by Kent for Chiswick House in about 1730, may be one of the earliest pieces made by Vile — or must, at any rate, be the kind of furniture from which his style derives. A suite of furniture, which was ordered by Sir Thomas Robinson[1] of Rokeby Hall, Yorkshire, is perhaps amongst the earliest pieces that can be attributed to Vile. It consists of a pair of *back-to-back* library tables (Pl. 2), a pair of commodes,[2] and a buffet. The owls on the Chiswick House example (Pl. 1) have now given way to scrolled consoles carved with acanthus foliage and consoles with overlapping money-pattern mouldings surmounted by lion-masks and rings (Pl. 2). The rosette-and-trellis, Greek key-pattern, and ribbon-and-rosette motifs which Vile favoured so much during later years are here first employed. The whole suite is still baroque in conception but Vile has already managed to stamp some of his individuality on the Kentian formula. There is a similar commode at Alnwick Castle, Northumberland, which also came from Yorkshire.[3] It was originally at Stanwick House in the bedroom of Lady Elizabeth Smithson (later Duchess of Northumberland). It can be dated exactly as it is mentioned in a letter to her mother, the Countess of Hertford, written on 8th August, 1740, in which she says that 'between the windows stands covered with marble a French set of drawers of mahogany much ornamented with brass gilt'. It will be seen that the lion-mask and ring-headed consoles (Pl. 2) were retained by Vile as important decorative and structural motifs until about 1760, and that they were then used in conjunction with some of his other more renowned forms of ornamentation. Thus they can be seen in the Ashburnham library table (Pl. 3).[4] This also displays his shell-clasped oval panels which will be discussed below. Another library-table (Pl. 4) of slightly earlier date and with folding top was in the Walter P. Chrysler sale but unfortunately no provenance is given in the catalogue.[5] The rosette-and-trellis design, which is employed on the borders, appears to have been one of Vile's favourite motifs; this was already present on the frieze of the Rokeby example. A commode with key-pattern borders is seen in Pl. 5 and the high quality of its gilt-metal escutcheons should be noted (Pl. 6).

However, by about 1750, Vile seems to have started to exchange the lion-and-ring masks, which surmount his earlier carved and scrolled consoles, for putto masks that are executed brilliantly and which possess great liveliness and charm. These laughing boys are seen on a pair of commodes at Goodwood House, Sussex (Pl. 7) and the authors of *Georgian Cabinet-Makers*,[6] while discussing them, write 'these commodes, with their splendidly modelled child-headed consoles, are Baroque in conception, but the carved detail

[1] Sir Thomas Robinson, at one time Governor of Barbados, was well known as an amateur architect and extravagant entertainer. He proposed Chippendale for the Society of Arts and was also one of the original subscribers to his *Director*.

[2] See Edwards, '. . . *Vile*', *loc. cit.*, pl. I.

[3] Ill. *D.E.F.*, Vol. II, p. 111, fig. 2.

[4] Sold Sotheby's, 16 December 1955, Lot 179, and in the Ashburnham House Sale.

[5] Park-Bernet Galleries, New York, Walter P. Chrysler, Jr. sale, 7 May 1960, Lot 535.

[6] *G.C-M.*, pp. 53–4.

suggests that they were made in about 1750. The escutcheons and handles are conspicuously fine, while the grace and liveliness so rarely found in Early Georgian figure sculpture are here present in a pre-eminent degree.' A knee-hole writing-table with similar child-headed consoles (Pl. 8) was also in the Chrysler Sale,[1] and a commode (Pl. 9) from the Earl of Shaftesbury's collection at St. Giles's House, Dorset, has similar consoles — the corner ones being paired in the same unusual shoulder-to-shoulder positions. It is carved with many of Vile's typical motifs, especially the rosette-and-trellis design on the frieze, the oval panels with foliate clasps, and the scrolled consoles carved with acanthus foliage from which hang overlapping money-pattern scales. Vile had a wide connection in Dorset and Wiltshire, for his accounts are preserved at Came House, near Dorchester, and at Longford Castle, near Salisbury, and he might well have been recommended to the Shaftesburys by the Hon. John Damer or by Lord Folkestone, the respective owners of Came and Longford. Furthermore a commode from St. Giles's House is also much in the style associated with Cobb (Pl. 48) and it therefore seems that the partners may well have been employed in the house.[2]

A plainer commode, which is perhaps five years later in date (Pl. 10) is in the Metropolitan Museum, New York.[3] Its decoration is restrained and the smiling boys, with their late baroque sympathies, have been left far behind; on the other hand the circular moulded panel in the middle seems rather to look forward to the ovals on the organ-roll cupboards in the Royal Collection (Pl. 16). A pair of cupboards, which should be compared with the Metropolitan commode, are in the collection of the Earls of Leven and Melville,[4] and another with lion-headed terminals is illustrated in *Georgian Cabinet-Makers*.[5] A dwarf cupboard (Pl. 11) again shows many of Vile's characteristics, and the strange manner in which the scrolled ovals are flanked by simulated drawer fronts on cupboards and commodes of this class is admirably illustrated here.

It is well known that some of Vile and Cobb's finest work was made for the Crown and, as much of it is fully documented and some of the examples, in fact, form the key to their style, it will be discussed in some detail. Vile is believed to have worked for George, Prince of Wales, before the latter's accession to the throne and it was not surprising, therefore, that he should be appointed cabinet-maker to the Royal Household, which occurred on 5th January, 1761, when he was granted a warrant from Earl Gower, Master of His Majesty's Great Wardrobe. He made some of his finest and most delicate furniture for Queen Charlotte; her jewel cabinet is perhaps justly the most celebrated of these pieces (Pl. 12). It was designed to hold her parure of Coronation diamonds, which were then valued at £50,000, and its secret rising top has a central panel of amboyna which is inlaid with the Queen's coat of arms in engraved ivory.[6] Vile probably supplied the cabinetwork and Cobb, who, as will become apparent below, was responsible for the firm's upholstery,[7] the velvet linings. It was supplied in the Autumn of 1761 to the seventeen-year-old Queen at a cost of

---

[1] Chrysler Sale (see p. 21, n. 5 above), 30 April 1960, Lot 249 — from Sir James Horlick's Collection.
[2] It should be noted that Chippendale is also thought to have worked at St. Giles's House, see p. 119.
[3] Its pair was in the collection of the late H.R.H. The Princess Royal, Harewood House, nr. Leeds.
[4] Ill. Margaret Jourdain and F. Rose, *English Furniture, The Georgian Period*, London 1953, fig. 118, p. 149.
[5] *G.C-M.*, p. 148, fig. 56.
[6] The Royal Arms of England impaling Mecklenburg with seven quarterings.
[7] Edward H. Pinto, 'The Furniture of William Vile and John Cobb', *Antiques*, January 1959.

£138. 10. 0., which was a high price indeed in those days. It is described in Vile's account as 'a very handsome jewel cabinet, made of many different kinds of fine wood on a mahogany frame richly carved, the front, ends and top inlaid with ivory in compartments neatly engraved'. At the same time (1761) a mahogany bureau-cabinet (Pl. 13) was also supplied for the Queen's apartment at St. James's. It cost £71. 10. 0. and was invoiced as 'an exceedingly ffine mahogy secretary with drawers and a writing drawer, a sett of shelves at Top, and the sides and back all handsome cuttwork'. It is one of the most exceptional pieces of furniture ever to have been made in this country and the *bombé* side panels in the lower section must have been technically extremely difficult to perfect, although greater skill must have been required by the cabinet-makers employed by Channon (see below) when they were constructing the three-dimensional curves so typical of his work (Pls. 60, 62). It has recently been restored, and I am most grateful to Mr. Francis Watson for allowing me to examine this piece and for pointing out that the crown surmount is almost certainly a Victorian replacement. It is also fascinating to note that the upper section bears carved neo-classical enrichments — e.g. paterae and husk garlands — at this early date. Ince and Mayhew (pp. 62–8) were not the only cabinet-makers to be influenced by Adam's work at this date, which was a year prior to the publication of the third edition of Chippendale's *Director* (1762).

During the following year the firm made a bookcase (Pl. 14) for the 'Queen's House in the Park' (Buckingham House, as the Palace was then called) which is amongst the finest pieces of case furniture that have ever been created; the quality of the carving is superb. The two central doors of the lower section are carved with the Garter stars within rococo foliate surrounds and these are flanked by two other doors each carved with a circular wreath of berries and laurels. These 'ovals of laurels', as Vile describes them in his account of the following year (see below), are typical of his work and style, as likewise are the trailing garlands which are suspended from the lion-mask mounts on the narrow outer doors of this monumental bookcase. It cost £107. 14. 0. and is described as 'A very handsome mahogany bookcase with plate Glass Doors (in) the upper part, and wood doors at bottom, a Pedement head with Pilastres and trusses, the whole very handsomely carved to match the Cabinett in the Queen's Bow Closet in St. James's'.

Another cabinet (Pl. 15), also of architectural conception, is of unusual interest as it was originally designed as a case for a mechanical organ and harpsichord — probably by Benjamin Goodison in about 1735.[1] Vile altered it into a cabinet towards the end of 1763 at a charge of £57, and it was then that he applied the 'ovals of laurels' and 'vine tree' ornaments that are so much the key to his style. The doors are again flanked by stiles and panels which are decorated with applied swags of flowers and foliage suspended from ringed lion-masks. This unusual cabinet is illustrated by Stephanoff in Pyne's *Royal Residences*[2] where it is shown at the end of the Queen's Gallery at Kensington Palace. In the same plate can be seen six of a set of nine dwarf cabinets (Pl. 16) which were made to hold organ rolls. The scrolled foliate sprays in the spandrels are again typical of Vile's 'vine tree ornament' (cf. the base of the pilasters on the converted organ case, Pl. 15) and

[1] See p. 134.
[2] W. H. Pyne, *The History of the Royal Residences*, Vol. II, 1819, Kensington Palace, pl. 32. Ill. H. Clifford-Smith, *Buckingham Palace*, London 1931, pl. 67.

these cabinets therefore have also been ascribed to him on stylistic grounds — but the attribution must remain uncertain as no documentary evidence has, to date, been discovered.

During the same year (1763), Queen Charlotte ordered a mahogany work table for her private apartments at Buckingham House and was charged £9. 18. 0. by Vile for 'a neat mahogany work table, with shape legs neatly carved and a scrole on the foot and a leaf on the knee . . .'. This comparatively simple piece (Pl. 17) is interesting as it illustrates the use of the scrolled toe in conjunction with acanthus decoration which has now also become accepted as being one of the characteristic features of Vile's work.

The young King however did not allow his wife to monopolise Messrs. Vile and Cobb, for he called them in to help him to furnish his libraries at St. James's and at Buckingham House. Thus in 1761 Vile invoiced 'for H.M. Library at St. James's . . . three very neat mahogany paper cases, the insides full of sliding partitions, the outsides richly carved with exceeding fine locks and 2 keys'. Two of these three cases have survived[1] and are now at Windsor Castle. In the following year he charged the King the sum of £24. 10. 0. for 'A very good mahogany Library table on castors, the top covered with leather, and exceedingly fine locks made to the King's key', which was destined for the 'King's Blue Library at Buckingham House'. It is an interesting entry, since it appears that the King, who was an amateur locksmith, had made a key and told Vile to produce locks to fit it. Mr. H. Clifford-Smith[1] tries to relate this description to a pair of *back to back* writing-tables (Pl. 18) which are now at Holyrood Palace. It seems unlikely that they are in fact the examples in question as they are not covered in leather and, moreover, there is a *pair* of them and not one, as described in the invoice. However that the pair of desks is the work of Vile himself or of his firm is evident, Clifford-Smith maintains, 'from their similarity to a writing-table formerly at Edgecote House, Northants (see below in text), and now the property of Captain C. A. Cartwright, R.N., which was made for his ancestor, Richard Chauncey, by Vile and Cobb in 1758'. It is no longer possible to verify this comparison, but the key-pattern friezes, acanthus scrolls, pendant garlands and rings on the Holyrood pair seem to be all in Vile's tradition.

A similar pair in the Mansion House (Pl. 19) have also been ascribed to Vile by Clifford-Smith[2] on stylistic grounds. This pair, which, in fact, belongs to a not uncommon type, is probably rather earlier in date, 1750–60, but the canted angles are again carved with garlands of flower-heads, fruit and foliage — all suspended from acanthus scrolls. The plainer desk shown in Pl. 20 is obviously a country cousin of such Royal pieces. It is inscribed *David Wright, Lancaster, August 17, 1751*, and it is interesting to compare the pilasters that flank the knee-holes and the carving in the spandrels above them (cf. Pl. 19).

A pair of globes,[3] which are now in the King's Library in the British Museum, are mounted on elaborately carved frames supported by fluted columns and tripods, carved with acanthus foliage and terminating in scroll feet. The frames and supports are fully in

---

[1] Ill. H. Clifford-Smith, 'Some Georgian Furniture from the Royal Collections', *Apollo*, May 1935, p. 275, fig. IV. The following few paragraphs are based on notes taken from this article.

[2] H. Clifford-Smith, 'Two hundred years of the Mansion House, London, and some of its Furniture', *Connoisseur*, December 1952.

[3] See Clifford-Smith, 'Some Georgian Furniture', *loc. cit.*, fig. VII.

Vile's tradition and, as they were originally in one of George III's libraries, they may well have been made by Vile's firm.

A great deal of research has been recently carried out by Mr. Delves Molesworth and Mr. Derek Shrub[1] into the history of the pair of mahogany medal-cabinets (Pl. 21), which for long have been considered the work of Vile for George III, when he was still Prince of Wales. This supposition was based on a statement by the Comte de Salverte,[2] who, without giving any form of supporting evidence, claims that Vile made for George III *un grand medaillier en bois d'acajou*. There is, in fact, no trace of an order for such a cabinet in the Royal tradesmen's accounts, although there is an entry concerning an alteration to '*His Majesty's Grand Medal Case*' in a bill from Vile of 1761, which includes the following:

> 'For 5 Mahogany Medal drawers with 9 Turned holes in each lined with Green Cloth with two neat Brass Rings fixed on Brass Plates to each Drawer.
> For 6 more Medal Drawers lined with Green Cloth and plate Rings as above
> For 3 diff[t] pieces of Work fitted in between the Legs of his Majesty's Grand Medal Case with carved doors and Ends and a New plinth to D[o] on a frame and two new Ingraved keys with his Majesty's Arms on each side with the Bar filed to pass the whole Set of Locks.'

Mr. Molesworth and Mr. Shrub have conclusively proved from these entries, which are part of a longer entry, and from careful study of the carcasses and construction of the pair of medal-cabinets (Pl. 21), that the pair in question originally formed the flanking sections of the *Grand Medal Case*. Vile, in 1761, must have been instructed to detach the end sections from the large cabinet, which was probably of break-front form, and make certain necessary alterations to them — the most important of which was to fill the space between the legs with '*carved doors and Ends and a New plinth to D[o] on a frame*'; to quote from Vile's 1761 account again the '*2 compartments within the doors*' were then '*fitted with Medal Drawers with more than 1,000 holes all lined with Green Cloth and neat brass Rings on plates . . .*'.

The pair of cabinets passed into the collection of the second Duke of Wellington at Stratfield Saye House, Hampshire — it being uncertain whether they were a direct Royal gift, or whether they had first been sent to the British Museum in 1825, when the Royal collection of medals had been ceded to the Museum as part of a deal with Parliament over the payment of George IV's debts. The Victoria and Albert Museum acquired one of the cabinets in 1963 and the Metropolitan Museum has acquired the other.

Another medal-cabinet in three sections (Pl. 22) is in the Untermyer Collection and, although it cannot be attributed to Vile, its general design is similar to the 'Stratfield Saye' examples.

Queen Charlotte died at Kew in 1818 and a few of her favourite pieces had been moved there from Buckingham House to furnish her apartments. Amongst them is a candlestand with two adjustable hinged brass branches which may be related to 'two neat brass swing jointed candlesticks made to fit the reading desk and take on and off with a thumbscrew', for which Vile charged £1 in 1763.[3]

---

[1] Delves Molesworth, Lecture at The Victoria and Albert Museum, 3 March 1965, 'Problem Pieces in Furniture'. Derek Shrub, 'The Vile Problem', *Victoria and Albert Museum Bulletin*, No. 4, October 1965.

[2] Comte de Salverte, *Les Ébénistes du XVIIIᵉ Siècle*, Paris, 1953, p. 313.

[3] See p. 24, n. 1.

Two *bonheurs-du-jour*[1] in the French taste have recently been in the market. The first (Pl. 23) is said to have been made by Vile for George III when he was Prince of Wales. The Prince gave it to Lady Pembroke, wife of Henry, 10th Earl of Pembroke, who was made Lord of the Bedchamber to the Prince in 1756 — Lady Pembroke was also a Lady-in-Waiting to Queen Charlotte.[2] The second example, which is almost a pair to the first, was in the Duke of Leeds' collection.[3] If it could be proved from a documentary source that either of these pieces was, without doubt, made by Vile and Cobb, the firm may well have been responsible for a whole series of similar pieces. It would also show that Vile and Cobb kept a keen eye open for new styles from Paris, just as did Chippendale and Ince and Mayhew.

It is often thought that Vile and Cobb only supplied furniture for the Royal Family at Buckingham House and Kensington Palace, but in fact a great deal of their work was carried out for St. James's Palace. Thus the celebrated bureau-cabinet and jewel-cabinet (Pls. 12 and 13) were originally destined for the Queen's apartments in St. James's. During 1761 and 1762 Vile also supplied the following strange assortment[4] to that Palace:

> 'thirteen carved cases with plate glass doors,
> four large gilt ovals with carv'd work (to) hang miniature pictures on,
> Mahog. stands for bird cages
> two mahogany houses for a Turkey Monkey.'

In 1763 Vile was paid £572. 12. 0. for 'making out all the old Japan brought from the Queen's House, new drawing and securing it, and making a quantity of new Japan to make out the old to fit the different walls'. It appears from this description that the firm panelled the room with the lacquer which had already been hanging in another room, and supplied additional panels to fill in the gaps. This room is also illustrated in Pyne's *Royal Residences*[5] under the title of 'the Queen's Breakfast Parlour' and the panels are described as being 'formed of beautiful Japan'. Vile also charged £2. 14. 0. for 'cleaning and new gilding Japan glass frames, and new drawing the ground in Japan' and these pier-glasses, one of which still survives,[6] can be clearly seen in Pyne's illustration.[5] A further rather humdrum task that Vile and Cobb undertook was the hanging of various rooms 'with strong cloth and cartridge paper pasted thereon to keep the dust from the damask hangings'. It is interesting to note that the entry for this work was made out to Vile and Cobb, and not to Vile alone — probably because it constituted an upholsterer's rather than a cabinet-maker's office. In Appendix A an account from Vile is quoted in full[7]: it is for one of a set of chandeliers that he supplied for the Saloon of Buckingham House in

---

[1] F. J. B. Watson in *Louis XVI Furniture*, London, 1960, tells us that such pieces were known as early as 1750 in France, but that the word itself first appears in 1770 in an inventory of the duc de Villar's property at Marseille.

[2] Lady Elizabeth Herbert, grand-daughter of the 10th Earl, was given the *bonheur-du-jour* on her marriage to the 3rd Earl of Clanwilliam in 1830 and it remained in the Clanwilliam family until sold.

[3] Sold Sotheby's, 14 July 1961, Lot 154.

[4] Quoted from H. Clifford-Smith, *Buckingham Palace*, London, 1931, p. 75.

[5] See p. 23, n. 2 above, pl. 77.

[6] H. Clifford-Smith, *Buckingham Palace*, London, 1931, pl. 230.

[7] Quoted from a letter from H. Clifford-Smith entitled 'Attributions to William Vile', *Country Life*, 4 November 1954.

1764. They can be seen in an engraving after a picture by Henry Singleton of the marriage of the Duke and Duchess of York in 1791 which took place in the Saloon (Pl. 24).

The firm also executed much work for non-Royal patrons. The earliest extant account[1] from Vile and Cobb appears to be that which they presented to Anthony Chute for work that they carried out for him at The Vyne, near Basingstoke, in 1752–3.[2] It totals £120. 16. 4¾. and the first entry for 19th May, 1752, is 'for repairing a stone cabinett . . . 17/–'. This probably refers to a Florentine *pietre dure* casket, contained in a glass-mounted case, which is supported by a superbly carved giltwood stand (Pl. 25). The latter is undoubtedly of the finest mid-eighteenth-century craftsmanship and is of the exacting standard that one associates with the workshop of William Vile; one might, however, easily date to the nineteenth century the glass case that it supports, even after a careful examination. It is fascinating, therefore, to read in an inventory taken at the Vyne in 1776 an entry which refers to 'a curious cabinet with glass cover with gilt frame'. This piece may be compared with a small lacquered work-box on a giltwood rococo stand at Longford Castle (see below), which has also tentatively been attributed to Vile (Pl. 26).

On 30th March, 1753, the firm charged Anthony Chute £5. 14. 0. for '6 neat mahogany chairs stuffed in linen at 19/– each', and four of these simple chairs still remain at The Vyne (Pl. 27). A set of eight stools (Pl. 28) are invoiced as '8 large mahogany stools with carv'd feet and carv'd bracketts, stuff'd and cover'd with leather welted quilted and finish'd with burnish'd nailes at £3. 12. 0. each'. Seven of the original eight remain and it is interesting to see that one had already been lost by 1776, as only seven are mentioned in the inventory that was taken in that year. There are several other pieces mentioned in the accounts which, although no longer in the house, are of sufficient interest to be more fully quoted here (Appendix B), as they help to illustrate how diverse were the tasks undertaken by a firm of cabinet-makers and upholsterers during the eighteenth century. It is interesting to read that in 1753 fashionable cabinet-makers were still making and selling bureaux in *walnut* and also were prepared to provide chamber bellows and hearth brooms.

The next record of the firm is in the accounts for the furnishing of Braxted Park,[3] in which it is recorded that Vile and Cobb were paid £4. 15. 6. 'for a mahogany frame for a marble table' on 8th May, 1755. In the following year they supplied 'a bookcase with part of yr. wood and glass doors at top and drawer at bottom' to the Hon. John Damer for Came House, near Dorchester. They continued to supply furniture for Came House until 1764. Various entries from the accounts which have already been published in *Georgian Cabinet-Makers*[4] are quoted in Appendix C. A mahogany settee and chairs, which still remain in the house, are probably part of the set referred to in these quotations.

Vile and Cobb were also working for Thomas Coke, the first Earl of Leicester, at Holkham, for an entry in the *Holkham Weekly Departmental Accounts*[5] on 17th June, 1758

[1] I am indebted to Captain A. V. Chute for his kind permission to publish these accounts which are on loan to the Hampshire Record Office.   [2] See p. 19, n. 4.

[3] Essex Record Office — Du Cane archives (D/DDC A 13, f.f.59, 121) 1754–6.   [4] *G.C-M.*, p. 118.

[5] I am indebted to Dr. S. O. Hassall for this information. See Anthony Coleridge, 'Some Cabinet-Makers at Holkham', *Apollo*, February 1964. In the *Holkham Household Accounts* for 1755, Vile is recorded as supplying :

'a pattern chair like ye Duke of Devonshire's	£8.	0.	0.
another pattern chair	6.	6.	0.
one to match ye parlour chairs lac'd bottom gilt	3.	10.	0.'

reads 'To . . . Mr. Cobb for 2 India two leaf'd screens . . . £3. 10. 0'. Yet this very fact may mislead the unwary student, for there is at Holkham a mahogany and gilt low cabinet (Pl. 368) with wire grill doors, the sides applied with foliated ovals (Pl. 369), which is typical of Vile's style, and so is a knee-hole writing-table which is *en suite* with it; in the *Departmental Accounts*, however, for the week-ending 11th June, 1757, we read 'Mr. Goodison for a mahog. table press carv^d and gilt with wire doors for ye Gallery . . . £14. 16. 0.' (see pp. 134–5). This is but another example of the danger of attributing furniture to cabinet-makers on stylistic grounds during the middle decades of the eighteenth century.

In the same year the partners were working for Richard Chauncey at Edgecote, in Northamptonshire, and their account in the estate ledgers, under the heading 'totl. bill from Messrs. Vile and Co.' amounted to £1,215. 7. 11½. Unfortunately no details as to individual pieces of furniture are given, only the cost of the furniture supplied for each room, but a pair of chair-back settees in the Gothic taste (Pl. 29), which have survived rom the house, are traditionally held to have been supplied by Vile's firm. There is also a reference to a library table from Edgecote which has already been discussed above.[1]

This must have been a very busy year for the firm, for in 1758 they were not only working at Edgecote, Came, Holkham and for the Prince of Wales, but they were also supplying furniture and furnishings to Sir Charles Hanbury-Williams Bart. for his house in Brook Street and for Coldbrook, his estate near Abergavenny in Monmouthshire.[2] Their account with Sir Charles totals £437. 19. 6. and is made out to 'Cobb and Vile, Cabinet-makers, Upholders etc. the Corner of Long Acre' — it covers the period from 15th April to 18th December, 1758. Details are given (Appendix D) of some of the many pieces of furniture that Sir Charles bought and he appears to have consulted Cobb, as well as Vile, on matters relating to upholstery, linen and interior decoration — all subjects of which Cobb had specialist knowledge. For instance there are entries :

'For making your damask into festoone curtaines made to open in the middle, lin'd and fring'd compleat.'
'For 90 yardes of sprig paper to hang a room.'
'For 72 yardes of flower potte Gothick paper to hange the Housekeeper's Rooms below stairs.'
'For man and woman's time to clean all your damask with bread and bran, 16/–.'

Vile's name is first mentioned in the 1st Lord Folkestone's accounts at Longford Castle in 1760 and an early entry is a protest against his high prices — 'Vile, Cabinet-Maker, a bill. N.B. He charges £7. 10. for two girandoles and £1. 15. for the 4 nozzles and I am to pay him these prices for all I am to have from him, £17. 5.' Frequent payments are made to the partners up to 1767 but no details are given as to which pieces of furniture they refer. One of the finest pieces attributed to Vile at Longford is a gilt chest which is superbly carved with many of the typical motifs associated with his style (Pl. 30). The satyr masks are particularly fine and should be compared with those carved on the giltwood stand shown in Pl. 25. Access to the upper part is gained by lifting the top which is inset with a panel of Oriental lacquer. Vile and Cobb seem to have specialised in the use of

---

[1] See p. 24.
[2] The information in this paragraph and in Appendix D. has been based on an article by Ralph Edwards entitled, 'A Bill from Vile and Cobb', *Country Life*, 1956, Vol. 119, p. 1222.

lacquer, as can be seen from the casket (Pl. 26), also at Longford, the '2 India two-leaf'd screens' made for Holkham, and the rehanging of the lacquered or japanned panels at St. James's. Another unusual piece at Longford is the open display-stand with fretted sides and back (Pl. 31), the canted angles and side-panels of which are enriched with pendant floral swags and garlands that are typical of Vile's work. There is also a set of shaped stands in the same room which can be attributed to the firm on stylistic grounds.

A most unusual commode (Pl. 32), which came from St. Giles's House, Wimborne, and is now in the Fitzwilliam Museum, has, by some, also been ascribed to Vile. It is veneered in rosewood and decorated with applied giltwood, and it displays many motifs that are characteristic of Vile's style, especially the oval mouldings on the side panels and the carved acanthus scrolls on the angles — and, again, the top is inlaid with a Chinese black lacquered panel.

The third year of George III's reign must have also been a very busy one for the firm, for in 1760 Vile's name first appears in the Strawberry Hill accounts. John Chute, who had inherited the Vyne from his brother Anthony in 1754, may have well recommended Vile and Cobb to his close friend, Horace Walpole, especially as both he and Walpole were so interested in the building, alteration, and furnishing of each other's houses. Walpole, in his *Description of Strawberry Hill*, refers to the furniture which Mr. Cobb made for the bed in the Holbein Chamber as 'of purple cloth lined with white satin, a plume of white and purple feathers on the centre of the tester'.[1] It is again of interest to note that Cobb's name alone is mentioned in connection with this work which is, of course, purely an upholsterer's by nature. In the Strawberry Hill accounts for 1770 is found the following entry which again illustrates how diverse was the work undertaken by the firm: 'Cobb's bill for furnishing the Round Room, tapestry chairs for the cottage, carpet for ditto . . . £99. 8. 6.' By this date Cobb was running the business by himself and we therefore find him providing the furniture as well as the carpets and other soft furnishings.

On 27th October, 1761, there is an entry in Lord Harrowby's account books[2] which reads 'Bill to Vile, cabinet-maker, including my travelling box £21. 12.', and on 23rd July, 1773, 'to Cobb, cabinet-maker, for Mrs. St. Andre'. The meaning of the second entry is not entirely clear but it shows that Vile and Cobb had yet another influential client in Lord Harrowby. No doubt more evidence of the extent of this relationship in such circles will come to light.

In 1762 the widowed Princess of Wales, George III's mother, was buying furniture from the firm,[3] and, at the same time, they were of course supplying furniture to the Royal family for Kensington and St. James's Palaces and Buckingham House. In 1763 Thomas Mortimer in the *Universal Director* describes the firm as 'Vile and Cobb, Long Acre, Cabinet-maker to H.M.'.

Before discussing Vile's Will, attention must be given to a series of bookcases and some other important pieces that can be attributed to his firm, or its emulators, on stylistic grounds. The only documented examples of the former are in the Royal Collection (Pls.

[1] Quoted from Sir Ambrose Heal, *The London Furniture Makers*, London, 1953, p. 38.
[2] I am indebted to Mr. Geoffrey Beard for lending me his notes on the Harrowby MS. The references are Ledger 326, folio 38, and Ledger 338, respectively.
[3] See *Connoisseur*, June 1957, p. 30.

14 and 15), but the break-front bookcase illustrated in Pl. 33 may be tentatively attributed to Vile, as it is decorated with many of his favourite motifs, the most obvious being the 'ovals of laurels' in the centre. It is once again surmounted by an architectural pediment as is the example from Lord Rockley's collection, which is thought to have originated from Charlemont House, Dublin (Pl. 34). This has a rather unusual motif on the central door in the lower section — the applied moulding being basically rectangular and not oval in shape. However the central lower panels on Queen Charlotte's bookcase (Pl. 14) are very similar, and so are the pendant floral swags on both bookcases. A third example (Pl. 35), which could almost be built-up out of the component parts of the three that have been illustrated, is among the furniture which Claude Rotch bequeathed recently to the Victoria and Albert Museum.

Several bureau-bookcases can also be attributed to Vile, or to his emulators, on stylistic grounds. The only documented one is the important example in the Royal Collection (Pl. 13), but another is illustrated in *Georgian Cabinet-Makers* (fig. 64, p. 153) which was probably made by Vile for George, Prince of Wales, or for his father, Frederick, Prince of Wales. It has a pair of glass doors above, flanked by a framework carved with blind-fret ornamentation, and is surmounted by an open-fret architectural pediment centred by the Prince of Wales' plumes. The Earl of Mansfield has an even finer example in his collection at Scone Palace (Pl. 36), although perhaps rather earlier in date; its chased rococo handles and escutcheons are almost identical to those on the Royal example. The use of gilt and gesso, which can be seen on the pilasters and pediment rosettes of the Scone piece, has already been noted on the Longford chest (Pl. 30) and the rosewood commode from St. Giles's House (Pl. 32).

One of the most unusual pieces that have been attributed to William Vile is a goldfish bowl stand[1] (Pl. 37). In the second quarter of 1762 Vile invoiced the following :

> 'For the Queen's Bow Closet at St. James's.
> For 2 mohog^y stands part carv'd and Gilt to set large Glass Basons of Gold Fish on, the Top lin'd with green cloth . . . £6. 0. 0.
> For a neat mohog^y handle to a Fish net . . . 2. 6.'

It is not surprising to find Queen Charlotte buying similar stands for her goldfish bowls after reading that she had already bought bird- and monkey-cages (see p. 26). The stand in question (Pl. 37) has its cabriole legs carved with acanthus foliage and terminating in scroll feet in a manner typical of Vile's work (cf. Pl. 17), and it is possible that his firm was responsible for its fabrication.

Vile retired in 1765, probably on account of ill-health, and died two years later in September 1767. In his will, dated August 1763, he describes himself as 'of the Parish of St. Martin's in the Fields, cabinet-maker and upholder'. He appoints William Hallett (see below) and Charles Smith[2] as trustees to sort out 'all manner of accounts depending between me and the said John Cobb', with whom he has described himself earlier in the will as being 'engaged with . . . in very extensive branches of trade'. He left his wife Sarah 'two houses now in my possession situate at Battersea Hill' and his furniture 'in

---

[1] This piece is fully discussed in 'A goldfish bowl stand by William Vile', *Connoisseur*, June 1960, pp. 25–6.
[2] Charles Smith, Upholsterer and Cabinet-Maker, had his premises in Portugal Street, Lincoln's Inn Fields in 1763 (R. W. Symonds, *Connoisseur*, April 1938).

my houses both in town and country'. From the wording, it appears that Vile must have been reasonably prosperous by 1763, when he made his will, with two houses on Battersea Hill and presumably a 'country' house in addition.

As has been stated above, John Cobb carried on the business after Vile's retirement in 1765. Rather more is known about his character and personality, than that of Vile's. J. T. Smith describes him in *Nollekens and his Times* as that 'singularly haughty character . . . one of the proudest men in England . . . he always appeared in full dress of the most superb and costly kind, in which state he would strut through his workshop giving orders to his men'.[1] However this high-handed behaviour earned him a rebuke from George III who, although he 'smiled at his pomposity', could not stomach his overbearing behaviour to his subordinates. Cobb on one occasion was giving instructions to one of his workmen whose ladder was standing in front of a bookcase in the King's Library at Buckingham House, and the King, who happened to be there, asked Cobb if he could hand him one of the books which was being hidden by the ladder. J. T. Smith,[1] who tells the story, continues thus, 'Instead of obeying, Cobb called to his man, "Fellow, give me that book!" The King with his usual condescension arose, and asked Cobb for his man's name "Jenkins, Your Majesty," answered the astonished upholsterer. "Then," observed the King, "Jenkins! You shall hand me the book!" '

Smith also tells us that Cobb was 'the person who brought that very convenient table into fashion that drawers out in front, with upper and inward rising desks, so healthy for those who stand to write, read or draw'. He continues, 'Sir Nathaniel Dance considered Cobb's tables so useful that he easily prevailed upon the adonised upholsterer to allow him to paint his portrait for [i.e. in exchange for] one; which picture, after it had remained in Cobb's show-room for some time "purposely to be serviceable", as he said, "to the poor painter", he conveyed in his own carriage to his seat at Highgate.'

If these descriptions are fair and unbiased, he appears to have been a bully by nature, condescending in the extreme and a social climber. The last of these three points is further borne out by a clause in his will which reads 'let it be noticed that the principal twenty thousand pounds stock is never to be broken into . . . my intent being that there should always be the interest aforesaid to support ye name of Cobb as a private gentleman'.

Cobb, who died in 1778, made two wills, the first is dated 3rd February, 1774, and the second, 17th July, 1776. Administration was granted to his wife, Mary Cobb, on 31st August, 1778, on the affidavit of William Hallett of Cannons and John Graham of St. Martin's Lane, upholder (see below). Cobb must have died a rich man, for he refers to 'all the furniture together with the plate, linen and china now being in my dwelling-house in Saint Martin's Lane', the similar contents in his house 'at Hygate', his house at Islington, and his chariot and horse. He bequeathed to his wife 'one half of a fortune amounting to upwards of £12,000 which I have on the 3% funds' secured 'in the firmest manner'. His bank-account is preserved at the Drummond's Branch of the Royal Bank of Scotland[2] and it is interesting to see that in 1770 there is a balance of £16,594. 19. 10. However in his second will of 1776, his 'fortune now being altered since my writing the first part of this paper', he referred to 'two and twenty thousand 3% stock'.

[1] *Nollekens and his Times*, Ed. 1829, Vol. II, p. 243.
[2] 49, Charing Cross, London, S.W. 1.

The business does not appear to have suffered on Vile's retirement except, of course, for the fact that the firm lost the Royal appointment to Bradburn.

There are few other contemporary references to Cobb, although Mrs. Neale writing in 1771 to Mary Cathcart at Kaminoi Ostroff in Russia refers to a 'Chamber horse' which Mrs. Bonfoy had intended to forward to Russia after purchasing it 'at Mr. Cobb's'.[1]

In the following year, 1772, we find Cobb in some trouble with the Commissioners of Customs,[2] as he, and others, were apparently selling furniture that had been imported, duty free, into the Country, probably on commission for Count Pignatelli, the Neapolitan Minister, and for the Venetian Resident, Baron Berlindis, both of whom, it was stated, were importing the furniture in the diplomatic bag. Many other members of the trade were so indignant about this that they presented a petition to the House of Commons on 26th May of that year on behalf of the 'Master and Journeymen Cabinet-Makers of London and Westminster' alleging that the employment of British Craftsmen was being imperilled. It took a year, and an initial defeat, before it was discussed by a committee and, on 2nd June, 1773, an appendix of the report was delivered to the House. It reads as follows:

> 'To prove the allegations of the said Petition, Mr. John Sharpe said, That, about the Beginning of the year 1772, a Number of Cases, full of Furniture of Various Kinds, and a Number of Clocks of great Value, were brought to Mr. Cobb's in Saint Martin's Lane — That the Contents of the said Cases were there exposed to Sale — That being informed they were imported under Privilege of a Foreign Minister, by one Beaumont of Wardour Street, the Witness, after taking the Marks and Numbers of the Cases, went to the Custom House, and being permitted to see the Custom House Books, he found the Marks and Numbers to agree — That, upon his Application, an Order was given for the Custom House Officers to seize the said Furniture, which was accordingly done, but that the goods were soon after claimed, formally, by Count Pignatelli, as the Furniture of his House; on which the officers relinquished their Seizure, and quitted the Premises.
>
> 'Mr. Thomas Wright, Watchmaker to His Majesty, informed your Committee, "That, in the Year 1772, being desired, by a Custom House Officer, to treat for some Clocks at Mr. Cobb's Warehouse, that the officer might seize them if offered to Sale, he went thither, but was told, they were removed to Count Pignatellis, and was directed to Mr. Beaumont, who was to introduce him. . . ." '

After taking the statements of other witnesses, the committee passed two resolutions — they stated that much furniture has obviously been imported in the alleged manner and they recommended that the regulations concerning the baggage of diplomats should be re-examined.

In an appendix to the report are given lists of the goods that were seized from the firms of cabinet-makers in question — Cullen's (see p. 161), Messrs. Riley and Wall's, and Cobb's. The Goods seized from Cobb's St. Martin's Lane premises, on 6th July, 1772, 'which the officers alledge they can prove were there to be sold' consisted of:

'A Writing Table.
One Do with a Cabinet on its Top.
A Commode, with a Marble Slab.

[1] E. Maxtone Graham, *The Beautiful Mrs. Graham*, 1927, p. 19; *G.C-M.*, p. 56.
[2] First published by Geoffrey Wills in 'Furniture-Smuggling in Eighteenth Century London', *Apollo*, August 1965.

A Coin [corner-cabinet] with a Marble Slab.
One Ditt⁰, with a Ditto.
A Writing Table.
A Coin, with a Marble Slab.
One Ditto, with a Ditto.
A Writing Table.
4 Architrave Glass Frames, in Pieces, gilt.'

Cobb appears to have accepted the confiscation of the furniture with little protest, and Mr. Geoffrey Wills, while discussing this, writes,[1] 'From this it might be thought that it was not uncommon to offer uncustomed furniture for sale, and if the goods were seized it was accounted a legitimate trading risk.'

It has been pointed out to me by Mr. Geoffrey Beard that Cobb's account is extant at Croome Court for a set of eight armchairs which he sold to the 6th Earl of Coventry in 1764, when the latter was altering and refurnishing Croome Court in Worcestershire. These chairs (Pl. 38) are described thus in his invoice, 'for 8 Mahogany armd chairs the seats stuffd and coverd with blue Morrocco Leather and finished with burnished nails and Carving all the Arms and 2 front feet, all the rest Carvd by Mr. Alkin'. It would thus appear that Cobb's firm was responsible for the carving of the chairs with the exception of the splats and toprails which were carved by Sefferin Alkin, or Alken, who carried out much of the specialist carver's work at Croome. This division of work on a set of chairs seems strange, but it has been suggested by Mr. E. H. Pinto[2] that Vile and Cobb were *cabinet-makers* and not *chairmakers*; perhaps that was the reason for their enrolling the services of a specialist to carve the intricate splats on these chairs with their pierced double-anthemion motifs. This theory may well be correct, and it is worth noting that the surviving chairs made by the firm for the Vyne (Pl. 27) are of a simpler nature, while those described in the firm's accounts for the Hon. John Damer and Sir Charles Hanbury-Williams (Appendices C and D) all appear to be of a relatively simple design, with 'stuff'd and quilted' backs and seats, and little intricate carved detail. In fact, chairs occur only rarely in the firm's accounts. However a further example of this specialisation is recorded when Sir Mathew Fetherstonhaugh bought a chair for Uppark, Sussex, as can be seen from a reference in his manuscript account book, which is extant at Uppark: 'Jan. 1st, 1764, Paid Mr. Cobb in full for Gouty chairs . . . £5. 13. 0.' These chairs unfortunately have not survived. Sir Mathew also employed Vile, for on 1st January, 1765, he recorded in his account book that he 'Pd. Mr. Vile in full . . . £17. 3. 6.' No details of his purchases are given.

John Cobb, however, is primarily remembered for his furniture, which is inlaid with marquetry in the early neo-classical tradition — much in the same style as that which Thomas Chippendale adopted during the later period of his career during his collaboration with Robert Adam. The key to identifying Cobb's furniture, most examples of which are commodes, is found in the 'extra neat inlaid commode' (Pl. 39) which was supplied by Cobb in 1772 to Paul Methuen of Corsham Court in Wiltshire. Cobb's receipted account, which is still at Corsham Court, shows that it cost £63. 5. 0., and the commode was made to Mr. Methuen's order — the sides being inlaid with the arms of Methuen and

[1] See p. 32, n. 2.　　　　[2] See p. 22, n. 7.

Cobb.[1] Its serpentine front is veneered with satinwood and inlaid with oval panels filled with vases of flowers executed in marquetry. The top is painted in imitation of marble and the whole is mounted in finely cast and chased ormolu. A pair of satinwood pedestals of baluster form (Pl. 40) were made *en suite* with the commode and the borders of the three pieces are inlaid with an unusual alternating design of rosettes and honeysuckle[2] which presumably derives from the characteristic Vile rosette-and-fret border. The pedestals each support a marble vase mounted in ormolu which were bought two years later in 1774.

Three very similar commodes have already been published[3] which are so closely related to the Corsham commode that they may be attributed to Cobb on stylistic grounds. The first is in the Victoria and Albert Museum[4] and the second (Pl. 41) was sold in the Parke-Bernet Galleries, New York[5] — they are a pair and were both originally in the collection of the 1st Baron Tweedmouth. The top of the second commode, which is identical to the other with the exception of the colour of the ground panels, is illustrated in Pl. 42; the marquetry subject of a bowl of fruit, in the centre, is extremely rare. A commode from Holland House, in Viscountess Galway's collection, is the third example. All of them have their front and side panels bordered with the same alternating rosette-and-honeysuckle design as the Corsham example. The marquetry inlay on these pieces is of the highest quality and reference is made, in Mrs. Thrale's French journal,[6] to the high reputation and French standards of Cobb's marquetry.

But it must again be stressed that caution should be exercised in the discussion and attribution of such commodes in the French taste. However, this is an appropriate place in which briefly to describe and illustrate a series of important examples in this *genre*. Whether they were made in the workshop of Cobb or one of his contemporaries is immaterial, and anyway the skilled designers and marquetry-cutters who were responsible for their creation and execution may well have changed firms on several occasions, thereby taking the secrets and techniques of their first master on to the next. Some, of course, were specialists who supplied the trade in general and worked from their own premises. Two commodes, which almost form a pair with one another, are now in the United States. The first (Pl. 43) is in the Metropolitan Museum and the second, the top of which is shown in Pl. 44, was sold in the Whitmarsh Collection at the Parke-Bernet Galleries.[7] The urns of flowers and key-pattern and rosette borders are reminiscent of Cobb's style, although by

[1] Paul Methuen was married to Catherine, daughter of Sir George Cobb, 3rd baronet, of Adderbury. Edwards and Jourdain, *G.C-M.*, point out that no connection has been traced between her and the family of John Cobb.

[2] This important suite of furniture is fully discussed in the following articles: O. Bracket, 'Documented Furniture at Corsham', *Country Life*, 28 November 1936; Ralph Edwards, 'Two commodes by John Cobb', *Country Life*, 22 May 1937.

[3] *G.C-M.*, p. 56; and Edwards, 'John Cobb', *loc. cit.*

[4] Ill. and described *D.E.F.*, Vol. II, p. 110 and pl. 111; *G.C-M.*, p. 56, pl. 70: sold at Christie's by the Earl of Portsmouth, 18 May 1922.

[5] Lillian S. Whitmarsh Sale, 8 April, 1961, Lot 361. Originally in the Leverhulme Collection, sold at the Anderson Galleries, New York, February 1926, Lot 595.

[6] Mrs. Thrale's French journal from MS. in the John Rylands library, 1932, p. 120.

[7] Lillian S. Whitmarsh Sale, 7 April 1961, Lot 181. Formerly in the Sir Anthony de Rothschild Collection, Aston Clinton, Bucks, and then in the Leverhulme Collection. Sold at the Anderson Galleries, New York, February 1926, Lot 338.

no means sufficiently akin to hazard any attribution. The musical trophy (Pl. 44) is particularly fine and is executed with ivory details; Vile and Cobb at times, of course, also used ivory in their marquetry inlay (cf. Pls. 12 and 39). A third commode (Pl. 45) is in the same tradition, notably in the marquetry borders and arabesques with their marked rococo flavour. There are two pairs of commodes at West Wycombe Park, Buckinghamshire, which have, in the past, been rather loosely attributed to Cobb and one of these is illustrated in Pl. 46. The diagonal linear striping of the wood which forms the borders to the two doors is highly unusual. Another commode (Pl. 47) may be compared with it: this has similar borders of striped wood and identical mounts on the feet. The latter is of superb quality and its ormolu rococo handles and mounts are as fine as the best that the French *ciseleurs* could produce. The curved back-edge is very French and unlike the more typical vertical edge usually found on English pieces.

The last, and possibly the most important, of these unattributed marquetry commodes that are being discussed here, is the example in the Metropolitan Museum, which was originally at St. Giles's House, Dorset (Pl. 48). A mahogany commode (Pl. 49) which was in the same house, has already been attributed to Vile and this fine marquetry example could equally well have been made in Cobb's workshops, especially as he is known to have employed engraved ivory in his inlay, as in the case of the Corsham commode. However, this is only a tentative attribution, since Chippendale is also thought to have worked in the house, and the Countess of Shaftesbury, to whose husband it belonged, was a subscriber to the first edition of the *Director*.[1]

It was not only commodes that were being made in the French taste at this date as the *bureau de dame* illustrated in Pl. 49 shows. Its sloping flap is inlaid with the arms of Walpole impaling Waldegrave. It may have been made to commemorate this marriage, as had been the case with Paul Methuen's commode (cf. Pl. 39). Its quality speaks for itself and it is one of the finest pieces of furniture made during this exacting age.

Chippendale must have been a great rival to Cobb, but the former was not the only other important cabinet-maker who was making inlaid furniture in the Louis XV and neo-classical tastes. Peter (or Pierre) Langlois[2] appears to have leased his premises in the Tottenham Court Road in about 1760 and from that date he must have been a sharp thorn in Cobb's elegant side.

He was presumably an immigrant French *ébéniste* who must have been apprenticed to one of the leading Parisian *maîtres* flourishing in Paris during the 1740's.

In Thomas Mortimer's *Universal Director*, which was published in London in 1763, it is stated that 'Langlois performs all sorts of curious inlaid work, particularly commodes in the foreign taste, inlaid with tortoiseshell, brass etc.' His trade card,[3] which is published in English and French and contained in an elaborate rococo cartouche, states that he 'makes all sorts of fine cabinets and commodes made and inlaid in the politest manner with brass and tortoiseshell, and likewise all rich ornamental clock cases and inlaid work

[1] This commode is fully described by James Parker, in 'Rococo and formal order in English Furniture', *Metropolitan Museum of Art Bulletin*, January 1957, pp. 134–7. Sold at Christie's, 12 May 1955, Lot 108.

[2] His work is also discussed by the present writer in 'Pierre Langlois, His Oeuvre and some Recent Discoveries', *Gazette des Beaux-Arts*, September, 1967.

[3] Ill. *G.C-M.*, p. 238, pl. 227, and Sir Ambrose Heal, *The London Furniture Makers*, p. 94.

mended with great care. Branch chandeliers and lanthorns in brass at the lowest prices.'

An early recorded reference to Langlois in this country is in the accounts of the Duke of Montagu in which 'Langlois cabinet maker' is paid £6. 6. 0. on 7th April, 1760. A commode and a pembroke-table at Boughton, Northamptonshire, are typical of his accepted *oeuvre* and may perhaps be related to this entry. Another reference dating from the later part of the same year is found in the Bedford accounts at Woburn Abbey.[1] Langlois sent the following receipt to the third Duke 'received December 18th, 1760 of his Grace the Duke of Bedford by Richard Branson Seventy eight pounds eight shillings in full for a large inlaid commode table . . . witness P. Beaumont'. This commode (Pl. 50) which is typical of the other examples by, or attributed to, Langlois (cf. Pls. 54–6), is now in the private apartments at Woburn. Its ormolu enrichments and marquetry inlay are of the highest quality. The angle and apron mounts should be compared with those on the Coventry commode (cf. Pl. 55).

The documented Woburn commode is very similar to a pair of commodes (Pl. 51) in the Marquess of Zetland's drawing-room at Aske Hall, his seat near Richmond in Yorkshire. Yet no documentary evidence relating to Langlois appears to be extant in the Dundas papers — the Marquess of Zetland is a direct descendant of Sir Lawrence Dundas — although they are so rich in material relating to other eighteenth-century cabinet-makers. The Zetland commodes can, however, on stylistic grounds and with confidence, be added to Langlois' *oeuvre*. A second pair of commodes at Aske, their tops inlaid with ivory, may also be attributed to Langlois[2]. Their ormolu angle-mounts are cast with the unusual and distinctive bud-like flower-heads, which are typical of his accepted style (cf. Pls. 50 and 55).

Another pair of commodes, again at Woburn, which are veneered in kingwood, inlaid with floral marquetry sprays within key-pattern borders, can, in Mr. Ralph Edwards' words 'be attributed, by irresistible inference, to the same [Langlois'] workshop. Rectangular and in the neo-classic style, fitted with drawers instead of doors and mounted with rams' heads and pendants in ormolu of very high quality, they closely correspond in design and decoration with a commode in the Fitzwilliam Museum, Cambridge (Pl. 52). But that commode has a top elaborately decorated in marquetry with architectural scenes, which is clearly not by the same hand as the rest of the inlay. . . . The tops of the Woburn pair are of *pietre dure* with designs of harbour scenes and picturesque ruins. . . .'[1] The Fitzwilliam commode is signed '*Daniel Langlois*' on the carcase of the top drawer (Pl. 53), and, Mr. Edwards continues, 'this signature is taken to relate to the mounts.' Daniel Langlois was apprenticed to a certain '*Dominique Jean of St. Pancras Water Gilder*', as Miss Dorothy Stroud informs us, and was later employed as an ormolu worker at Buckingham Palace. The relationship between Daniel and Peter Langlois is not established.

In this same article, Mr. Edwards published, for the first time, a bill of May 1759 to the Duke of Bedford from 'Cabinet Maker Pierre Langlois', which reads 'Une table de vide poche incruste de fleur de bois violette des indes injolivee de ornement de bronze doree du prix de neuf guinee.' This, to date, is the earliest reference to Langlois in this country so

---

[1] G. Scott Thomson, *Family Background*, London, 1949, p. 53 — also Ralph Edwards, 'Patrons of Taste and Sensibility, English Furniture of the Eighteenth Century, Woburn Abbey', *Apollo*, December 1965.

[2] The inlay is very similar to the work of the contemporary cabinet-maker, Pietro Piffetti.

B. A lacquered commode, from a set of four, at Uppark. *Mrs. R. Meade–Fetherstonhaugh,*
Uppark, Sussex.
Photograph and block courtesy of The Connoisseur.

far published. There is also a receipt from him in the Woburn Abbey archives, dated 1760, for 'an inlaid writing-table'.

In 1763 Horace Walpole bought from him 'two commodes and two coins' (encoignures),[1] and 'an inlaid writing box by Langlois' is mentioned in the *Description of Strawberry Hill* as 'being on the writing-table in the Breakfast Room'. There is a further link between Walpole and Langlois for George Montagu, in a letter of 12th March, 1766, to the former writes, 'I will take my corporal oath that three parts of the japan you gave Langlois to make into commodes is still there, and so will Mr. Chute. He carried me to see his *things* and there it was flowing about the rooms in panells and in the staircase, 'tis a burning shame.' Mr. Chute's *things* are almost certainly a pair of commodes that still remain at The Vyne, Hampshire.[2] They (Pl. 54) are inlaid with musical trophies and floral marquetry sprays, the stalks knotted together with ribbon-ties, in a manner typical of Langlois' style (cf. Pls. 55 and 56), and the ormolu corner mounts are identical to those on the Croome Court and Royal commodes (see below). They are somewhat unusual in the fact that they contain drawers and not doors, and it is tragic that the drawers in both cases have been divided vertically at a later date.

On 21st March, 1763, Caroline, Lady Holland, writing about a present for her sister, Lady Louisa Conolly, to another sister, Emily, Countess of Kildare,[3] said,

> 'I hear she likes L'Anglay's inlaid things very much, and I should wish to send her something that might suit some of her rooms, whether the commode table, bureau or *coins*, which to be sure one might vulgarly call corner cupboards; but really they are lovely and finish a room so well. I have *two* beauties in the Salon at Holland House.' [*One of these, at Holland House until the fire, is in Viscountess Galway's collection at Melbury House, Dorset.*]

Lady Holland appears to have carried out her wish and sent Lady Louisa Conolly a pair of Langlois' commodes as a present; for, until their recent sale at Christie's,[4] a pair of magnificent commodes in Langlois' full tradition were to be seen in the Red Drawing-Room at Castletown, Co. Kildare, the Conollys' Irish house.[5]

This supposition is further strengthened by a letter which Mr. Desmond Guiness has recently discovered at Castletown and kindly brought to my attention. It is written to Tom Conolly, Lady Louisa's husband, by his mother:

London February ye 3rd 1763.

Dear Tom

> ... I beg my love to Lady Louisa and dear Fanny's. I hope Lady Louisa will get the commode soon and that she and you will like it. I paid Mr Langlois and have paid the other things you desired me to pay ...

Yours most affectionate Mother

A. Conolly.

Perhaps the most important documented piece by Langlois is the commode (Pl. 55), which is described in his account of 20th July, 1764, to the 7th Earl of Coventry as being

[1] Mr. John Hardy has drawn my attention to a contemporary engraving by J. C. Stadler of the Gallery at Strawberry Hill which includes the commodes and *coins* in question.   [2] See p. 19, n. 4.

[3] *Correspondence of Emily, Duchess of Leinster*, edited by Brian FitzGerald, Irish MSS. Commission, Vol. I, 1949.   [4] Christie, Manson and Woods Ltd., April 21, 1966, lot 118.

[5] This pair, and a very similar commode, decorated with the armorial bearings of Thomas Villiers, Baron Hyde of Hindon, are discussed by Mr. Ralph Fastnedge in 'An unpublished Commode attributed to Pierre Langlois', *The Journal of the Furniture History Society*, Vol. III, 1967. Another was sold at Sotheby's on Jan. 26, 1968.

in floral marquetry with gilt bronze mounts. It was still in the room, for which it was made at Croome Court, Worcestershire, in about 1880, as can be seen from an old photograph of that date.[1] Its two doors are inlaid with his distinctive sprays of floral marquetry tied with ribbons, and its shaped apron is centred by an unusual ormolu mount cast as a lion-mask flanked by acanthus scrolls. There is a pair of commodes in the Royal Collection at Windsor[2] (Pl. 56) which display many similar features, notably in the drawing of the floral marquetry bouquets, again tied with ribbons. Yet another example was sold at Christies in 1961,[3] again with the unmistakable floral marquetry inlay. The tops of most of these commodes are decorated with marquetry panels of musical trophies. Noteworthy also are the corner ormolu mounts of all these commodes (Pls. 54–6) which take the form of acanthus foliage combined with an unusual design of bud-like flower-heads. Mr. Peter Thornton has pointed out to me, in this connection, that many of Langlois' commodes have bifurcated scrolled toes in ormolu (Pls. 50–56) — this form of toe was, in fact, often used by the celebrated French *ébéniste*, Jean-François Oeben.

Another commode in the Royal Collection (Pl. 57), which is veneered with kingwood, has mounts on the apron and at the corners of the drawers identical to those on the Croome example (cf. Pl. 55). This Royal commode is one of a set of four. The top is inlaid in engraved brass with a basket of mixed flowers, which is signed *G. M. Dutton*, and is bordered with a wide band of rosette-and-trellis marquetry. The set was purchased in 1818 at the sale of the effects of a Mr. Squib by Lord Yarmouth on behalf of the Prince Regent for Carlton House, and there is, therefore, no documentary evidence as to the maker. As far as is known Langlois' name does not figure in the Royal accounts, but as these particular commodes appear to have been bought from the collections of private individuals, rather than direct from the cabinet-makers themselves, this would be the obvious explanation.

There is another fine mahogany commode in the French taste at Windsor (Pl. 58), the quartered veneers of which are contrasted with finely chased ormolu mounts and borders. The top is inlaid with a design of scrollwork in brass. Its history has not been traced prior to 1868 when it was in the Queen's Audience Chamber.

A series of tables in a totally different style and medium have been attributed to Langlois on the grounds of a note in the Duchess of Northumberland's memorandum book concerning the purchase of 'a table inlaid wood by L'Anglois'. There is a pair of carved and gilded folding card tables at Syon House, Isleworth, which may possibly be the ones referred to in the Duchess's memorandum,[4] and, until recently,[5] a pair of pier tables (Pl. 59) and a set of painted and gilt furniture at Audley End, Essex, have also been attributed

---

[1] This commode is discussed by James Parker in 'Croome Court, The Architecture and Furniture', *Metropolitan Museum of Art Bulletin*, November 1959, pp. 90 and 92.

[2] Purchased privately for George IV's use at The Royal Pavilion, Brighton: described by G. F. Laking, *Windsor Castle Furniture*, p. 77.

[3] Christie's, 20 April 1961, Lot 51, the property of L. Ambridge, Esq.   [4] Ill. *G.C-M.*, p. 238, pl. 299.

[5] In fact Mr. John Hardy has recently pointed out to me that the Audley End seat-furniture and tables were supplied by Gordon and Taitt (see p. 51) in 1771 to the Hon. Sir John Griffin Griffin — the account (in the Essex Record Office, D/D By A365) is published by J. D. Williams in *Audley End*, Chelmsford, 1966:

'To 2 Table frames under the Glasses, carved & gilt in burnished gold & picked in greene [?]   £16. 16. 0.
To 2 very rich Inlaid Tops for do   £30. 0. 0.'

to his workshops on stylistic grounds. The inlaid tops and decoration of the giltwood frames on the Syon and the Audley End tables, although similar to each other, are totally different to Langlois' marquetry work of ten years earlier and, if he really was responsible for them, he must have quickly and adeptly learnt to adapt his style from the *rococo* to the *neo-classicism* of the Adam tradition.[1]

This is a suitable point at which to discuss a series of pieces of furniture which have caused a great deal of interest and speculation since the war. During the second quarter of the eighteenth century, several examples of brass-inlaid furniture, lavishly mounted in ormolu, were made, probably in London. All the known surviving pieces in this small group are of the highest quality, both as to the choice of woods and the casting and chasing of the mounts (Pl. 62).[2]

The identity of the cabinet-maker responsible for these highly individual creations has for long remained a mystery. It was supposed at one point, largely on the evidence of his trade card (p. 35), that they may have been made by Pierre Langlois, but this theory was largely refuted in an article by R. W. Symonds, in which he pointed out that Langlois must have been far too young to have made these pieces of furniture as, on stylistic grounds, they cannot be dated later than the fourth decade of the century.[3] It was then thought that Abraham Roentgen,[4] who was working in England from 1731 to 1738 — perhaps with a London cabinet-maker of German origin named Gern — may have made them. However, in spite of definite stylistic similarities, it has not yet been possible to establish an undisputed connection between Roentgen and the maker of the group of pieces under discussion — whose identity is disclosed below.[5]

All the available evidence relating to this series was published in January 1965 by Mr. John Hayward in an article in the *Victoria and Albert Museum Bulletin*.[6] In this he listed the examples known at that date :

A cabinet-on-stand (Pl. 60)	— *The Victoria and Albert Museum*
A table	— *The Victoria and Albert Museum*
A bureau-cabinet	— *The Victoria and Albert Museum*
An armchair	— *The Victoria and Albert Museum*
A library-desk[7] (Pl. 61)	— *The Victoria and Albert Museum*
A commode (Pl. 63)	— *The Fitzwilliam Museum, Cambridge*
A commode	— *Temple Newsam House, Leeds*
A bureau-cabinet	— *London County Council at Kenwood*
A bureau-cabinet (Pl. 66)	— *The City Art Gallery, Bristol*
3 writing-cabinets (Pl. 64)	— *Private Collections*
A bureau-cabinet	— *London Art Market*

These pieces, on stylistic grounds, all appear to have come from the same stable. Two

[1] See p. 38, n. 5.

[2] The most favoured woods were rosewood, amboyna and a mahogany of a particularly rare type with a fine figure : the quality and finish of the ormolu mounts is superb (pl. 62).

[3] R. W. Symonds, 'A Magnificent Dressing Table', *Country Life*, 16 February 1956.

[4] Founder of the famous cabinet-making business at Neuwied on the Rhine.

[5] This possible relationship was first raised and discussed by Messrs. Peter Thornton and Desmond FitzGerald in 'Abraham Roentgen "Englische Kabinettmacher" ' and 'Some further reflections on the work of John Channon', *Victoria and Albert Museum Bulletin*, October 1966, Vol. II, No. 4.

[6] *English Brass-inlaid Furniture*, Vol. I, no. 1.   [7] Its pair was sold at Sotheby's, 12 February 1965.

of them, moreover, give us some clue as their possible maker. The bureau-cabinet, which was then in the London Art Market, has the name J. Graveley branded on its base. Mr. Hayward, while discussing this, suggested that, as nothing further is known of this man, that he was one of the workmen, employed by the unknown master cabinet-maker, who was allowed to stamp his name on the pieces that he finished. Secondly, the cabinet-on-stand (Pl. 60) has the workman's emblem — *a Ram pendant from entwined snakes* — engraved on the hinge plates. This almost certainly means that the cabinet-maker was working 'At the Sign of the (Golden) Fleece'. Mr. Hayward, however could draw no definite conclusions as to the identity of the makers of this group of furniture, and the mystery remained unsolved.

But in a subsequent article,[1] the same author was able to write 'the name of the maker of this particular group has come to light'. He illustrated one of a pair of outstanding bookcases of architectural form (Pl. 65) which are at Powderham Castle, near Exeter, in Devon. Each of these is signed 'J. Channon 1740', on a brass plaque. There is, furthermore, a payment of £50 'part on account' to John Channon on 29th April, 1741, recorded in the Account Books of Sir William Courtenay of Powderham, which presumably refers to the bookcases. Comparison of the mounts, wood, inlay and other decorative details between these and the pieces illustrated in Pls. 60 to 64 leave little doubt that the same maker was responsible for them all.

Mr. Hayward's researches have shown that John Channon, a member of an Exeter cabinet-making family, moved to London after 1733, and had started practising on the West Side of St. Martin's Lane by 1737. He lived there until 1783, and in the following year was succeeded by Hughes Channon who left after only a year. Mr. Hayward writes 'The Polling List of the Westminster Election of 1749 includes a George Channon of St. Martin's Lane, cabinet-maker. As there is no other mention of a George Channon, we are probably justified in assuming that the clerk of the poll made a mistake in the christian name and wrote George instead of John. . . . John Channon's name is found in the London Insurance Registers for 1760 and there are records of apprenticeships to him in 1741, when he was described as a joiner and in 1752 when he was described as a cabinet-maker of St. Martin's Lane. He charged a fee of £25 and £15 respectively on these occasions, but when in 1762 Edward Henry Williamson was apprenticed to him, he had to pay the considerable sum of £50. In 1754 the famous Thomas Chippendale charged no more than £20 as an apprenticeship fee.'

It is not surprising that we should find the name of a cabinet-maker of his calibre amongst the subscribers (pp. 82–3) to the first edition of Chippendale's *Director* (1754) — 'Channon Senior' and 'Channon Junior' are both listed. The Channons probably quickly realised that the new craze for the 'Rococo' was bound to date their rather ponderous, ormolu-mounted creations of architectural form, and, thus, after careful study of the *Director*, they must have abandoned their original style and jumped on the rococo 'band-waggon'. This would, of course, explain why the later Channon furniture — we know that his workshop was still operating in St. Martin's Lane in the 1760's[2] — has not

---

[1] 'The Channon family of Exeter and London, chair and cabinet-makers', *Victoria and Albert Museum Bulletin*, April 1966, Vol. II, no. 2.

[2] John Channon's name is found in the London Insurance Registers for 1760.

yet been distinguished from that made by his rivals. Mr. Hayward, through his researches, has unearthed the identity of yet another cabinet-maker of the highest importance, who specialised in the continental technique of engraved metal inlay contrasted with elaborate cast and chased metal-gilt mounts, and in the selection of rare and finely figured woods. A further piece — a medal or specimen cabinet (Pl. 60) — which has also recently been discovered, aptly illustrates his proficiency in the handling of all of these.

It has already been seen that John Graham and William Hallett swore affidavits to Cobb's will on 31st August, 1778, and it appears that Graham, who may well have been a member of Cobb's firm, eventually took over the premises in St. Martin's Lane. Thus in 1790 'Messrs. Graham and Litchfield, upholders' are listed in the *London Directory* as having premises at 'No. 72, St. Martin's Lane, Charing Cross', which was, of course, Vile and Cobb's business address. The famous partners' employees seem to have had little difficulty in setting up in business on their own account for, in 1774, John Jenkins, who described himself as 'late foreman to Mr. Cobb', and who was probably the man on the ladder in the incident in George III's library (see p. 31), opened his doors in his new premises at 75 Long Acre. In 1780 he was joined by a Mr. Strickland who was 'nephew to the late Mr. Vile', and who appears to have taken with him some of his late uncle's clients, for in the Strawberry Hill accounts for the year 1773 'details are given of the costs of an elaborate plumed bed hung with Aubusson tapestry for the Great North Bedchamber and a set of white or gold elbow chairs which were brought over from Paris through the Agency of Madame du Deffand in 1770 and supplied to Strawberry Hill by Strickland'.[1] It is probable, therefore, that many of the pieces in Vile and Cobb's tradition, which are often so freely attributed to them, were in fact made by men like Jenkins, Strickland, or Graham — or perhaps even William Hallett who, as will be shown below, was closely associated with the celebrated partnership.

William Hallett, who had become a fashionable cabinet-maker during George II's reign, numbered many of the great amongst his clients. He was paid considerable sums by Lord Folkestone, between 1737 and 1740, for work that he had carried out at Longford Castle,[2] and, in 1735, he supplied Arthur, 6th Viscount Irwin, with furniture at a cost of £45. 13. 6. as is shown by the extant account.[3] Amongst the pieces that he invoiced were :

'August 9th	£	S	d
For 18 carved walnutree chairs at 23s.	20.	14.	0.
For 2 settees to do.	4.	18.	0.'

These chairs and settees were originally purchased for Lord Irwin's London house, but were later taken to the family seat at Temple Newsam near Leeds in Yorkshire. They were sold by auction in 1922, and the eighteen chairs and one settee were, until recently, in the collection of Mr. Patrick Hall of Longford Hall, Shropshire — his father having acquired them after the sale.[4] They were again offered at auction in 1966.[5]

[1] See Sir Ambrose Heal, *London Furniture Makers*, 1953, p. 176.   [2] *Country Life*, 12 December 1931.
[3] TN/EA 12/5 — The Temple Newsam Papers (now in the Archives Dept. of Leeds Reference Library).
[4] I am indebted to Mr. Christopher Gilbert, assistant Keeper of Temple Newsam House, Leeds, for all the information relating to this suite — an article by him on this suite was published in *The Connoisseur*, December 1964.
[5] Sotheby's, 24 June 1966, lot 127.

VILE, COBB, LANGLOIS, CHANNON, AND HALLETT

In 1732, Hallett was established in Great Newport Street, Longacre,[1] and between 1736 and 1738 he sold, from this address, a good deal of furniture to Leak Okeover of Okeover Hall, Staffordshire.[2] He supplied two mahogany chests, which may be related to those now in the New Entrance Hall at Okeover, and also 'a Handsome glass in a Carved and gilt frame in Burnish gold' at a cost of £19. 10. 0. This is probably the mirror at Okeover Hall in a gilt gesso frame, the carved and scrolled cornice centred by the Okeover Crest.[3] We come across Hallett's name again in 1742 in the Wilton House books[4] where an entry under the date, 7th April, reads 'To Hallett, 3 pair of candlestands silvered nozzles . . . £5. 8. 0.'. These, unfortunately, have not survived, but Hallett's firm may well have supplied other pieces of furniture to the Earl of Pembroke,[5] to harmonise with William Kent's grandiose baroque interiors.

In the same year, he was working for Ditchley Park House, near Oxford, and there is a note of an account which reads 'From William Hallett, cabinet-maker, in Great Newport Street near Long Acre, for tables, stands and screen, work done in 1742'.[6] Three years later, in 1745, his name is mentioned in the 4th Earl of Cardigan's account books.

In 1756 the poet Richard Cambridge couples Hallett's name with that of Thomas Bromwich, a highly successful specialist in wall-papers, who had his premises at the sign of the Golden Lyon, Ludgate Hill, and writes in his *Elegy Written in an Empty Assembly Room*,

'. . . *In scenes where Hallet's genius has combined
With Bromwich to amuse and cheer the mind.*'

It is exciting, therefore, to find *both* Hallett and Bromwich mentioned in the Holkham and Uppark archives relating to the furnishing of these two houses. Thus in the *Holkham Weekley Departmental Accounts* for March 1738, we read that £3. 5. 0. was paid to 'Mr. Hallett for a pattern chair for Holkham'. While discussing this entry in an article in the *Apollo*,[7] the present author writes, 'It would be folly to hint that the superb chair [Pl. 67] — in the Library at Holkham — might be the pattern chair in question, but it is of about the right date, is the only one of its kind in the house and is of such high quality and perfect execution that only one of the greatest craftsmen of the time could have been responsible for its production.' In a later entry in the *Departmental Accounts* we see that £3. 13. 0. was paid to 'Mr. Bromwich for printed paper and border'.

Both Hallett and Bromwich are also mentioned in the Account Book which was studiously compiled by Sir Matthew Fetherstonhaugh, Bt., who started to refurnish and redecorate his house, Uppark, in Sussex, after his marriage in 1745. There is an entry, dated 1st January, 1748 — 'Pd. Mr. Bromwich in full . . . £20. 16. 1.' and another, dated 27th March, 1754, 'Pd. Mr. Hallett for a cabinet . . . £43. 5. 6.'. The wall-paper is perhaps the remarkable red flock wallpaper in the Drawing-Room, and the cabinet may

---

[1] In the 1749 Poll for Westminster, he is listed as 'William *Halliott*, Newport Street, *Cabinetmaker*.'

[2] See Arthur Oswald, 'Okeover Hall, Staffordshire, (Part II)', *Country Life*, 30 January 1964.

[3] *ibid*. fig. 15.   [4] At Wilton House, Wiltshire, in the Collection of the Earl of Pembroke.

[5] See Anthony Coleridge, 'Chippendale At Wilton', *Apollo*, July 1964.

[6] Oxfordshire Record Office — Dillon Collection, Cat. no. 1/p/3bl.

[7] Anthony Coleridge, 'Some Mid-Georgian Cabinet-Makers at Holkham', *Apollo*, February 1964. However there is a subsequent entry in the Holkham Accounts, for April 15, 1738, in which £2. 5. 0. was paid 'to Mr. Hallett in exchange of a pattern chair which he received £3. 5. 0. for on the 18th of March last.' These entries are somewhat obscure.

possibly be the example which is now on the Main Landing (Pl. 68). It is of architectural form and is much in the tradition of the case furniture that Hallett is thought to have been producing at this period. Although the entry is dated 1754, the year in which Chippendale published the first edition of his *Director*, the style of this piece is of Kentian architectural form and one would have expected it to have been made in about 1740. Hallett's style, however, was obviously little affected by the rococo phase in this country, as is demonstrated by the cabinet illustrated in Pl. 69, which is signed by Hallett and which, in spite of its pilaster-like uprights and key-pattern frieze, is dated 1763 (Pl. 71). The detail of its carved decoration (Pl. 70) is of the highest standard. This cabinet was in the collection of Lord Wharton of Halswell Park, near Bridgwater, in Somerset, and the inscription in pencil on the carcase of its base, 'William Hallett, 1763, Long Acre', is of the greatest interest — Why it should have been scrawled in such an ill-formed hand must remain a matter for conjecture; perhaps an apprentice wrote it in a moment of pride. It should anyway be compared with another cabinet, or bookcase, which is in the same tradition, with an architectural cornice and key-pattern frieze (Pl. 72). It is more than probable that Hallett's firm was producing pieces of case furniture of this general type even during the 1750s and '60s.

Hallett is referred to by Horace Walpole in a letter written to Richard Bentley on 5th July, 1755, in which he speaks of his 'mongrel Chinese' (furniture), and in the same letter writes, 'I want to write over the doors of most modern edifices "Repaired and beautified: Langley and Hallett, churchwardens".' These cryptic remarks of Horace Walpole's indicate that Hallett, in spite of his allegiance to the classical dictates of Palladianism, did in fact show some interest in the prevailing Chinoiserie and Gothic mania. The Langley brothers' pioneer designs in the Gothic taste are discussed in Chapter 2.

In 1745, Hallett bought the site of Canons, the Duke of Chandos' house at Whitchurch in Middlesex, and 'built himself a house on the centre vaults of the old one'. He had known the old house and estate well, as he had frequently been employed by the Duke to furnish and refurbish it. There is a reference to the sale and subsequent history of Canons in *The Ambulator, or a Pocket Companion in a Tour Round London.*[1] '. . . as no purchaser could be found for the house, who intended to reside in it, the materials of the building were sold in auction, in 1747, in separate lots, and produced, after deducting the expenses of the sale, £11,000. The marble staircase was purchased by the Earl of Chesterfield, for his house in May Fair; the fine columns were bought for the portico of Wanstead House; and the equestrian statue of George I, one of the numerous sculptures that adorned the grounds, is now the ornament of Leicester Square. One of the principal lots was purchased by Mr. Hallett, a cabinet-maker in Long Acre, who having likewise purchased the estate at Canons, erected on the spot the present villa, with the materials that composed his lot. . . . Mr. Walpole mentions the sale of this place to a *Cabinet-Maker*, as mockery of sublunary grandeur.'

William Hallet married a daughter of James Hallett of Dunmow who may have been connected with the family of goldsmiths of Cheapside, who bore the same name and who also lived in Dunmow. Hallett was twice described as being 'eminent' — the first occasion

---

[1] *The 6th edit., corrected and improved, printed for Jane Bew, Widow of the original Proprietor, 1793* — I am indebted to Mr. Cyril Staal for this information.

being in a report in the *General Advertiser* of 4th March, 1747, which describes an unsuccessful attack made on his party by a highwayman near Kensington Gore; and the second statement was made by his foreman who, in an advertisement in a New York newspaper in 1771, described his former employer as 'the great and eminent cabinet-maker'.

In view of his eminence, it seems extraordinary that so few pieces of furniture have, so far, been proved to have been made by his firm. Why should so many pieces by Chippendale and Vile and Cobb have survived, and so few by Hallett? If and when it is possible to isolate more of the furniture that he made, it may well transpire that his later style was similar to Vile and Cobb's. There are anyway many reasons for suspecting that there was a close business liaison between these three cabinet-makers.

In the first place Hallett and Vile, and (or) Cobb, worked for Thomas Coke at Holkham, for Lord Folkestone at Longford Castle, for Sir Matthew Fetherstonhaugh at Uppark, and for Horace Walpole at Strawberry Hill. Secondly, Hallett swore an affidavit to prove Cobb's will, and was appointed a trustee by Vile who had the highest opinion of his 'honour, ability and integrity'. Thirdly, in 1752, Hallett moved from Newport Street and bought the premises next to Vile and Cobb in St. Martin's Lane. Fourthly, between 1760 and 1770, there are a number of 'out payments', from Cobb to Hallett, noted in the former's bank account which is preserved at Drummond's Bank in Charing Cross.[1] Lastly there is a notice in *The Gentleman's Magazine, 6th September, 1783,* in which Cobb is said to have been 'formerly partner with the late Mr. Hallett of Cannons'. Added to this there is a note in *London Furniture Makers* in which Sir Ambrose Heal writes, 'I am informed by R. W. Symonds that he has found reason for thinking that there was a business connection between Hallett and his next door neighbours, the firm of Vile and Cobb.' Whether these reasons were the same as those given above will unfortunately now never be known, but the evidence produced here is strong enough to suggest there was a partnership or business connection between the two firms. If this was the case, Hallett's style may well have been very similar to that of Vile and Cobb.[2]

APPENDIX A

Extracts from the Lord Chamberlain's account for furniture supplied by Vile for Buckingham House:

No. 29. Wm. Vile Cabinet-Maker. For the Queen's House in St. James's Park. Bill for Quarter Day ending Lady Day, 1764.

'For taking down the lustre and bringing it home to be altered	£1. 14. 0.
For making a drawing of the lustre for the King's approbation	0. 13. 0.
For taking the lustre to pieces, cleaning all the old glass new wiring the whole after cleaned, putting to gr. again	24. 0. 0.
For making lead patterns for the branches	8. 0. 0.
For making four new brass branches with three lights each for 4 ditto with 2 ditto	12. 0. 0.
For 2 large nossels, sockets, 8 pillars and 8 large gadroon pans and 10–20 roses to ditto	3. 10. 0.

---

[1] I am indebted to Mr. Geoffrey Beard for this information.

[2] The substance of the text discussing William Hallett has already been published by the author in *The Journal of the Furniture History Society*, Vol. I, 1965, in his article 'A Reappraisal of William Hallett'.

For new silvering the whole lustre compleat conts. 127 pieces.	42. 0. 0.
For 650 new pieces of cut glass, repairing nine old ornaments.	41. 3. 0.
For 11 yards of strong chain and strong hooks with one end of each divid'd. into 4, a hole in each for fixing silk lines to ye 2 wood caps with 4 holes in each for the Line to pass to stiffen the iron Hook painted green	2. 12. 0.
For porterage home of the lustre carrying up the weights to the top of the house, the wheels, fframes, getting them in the roof fixing the fframes and wheels there fixing up the ceiling tassel with two iron Bolts, Screws, nutts to go thro' the Ceiling and a strong oak plank for fixing do. casing up the Weight on the Gallery with Holdfasts and screws for Fixing Ditto, and Hanging	7. 10. 0.'

See p. 26, n. 7.

APPENDIX B

Extracts from account, totalling £120. 16. 4¾. which was presented by Messrs. Vile and Cobb to Anthony Chute Esq. of The Vyne, near Basingstoke, for work carried out between 1752 and 1753 :

'*For a good mahogany chamber table with a drawer*	£1. 13. 0.
For a good mahogany cornor table	1. 5. 0.
For a good wallnuttree buerow on castors	5. 10. 0.
For a pair of chamber bellows and 3 hearth brooms.	0. 15. 0.
For a japanned hearth broom.	0. 3. 0.
For 5 yards of carpett border at 5/6.	1. 7. 6.
For a globe lanthorn. }	
For 2 glass shades and brass hooks. }	0. 15. 0.
For 2 globe lanthorns on mahogany fluted pillers	2. 10. 0.
For 2 bell lanthorns on brass armes	1. 10. 0.'

(Careful note was also kept of the expenses) :

'*For a man 6 days 6 hours going into the Country puting up the bed window curtains and hangings*	1. 2. 9.
For coach hire and expences	1. 10. 0.'

See p. 27, n. 1.

APPENDIX C

Extracts from MS. account for furniture made by Wm. Vile and John Cobb for the Hon. John Damer for Came House, near Dorchester :

'*For 2 Rich carved and Burnish'd gold Terms*	£26. 13. 0.
For 2 wrot Brass gerondoles neatly lacquered	11. 0. 0.
For a gilder's time 26 weeks, 3 days in the Country, gilding and painting a room.	27. 16. 6.
For a mahogy cheese board made to Turn Round	1. 1. 0.
For Mr. Vile's post chase and expenses	14. 14. 0.
For 10 good mahogy Back stool chairs with carv'd feet, stuf't and covered with damask and finished compleat with Burnish nails	23. 0. 0.
For a good mahogy sopha on castors with carv'd feet to match the chairs	8. 8. 0.'

See p. 27, n. 4.

APPENDIX D

Extracts from MS. account for furniture and furnishings supplied by Vile and Cobb, between 15th April and 18th December, 1758, to Sir Charles Hanbury-Williams Bart. for his house in Upper Brook Street and for Coldbrook, near Abergavenny, Monmouthshire :

'2 *good mahog. double close stoole night tables on castors and stone pans for do.*   5. 10. 0.

2 good mahog. card tables with brackets to the feet, lin'd with cloth and made with folding frames   5. 10. 0.

A pair of neat mahogy. Toy light (toilet) tables with cuttwork sides   6. 6. 0.

Large mahog. Dining tables made to joyn together with a leave made to take off   6. 10. 0.

8 good mahogany chairs, the seats stuff'd and cover'd with figured hair cloth and brass nail'd for the back bow parlour   8. 8. 0.

A pair of arm'd chairs on castors, stuffed, quilted and covered with the same material   6. 0. 0.

An extra fine mahogy. sideboard table with a fret carv'd on the front and bracketts to do.   7. 0. 0.

A good mahog. cistern in a frame Pedestall . . . a paile at top with a lock and one ditto att bottom, lin'd with lead to lift out and carv'd mouldings.

A large globe Lanthorne with a glass shade at top and a branch for 3 candles to take out.

An extra large mahog. Double cloaths press with 12 shelves for the cloaths and bays flaps to do.

For a mahog. 2 leav. screen wth frett at bottom, cover'd with India paper   1. 10. 0.

For man and woman's time to clean all your damask with bread and bran   0. 16. 0.'

See p. 28, n. 2.

CHAPTER II

English Rococo Designers (excluding Chippendale)

We have already dealt with some of the principal cabinet-makers, who flourished during the period under discussion, in the first chapter. As far as we know, none of these published designs for furniture. However, they must certainly have been proficient draughtsmen themselves, or they must have employed skilled designers, in order to provide working drawings for their own establishments; but they do not appear to have taken the further step and *published* such designs. So, such influence as these men may have had must largely have been through the examples that the finished product provided, as they stood in the great houses of the day — or through the movement of workmen from the workshops of such masters to those of other makers.[1]

However, a very important influence was exerted on the forms of English furniture by designs that were published by various people — in some cases, by independent designers, in others, by designers attached to cabinet-making businesses, and sometimes by the firms of cabinet-makers themselves. In the present chapter we try to trace the influence of such designs on English furniture from about 1740 to 1765, in the light of such published designs. However, the work[2] of the most important of all the designers in this group, Thomas Chippendale, is dealt with separately in the chapter succeeding this.

The growth of the *rococo* style in this country can only be studied through the publications of the designers who popularised it, which is, as has been explained, the primary aim of this chapter. English designers were many years behind the French in this field and, in about 1730 when the first phase of the French *rococo* was almost over in Paris, its earliest tremors had barely been felt in London. In France it had been engendered by Jean Bérain with his stylised designs of linear arabesques, and a few years later developed through the asymmetrical and naturalistic designs of Bernard Toro which were published as early as 1716.[3] These were shortly followed by the engraved designs of Nicolas Pineau, Juste-Aurèle Meissonnier, François Cuvilliés and Jean Mondon, and it was they who

---

[1] Apprentices also helped greatly to publicise their master's designs when they set up in business on their own account: e.g. Ince and Mayhew, see pp. 62–3.

[2] *The Gentleman and Cabinet Maker's Director* [1st edition, 1754; 2nd edition, 1755; 3rd edition, 1762].

[3] The designs of both Bérain and Toro were freely drawn upon by Thomas Johnson.

I am much indebted to Helena Hayward's *Thomas Johnson and English Rococo*, p. 9, for much of this information on the sources of the English *rococo*.

brought the *genre pittoresque*,[1] as the rococo was then called in France, to its full bloom with its riot of curves, scrolls, shells, flowers and other decorative motifs culled from nature's rich garden. This, then, was the form that the rococo took when it was first introduced into England in the early 1730's, when the Palladianism of Burlington and Kent was still very much at its zenith. For it was in this year that the Huguenot goldsmith, Paul de Lamerie, is first recorded as using rococo engraved decoration on his plate.

The English designers never fully understood the subtler nuances of the French rococo style, and in many cases they were content to graft its more obvious forms and motifs, such as birds, shells, foliage, water and rocks, 'C' scrolls and *Rocaille* work — or, as Mr. Ward-Jackson[2] describes that favourite ornament of the rococo designers 'an amorphous-looking substance which could be moulded into any shape the artist's fancy suggested', on to the still barely disguised baroque bones of their creations. The growth of the French rococo movement was slow and gradual and it had passed through several phases, being tended by two or three generations of designers and craftsmen, before it reached maturity. In England, on the other hand, it was, with some notable exceptions, such as Hogarth, transplanted from the Continent in its fully developed state, and foisted on to a novelty-conscious society by artists, who, in many cases, little understood the principles, let alone the subtleties, of the movement that they were purveying.[3]

The silversmiths, however, many of whom patently *had* assimilated 'the grammar and syntax' of the rococo style, appear to have been the spearhead of the movement in this country. For instance, already, in 1735, a silver table-centre and a pair of terrines were made for the Duke of Kingston which were inspired by one of Meissonnier's exaggerated rococo designs. The first furniture designs, incorporating rococo motifs were published in 1736 by an Italian painter, Gaetano Brunetti, who had been working in Paris in 1730. Six years later he published a book in London entitled *Sixty Different Sorts of Ornaments*.[4] Six of these plates show designs for furniture and, although they are Italianate in style and baroque in conception, some of them incorporate rococo motifs such as shellwork and scrolling foliage, which probably helped to introduce the Continental rococo to English designers. It is rare to find furniture taken from these designs, but a pair of chairs in the collection of Mr. John Hayward (Pl. 73) is inspired by one of them. An early set of engraved designs in the full rococo tradition, which were published in 1741 in this country, was included in De La Cour's *First Book of Ornament*. Its title page[5] includes a female figure with her left arm pointing to the dedication to Lord Middlesex — this figure, with slightly altered pose, was later plagiarised by Thomas Johnson and used as a support for a candlestand.[6] Other rococo pattern books were published at an early date by P. Glazier, Chatelin, A. Heckell and J. Collins.[7]

[1] The history of the rococo style in France is fully discussed by Fiske Kimball in *The Creation of the Rococo*, Philadelphia Museum of Art, 1943.

[2] P. Ward-Jackson, *English Furniture Designs of the Eighteenth Century*, 1958, p. 12.

[3] Ward-Jackson, *op. cit.*, p. 13.

[4] *Sixty Different Sorts of Ornaments by Gaetano Brunetti, Italian painter. Very useful to painters, sculptors, stone carvers, wood-carvers, silversmiths etc.* . . .

[5] Ill. Ward-Jackson, *op. cit.*, pl. 29.   [6] Ill. Ward-Jackson, *op. cit.*, pl. 346, and *Hayward, op. cit.*, pl. 177.

[7] P. Glazier — designs for metalwork dated 1748 and 1754. Chatelin, *A Book of Ornaments . . . from the drawings of Messrs. Germain, Meissonnier, Si Cattarello etc.*; A. Heckell, *A New Book of Shields*; J. Collins, *A New Book of Shields*.

During these early formative years, when the transplanted rococo style was beginning to take root and blossom in this alien country, the English Palladianism, as prescribed by Lord Burlington and William Kent, was at its apogee. Kent, who had returned from Italy with Burlington in 1719, began to practise seriously as an architect in about 1730. He had adopted Burlington's ideal — namely, that of establishing a classicising Palladian style in England. He was a man of wide tastes, and was not only the first English architect to take a serious interest in interior decoration and furniture, but also fully realised the visual impact that could be obtained by relating the architecture and decoration of a room to the furniture that it contained. His primary commissions in this field were at Holkham, Houghton and Wilton and much of the furniture that he designed for the state apartments of these houses still remains in them. It is unlikely that he provided detailed designs for every piece of furniture associated with his style in these houses, because very few actual furniture designs from his hand survive. It is more probable that he described, or sketched, the kind of pieces that he visualised for the grandiose settings that he had created, leaving it to one of the professional furniture designers to develop his basic conceptions. For the leading cabinet-makers, such as Hallett, Goodison or Haddock must have retained such specialist designers.[1] However, some of his designs have survived and one, for a table which still remains at Houghton, is signed on the reverse by the artist.[2]

Other designs by Kent were published in 1744 by the architect, John Vardy, in a book entitled *Some Designs of Mr. Inigo Jones and Mr. William Kent*. Most of these are in the rather ponderous and heavy tradition that has become associated with Kent and the Burlingtonians. These include *'a chandelier for the King'*, a table designed for Lord Burlington's villa at Chiswick House, an organ case, chairs and settees.[3] John Vardy was an architect and designer who spent most of his career in the Office of Works. It was there that he doubtless became acquainted with Kent who had held important posts in that organisation from 1725.[4] The Office of Works was situated in St. Martin's Lane and this was doubtless one of the reasons why the leading cabinet-makers tended to have their premises in the same street or in the vicinity.

Vardy's most important surviving building is Spencer House, Green Park. In a proposed design for the interior elevation of the Great Dining-Room at Spencer House, dated 1757, a pair of girandoles carved with lion-masks is clearly visible. This design was, in fact, never executed, but detailed drawings were made by Vardy in the following year for 'Two Tables and Two Glasses at each end of Great Dining Room and Parlour Room' (Pl. 74), and a 'Table and Glass as Designed for the Little Dining Room' (Pl. 75). The former is fully in the style that has become associated with Vardy's designs for carvers and is, undeniably, in the Kentian tradition; the sphinx support of the table in the latter is, however, very *avant-garde* and seems to look forward to some of the *antique* designs of Percier and Fontaine dating from the early years of the 19th century and incorporating this hybrid beast, rather than to hark back to Kent's more baroque beasts.[5] It is not known

[1] See Anthony Coleridge, 'Chippendale at Wilton', *Apollo*, July 1964, for a fuller discussion of this theory.

[2] Ill. Ward-Jackson, *op. cit.*, pl. 18.   [3] *Ibid.*, pls. 13–17.

[4] He was *Master Carpenter* from May 1725 until July 1735 when he succeeded Dubois as *Master Mason*. He was Deputy to the Surveyor-General from 1737 to 1742 and continued as a Commissioner until his death.

[5] *e.g.* the female sphinx figures supporting the settees in the Double Cube Room at Wilton, and those supporting a side-table at Houghton, ill. Margaret Jourdain, *The Work of William Kent*, 1948, fig. 142.

whether these designs were, in fact, carried out, although the highly finished state of the drawings suggests that they were.

John Vardy's brother, Thomas, was a carver of Park Street, Grosvenor Square, and it was, presumably, he who executed John's *'carvers' designs'*. John's will,[1] dated 13th April, 1762, also mentions his son, John, to whom he left all his books, drawing instruments and matters relating to architecture. It therefore seems probable that there was a family firm, which he ran as a sideline in his capacity as architect and civil servant at the Office of Works. With the help of his son, he perhaps designed furniture which his brother then produced in his Park Street workshop. This may explain why Vardy had such a predilection for designing furniture that required the talents of the carver, rather than the joiner.

Much of the furniture from Spencer House has been moved to Althorp, Earl Spencer's country house in Northamptonshire.[2] Many of these pieces may be attributed to Vardy on stylistic grounds. Until he was succeeded by James (Athenian) Stuart, Vardy was entirely responsible for the interior decoration of Spencer House. The first piece illustrated here is a pier-glass (Pl. 76), which is surmounted by an architectural pediment centred by a shell. Similar cornices are found in pier-glasses and over-mantels designed by Vardy, the original drawings of which are in the Royal Institute of British Architects.[3] The uprights are over-carved with entwined frond-like acanthus foliage of a most unusual nature. Similar fronds are found on the design for a pier-glass and table (Pl. 77),[4] the frieze of the latter being adorned with the arms of the Bolton family — *Three swords in pile*. This design, although drawn in 1761, four years before Vardy's death, and when the rococo in this country was at its zenith, still shows a close adherence to the more formal principles of Burlington's Palladianism. However, another design (Pl. 78) for a pier-glass and side-table is more in the rococo manner, and the mirror plate is overlaid in giltwood with similar strange, frond-like, palmettes, which are very similar to those found in French designs of about 1745. A pair of pier-glasses and tables (Pls. 79 and 80) made from these designs still remain in the Saloon at Hackwood Park, Basingstoke, where they were delivered to the 3rd or 4th Dukes of Bolton.[5] A giltwood and metal hexagonal lantern (Pl. 81), probably designed by Vardy for the Entrance Hall at Spencer House, is also at Althorp, and its uprights terminate in splayed palm foliage, carved with berries — a refinement found on the pier-glass from the same house (cf. Pl. 76).

There are also many pieces of seat and case furniture at Althorp, which have come from Spencer House, and which must have been supplied by chair or cabinet-makers as opposed to carvers. One of a set of twenty-three single chairs (Pl. 82) has a most unusual splat carved with the splayed acanthus foliage which has been associated with Vardy's style. In the same way Pl. 83 illustrates a hall-chair from a set of twelve which has a porter's chair of similar design to it. On the seat-rails are carved bucrania similar to those which appear in

[1] P.C.C. 239, Rushworth.

[2] I am deeply indebted to Lord Spencer for the information that he has given me relating to Vardy and Spencer House, and the work of Gordon and Tait, and also for his photographs of furniture at Althorp.

[3] R.I.B.A. Library K9/6 and K9/21 — The former, an overmantel mirror, inscribed *This design for Lady Milton's Dressing Room Frame over the Chimney. J. Vardy, 1761.* Ill. *Ward-Jackson, op. cit.,* pls. 40, 42.

[4] A pair of tables made from this design are in the Collection of Lord Bolton at Bolton Hall, Yorkshire.

[5] Charles, third Duke of Bolton, 1721–54; Henry, fourth Duke, 1754–9; Charles, fifth Duke, 1759–65. For a full description of the Hackwood Suite see Anthony Coleridge, 'John Vardy and the Hackwood Suite', *Connoisseur,* January 1962, pp. 12–16.

the frieze in the hall at Spencer House, where they originally stood, and which was designed by Vardy in 1758. These chairs were repaired in 1772 by the firm of cabinet-makers and upholsterers, Gordon and Taitt who, in that year, had moved from King Street, Golden Square, to Little Argyle Street. Other accounts from the firm, dated between 1774 and 1776, are in the Althorp archives, and it is probable that some of these sets of chairs, originating from Spencer House, were, in fact, made by William Gordon at an earlier date, when he was working alone in Golden Square, about 1754, prior to the formation of the partnership. This supposition is strengthened if the chairs illustrated in Pls. 84 and 85, which belong to sets originally delivered to Spencer House, are compared with those shown in Pls. 86 and 87,[1] which were ordered from John Gordon[2] of Swallow Street, Argyle Buildings, by the 2nd Duke of Atholl for Blair Castle in 1753. Like the examples at Blair, the open armchair (Pl. 84) is superbly carved; it belongs to a suite of two settees, two armchairs, eight single chairs and a waisted library table. The toes of the set of eight *dolphin* chairs from Blair Castle (Pl. 87) which Gordon describes in his account of 17th June, 1765, as '8 mahogany chairs, carv'd frames in fish scales, with a French foot and carv'd leaf upon the toe', should be compared with those on the Spencer House example (cf. Pl. 85), which is one of a set of five similar chairs and three stools. The shape and design of the seat-rails and legs of the two sets are also very similar. It would therefore appear that William and, or, John Gordon were probably supplying seat and case[3] furniture to Spencer House, when it was being furnished, under Vardy's direction, during the late '1750's'. It has been demonstrated that the chairs illustrated in Pls. 82 and 83 may have been designed by Vardy and that those in Pls. 82 to 85 were probably made by John Gordon. In conclusion, therefore, it is suggested that John Vardy commissioned his brother to execute his designs for *carvers'* pieces while he engaged Gordon, in the case of Spencer House, to execute the seat and case furniture.

This discussion of the work of John Vardy, and that of Gordon and Taitt, stemmed from a brief review of William Kent's influence on English furniture design. No such review would be complete without a study of the designs of William Jones and the brothers Langley. The former, who died in 1757, was also an architect and designer, and in 1739 he published *The Gentlemens or Builders Companion* . . .[4] which contains twenty designs for tables and mirrors. Most of these are derived from the work of Inigo Jones, and William Kent, although some of them betray Continental influence and one (*plate 32*)[5] is clearly derived from the engraved designs of Nicolas Pineau. A mahogany side-table (Pl. 89) in the Victoria and Albert Museum owes much to Jones' design, and the cabinet-maker had the good sense to simplify it, eliminating the garlands that unite the caryatid supports to the mask apron. It is also clearly derived from a design (*plate 143*) in *the City and Country*

---

[1] These sets of chairs are fully discussed by Anthony Coleridge, 'Chippendale, *The Director*, and Some Cabinet-Makers at Blair Castle', *Connoisseur*, December 1960, pp. 252–3.

[2] It appears that John Gordon was related to William Gordon and that later they were both partners in the firm of William Gordon and John Taitt.

[3] A set of three break-front bookcases from Lord Spencer's Library at Spencer House was also probably made by William Gordon — the mouldings on the bookcases are *en suite* with those on the Library doors.

[4] *The Gentlemens or Builders Companion containing variety of useful designs for doors, gateways, peers, pavilions, temples, chimney-pieces, slab tables, pier glasses, or tabernacle frames, ceiling pieces &c. Explained on copper plates by Wm. Jones, architect. . . . 1739. London. . . .*

[5] Ill. Ward-Jackson, *op. cit.*, pl. 23.

Builder's and Workman's Treasury of Designs . . .[1] by Batty Langley, printed in 1740, and engraved by his brother Thomas. The design in question, which is signed *Thos. Langley Invent delin and Sculp 1739*, is clearly also plagiarised from Nicolas Pineau's *Nouveaux Desseins de Pieds de Tables*. Batty Langley, the elder brother, was a designer, architect and landscape gardener, whilst Thomas was an engraver and draughtsman. They published numerous trade pattern books for builders and gardeners, the most important of which, containing twenty-five designs, was the work just mentioned.[1] They freely copied from Continental sources — six designs for tables being taken from Pineau, while others are after designs by Johann Jakob Schübler and Johann Friedrich Lauch. They also published a book on Gothic architecture[2] in 1742, which is the only other of their many publications that has a bearing on furniture and interior decoration. Batty Langley died in 1751 and his obituary in the *London Advertiser* is as amusing as his name (Appendix A).

To complete this survey of the Kentian tradition, the designs of the carpenter and joiner, Abraham Swan, fl. 1745–65, should also be mentioned. In 1745 he published[3] *The British Architect; or the Builder's Treasury of Staircases*, which includes designs for chimney-pieces with rococo motives grafted on to classical frames. These designs, however, can have had little influence and are of no great importance.

We now come to the period immediately prior to the publication of the first edition of Chippendale's *Director* in 1754, during which a whole mass of furniture designs were to be published. Mathew Darly, who was responsible for the majority of the engraved plates in the three editions of Chippendale's *Director*, published his first book of designs in 1751[4] entitled *A New Book of Chinese, Gothic and Modern Chairs. . . .* The designs for these chairs are bizarre and eccentric in the extreme and it is difficult to distinguish between the Chinese, the Gothic and the Modern. His next book, which he published in collaboration with an artist named Edwards, came out in 1754 under the title *A New Book of Chinese Designs. . . .*[5] It includes a few designs for pieces of furniture in the Chinese and rustic styles, some of which are ludicrous in conception as they are formed from gnarled and twisted roots, whilst others are more practical and resemble Chinese bamboo *Export* furniture of the early nineteenth century. These latter designs[6] also resemble those published by Sir William Chambers in 1757 as plates 13 and 14[6] in his folio book entitled *Designs of Chinese Buildings, Furniture. . . .*[7] Chambers,[8] who was one of the most important British architects of the period, had visited China in his youth when he was a cadet in the Swedish East Company. He had executed a series of drawings when he had visited Canton

---

[1] *The City and Country Builder's and Workman's Treasury of Designs: or the Art of drawing and working the ornamental parts of architecture. . . . By Batty Langley. London . . . 1740.*

[2] *Ancient Architecture restored and improved by a great variety of grand and useful designs, entirely new, in the Gothic mode, for the ornamenting of buildings and gardens . . . 1742.*

[3] 1st edition, 1745; 2nd edition, 1750; 3rd edition, 1758.   [4] The plates are dated 1750 and 1751.

[5] *A New Book of Chinese Designs calculated to improve the present taste, consisting of figures, buildings, Etc. furniture, landskips, birds, beasts, flowrs and ornaments Etc. . . . By Messrs. Edwards, and Darly. Published . . . & Sold by the authors, the first house on the right hand in Northumberland Court, in the Strand MDCCLIV —* (Darly had taken this house over from Chippendale on Lady Day 1753).

[6] Cf. *Ward-Jackson, op. cit.*, pls. 132 (Darly) and 135, 136 (Chambers).

[7] *Designs of Chinese Buildings, Furniture, Dresses, Machines and Utensils. . . . From the originals drawn in China by Mr. Chambers, Architect . . . to which is annexed a description of their temples, houses, gardens etc. London . . . 1757.*

[8] His life is fully discussed by Mr. John Harris in his book *Sir William Chambers*, London, 1968.

during this voyage, and it was these that he published in 1757. The furniture he illustrates is clearly intended to represent actual examples of Chinese furniture and is very different from the essays in chinoiserie of men like Chippendale and Thomas Johnson.

Matthias, or Matthew, Lock is the next designer whose work is to be discussed and he is a figure of some importance. Very little is known of his life apart from a few facts, which can be gathered from his published works, and a good deal of supposition has been built-up from, and around, these. Mr. Geoffrey Wills in *English Looking Glasses*[1] has, however, recently published an entry from the Apprentice Records of 1724 which may refer to him: 'Math [Son of] Math [of] St. Paul's Shadwell join[er] to Ric[hard] Goldsaddle [of] St. Mart/Fields carv[er].' His design books are listed in some detail below, as they are the first designs in the full rococo manner of importance and originality to be published in this country. With his collaborator, H. Copland, Lock 'took up the style with extraordinary aptitude and handled it with the greatest facility and freedom. So far as the French models are known to us, there is no literal or slavish copy of individual French examples but a new and genial creation along the general lines established by the French designers'.[2] The list[3] of their publications, in shortened form (the publisher being omitted from some titles), is as follows:

1740.   *A New Drawing Book of Ornaments, Shields, Compartments, Masks, etc., drawn and engraved by M. Lock.*

1744.   *Six Sconces by M. Lock . . . published March 1744.*

1746.   *Six Tables by Matths. Lock . . . published April ye 10, 1746.*

No Date. *A Book of Ornaments, drawn and engraved by M. Lock, principally adapted for carvers, but generally useful for various decorations in the present taste . . . London. Published by John Weale . . . M. Lock, invt.*
         (title as given in Weale's Restrikes in 1835)

1752.   *A New Book of Ornaments, with twelve leaves, consisting of chimneys, sconces, tables, spandle pannes, spring clock cases, etc., stands, a chandelier, etc., gerandole etc., by M. Lock and H. Copland . . . Published . . . Nov. 13, 1752 & Sold by the proprietors M. Lock near ye Swan, Tottenham Court Road & E. Copland Gutter Lane Cheapside.*

1768.   *A New Book of Ornaments consisting of tables, chimnies, sconces, spandles, clock cases, candle stands, chandeliers, girandoles, etc. By Matt. Lock and H. Copeland . . . published Jany 1, 1768 by Robert Sayer at No. 53 Fleet Street.*

1768.   *Six Sconces by M. Lock.*
         (2nd edition of the work of 1744, plates unchanged).

1768.   *A Book of Tables, Candle stands, Pedostals, Tablets, Table Knees etc. by Matt. Lock. . . .*
         (2nd edition of the work of 1746, plates unchanged).

1769.   *A New Book of Pier-Frame's, Ovals, Gerandole's, Tables etc. by M. Lock. . . .*

1769.   *A New Book of Foliage for the Instruction of Young Artists by M. Lock. . . .*

No Date. *A New Book of Ornaments for Looking Glass Frames, Chimney Pieces etc. in the Chinese taste by Matt. Lock. Useful for carvers. . . .*
         (probably a 2nd edition of an earlier work, issued in about 1768).

No Date. *A New Drawing Book . . . Printed for Robert Sayer. . . .*
         (2nd edition of work of 1740, issued about 1768, plates unchanged).

[1] London, 1965.

[2] Quoted from Fiske Kimball and E. Donnell, 'The Creators of the Chippendale Style', *Metropolitan Museum Studies*, I, May 1929. This pioneer essay has afforded me much information on the designs of Lock and Copland.

[3] Based on that given by Mr. Ward-Jackson in *English Furniture Designs of the Eighteenth Century*, pp. 38–9.

No Date. *The Principles of Ornament, or the Youth's Guide to Drawing of Foliage . . . by M. Lock. London. Printed for Robert Sayer near Serjeant's Inn Fleet Street.* (Title page only in Victoria and Albert Museum. No complete copy recorded).

A number of Lock's original drawings have also survived, some being in the Metropolitan Museum, New York, while the majority are in the Victoria and Albert Museum. In 1920 the Metropolitan Museum acquired two folio scrap-books, formerly in the collection of Lord Foley, containing two groups of drawings. The first includes nearly all the designs for the plates in the first edition of Chippendale's *Director* (1754) with many for the third edition (1762), and the second consists of a number of unpublished designs for carvers' pieces that have been attributed to Lock on stylistic grounds, after comparison with others in the Victoria and Albert Museum. The Victoria and Albert drawings were acquired in two separate groups from George Lock of Edinburgh, the grandson of Matthias Lock. The first, consisting of seventy-eight sheets, was bought in 1862, forty-six of these drawings being ascribed to Lock and thirty-two to Chippendale.[1] Amongst the designs attributed to Lock are seven small sketches of pieces of furniture covered with notes relating to the number of days taken to produce the pieces and the wages due for the work carried out by Lock and other craftsmen.[2] Two of these sheets are on the reverse sides of the leaves of a diary, which can be dated to 1752 as it was leap year. The sketches are annotated as follows 'A Sconce and a Table for Lord Holdernest', 'to Chimney, Mr. Bradshaw', 'to Table Ld. Northumb'ld.'.[3] The second group, which was acquired by the Museum from George Lock a year later, contains a hundred and sixty-eight drawings, most of which are by Matthias Lock, entitled *Original Designs by Matts. Lock Carver 1740–1765.* The album also contains ten more annotated sketches drawn by Lock recording commissions for carving executed between 1742 and 1744. Finally a drawing by Lock of the cartouche in the title page of his *Six Tables* of 1746 was included in the collection of Chippendale drawings that the Victoria and Albert Museum acquired in 1906.

An important reference to Lock was found by the author in 1964 in the Hopetoun House archives which, almost certainly, refers to designs for some of the carver's pieces of furniture which were sent by the cabinet-maker James Cullen (see pp. 160–9) to the Earl of Hopetoun. It is written on a loose scrap of paper and reads, 'The enclosed drawings are valuable being designed and drawn by the famous Mr. Matt Lock recently deceased who was reputed the best Draftsman in that way that had ever been in England.' It is thought that Lock died in 1770, his last dated books being published in 1769, and the designs were obviously sent by Cullen to his client almost immediately after Lock's death. It would appear, therefore, that Lock was designing for Cullen after he left Chippendale's employ. Thus, in a letter dated 18th January, 1768, written by Cullen to the Earl, we read, 'Herewith I enclose your Lordship the two small drawings for the State Bed *which are just come to my hands.*' Whether they had come from Lock's hand, or not, will never be known,

---

[1] Seven of these are original designs for the third edition of the *Director* (1762).

[2] These sketches, which were for furniture at Hinton House, Somerset, are fully discussed in the text below.

[3] Lord Holdernest was Robert, Earl of Holderness, succeeded in 1722 and died in 1778: Mr. Bradshaw may have been William Bradshaw, the cabinet-maker: there is no furniture at Alnwick or Syon which can with certainty be related to Lock's designs for the Earl of Northumberland.

but it seems more than likely that he was in fact retained by Cullen; this whole complex question is more fully discussed in connection with the career of James Cullen. At any rate, it cannot be denied that the lines quoted above make an admirable obituary for Matthias Lock as a designer — one which his surviving work shows that he richly deserved.

It was first pointed out by the authors of *The Creators of the Chippendale Style*[1] that Lock, who had been a prolific publisher of decorative and carvers' designs from 1740 to 1752, brought out nothing new between 1752 and 1769. They claim that during this period he may well have been employed by Thomas Chippendale, who published the three editions of his *Director* between 1754 and 1762. They suggest that Lock was retained by Chippendale during these years in an advisory capacity, for even at that early period he was probably accepted as the leading draughtsman working in the rococo style on account of his many publications. The author's further maintain that Chippendale employed Lock as a carver and as his resident designer of carver's pieces for important clients who wished to commission exclusive designs for themselves. It has never been suggested that Lock was responsible for any of the designs published in the *Director*, although, of course, he may have outlined many of them to Chippendale or to his draughtsmen.

By 1766 Chippendale had lain aside the rococo style and was furnishing Adam's rooms at Nostell Priory with furniture in the neo-classical tradition or *antique* taste. This phase is fully discussed by Mr. Clifford Musgrave in *Adam and Hepplewhite Furniture* in this series. Robert Adam, during the period when he was furnishing Luton Hoo between 1764 and 1768, had sounded the death knell to the rococo when he described his accessories there 'as an attempt to banish the absurd French compositions of this kind, heretofore so servilely imitated by the upholsterers of this country'. Lock, following Chippendale's example, also read the writing on the wall and in 1768, published his *New Book of Pier Frames* and *New Book of Foliage, in the neo-classical style*, and thus preceding Darly's *The Ornamental Architect or Young Artist's Instructor* of 1770 and Adam's publications of 1773 to 1778 by two and five years respectively. His career as a designer had thus spanned the life-period of the English rococo style and he was attendant at both its birth and its death.

Lock's career as a carver now remains to be discussed. Matthias Lock, in two trade cards dated 1746, is referred to as a *carver* and *designer*, while his address is given as being in Nottingham Court, Castle Street, near Long Acre: whereas, in 1752, his premises were near Ye Swan in Tottenham Court Road. It has already been suggested that he may have joined Chippendale's firm sometime after 1752, when he and Copland had brought out their *New Book of Ornaments*, and it will be remembered that it was during this year that he was supplying furniture to *Lord Holdernest, Mr. Bradshaw and Ld. Northumb'ld.* Whether this was before his suggested alliance with Chippendale, or after, is not known. Among the seven small annotated sheets of sketches in the Victoria and Albert Museum already referred to are three showing a looking glass, a table (Pl. 90) and a stand. The drawings, which are rapid sketches in pencil, are respectively inscribed *A Large sconce, a Table* and *Two Stands* and each were *in the Tapestry Roome*. It has recently been discovered[2] that these pieces were made for Hinton House, Hinton St. George, Somerset, the home of

[1] Fiske Kimball and E. Donnell, see p. 53, n. 2.
[2] See J. F. Hayward, 'Furniture designed and carved by Matthias Lock for Hinton House, Somerset', *Connoisseur*, December 1960, pp. 284–6.

the Earl Poulett and, until a few years ago, all of them had remained in the house [see also p. 54]. It is probable that they were designed by Lock for the second Earl Poulett, who succeeded in 1743, and they are certainly in his early rococo style. The pair of stands are still at Hinton House, the table[1] and the *Large Sconce*, or pier-glass, is in the Victoria and Albert Museum (Pl. 91). The pier-glass is partly gilded which contrasts favourably with the carved heads and background, which were painted to simulate bronze during the early nineteenth century to harmonise with the Regency decoration of the room. The execution of the carved detail and general conception of these pieces are still baroque in feeling although the spontaneously sketched designs display all the lively airiness of the rococo style. The design for the *Large Sconce* corresponds in style to those published by Lock in 1744 in his *Six Sconces* (Pl. 92), and this may be taken as being about the date for the suite. Another pier-glass of similar date and much in Lock's tradition is at Temple Newsam House, Leeds (Pl. 98). Mr. Hayward, while discussing the Hinton House suite,[2] writes, 'A particularly interesting feature of Lock's drawings for this suite of carved furniture is that he has noted against them the number of days worked by himself and each of his assistants, and also the price charged. No figure is given for gilding and presumably a separate charge was made for this. The mirror cost £36. 5. 0., of which £34. 10. 0. was charged for carving and the remainder for the joiner's work. Lock spent 20 days work on it, while his assistants (Loman, Wood and Low) spent 40, 15 and 14 days respectively. The distribution of the remaining days, spent on making the mirror, amounting to 49, is not given. The table took 89 days work and cost £22. 5. 0. . . . The pair of stands were, somewhat unexpectedly, the most expensive item, costing £50 the pair and taking 188 days work.'

It is important to remember that, in the case of the pier-glass, the £36. 5. 0. only included the cost of the carving and joiner's work and did not include that of the gilding; nor that of the glass plate — a far greater expense, as we can see from Samuel Norman's account,[3] presented on 13th September, 1760, to the Duke of Bedford for a pair of pier-glasses (Pl. 384) that now hang in the Blue Dining-Room at Woburn Abbey, Bedfordshire:

'William Norman[4] for 2 large glass frames in burnished gold	£229. 0. 0.
For a plate of glass	183. 5. 0.
	£412. 5. 0.'

One of the reasons for the high cost of these mirror plates is that it was the fashion during the middle decades of the century to use plates cast in France. In this connection we read of Chippendale in 1769, in the character of a dealer in glass plates, supplying ten plates for pier-glasses at Kenwood for Lord Mansfield.[5] He was to deliver them to Robert Adam

---

[1] The table, which was in the collection of the late Mrs. Rhodes, Thorpe Underwood Hall, Yorks, is now reunited with the pier-glass in the Victoria and Albert Museum.

[2] See p. 55, n. 2.

[3] See G. Scott-Thomson, *Family Background*, 1949, pp. 67–8, 74–8.

[4] William Norman was probably a relative of Samuel Norman, the latter signing the guarantee that accompanied the account. See pp. 140–5 for a full description of Samuel Norman's life and work.

[5] Accounts etc. for Kenwood House — quoted by Oliver Bracket, *Thomas Chippendale*, pp. 69–70.

who had retained the cabinet-making firm founded by William France,[1] to carve and gild the frames, Chippendale's estimate and promissory note for this work, dated 14th June, 1769, is as follows :

'I promise to deliver in about Two Months from this Date to Mr. Adam Architect The Following *French* plate Glass, in London silver'd and ready to be put up.

Two plates 74 ins. by 44 ins. at £69. 10. ea.	£139. 0. 0.
Four Dos. 74 by 26	at £35. 0. ea.	£140. 0. 0.
Four Dos. 74 by 13	at £15. 5. ea.	£ 61. 0. 0.
		£340. 0. 0.

The above dimensions are in English measures.

Robert Adam.   P. Thos. Chippendale.

Received Jan. 27, 1770, the full contents of this bill by the hand of Mr. France and My Sun in full of all demands.

P. Thos. Chippendale.'

The freight of these mirror panels from Paris would not only have been expensive, but the insurance would have been high as the risk of breakage was considerable. Thus, in 1767, in Chippendale's accounts to Sir Edward Knatchbull, for work that he had carried out at Mersham-le-Hatch near Maidstone, there is a charge of 11s. 'to freight paid of 4 cases with Glass'. Further details of freight and insurance costs are given in Robt. Gillow and Co. of Lancaster's account to the Duke of Atholl for furniture delivered to Castle Mona, Isle of Man.[2] Although it is dated 1805, the value of money had not greatly changed since the mid-eighteenth century and it gives some indication of relative costs :

'To cash paid for stamp'd bill of lading cartage to the Kay and Towns(?)

Duty . . .	£0. 15. 0.
To cash paid Captain Faraquer on account of freight . . .	£3. 13. 6.
To cash paid duty at the Custom House, Report and Entry . . .	£5. 9. 0.'

In an account of the following year, from the same firm, the Duke was charged 3 gns. insurance premium on furniture invoiced at £272. 7. 6½., which is a rate of little over a guinea per cent to insure furniture, presumably against all risks on this occasion, from Lancaster to London; the highest rate today would be about 5s. per cent. Another indication of the value that was put on these plates during the eighteenth century can be seen from the wording of Benjamin Rackstrow's trade card, engraved by H. Copland, in 1738 — Rackstrow being a *Cabinet* and *Picture frame maker* at Sir Isaac Newton's Head, at the corner of Crane Court in Fleet Street. He offered 'all Sorts of Cabinet Work, Picture Frames, Looking and Coach Glasses, Window Blinds etc. after ye newest Fashions *Exchanges New Glasses for Old Makes Old ones fashionable . . .*'. It can thus be clearly seen from the wording of this trade card that it was the custom to have new frames made for old plates, obviously on account of the high cost of the latter. In fact a number of other furniture dealers and cabinet-makers advertised their willingness to accept old plates for reworking or in part exchange.

[1] William France, related to Edward France of 101 St. Martin's Lane — see pp. 145–50 for a full description of his career.

[2] See Anthony Coleridge, 'The firm of Gillow and Co. at Blair Castle', *Connoisseur*, October 1964.

Returning to Lock's seven sketches for the Hinton House furniture, the four other annotated drawings appear to have been executed at the same time and for the same client. They represent a *lantern*, a *side-table, a bracket for a glass case* . . . and a *wall bracket* described as *a piece of Carving Work in a Closet in the Dressing Roome*. Two of the pieces have disappeared, the wall bracket is still remembered but is no longer there, and the table remains at Hinton House. It appears that Lock must have made at least two tables to this design (Pl. 93), as there is a table in the Earl of Dartmouth's collection[1] (Pl. 94) which is a close replica of the Lock sketch and is almost identical to the table at Hinton House. The carver's work for the Hinton table is noted as having cost £7. 5. 0. and the joiner's time and work 16s. : 29 days were spent on its production. The average cost was therefore a little over 5s. per day, which is about the same rate as that which was charged for some of the more elaborate examples made for Hinton House.

A few other pieces that have been attributed to Lock remain to be discussed. The first group consists of a series of tables which have a baroque flavour, more like that associated with Kent and the Palladian taste than with Lock's interpretation of the *genre pittoresque*. The design for these tables (Pl. 95) was produced by Lock in about 1740 and it is highly distinctive, the friezes being decorated with the mask of Hercules draped with the pelt of the Nemean lion. A pair of tables after this design, which were formerly at Ditchley House, Oxfordshire, are now at Temple Newsam House, outside Leeds,[2] and another is in the Metropolitan Museum, New York (Pl. 96). The latter was originally at Hamilton Palace, Lanarkshire, and is painted black and partly gilded. A related table is in the Duke of Atholl's collection in the State Dining-Room at Blair Castle, Perthshire (Pl. 97). It has been painted green at a later date, but the carving is of the highest quality and there is an added refinement in the manner that the lion's tail is entwined with the pelt. Apart from these tables there is a carved and painted chimney-piece taken from a design in Lock and Copland's *New Book of Ornaments*, 1752, and in their full rococo manner. It is in the Drawing-Room at Stedcombe House, Devon, in the collection of Mr. and Mrs. Robert Mathew.[3] Both the design and chimney-piece admirably illustrate Lock's skill and versatility as designer and carver alike.

Lock and Chippendale were not, however, the only exponents of the English rococo style at this period; they had a serious rival in Thomas Johnson, who was also both a carver and gilder and a *designer*. Johnson published his first set of designs, entitled *Twelve Gerondoles*, all engraved by W. Austin, on 1st September, 1755, from his address in Queen Street, near Seven Dials, London. These designs, although still conforming to the current English interpretation of the French rococo, are highly individual and 'spikey and jagged, the outlines (being) pierced and darted by leafless twigs, spurting water or dripping weeds. Scrolls and columns carry the mounting structure. Chinese motifs are hardly present. Instead a rustic mood is dominant. One includes a watermill with a peasant leading a donkey. The most marked characteristic of the designs, however, is Johnson's

---

[1] See Anthony Coleridge, 'Furniture in the Collection of Viscount and Viscountess Lewisham', *Connoisseur*, November 1962.

[2] Exhibited in the *English Taste in the Eighteenth Century* exhibition, The Royal Academy, 1955–6, Cat. No. 43, and Ill. *D.E.F.*, III, 1927, pp. 123–4, fig. 3 and *G.C-M.*, pl. 82.

[3] The chimney-piece and the design are illustrated in an article by Mark Girouard, 'Stedcombe House, Devon', *Country Life*, Vol. CXXXIV, p. 1741.

frequent recourse to Francis Barlow's illustrations to *Aesop's Fables*.[1] In plate 2 of *Twelve Gerondoles* Johnson has used Barlow's design of Aesop's Fable *A Wolf in Sheep's Clothing* as a basis for his design. A table (Pl. 99) from the Earl of Dartmouth's collection, recently at Patshull House, Wolverhampton, is based on Johnson's design for 'a Gerondole'. The carving may well be by Johnson himself, although there is no documentary evidence, apart from the design, to support it. A console table of somewhat similar design is at Corsham Court. It is supported by a tree trunk and slender colonettes and, as in the case of another pair of tables in the same tradition, which are at Curraghmore, Co. Waterford,[2] this is based on one of Johnson's designs from his next publication. These Curraghmore tables, together with some pier-glasses and tables now at Powerscourt House, Co. Wexford, came from Tyrone House, Dublin. Although they are inspired by Johnson's designs, they are probably of Irish workmanship since their design and form are highly exaggerated — which is a characteristic feature of much Irish furniture of the period.

In 1756 Johnson began to issue a series of designs for 'carver's pieces', in monthly parts, and these were issued, bound together in one volume, in 1758. There was no title but the first page bears a dedication to *The Right Hon.ble Lord Blakeney,*[3] *Grand President of the Antigallican Association and the Rest of the Bretheren of that most Honourable Order, and Sold by T. Johnson carver, At the Golden Boy, In Grafton St. St. Ann's Westminster . . . 1758.* It can thus be seen that sometime before 1st May, 1757, he had moved to No. 28 Grafton Street. He was, during this period, living at No. 16 St. Giles's Court. These designs were not directed to the public, as Chippendale's *Director* had been to some extent, but towards large firms of cabinet-makers who might call upon his specialist skill as a designer and carver. He must have been reasonably successful in this aim, for a second edition was published in 1761, issued in four parts with separate title pages, containing the same plates, re-arranged, and with one additional design (no. 48). It was entitled *One Hundred and Fifty New Designs, by Thos. Johnson carver . . . ,*[4] and, eccentric as these designs may appear, several of them have been faithfully executed in wood, glass and metal by Johnson himself, or by other carvers, copying his designs. Before these pieces are discussed, and we consider Johnson's importance as a specialist in carving, mention must be made of his last book of designs, apparently published in 1760 under the title *A New Book of Ornaments by Thos. Johnson . . . 1760.* Unfortunately only the title page of this work appears to be extant, although, in 1835 and 1858, some of these plates, as well as a number from *One Hundred and Fifty New Designs*, were republished by a certain

---

[1] Quoted from *Thomas Johnson and English Rococo*, London, 1964, p. 15. I am much indebted to the author, Mrs. Hayward, for some of the information on Johnson in this chapter. *Aesop's Fables*, illustrated by Francis Barlow, was published in 1665 and reissued in 1687.

[2] Ill. Mark Girouard, 'Curraghmore, County Waterford — III', *Country Life*, Vol. CXXXIII, p. 370, fig. 6.

[3] William Blakeney was one of the military heroes of the time. He had defended Minorca against the French, after being abandoned by Admiral Byng, and had helped to defeat the Highlanders in the 'Forty-five Rebellion. He was thus an admirable choice as Grand President of the *Laudable Association of Anti-Gallicans* founded in 1745 'to oppose the insidious arts of the French Nation'.

[4] *One Hundred and Fifty New Designs, by Thos. Johnson carver. Consisting of ceilings, chimney pieces, slab, glass and picture frames, stands for china Etc., clock & Watch cases, girondoles, brackets, grates, lanthorns etc. etc. The whole well adapted for decorating all kinds of ornamental furniture, in the present taste. Engraved on 56 copper plates. . . . Sold by Robert Sayer . . . , London, 1761.*

John Weale in a book of designs entitled *Old English and French Ornaments*.[1]

As no account from Johnson has to date been found for any work carried out by him or his firm (for he must presumably have employed many assistants), pieces can only be attributed to him that are either after, or in the tradition of, his published designs. This lack of documentary evidence relating to his work is not surprising, when it is remembered that he did not run a cabinet-making business and shop, as did Chippendale or Vile and Cobb, but that he was a free-lance designer and carver who, in the same way as Lock, relied almost entirely on commissions from the bigger firms. As he was a rival to Chippendale and Ince and Mayhew, both of whom were also publishing designs for carver's pieces at the same time as he was, he must have looked elsewhere to other cabinet-makers for his clients in the trade, and Mrs. Hayward suggests that he found one in George Cole of Golden Square.[1]

In the Day Books for Corsham House, Wiltshire, are payments *to Mr. Cole the Upholsterer* by Mr. Paul Methuen, the owner, for the sums of £130. 14. 0. on 10th March, 1761, and of £103. 8. 0. on 25th November, 1763. It is not known to which pieces these payments refer as there are no detailed accounts extant from Cole at Corsham. However, during 1761, Cole delivered a pier-glass (Pl. 100) to the Duke of Atholl for Dunkeld House, Perthshire, and the original instructions to Cole, dated 28th September of that year, still remain in the Archives at Blair Castle.[2] It was to cost about £50 and it begins 'The Drawing fixed upon is a man with a Gun upon the Top, a Ducal Coronet below and at the bottom of the Frame a *Squiral...*' (Pl. 101). The Duke was obviously delighted with the pier-glass as he ordered three others of similar design, with three console tables *en suite*, for his main Highland seat, Blair Castle, two years later. Cole's account for these is also extant and reads :

'1763
> Feby 28 To 3 rich carved and gilt tables with mahoy tops ...   £43. 0. 0.
> Nov 4   To 3 very rich carved and gilt glass frames to take to pieces with
>   glass *as before* ...   £168. 0. 0.'

A detail of the carving on one of the console tables is shown in Pl. 102. These now have marble tops in place of the original mahogany ones. The words *as before*, of course, refer to the Dunkeld pier-glass, which had been delivered two years previously.

Mrs. Hayward has shown that the pier-glasses at Blair Castle include many decorative motifs which suggest the hand of Thomas Johnson, and has shown that the 'man, in ragged dress, with a leaf hat and a long moustache, holding a gun, recalls in pose the figure of a hunter used as a central feature in one of Johnson's designs for a sconce (plate 2, *Collection of Designs*, 1758). . . . The dead hare also features in the same Johnson design for a sconce and again on a side table and a girandole (*Twelve Gerandoles*, 1755, title page).' It would thus appear that Cole submitted to the Duke of Atholl a design specially commissioned from Johnson (the coronet would not have been incorporated in a stock in trade design), for his approval and, having received this, instructed Johnson to carve the frame from his own design. It is unlikely that the Duke would have bothered to seek out Johnson

---

[1] All of Johnson's known designs are published by Mrs. Hayward in *Thomas Johnson and English Rococo*, London, 1964.

[2] See Anthony Coleridge, 'The Director and Some Cabinet-Makers at Blair Castle', *Connoisseur*, December 1960, pp. 254–5 for a full discussion of these mirrors and tables.

personally and give him the commission direct. He would have preferred to deal with Cole who was an established cabinet-maker, specialising in the sale of carvers' pieces such as pier-glasses, console-tables and girandoles.

It has already been shown that George Cole delivered furniture — and, perhaps, soft-furnishings[1] to Mr. Paul Methuen at Corsham House in 1761–3,[2] and it is not surprising, therefore, to find examples of carved furniture after designs in Thomas Johnson's publications in the same house. It has been shown that Cole probably employed Johnson to carry out his commissions from the Duke of Atholl in 1761, and it is, therefore, reasonable to suppose that he should also have employed him at Corsham Court in the same year. A gilt console-table supported by a tree trunk at Corsham which, like the related tables at Curraghmore[3] and Patshull House (Pl. 99), are all in Johnson's style.

There are further important pieces still at Corsham which may be attributed to Johnson and which may have been delivered by George Cole. They include a pair of girandoles which are inspired by an engraving in the *New Book of Ornaments* (1760) (cf. plate 4, from Weale's reprint) and two pairs of pier-glasses. The first (Pl. 104) is copied directly from a design in Johnson's *Collection of Designs* (Pl. 105) published in 1758, and reprinted in *One Hundred and Fifty New Designs*, 1761. The second pair (Pl. 106) is closely linked with the first, although they have rectangular and not oval frames.

Other carved work has been attributed to Johnson on stylistic grounds but, although many of these examples may in fact have been carved in his own workshop, it must always be remembered that he had published his designs for the trade, so that his rivals, and even some of his trade clients, would not have hesitated to use them should the demand and occasion have arisen. There is a pair of oval pier-glasses at Curraghmore[3] which may be compared with the oval examples (Pl. 104) at Corsham, as they are all suspended from similar knotted ties. There is also a chimney-piece,[4] originally at Halswell Park,[5] which follows a Johnson design (plate 9, right, *Collection of Designs*, 1758). Girandoles after Johnson's designs are rarer but an interesting pair, which originated at Hagley Hall, Worcestershire, are now in the Philadelphia Museum of Art (Pl. 107). They were inspired by plate 48, right, of the *Collection of Designs*, 1758 (Pl. 108) and they are of interest being coloured and not gilded. Another pair, which were recently on the London art market,[6] are also thought, without definite proof, to have come from Hagley, and their whole composition and design are entirely in Johnson's tradition (Pl. 109). An important set of four candlestands from the same house (Pl. 107) are also taken directly from a design (Pl. 110) in the *Collection of Designs*, 1758 (plate 13, right). These too are coloured. The set has, unfortunately, been split up, a pair being in the Philadelphia Museum of Art, a third is in the Victoria and Albert Museum, while the fourth is at Temple Newsam House,

[1] George Cole is described as *the Upholsterer* in the Corsham Day Books and as *an Upholder* in the London Polling Lists and contemporary newspaper advertisements: it is important to realise that an *Upholder* was probably an interior-decorator, there being a *Company of Upholders*, whilst an *Upholsterer* has, to this day, retained its eighteenth-century usage.

[2] There is also a small entry in the Corsham account books for 20 December 1777, recording a settlement of 10s. 6d. to the Administrator of Cole's estate — he must have died shortly before this date.

[3] See p. 59, n. 2.

[4] See p. 60, n. 1.

[5] See 'Rococo Mirrors and a chimney piece', *Apollo*, September 1956.

[6] Sotheby's, 5 July 1963, Lot 161 — Mrs. Derek FitzGerald's collection.

Leeds. These were originally attributed[1] to Chippendale, because the third edition of the *Director* includes a design for a candlestand with dolphin supports, plate 145, but Johnson's authorship was recognised by the compilers of *The Dictionary of English Furniture*.[2]

Some pier-glasses at Temple Newsam House may perhaps also be added to Johnson's *oeuvre*. There is a mirror from Brinkburn Priory, Northumberland, which has many decorative details, such as the *ho-ho* birds, taken from his designs (Pl. 111), and there is a pair of pier-glasses from Newburgh Priory, Yorkshire, which are based on a design of Johnson's in the *Collection of Designs*.

To complete the list of furniture attributed to Johnson, there is a pier-glass in the Assembly Rooms at York, another in the collection of Mr. Ferry at Uxbridge, an over-mantle at Buscot Park, Berkshire, in Lord Faringdon's collection, and two others, similar, in the Victoria and Albert Museum.[3] Then there are some girandoles — one pair (Pl. 112) being taken directly from a design in his *Twelve Gerondoles*, 1755, which is an important, hitherto unpublished, addition to his *oeuvre*. Another pair (Pl. 113), although their architectural backgrounds are rather more ponderous than Johnson's usual designs, is inspired by one of Aesop's Fables as are so many of the designs in Johnson's *Twelve Gerondoles*. Perhaps they were carved by another craftsman utilising an unpublished design of Johnson's. The example illustrated in Pl. 114, which is one of a pair at Temple Newsam, was formerly attributed to Johnson. Mrs. Hayward, however, while discussing this pair,[4] writes, 'There appears, in fact, to be no stylistic evidence upon which such an attribution could be based. They are probably the work of Matthias Lock. An unpublished drawing[5] by Lock in the Victoria and Albert Museum introduces the theme of a hound attacking a stag which is the subject of the Temple Newsam pair. In the carved pieces, tall bull-rushes are also a dominant feature. This motif appears in Lock's unpublished drawings in the Victoria and Albert Museum and is inspired by Barlow's illustrations.' The girandoles in question (Pl. 114) were probably made for Henry Ingram, 7th Lord Irwin, for the positions that they still occupy in the Saloon at Temple Newsam. However, Vardy, Lock, Johnson and Chippendale were not the only important carvers and designers during this period; they had serious rivals in Ince and Mayhew and the Linnells, both of which firms were specialist designers in this field.

The Public Advertiser of 27th January, 1759, announces that 'Messrs. John Mayhew who served his time with Mr. Bradshaw[6] and William Ince, who served his time with the late Mr. West,[7] have taken the house of Mr. Charles Smith, cabinet-maker and upholsterer, opposite Broad Street, Carnaby Market . . . begs (sic) leave to inform . . . [customers, etc.] . . . commands executed in the neatest taste'. John Mayhew had, for a short period

[1] O. Brackett, *Thomas Chippendale*, London, 1930, plate XLVII.

[2] *D.E.F.*, 1927, Vol. III, p. 55; Ralph Edwards in *Country Life*, 13 April 1929, p. 538.

[3] W23 and A — 1949: other chimney-pieces in Johnson's tradition are at Fairlawne, Kent, and Fonmon Castle, Glamorgan — both discussed *G.C-M.*, pp. 57–8, pls. 78–9. See also Helena Hayward, 'Thomas Johnson and Rococo Carving', *Connoisseur Year Book*, 1964. Pier and overmantel glasses are also at Melbury House, Dorset.   [4] *Thomas Johnson and English Rococo*, p. 40, note 69.

[5] Dept. of Engravings, Illustration and Design, Lock Collection No. 2550. Ill. *English Furniture Designs of the Eighteenth Century*, fig. 58.

[6] See William Bradshaw and George Smith Bradshaw, pp. 137–40.

[7] John West, cabinet-maker, of King Street, Covent Garden, died in 1758. He was succeeded by Samuel Norman, of Whittle, Mayhew and Norman.

prior to this announcement, been in partnership with James Whittle and Samuel Norman, as can be seen from an advertisement published in 1758 which read, 'Having purchased the lease of the late Mr. West's[1] house and warehouses in King Street, [Whittle, Norman and Mayhew] beg leave to acquaint the Nobility, Gentry and Others that they continue to carry on the Upholstery and Cabinet as well as the Carving and Gilding Businesses in all their branches. . . .' Mayhew cannot have stayed there long, for, as we have seen, early in 1759, we find him announcing the formation of his partnership with William Ince, who had been apprenticed to West, whose premises Mayhew had taken over with Whittle and Norman. Ince and Mayhew had probably met during this period.

As soon as they had started business in their new premises, opposite Broad Street, Carnaby Market, they began to advertise their stock in much the same way as Chippendale was doing through the medium of the first and second editions of his *Director*. They too published their designs, for both case furniture and carvers' pieces, but as separate sheets, and thus unbound. In a list of new books published in the *Gentleman's Magazine* for 13th July, 1759,[2] the following entry occurs : *A general system of useful and ornamental furniture. By Mess. Ince and Mayhew, publishing in numbers 1s. each.*[3] The sixteenth number was announced in the Public Ledger for 13th February, 1760. In April, that same year, through the columns of *The Gentleman's Magazine* (for the 12th of that month), the firm 'return their utmost thanks for the kind reception their designs have met with and assure them [their patrons] that no pains shall be spared to render them preferable to any like Performance both for the choice of the gentleman and the use of the workman'.[4] They finish by stating that only a few sheets of the first impression remain unsold. Sometime during this period they took additional premises in Marshall Street, Carnaby Market, and they issue an invitation to their customers to inspect 'An Assortment of French Furniture consign'd from Paris, for immediate Sale, very much under the original Cost, which may be seen at their Warehouse, Broad Street, Soho'.[5] The partners obviously were involved in all aspects of the trade and were not above a little dealing.

Their designs were later published in a large folio edition which was dedicated to the Duke of Marlborough and, although it is undated, R. S. Clouston[6] has deduced that it can probably be dated to 1762 on the grounds that, in some copies, the Duke is described as Lord Chamberlain, a post to which he was appointed in that year. The Duke is described as 'ever willing to promote and encourage Industry and Ingenuity'. Its title is quoted here in full and it is interesting to compare its wording with that of Chippendale's *Director* (see Appendix B, Chapter III), which the entire publication emulates in so many ways.

> *The Universal System of Household Furniture. Consisting of above 300 designs in the most elegant taste, both useful and ornamental. Finely engraved, in which the nature of ornament and perspective, is accurately exemplified. The whole made convenient to the nobility and gentry, in their*

[1] See p. 62, n. 7.

[2] Vol. XXIX, p. 338.

[3] Quoted from *Ward-Jackson, loc. cit.*, pp. 49 and 50 respectively.

[4] Quoted from *G.C-M.*, p. 73. I am indebted for much of the information in these paragraphs to the authors of the above and also to Mr. Ralph Edwards' foreword to *The Universal System of Household Furniture, 1762*, published by Alec Tiranti, 1960.

[5] Quoted from Ince and Mayhew's trade label on the bookcase (pl. 120) in the Museum of Decorative Arts, Copenhagen.

[6] R. S. Clouston, *English Furniture and Furniture Makers of the Eighteenth Century*, London, 1906, p. 158.

choice, and comprehensive to the workman, by directions for executing the several designs, with specimens of ornament for young practitioners in drawing. By Ince and Mayhew cabinet-makers and upholders, in Broad Street, Golden Square, London. Where every article in the several branches, treated, of, is executed on the most reasonable terms, with the utmost neatness and punctuality. Sold by Robt. Sayer,[1] map and print-seller near Serjeant's Inn, Fleet Street.

The title page and notes to the plates are translated into French which shows that the partners hoped to attract a Continental market. It has already been pointed out that they imported French furniture, unless they bought the consignment on arrival, and they thus appear to have been trying to encourage a two-way trade — a far cry from Johnson with his dedication to the Brethren of the Anti-Gallican Association which had been founded in 1745 'to oppose the insidious arts of the French Nation'.

The lay-out of the *Universal System* is based, to a considerable extent, on the *Director* and both works have a preface, and notes to the plates. Compared with two hundred plates in the third edition of the *Director* (1762), the *Universal System* contains a hundred and one plates. Mathew Darly, who was responsible for most of the plates in the *Director* (see pp. 85–6), engraved all these plates. The designs are divided into case and carvers' pieces, and include plates of chairs, lanthorns, therms, tables, bookcases, desks, library-tables, beds, night-tables, commode chest of drawers, china-cases, card-tables, an organ case, sofas, candlestands, girandoles, chandeliers, console-tables, pier-glasses and chimney-pieces. Certain types of furniture are included which are not illustrated in the *Director*, such as tripod or 'claw' tables (Pl. 115), library steps and designs for corner shelves, or 'Ecoineurs' as they are called (Pl. 116), and 'voiders', or trays. The plates finish with a section devoted to metalwork, including stoves, fenders, grates, fire-dogs, staircase railings and brackets. It has been suggested that these were added later but this theory cannot be entirely accepted, as in *The British Chronicle*, 15th–18th August, 1760, on page 168, we read:[2]

> '*This day is published* price 1s. Number XVIII (containing four plate folio) INCE AND MAYHEW'S ORIGINAL DESIGNS FOR FURNITURE in which, and the former Numbers are introduced, New Designs for Grates . . . Brasswork &c. &c. To be had of *Darley in Long Acre, Webley in Holbourn*, and of the Authors, Cabinet-Makers and Upholsterers, *Broad Street, Golden Square*, where every article is executed on the most reasonable terms. Glass and Furniture for exportation.
>
> N.B. As this work has sufficiently proved its great Utility both to the Gentleman and Workmen, there need no other Force to reccomend it than the candid Judgment of the Publick.'

The note referring to export of Glass (presumably pier-glasses) and Furniture is of great interest, as it is another example of Ince and Mayhew's efforts to attract the Continental markets.

---

[1] Robert Sayer, a Fleet Street printseller, seems to have specialised in the sale of Furniture Design books — amongst others he sold: 1. *Household Furniture in Genteel Taste for the year 1760. By a Society of Upholsterers. . . .*; 2. *One Hundred and Fifty New Designs, By Thos. Johnson . . . 1761*; 3. *The Chair-Maker's Guide. . . . By Robert Manwaring . . . (1766)*; 4. *Six Sconces by M. Lock (2nd edition) . . . 1768*.

[2] I am deeply indebted to Mr. A. G. Lewis who pointed out to me the existence of this advertisement.

While discussing *the Universal System*, Mr. Ward-Jackson writes,[1] 'The style of the designs is likewise influenced by the *Director*, but they possess certain characteristics of their own, the most marked being the frequent use of elaborate symmetrical patterns, half Gothic and half rococo, executed in fretwork and applied blind to panels or used as an openwork filling for a frame.' Ince and Mayhew were probably also influenced by Lock and Copland's rococo designs, a conjecture which is strengthened by the fact that five of Lock's plates were interleaved in Mayhew's copy of Langley's *Treasury of Designs* which is now in the Metropolitan Museum.

There are several references to the firm in contemporary letters and diaries, thus on 5th March, 1766, Lady Louisa Fermor writes to her niece Lady Shelburne that she has been 'to see . . . a famous table at Mayhew's in which I was disappointed'.[2] An entry in Lady Shelburne's diary of 1768, during the furnishing of Shelburne (now Lansdowne) House, shows that it was the custom to visit several artists and cabinet-makers before making any purchases. It reads,

> 'My Lord being to carry us to Cipriani's, Zucchi's, and some other people employed for our house in town, called my Lord with whom we went first to Zucchi's, where we saw some ornaments for our ceilings. . . . From there to Mayhew and Inch where is some beautiful cabinet work, and two pretty glass cases for one of the rooms in my apartment, and which, though they are only deal, and to be painted white, he charges £50 for. From thence to Cipriani's. . . . From thence to Zuccarelli's . . . and from thence home it being half an hour past four.'[3]

Lady Shelburne was not alone in patronising Ince and Mayhew at this time, for on 5th October, 1769, the Earl of Coventry received a bill for £35 from the partners for 'A large Architect Pier Frame, fluted, richly carv'd with shell on top, festoons and drops of double husks down the sides, goates head at bottom gilt in the very best Double Burnish'd Gold',[4] that he had ordered for Croome Court in Worcestershire which he was furnishing. This pier-glass, which is already in Robert Adam's neo-classical style, is now in the Croome Court Tapestry Room in the Metropolitan Museum, as are a set of six armchairs (Pl. 117) and two settees, which were also made by Ince and Mayhew for Croome Court. They are described in the same account as '6 Large Antique Elbow Chairs with oval Backs carv'd with Double husks and ribbon knot on top, Gilt in the Best Burnish'd Gold, stuffed with Besthair, in Linen — Backt with Fine Crimson Tammy — proper for covering with Tapistry in the Country . . . the pattern included £77. 8. 0. . . . 2 settees for Each Side the Chimney, richly carv'd and Gilt Stuff'd and Cover'd to match the Chairs £56. 10. 0.' They are covered in Gobelins tapestry, which the Earl had ordered in August 1764 from Jacques Neilson, the superintendent of the low-warp *atelier*, who was a Scot and whom Adam personally knew. They were to match the set of tapestries that were being woven to his and Robert Adam's designs and specifications — now also in the Metropolitan Museum.[5] These were the tapestry seat-covers referred to by Ince and

---

[1] Ward-Jackson, *op. cit.*, p. 50.   [2] Fitzmaurice-Villars, *Earl of Shelburne*, 1912, Vol. I, p. 273.
[3] A. Bolton, *Robert Adam*, Vol. I, p. 312.

[4] Quoted from James Parker, 'Croome Court, The Architecture and Furniture', *The Metropolitan Museum of Art Bulletin*, Vol. XVII, No. 3, November 1959, p. 88.

I am indebted to the authors of this article for other information on the firm's dealings with the Earl of Coventry.

[5] See Edith A. Standen, 'Croome Court, The Tapestries', *The Metropolitan Museum of Art Bulletin, loc. cit.*

Mayhew in their 1769 account as 'proper for covering with Tapistry in the Country'. There is also a carved giltwood side-table of neo-classical design (Pl. 118) in the Croome Court Room in the Metropolitan which was probably made by Ince and Mayhew for Lord Coventry. It supports a black marble slab inset with 176 squares of specimen marbles and coloured stones for which John Wildsmith charged the Earl £46. 3. 0. in July 1759.[1] It is interesting to find that tables of this nature were made in London and not only in Florence and Rome, as is often supposed. Ince and Mayhew must have later been commissioned to make the stand to support the slab. Its apron is carved with a guilloche frieze which resembles the similar decoration around the window frames in the Tapestry Room at Croome Court which was executed between 1763 and 1765.

A pair of commodes (Pl. 119), also from Croome Court, were supplied by Ince and Mayhew at the surprisingly early date of 1761. This was a year before the *Universal System* was published as a collected folio volume and a year before Chippendale published the third edition of the *Director*, both publications being devoted to rococo designs. The commodes, which are neo-classical in form and inlay, are described in an account from Mayhew and Ince dated 15th–21st September, 1761, as 'two very fine satinwood and holly commodes, neatly gravd and inlaid with flowers of rosewood, the one with drawers, the other with shelves lin'd with paper and green bays falls to ditto brass nailed'. The green baize and the brass nails have disappeared though traces of them are still to be seen. There seems to be little doubt that this description refers to the pair of commodes (Pl. 119) which are on loan to The Iveagh Bequest, Kenwood House, Hampstead, and, if this is so, they must be amongst the earliest examples of furniture in the neo-classical tradition made in this country. Lord Coventry had engaged the services of Robert Adam early in his career, and we thus first find him at Croome in August 1760, which was only two years after he had returned from Italy in January 1758. Adam designed a chair for Croome as early as 1761,[2] and it is possible, therefore, that he supplied Ince and Mayhew with a design for the pair of commodes in question in that year. It is interesting that he may have commissioned the partners, who, like himself, were both young men at the threshold of their careers, to execute this novel and daring design.

In 1762, on 20th February, the two partners married two sisters at St. James's, Piccadilly. This was a fashionable church and they were obviously on the way up in the world. They had published their own book of designs, may well have been associated with Robert Adam in business and were treating with such fashionable clients as Lady Shelburne and the Earl of Coventry. It must also be remembered that Robert Adam was called in to advise on the furnishing of Bowood House, Wiltshire, in 1765, and Lansdowne House, Berkeley Square, in 1768,[3] both for the Earl of Shelburne, and that he may well have

[1] The full account reads 'The Right Honourable the Earl of Coventry to John Wildsmith, 1759 July 28th, To a Rich fine and marble Table in squairs of all the curious sorts of marble No: 176 Sqrs. in Do. To 41 squairs cut out and others fixt in there places £42.10. 0d. By paid for 1 squair of Lapuis Lazer and 1 sq. of Plumb pudding stone £3.13. 0d. . . . .'
Little is known of John Wildsmith except that he became a bankrupt in 1769, when he had to sell the contents of his yard near Saint James's Church, Piccadilly.
[2] Soane Museum 50(21).
[3] There is a design by Adam for a mirror for Bowood in the Soane Museum 20(19) dated 1765, and others for tables 3 (40, 87, 88) for Lansdowne House dated 1768.

recommended Ince and Mayhew to the Shelburnes, or merely commissioned them to execute some of his furniture designs.

In 1763 John Mayhew was elected a Director of the Westminster Fire Office and he served for two years being re-elected in 1790. William Ince was elected in 1771, 1780, 1789 and 1798, serving for two years on each occasion.[1] Thus on 7th June, 1792, we read that the Directors met, Mayhew being one of them, and 'ordered that Mr. Ince do make 18 new chairs for the directors to be placed in the office also a new chair for the chairman'. Ince appears to have rather overplayed his hand, for on 13th June, 1793, the directors 'ordered that the Clerk do write to Messrs. Mayhew and Ince informing them that it is the unanimous opinion of a full board of Directors [*Mayhew had retired in 1792 after serving his two year term*] that the charge of making the desk and chairs is high and wish to refer it to their consideration'. Amongst the bills discharged on 20th June for that year was one to Mayhew and Ince for £102. 9. 0. It is not recorded whether they reduced their original account, but it is worth noting that Ince was elected a Director of the Company five years later, so perhaps they did. Anyway there are now twenty-two single chairs and two armchairs at 27 King Street, Covent Garden, the premises of the Fire Office. Eighteen of these were supplied in 1793 and six in 1813.[2]

Ince appears to have evinced an interest in furniture designs at an early age for he was a subscriber to the first edition of the *Director* in 1754. In 1760 Ince and Mayhew had contributed some designs to a work entitled *Household Furniture in Genteel Taste for the year 1760. By a Society of Upholsterers . . .*, which shows that they must, at that early date, have been held in esteem by their colleagues and rivals, for this book was a joint venture, published by a body that included some of the leading London furniture-makers of the day (see pp. 69–70).

Little furniture has, to date, been ascribed to the firm, but before some of these *book-pieces* are described, mention must be made of a bookcase (Pl. 120) bearing their trade label (quoted above p. 63, n. 5) in the Museum of Decorative Arts, Copenhagen. It can be dated to about 1760 and should be compared with their design for *Bookcases for Recesses* in plate 19, right, of the *Universal System* which it somewhat resembles (Pl. 121). A pair of pier-glasses of chinoiserie design in the Metropolitan Museum (Pl. 122) have cornices, each with a chinaman standing in a pagoda, similar to that in a design for a *chimney-piece*, plate 85, in the *Universal System* (Pl. 123). A pair of giltwood wall-brackets (Pl. 124) in the collection of Mr. K. Galliers-Pratt should also be compared with the upper part of plate 85 in the *Universal System* (cf. Pl. 123). The centre of the back of a hall-seat of unusual design (Pl. 125) may have been inspired by the unusual tracery decoration in Ince and Mayhew's plate for an *Ecoineur* (cf. Pl. 116, left). An artist's table in the Victoria and Albert Museum[3] may well have been inspired by designs in the *Universal System*. Finally, there is recorded a mahogany stool[4] which is of similar design to a *Lady's Dressing Stool*, plate 34, in the *Universal System*.

[1] Vile and Cobb were both also Directors of the Westminster Fire Office — see Hugh Phillips, *Mid-Georgian London*, London, 1964, p. 116.

[2] Ill. *G.C-M.* (pl. 158); these chairs are also discussed by C. Hussey in *Country Life*, 21 December 1951.

[3] W31 — 1912.

[4] Ill. *G.C-M.*, pls. 159 and 160.

It is interesting to find two sets of chairs which can both be dated to about 1760, all of them stamped with the initials I.M. The first set (Pl. 126) has splats of a form very similar to that of one of the four *Parlour Chairs* illustrated on plate 9 of the *Universal System*. The other set consists of mahogany latticed-back chairs of chinoiserie design at Pwllywrack, Glamorgan, which are again stamped with the same initials, although they bear no close resemblance to any of the Ince and Mayhew designs. The presence of these initials does not, of course, constitute sufficient evidence to add these chairs to Ince and Mayhew's proven *oeuvre*.

As it has already been seen, the partnership which was often referred to as 'Mayhew and Ince', continued until 1803 at Broad Street, Golden Square, when Ince must have retired or died. Mayhew, who died in 1811, also owned other premises at No. 20 Marshall Street, Carnaby Market, from which, according to the *London Directories*, he traded from 1774 until his death in 1811. The later work of the firm, which survived into the opening years of the nineteenth century,[1] is well beyond the scope of this book. It has thus been shown that Ince and Mayhew ran a highly successful and vigorous partnership for over forty years, and it is interesting to read that Sheraton pronounced the *Universal System* 'to have been a book of merit in its day, though much inferior to Chippendale's which was a real original, as well as more extensive and masterly in design'. A further link between Robert Adam and Ince and Mayhew has just been published by Dr. Lindsay Boynton in *The Furniture History Society Bulletin* (Vol. II, 1966) in his article 'An Ince and Mayhew Correspondence'. In it he discusses the correspondence between Ince and Mayhew and Boulton and Fothergill of Soho, Birmingham. Amongst it are letters of 1775 to 1776 referring to the ormolu mounts which Boulton and Fothergill had made for the Duchess of Manchester's cabinet (now in the Victoria and Albert Museum). These were sent to Ince and Mayhew who presumably made the cabinet to Robert Adam's design of June 1771, which is extant in Soane Museum. It may well transpire that the partners were responsible for much of the fine furniture made to Adam's designs.

Another firm of carvers and cabinet-makers who must have been serious rivals to Chippendale, Lock, Johnson, and Ince and Mayhew, especially in the designing and carving sections of the profession, was that of William and John Linnell. The work and life of William, who flourished 1720–63, is discussed elsewhere[2] as he is primarily remembered as a carver and cabinet-maker. John, however, who was undoubtedly William's son, took over the premises at No. 28 Berkeley Square, after the auction of William's stock in 1763 following the latter's death, was not only 'in the first line of his profession' as carver, cabinet-maker and upholsterer,[3] but was also a prolific designer. A large collection of his original drawings is in the Victoria and Albert Museum, mostly assembled and collected by Charles Heathcote Tatham, the famous antiquarian and designer, who apparently intended to publish them. The majority of these are in the neo-classical style, and need not concern us here, but some of John Linnell's earlier drawings are in the rococo manner, and they include a set of engraved designs by him for vases which show that he was influenced by Meissonnier. These can be dated to 1760.[4] After discussing these designs, Mr. Ward-

---

[1] See *G.C-M.*, p. 74.   [2] See pp. 150–1.

[3] A note by the architect, Charles Heathcote Tatham, quoted in *G.C-M.*, p. 76.

[4] The dates have been cut out from the Museum's examples but a set was sold at Sotheby's, Nov. 18. 1914, dated 1760.

Jackson writes[1] 'Many of his furniture designs are spirited fantasies in the same vein, and a comparison between his work and that of François Cuvilliés suggests that, like Lock, he had studied French models with more understanding than most English artists. Before adopting the neo-classical style in all its vigour, as he eventually did, he passed through an intermediate phase, in which a chastened type of rococo ornament was combined with classical forms to produce a charming and individual synthesis.'

A design for a side-table with dragons writhing around the scrolled supports (Pl. 127) can be dated to about 1760, and is rather like a design for a table decorated with dragons drawn by Cuvilliés.[2] A chimney-glass (Pl. 128) from one of the bedrooms at Osterley Park was designed by Linnell (cf. Pl. 129), and must also have been carved in his workshops since, from 1767 onwards, his firm was supplying fine furniture to Mr. Child at Osterley — many of his accounts having survived to prove this. Another amusing rococo design (Pl. 130) was drawn by him in about 1760, and the pier-glass and table that are depicted in it are as exaggerated and naturalistic as some of Thomas Johnson's most daring essays in this vein.

John Linnell had many important clients, as can be seen from study of his annotated designs in pen, wash and watercolour, dated between 1773 and 1781, which are in the Victoria and Albert Museum. Although this period is beyond the scope of the present book, it is worth quoting the names of some of the clients for whom these drawings were made — 'the Dukes of Cumberland, Queensberry, Grafton, and Chandos, The Duchess of Ancaster, the Marquess of Donegall, the Earls of Haddington, Lichfield, Pembroke, and Lisburne, Earl Poulett, Lord Cadogan, and W. Blathwayt of Dyrham.'[3] In 1763 he began to provide furniture to William Drake for Shardeloes, much of which was in the neo-classical style,[4] and, sometime before 1761, he started to work for Sir Nathaniel Curzon (created Baron Scarsdale in 1761) providing furniture for his house Kedleston in Derbyshire. There is a sofa[5] at Kedleston which was made, in about 1765, from a design[5] of John Linnell's. Robert Adam had designed a similar sofa[6] for Kedleston which is inscribed 'Lord Scarsdale and also executed for Mrs. Montagu in Hill Street'.[7] Lord Scarsdale appears to have preferred Linnell's design, which is heavy and Kentian in feeling with its entwined dolphin and merfolk supports. It is very different to some of the rococo fantasies (cf. Pl. 129) that he had designed about five years earlier. John Linnell was yet another cabinet-maker, carver and designer of the first flight who, like Ince and Mayhew and later, Thomas Chippendale, had allied himself at an early age to the rising star of the gifted and highly successful Robert Adam.

In 1760 some of the leading designers seem to have banded together into a *Society of Upholsterers* and to have published a design book under the title :

'Household Furniture in Genteel Taste for the year 1760. By a Society of Upholsterers, Cabinet-Makers, etc. containing upwards of 180 designs on 60 copper plates. Consisting of china, breakfast,

[1] Ward-Jackson, *op. cit.*, p. 55.

[2] Ill. Ward-Jackson, *op. cit.*, pl. 354 (bottom).

[3] *G.C-M.*, p. 78.

[4] *G.C-M.*, plates 170–1 : By the end of 1768 his account totalled £1,056.

[5] Ill. *G.C-M.*, pls. 162–3; Clifford Musgrave, *Adam and Hepplewhite Furniture*, 1966, pls. 29–34.

[6] Ward-Jackson, *op. cit.*, pl. 203.

[7] Two other very similar sofas may be associated with these designs of Linnell and Adam — one of these, in the Philadelphia Museum (pl. 131) is illustrated.

side-board, night tables, chairs, couches, French stools, cabinets, commodes, china shelves and cases, trays, chests, stands for candles, tea kettles, pedestals, staircase lights, bureaus, beds, ornamental bed-posts, corniches, brackets, fire-screens, desk, book and clock-cases, frames for glasses, sconce and chimney-pieces, girandoles, lanthorns, chandalears etc. etc. London, Printed for Robt. Sayer, map and printseller, at the Golden Buck in Fleet Street.

There was also an undated second edition and a later edition entitled *Household Furniture for the year 1763.*

It is neither known why the Society was formed nor who was the moving spirit behind it, but it was probably felt that, if some of the leading members of the profession joined together and published some of their designs, business and prestige would be harvested by all concerned. Thomas Chippendale contributed some designs, as can be proved from the fact that three designs for plates in *Household Furniture* were found amongst Chippendale's drawings acquired by the Victoria and Albert Museum in 1906. Furthermore, in the Chippendale Albums in the Metropolitan Museum, among the few drawings which are not published in the *Director*, is found the original drawing for a sideboard table in plate 8 of the first edition of the Society's book. These drawings can be attributed to Chippendale's firm, as they are by the same hand as the *Director* drawings, and several other plates have also been attributed to the same firm on stylistic grounds.[1] Ince and Mayhew also appear to have been involved in the Society, as one would expect from two young men of such drive and awareness — nineteen plates being variations of designs published in their *Universal System*. Eight other plates have been attributed to Thomas Johnson who would also have been eager to be included in this venture.

The only other known contributor to the Society of Upholsterers' *Household Furniture in Genteel Taste* was Robert Manwaring, cabinet and chair-maker, who had business premises in the Haymarket. It is thought that he was responsible for the first twenty-eight plates in *Household Furniture*, with the exception of plates 12 and 13, which are copied from Ince and Mayhew's *Universal System, Plates 57 and 60*, and these were reprinted in 1766 in Manwaring's third publication *The Chair-Maker's Guide. . . .*

Manwaring published three books between 1765 and 1766 with the following titles :

(1) *The Carpenter's Compleat Guide to the Whole System of Gothic Railing, consisting of twenty-six entire new designs for paling, and gates of different kinds etc. . . . Printed for A. Webley, in Holborn, near Chancery Lane, 1765.*

(2) *The Cabinet and Chair-Maker's Real Friend and Companion, or, the whole system of chair-making made plain and easy; containing upwards of one hundred new and useful designs for all sorts of chairs. . . . Also some very beautiful designs, supposed to be executed with the limbs of yew, apple or pear trees, ornamented with leaves and blossoms, which if properly painted will appear like nature; these are the only designs of the kind that ever were published. . . . The whole invented and drawn by Robert Manwaring, cabinet-maker; and beautifully, and correctly engraved on forty copper plates by Robert Pranker London: Printed for Henry Webley, in Holborn, near Chancery Lane, 1765*[2]

(3) *The Chair-Maker's Guide; being upwards of two hundred new and genteel designs . . . for Gothic, Chinese, ribbon and other chairs, couches, settees, burjairs, French dressing and corner*

---

[1] The whole question is fully discussed by Fiske Kimball and Edna Donnell in *The Creators of the Chippendale Style — Chippendale Designs in the Book of the Society of Upholsterers*, Metropolitan Museum Studies, II, 1929, pp. 41–59.

[2] A second edition was brought out in 1775.

stools. . . . Many of the rural kind may be executed with rude branches, or limbs of trees etc. By Robert Manwaring, cabinet-maker and others . . . on seventy-five copper plates. Printed for Robert Sayer . . . at the Golden Buck, near Serjeants-Inn, Fleet Street. MDCCLXVI.

In the preface to the *Chair-Maker's Real Friend and Companion*, he claims, 'I have made it my particular Study to invest such Designs, as may be easily executed by the Hands of a tolerable skilful Workman . . .' and later 'the Author doth with the greatest Truth assert, that there are very few Designs advanced, but what he has either executed himself, or seen completely finished by others . . .'. He also asserts that they were 'Actually Originals, and not pirated or copied from the Designs and Inventions of others, which of late hath been too much practised'. Was he sniping at Ince and Mayhew, here?

From the titles to *The Chair-Maker's Friend* and *The Chair-Maker's Guide*, it can be seen that he was proud of his designs for chairs 'of the rural kind', and in the preface to the former work he writes, 'The Designs given for rural Chairs for Summer-houses, Gardens and Parks, are entirely new, and are the only ones that were ever published. . . .' Two designs for these chairs are illustrated in Pl. 143; a set of chairs (Pl. 144) in this style is in the Victoria and Albert Museum.

Although many of Manwaring's designs were executed by his own firm, as he himself tells us, he also informs us that some of the designs were 'finished by others'. Thus it would be particularly rash to attribute a particular piece of furniture to Manwaring's business, merely because it resembled a design in his unpublished works. Furthermore, examples of chairs in Manwaring's manner are not uncommon, and it must be remembered that many of his designs are similar to those published by Chippendale and Ince and Mayhew. Thus the chairs that are discussed here, as being after Manwaring's designs, owe much to Chippendale's designs in plates 26–29 in the third edition of the *Director*, and to Ince and Mayhew's designs for Dressing chairs in Plate 35 of the *Universal System*. An armchair in the Metropolitan Museum (Pl. 132) has affinities with the design by Manwaring from *The Chair-Maker's Friend* illustrated in Pl. 133. A similar chair (Pl. 134) also owes much to the same design and its back is inset with the crest of the Lane family. It is one of four from a larger set and is a fine example of its kind. Another armchair in the Victoria and Albert Museum (Pl. 135) stems from another plate in *The Chair-Maker's Friend* (Pl. 136) while a plainer example is in the Earl of Mansfield's collection at Scone Palace (Pl. 137). Another variation of this design is found in the backs of a set of eighteen chairs that were originally in the Summer Dining-Room at Stowe (Pl. 138). Finally there is a set of six single chairs and two armchairs, illustrated in Pl. 139, which are based on one of Manwaring's designs for *Gothick Chairs*. The very different qualities of these examples would seem to demonstrate that Manwaring's designs were utilised by other members of the trade and not only by himself.

It has been shown by Mr. Ward-Jackson[1] that Manwaring, in *The Chair-Maker's Guide*, *1766*, included several designs similar to those in Mathew Darly's *New Book of Chinese, Gothic and Modern Chairs, of 1750/51*, and that the former work can, in fact, be attributed to Darly. Although Manwaring claimed these designs as his own, it must be admitted that he did not pirate them outright, for in the title, he states that the designs are by 'Robert Manwaring Cabinet-Maker *and others*'. In Plate 41 of *The Chair-Maker's Guide* designs for

---

[1] Ward-Jackson, *op. cit.*, p. 53.

two *Parlour chairs* are shown, and, if these are compared with plates from Darly's *New Book of Chinese, Gothic and Modern Chairs* it will be obvious that Darly is the author. Chairs of this type (Pls. 140, 141, 142) are often attributed to Manwaring when, in fact, the designs were almost certainly drawn by Darly — a fact which has not been generally recognised before.

Manwaring appears to have had a rival in Charles Over who also published in 1768 designs for garden furniture in a book entitled '*Ornamental Architecture in the Gothic, Chinese and Modern Taste, being above fifty intire new designs* (Many of which may be executed with roots of trees) for gardens, parks, forests, woods, canals etc. . . .'. This was, in fact, published seven years before Manwaring's *Chair-Maker's Companion*, and the latter may have been casting covetous eyes at some of these designs when, in the preface, he wrote that his own were 'not pirated or copied from the Designs and Inventions of others . . .'.

With the important exception of Chippendale's and Copland's work which is discussed in Chapter III, the published work of the leading furniture designers in this Country during the so-called 'Rococo Period', has now been examined, and, at the same time, we have surveyed some of the furniture which derives from these designs or was inspired by them.

APPENDIX A

Batty Langley's obituary published in the *London Advertiser* on 6 March, 1751.

> '*Some days ago died Mr. Batty Langley, well known to the Public for his excellence in Surveying, Architecture, Designing, Drawing, etc. It is not easy to determine whether the loss of this eminent and honest Man is more regretted on account of his use to the World, from his extensive knowledge in the above Sciences, or for his great Integrity (when applied to) in reducing the exorbitant Bills of such Workmen who endeavoured to impose on their Employers*'.[1]

[1] I am indebted to Mr. Alex Lewis for drawing my attention to this.

CHAPTER III

Thomas Chippendale (1718-79)

PART I HIS LIFE

There have for many years been two distinct claims as to where Thomas Chippendale was born. One was published for the first time by Samuel Redgrave in his *Dictionary of Artists* in 1874 when, referring to Thomas Chippendale I, the supposed father of the famous cabinet-maker, he writes: 'He was a native of Worcestershire, came to London, where he first found employment as a joiner, and by his own industry and taste was, in the reign of George I., most eminent as a carver and cabinet-maker.' If Redgrave's statement, which is unsupported by any form of evidence, is accepted, then it must be supposed that Thomas Chippendale II was either born in Worcestershire, shortly before his father left for London, or was born in London shortly after his father's arrival. However, no record of his birth or baptism has been found in either London or Worcestershire, in spite of searches, and so it is unlikely that either of these events occurred in either of these places. Redgrave cannot be accepted as an *a priori* source, and Layton who supports his theory in his *Thomas Chippendale*[1] has been thoroughly discredited.

The alternate theory, on the other hand, which claims that Thomas Chippendale was born in Otley in Yorkshire, is backed by sound evidence. Redgrave's statement had been accepted by all authorities on the subject until, in 1912, Colonel W. H. Chippindall, of Kirkby Lonsdale, published in *Notes and Queries* a *Lease and Release*, dated 30th April, 1770.[2] The former bears the names of William Chippendale of Farnley, Yorkshire, carpenter, and of Thomas Chippendale of St. Martin's Lane, London. The release has the names of William Chippendale, Samuel Harper of Leeds, Christopher Elward of Horsforth, Thomas Chippendale and John Fletcher of Otley. The documents are in connection with buildings and an orchard in Boroughgate, Otley. They are of importance as they prove that there was indeed a link between Thomas Chippendale of St. Martin's Lane and the Chippendales, or Chippindales as they are often called in contemporary documents, of Otley in Yorkshire. Thomas Chippendale's connection with Otley is further strengthened when the Otley Parish Church birth registers are consulted and it is seen that on 5th June, 1718, 'Thomas, son of John Chippendale, of Otley, joyner', was born. Thomas Chippen-

---

[1] Edwin J. Layton, *Thomas Chippendale*, London, 1928.

[2] In the West Riding Registry of Deeds at Wakefield. Quoted in full in O. Bracket, *Thomas Chippendale*, London, 1930, p. 12.

dale's mother, whose maiden name was Mary Drake, died in February 1729, when Thomas was eleven years old, and it may have been shortly after this time that he left home. It has been suggested that he worked at an early age at Farnley Hall, near Otley, and there are still examples of mahogany furniture dating from the fourth decade of the eighteenth century in the house.

Thomas may then have worked as an apprentice for some years in Yorkshire and it is traditionally held that, during this period, he made the dolls'-house at Nostell Priory (Pl. 146). In 1739 Mr. Henry Lascelles purchased the Harewood estate outside Leeds, and, in *The Cabinet-Maker*, 31st March, 1923, the following entry is published: 'Thomas Chippendale worked with his father, John Chippendale (or Chippindale), the joiner and cabinet-maker at Otley. We[1] quote Mr. Chippendale regarding this matter and he stated: "at an early age his genius became recognised by the Lascelles family, of Harewood House", and apparently father and son made furniture from the oak grown on the Harewood House estate. "Later, by the influence of that distinguished family, he, Thomas Chippendale, commenced business in London, where his art appealed to noblemen, and soon his name became famous." ' Of course this is pure conjecture, but Chippendale certainly returned to Yorkshire at a later period in his life and made important and large quantities of furniture for both Nostell Priory and Harewood House — he may well have gained the support of these influential clients at an early stage in his career. Furthermore, it is probable that he had some sponsor who sent him to London, as it seems hardly credible that the son of a Yorkshire joiner should have gone to London at an early age without any introduction and little money, and moreover, that, by the age of thirty-five, he should have been running his own business from St. Martin's Lane — which was fast becoming the street in which the principal London cabinet-makers had their headquarters. Although it should be remembered that John Channon was also trading from St. Martin's Lane at the age of *twenty-six* (see p. 40).

Nothing, to date, has been recorded of Chippendale's career between his birth in 1718 and his marriage, on 19th May, 1748, to Catherine Redshaw of St. Martin's-in-the-Fields at St. George's Chapel, Hyde Park.[2] Catherine died in 1772 and on 5th August, 1777, he married his second wife, Elizabeth Davis, at the Parish Church, Fulham.[3] His eldest son was baptised on 23rd April, 1749, at St. Paul's, Covent Garden, and his second son, Edward, was born on 20th July, 1750. He was baptised at St. Martin's-in-the-Fields, on 12th October of that year. Chippendale had eleven children in all, seven of them boys, and the last was probably born in 1763.[4] It is not known therefore how old Thomas Chippendale was when he left Yorkshire and started his new life in London, although he was probably in his late 'teens' or early 'twenties'. He can hardly have been any older because by Christmas 1749, at the age of thirty-one, we find him married with a child and living at the sixth house in Conduit Court, Long Acre. It is not recorded whether he was working

---

[1] A contemporary member of the family writing on the grounds of family tradition, shortly after the First World War.

[2] Register of St. George's Chapel, Mayfair.

[3] Register of Fulham Parish Church.

[4] The baptisms of his tenth and eleventh children are not recorded but John and Charles, the two children in question, are mentioned in a document at Somerset House, dated 25 January 1784, as being entitled to administer with others in their father's estate.

in those premises, as well as living there, but it is known that they were rated at £10 per annum. He must have been a young man of great talent and single-mindedness, because it is almost past belief that, in a period of little over ten years, he could learn and earn enough to set himself up on his own account as a cabinet-maker in the centre of London during this highly competititive period. We do not know to whom he was apprentice when he came to London — if he had not already served his entire apprenticeship before he left Yorkshire — but details of the terms of indenture of one of his own apprentices throws some light on the question. Chippendale is recorded, on 11th April, 1754, as accepting a premium of £20 for an apprentice named Nath[1]. Hopson.[1] This was not a high price, for during the same period Giles Grendey took £43 and Seddon £55 as a similar indenture. Whether this meant that Chippendale was more philanthropic than his rivals or that he was unable to demand as high a premium as them is a matter of conjecture. Perhaps further search through the Apprentice books will, one day, fill in some of the blanks in these vital ten years of Chippendale's career.

He paid rates for his house in Conduit Court until midsummer, 1752 — the rates being raised to £14 during the previous year. At midsummer he took the first house on the right-hand side down Somerset Court, in the Strand, adjoining Northumberland House — a place called alternatively Northumberland Court. It was rated at £24, a sum which was later reduced to £21. He probably moved into this house before 7th June, as Edward, his second son, was buried at St. Martin's Church on that day, and the register gives his address as Northumberland Court. Conduit Court had been described by Strype in 1720 as 'indifferent broad with a free-stone pavement . . . indifferently well-build and inhabited', and Chippendale was, therefore, climbing up in the world when he moved to Somerset Court which Strype described as 'a handsome new-built Court with houses fit for good inhabitants'.[2] The rates that Chippendale paid for these premises have already been discussed, and a deed of trust recorded in the *Middlesex Register*, 1757, states that it was 'formerly in the Tenure of Thomas Chippendale at a yearly rent of Twenty Seven Pounds'. In a plan, dated 1759, these premises are shown to have been 20 ft. wide and about 45 ft. long, the back set against the south wall of Northumberland House. Mr. Hughes suggests[2] that Chippendale probably became acquainted with the Earl of Northumberland during this period, as they were neighbours, and this may have been one of the reasons why he dedicated his *Director* to the Earl. He gave up possession of the house in Somerset Court on Lady-Day, 1753, to Mathew Darly, the artist, engraver, designer, publisher and caricaturist, who was then in Chippendale's employ, as the latter was in the midst of engraving the plates for the first edition of the *Director*, which was to be published during the following year.

Chippendale probably took a sub-tenancy of No. 60 St. Martin's Lane for the next few months, and, at Christmas 1754, he took possession of the premises afterwards numbered as Nos. 60 and 61 St. Martin's Lane (Pl. 147), on a sixty years' lease, at the rateable value of £124 per annum. Mr. Hughes writes,[2] 'The *Middlesex Registers* for 1754 show that Chippendale acquired possession of Nos. 60 and 61, two houses separated by a covered

[1] Inland Revenue Papers, Public Record Office — apprenticeship books, 1752–4, City (Town) Registers (ref. 1/19). I am indebted for this information to Mr. E. T. Joy.

[2] Much of the information relating to Chippendale's premises' and workshops is taken from 'Thomas Chippendale's Workshops', by G. Bernard Hughes, *Country Life*, 14 June 1956, pp. 1290–1.

cartway entrance passage giving access to a stable yard; the land measured about 250 ft. long and at its widest about 180 ft. The owner of the property was James, Earl of Salisbury: in July 1753, he leased it to Robert Burges, who in the following December sub-let to Thomas Chippendale. In August 1754, a new lease was issued in favour of Thomas Chippendale and a financing partner, James Rannie; hitherto it has been thought that this partnership dated from 1755. It has always been stated that No. 62 was also leased by Chippendale. The rate books, however, show Robert Burges to have been the occupier from 1753 to 1777 . . . only in 1793 were the premises acquired as a personal residence by Thomas Chippendale the younger.' St. Martin's Lane and Long Acre were the centre of the cabinet-making, upholding and upholstering trades during the eighteenth century and the proximity of the Ministry of Works, from where many of the most important commissions were to be gleaned, was doubtless a paramount reason for this. William Hallett had his premises at No. 71 St. Martin's Lane, and Vile and Cobb had their premises next door on the corner of the Lane and Long Acre.

Chippendale altered the lay-out during the year 1754 and adapted it for his business, building workshops, warehouses, a shop and offices. He retained No. 60 as his residence. On 4th February, 1755, he insured his entire premises against fire for £3,700.[1] The policy, which is extant, is numbered 144850, and the first premium was £8. 9. 0. The annual premium was £7. 9. 0. and renewal date was Lady Day, 1756. The wording of the policy was first published by Mr. Hughes in 1956:[2]

'Thomas Chippindale of St. Martin's Lane in the Parish of St. Martin's in the Fields and James Rannie of . . . Cabinetmakers and upholsterers on the now Dwelling House of the said Thomas Chippindale Situate as aforesaid with a warehouse behind adjoining and Communicating on the Right Hand Side of the yard not Exceeding Eight Hundred Pounds   £800.

On their Household Goods utensils and Stock in Trade and Goods in Trust therein and under the said Warehouse and over the roof thereof not exceeding Sixteen Hundred and Fifty pounds   £1650.

Glass therein only not Exceeding One hundred pounds   £100.

Wearing apparel in the Dwelling house the property of Thomas Chippindale not Exceeding Fifty pounds   £50.

On a warehouse only intended to be built at the End of the yard to adjoin and Communicate with the aforesaid Warehouse not Exceeding Two Hundred and Fifty pounds   £250.

On their shop only Situate On the Left Hand side of the said yard Opposite to the first and adjoining the Last mentioned warehouse not Exceeding One Hundred and Fifty pounds.   £150.

Utensils Stock in Trade and Goods in Trust Therein only not Exceeding Two Hundred pounds   £200.

On their Utensils Stock in Trade and goods in Trust in their Back yard and in the Shops therein adjoining Each other behind the Intended warehouse with a Brick Wall between not Exceeding Five Hundred pounds.   £500.

All brick and Timber buildings.   £3,700.'

[1] For the value of the pound today multiply by approximately twelve.
[2] See p. 75, n. 2.

This (1754) must have been a busy year for Chippendale and in many ways a vital one. James Rannie had become his partner during the previous year and appears to have invested a considerable sum in the business. He is described as *Upholder and Cabinet-Maker* and probably specialised in the *upholding and upholstering* side of business. It can be seen from the insurance policy that, in 1755 'a warehouse only intended to be built at the End of the yard' was not yet completed and it was probably being built with some of the funds that Rannie had invested in the firm. The first edition of the *Director* had been published during the previous year and orders were probably pouring in. On Saturday, 5th April, the partners suffered a serious set-back, for it is reported in the *Gentleman's Magazine* of that month 'that a fire broke out in the workshop of Mr. Chippendale, a cabinet-maker near St. Martin's Lane, which consumed the same, wherein were the chests of 22 workmen'. It was lucky that they had insured them for £500 less than three months previously, and they were thus immediately rebuilt, 'together with a three-storeyed building extending the full 180 ft. width of the site and joining the shop and warehouse.'[1]

The Sun Insurance Company also made a plan of Chippendale's premises, the original of which has now unfortunately been lost. However, a copy was taken by the London County Council in the 1930's and a great deal can be learnt from study of it. It included 'counting-rooms, the dwelling house. . . . Upholsterers' shop and ware room heated with a German stove; stacks for the drying of wood in the roof . . . glass-room . . . feather room with an open cockle stove . . . three-storeyed building : all cabinet-makers' shops. . . . Veneering-room with feather-room over. . . . Drying-room with stone floor for charcoals, containing a japanning stove and German stove; carpet-room above. . . . Store-room and show-room. . . .' It can thus be seen that Chippendale's staff included specialist craftsmen of every kind and it is more than probable that he often cast and silvered his own glass mirror-plates, and he certainly sold carpets, stuffed his own mattresses with feathers, and dried the japanning on his furniture in a room heated by a German stove. It must have needed a first-class business brain to build-up, manage and organise an undertaking of so diverse and complex a nature; and it should be noted that it was shortly after the fire that he published the second edition of the *Director*.

His social standing seems also to have risen rapidly, for in 1760, when he was aged forty-two, he was elected a member of the Society of Arts. He was proposed by Sir Thomas Robinson of Rokeby Hall in Yorkshire, the well-known collector and patron of the Arts. The Society was founded for the 'encouragement of Art, Manufactures and Commerce', and membership was unlimited, including men of all professions from peers to waiters. Chippendale appears to have been the only cabinet-maker to have been made a member, but he was not in fact entered in the book in the same manner as the majority of the other members — he was referred to as 'Mr', the other untitled members being 'Esquires'. Sir Thomas Robinson had subscribed to the first edition of the *Director* and was doubtless a client of Chippendale's. He probably met many of his clients through membership of the Society and the signatures of the Duke of Portland and Lord Pembroke, both of whom later retained him, are found on the same page as that of Chippendale in the Society's book of members.

James Rannie died in 1766, four years after the publication of the third edition of the

[1] See p. 75, n. 2.

THOMAS CHIPPENDALE (1718–79)

Director, and was buried at St. Martin's on 29th January of that year. Chippendale carried on the business by himself for the next five years and, probably in order to wind-up Rannie's estate, a notice of the sale of the stock of furniture at 60 St. Martin's Lane appeared in the *Public Advertiser* for 3rd March, 1766. It must have also been an ideal opportunity for Chippendale to rid himself of many of the pieces in stock, in the French, Gothic or Chinese styles popularised by his publications of the *Director*, which were now rapidly becoming old-fashioned and obsolete on account of the rage for Robert Adam's neo-classical or 'Antique' taste. The advertisement for the sale is as follows:

'TO BE SOLD BY AUCTION
BY MR. PERVIL

some Time this Month, on the Premises in St. Martin's Lane;

All the genuine Stock in Trade of Mr. *Chippendale* and his late Partner Mr. Rennie, deceased, Cabinetmakers, consisting of a great variety of fine Cabinet Work, Chairs, and a Parcel of fine season'd Feathers; as also the large unwrought Stock, consisting of Mahogany and other Woods, in Planks, Boards, and Wainscot.

Of which Sale timely Notice will be given in this and other Papers.

The Business to be carried on for the future by Mr. Chippendale, on the Premises, upon his own Account.'

On 17th March, when the date of the sale was announced, a fuller notice was included worded as follows:

'TO BE SOLD BY AUCTION
BY MR. PERVIL

On Monday, the 24th instant, and the following Days.

The entire genuine and valuable Stock in Trade of Mr. Chippendale and his late partner Mr. Rennie, deceased, Cabinetmakers and Upholsterers, at their House in St. Martin's Lane, consisting of a great Variety of fine Mahogany and Tulup Wood, Cabinets, Desks, and Book-Cases, Cloaths Presses, double Chests of Drawers, Commodes, Buroes, fine Library, Writing, Card, Dining, and other Tables, Turky and other Carpets, one of which is 13 Feet by 19 Feet six, fine pattern Chairs, and sundry other Pieces of curious Cabinet Work, a large Parcel of fine season'd Feathers; as also all the large unwrought Stock consisting of fine Mahogany and other Woods, in Plank, Boards, Vanier and Wainscot.

The whole to be viewed on Friday next to the Hour of Sale (Sunday excepted) which will begin each Day punctually at Twelve.

Catalogues to be had the Days of Viewing at the Place of Sale, and at Mr. Pervil's, the Upper End of Bow-Street, Covent Garden.

The Business to be carried on for the future by Mr. Chippendale, on the Premises, on his own Account.'

This sale really brings to an end the first important phase of Chippendale's career when he was a champion of the rococo taste in England. As far as he was concerned it had served him well and, through the publication of the *Director*, he had attracted to his premises a large and influential coterie of clients. However, Thomas Chippendale was primarily a business-man, and he must have quickly realised that the rococo was doomed to fall before the neo-classical style, which was by this time so ardently being canvassed by Robert Adam, Athenian Stuart and some of their clients — not to speak of the echoes of a similar movement which were reaching this country from Paris. Adam had forecast its defeat with his accessories at Luton, 1764–8, intended, he says 'as an attempt to banish the absurd French compositions of this kind, heretofore so servilely imitated by the upholsterers of this country'. Chippendale rapidly joined Adam and now became a leading exponent of the *Antique* taste.

Chippendale's career in collaboration with Robert Adam and the outstanding marquetry, gilt, painted and japanned furniture that he made in the neo-classical tradition are beyond the scope of this book, but a few biographical details from this latter part of his life are included. In 1771, he made James Rannie's clerk, Thomas Haig, his partner. Haig appears to have taken over much of the administrative and financial side of the business. He continued in partnership with Chippendale's son, after Thomas's death in 1779, and only left the business in 1796.

There is an interesting reference[1] to Chippendale in August 1773, in a letter written by Sir William Chambers to Lord Melbourne, whose house Chambers was building at the time on the site where the Albany now stands, in Piccadilly. Chambers writes 'Chippendale called up me yesterday with some Designs for furnishing the rooms wh.upon the whole seem very well but I wish to be a little consulted about these matters as I am really a Very pretty Connoisseur in furniture. Be pleased therefore if it is agreable to Your Lordship & My Lady to order him to show me the Drawings at large for tables, Glasses etc. before they are put in Hand as I think from his Small Drawings that some part may be improved a little.'[2] Chambers and Chippendale had obviously just had an acrimonious quarrel, and this affords an important insight into the professional relationship between architect and cabinet-maker. It would be interesting to know more about that maintained between Adam and Chippendale (see p. 122). The many clients who patronised Chippendale's firm are discussed separately at the end of this chapter.

Chippendale's first wife, Catherine (*née* Redshaw), had died in 1772, and in 1777 he married a second wife, Elizabeth Davis. He died two years later of consumption and was buried on 13th November, at St. Martin's Church, aged sixty-two years. The appropriate entry in the sexton's book reads,

'Cons. M.62y. Thomas Chippendale, St. Martin's Lane, N.O.G., and Prays, £2. 7. 4.'.[3]

His second wife died in 1799. A memorial plaque, which was erected to commemorate Thomas Chippendale, was unveiled in November 1962 on the wall of the Building Society Offices in Boroughgate, Otley.[4]

Mr. Edward Joy has drawn attention to an interesting, and illuminating, episode in Chippendale's career, in his article *Chippendale in trouble at the Customs*,[5] which shows that the great cabinet-maker's business scruples were far from being beyond reproach. Chippendale was apparently importing French chairs in an unfinished state, which he was

[1] 14 August 1773, Letter book, Add. 41133, pp. 107–107V.

[2] Quoted from Heather Martienssen, 'Chambers as a Professional Man', *Architectural Review*, April 1964, No. 806, Vol. CXXXV, p. 280.

[3] Meaning 'Died of Consumption, Man, 62 years old, Thomas Chippendale, St. Martin's Lane, North Old Ground, and Prayers £2. 7. 4.'.

[4] I am indebted to Mr. R. D. Biss, Editor of the *Wharfedale and Airedale Observer* for this information.

[5] *Country Life*, 24 August 1951.

declaring at a very low value for import duty purposes and which he was then intending to finish in his own workshops. The Customs officers detected this ruse and confiscated some chairs, paying Chippendale his declared value on them, plus the duty payable and an additional ten per cent of the value — this shows to how great a degree he had under-declared the value of the chairs. The whole matter is recorded in the minutes to bench officers in the Customs House library and the commissioner's minute in question, dated 14th November, 1769, reads as follows:

> 'Messrs. Robson and Gibbs officers of the Warehouse having by their Memorial represented that on the 3rd Instant Thomas Chippendale entered on board the Calais Packet, John Gilby from Calais, one case containing, five Dozen of chairs, unfinished Value Eighteen pounds all (French) but that on Examination they have Reason to believe, the same is greatly under Valued, and have therefore stopped them for the Boards Directions; The Commissioners direct the Collector Inwards to take the said Chairs, and out of the Money in his Hands arising by Customs and other Duties, to pay the Importer or Proprietor, the Value Sworn to, together with the Customs or other Duties paid by him, and ten per cent on such value, and the Warehouse Keeper is to sell the Same, and pay the Produce thereof to the Collector Inwards, who is with the privity of the proper Chequer to apply the same as the Law directs.'

Chippendale had doubtless done this on several occasions before being detected and the whole business, as was the case with Madame Cornelys' bankruptcy (see p. 109), shows him up in a bad light. But in all fairness, his business principles appear to be no worse than that of his contemporaries. It is interesting that Chippendale's name was linked with James Cullen's in the Cornelys' bankruptcy, and that Cullen was also in trouble with the Customs over the misuse of the diplomatic bag by Count Pignatelli and Baron Berlindis (see p. 161). John Cobb, moreover, was no better (see p. 32), as he was also mixed up in the same dubious affair. The business morals of the leading cabinet-makers in London during the mid-eighteenth century seem to have been lax, to say the least.

PART II *THE DIRECTOR*

A — THE PUBLICATION

Thomas Chippendale brought out the first edition of his famous publication which is always known simply as '*The Director*' on 23rd March, 1754, under the title:

'THE GENTLEMAN AND CABINET MAKER'S
DIRECTOR

Being a large collection of the most Elegant and Useful Designs of Household Furniture in the Gothic, Chinese and Modern Taste.

Including a great variety of Book-cases for Librairies or Private Rooms, Commodes, Library and Writing-Tables, Buroes, Breakfast-Tables, Dressing and China-Tables, China-cases, Hanging-Shelves, Tea-Chests, Trays, Firescreens, Chairs, Settees, Sopha's, Beds, Presses and Cloaths-chests, Pier glass sconces, slab frames, Brackets, Candlestands, Clock-cases, Frets and other ornaments.

To which is prefixed a short Explanation of the Five Orders of Architecture, and Rules of Perspective; with Proper Directions for executing the most difficult Pieces, the Mouldings being exhibited at large, and the Dimensions of each Design specified: the whole Comprehended in 160 copper-plates, neatly Engraved, calculated to improve and refine the present Taste, and suited to the Fancy and Circumstances of Persons in all Degrees of Life.
Dulcique animos novitate tenebo. — Ovid
Ludentis speciem dabit et torquebitur. — Hor.

BY
THOMAS CHIPPENDALE
of St. Martin's Lane, Cabinet-maker
London

Printed for the Author and sold at his House in St. Martin's Lane, MDCCLIV.'

The book, which is a large folio volume, is dedicated to the Earl of Northumberland. The Earl was a keen patron of the Arts and in October 1752 Walpole had written of the Northumberlands, 'They are building at Northumberland House, at Sion, at Stanstead, at Alnwick and Warkworth Castles.' The Earl, with this flurry of building in progress, was an obvious target for the leading cabinet-makers of the time and Chippendale probably dedicated his design book to Northumberland with the aim of enlisting his patronage. It is not known whether he succeeded, as there are no extant accounts from Chippendale's firm in the Northumberland family archives. However on 9th February, 1752 — that is, some two years before the *Director* made its appearance — Matthias Lock, who may well have been in Chippendale's employ at the time (see p. 55) made a note which reads, 'A Sconce and a Table for Lord Holdernest, to Chimney Mr. Bradshaw, *to Table Ld. Northumb'ld.*' (see p. 54, n. 3). It is probable, therefore, that Chippendale was, in fact, providing furniture for the Earl at this juncture. The dedication in the *Director*, which is printed below the Earl's Coat of Arms, is couched in the usual sycophantic language of the time, and reads as follows :

'*The Right Honourable Hugh, Earl of Northumberland*, Baron Warkworth of Warkworth Castle, *Lord Lieutenant* and Custos Rotulorum of the County of Northumberland, *and one of the Lords of the Bed Chamber to His Majesty &c.*
My Lord, Your intimate acquaintance with all those Arts & Sciences, that tend to perfect or adorn life, and your well known disposition to promote them give the following Designs a natural claim to your protection, they are therefore with great respect laid at your feet by — *My Lord, Your Lordships Most Humble and obedient Servant*
Thomas Chippendale.'

The dedication is followed by a preface, the full text of which is given in Appendix A. This is primarily of interest as it shows that Chippendale intended that it should appeal to the amateur and the cabinet-maker alike. He thus writes :

'*The Title-page has already called the following work*, The Gentleman and Cabinet-Maker's Director, *as being calculated to assist the one in the choice, and the other in the execution of the Designs. . . .'*

The preface also reveals Chippendale's ambition to advertise his business, as widely as possible. The last paragraph, which demonstrates this particularly clearly, is also of importance :

> *'Upon the whole, I have here given no design but what may be executed with advantage by the hands of a skillful workman, though some of the profession have been diligent enough to represent them (especially those after the Gothic and Chinese manner) as so many specious drawings, impossible to be worked off by any mechanic whatsoever. I will not scruple to attribute this to malice, ignorance and inability; and I am confident that I can convince all Noblemen, Gentlemen, or others, who will honour me with their commands, that every design in the book can be improved, both as to beauty and enrichment, in the execution of it, by Their Most Obedient Servant, Thomas Chippendale.'*

It is obvious that many of his rivals in the trade had seen his designs before they were published and had scoffed at them and said that they were impracticable. This is further borne out by an earlier paragraph in the preface where he writes :

> *'I am not afraid of the fate an author usually meets with on his first appearance, from a set of critics who are never wanting to show their wit and malice on the performances of others: I shall repay their censures with contempt. Let them unmolested deal out their pointless abuse, and convince the world they have neither good nature to commend, judgment to correct, nor skill to execute what they find fault with.'*

From this it would seem that *a set of critics had in fact* already been showing *their wit and malice.*

During the preparation of the book, which took at least two years, if not longer, it is probable that a considerable amount of advertising and propaganda must have taken place. However no advertisement has, to date, been recorded, as far as I am aware, prior to that in an April number of the *Gentleman's Magazine* of 1754 which, among its 'New Publications' announces 'Thomas Chippendale published the *Gentleman and Cabinet-Maker's Director . . . £2. 8. 0.'* This was a very high price for a book of this nature and probably explains why Chippendale went to such great lengths to collect so many subscribers whose names are published in a list after the preface in the first edition.

How he managed to collect together this imposing list of subscribers is not recorded, but some sort of appeal must have been sent out, as it is hardly credible that Chippendale, or members of his staff, should have known personally or been recommended to all of them. He obviously could rely on a small number of his clients to subscribe to the publication and many of the tradesmen and cabinet-makers would have been known to him, but the remainder must have been enlisted in some other way. They include cabinet-makers, carvers, joiners and upholsterers. Amongst these are many familiar names such as Samuel Agar, *carver,* John Bladwell, *upholder,* William Gordon, the Channons, Richard Gillow, William Ince, *cabinet-maker,* Benjamin Parran, *cabinet-maker,* James Rannie, *cabinet-maker,* George Seddon, *cabinet-maker,* John Trotter, *cabinet-maker,* Thomas Whittle, *carver.*[1] Not

---

[1] Samuel Agar, *carver,* Church St., St. Anne's, Soho, fl. 1749–63. His address is given as Litchfield St. in the 1749 Westminster Poll Lists.

John Bladwell, *upholder,* Bow St., Covent Garden, fl. 1725–68.
  Accounts, dated 30 March 1752, for furniture at Woburn — see Gladys Scott Thomson, *Family Background,* 1949, pp. 49 and 59.
William Gordon, *Cabinet-Maker,* Swallow Street, Argyle Buildings, 1748. See p. 51.
Richard Gillow of Lancaster, 1734–1811, eldest son of Robert Gillow, founder of the firm, 1703–73. See pp. 154–6.
William Ince, *cabinet-maker,* was apprenticed to Mr. West, of King Street, Covent Garden, at this time.

all of them, however, were members of the London trades, for amongst others, are listed, Robert Barker, *Upholder at York*, Robinson Cook, at *Liverpool*, Richard Farrer, *Upholder*, *York*, Thomas Malton, of *Nottingham, cabinet-maker*, Hugh Underwood, *cabinet-maker*, *Scarborough*, Richard Wood, *in York, 8 Books*. The connection with York and Scarborough can be explained by Chippendale's family link with Yorkshire, but Liverpool and Nottingham are further afield. However, it was not only cabinetmakers and upholsterers who subscribed, for members of other professions are also listed — plasterers, engravers, booksellers (probably accounting for the eight copies ordered by Mr. Wood of York), a bricklayer, a founder, a painter, an architect, a merchant, a watch-maker, a chemist, an organ-maker[1] and two professors of philosophy. Oliver Bracket, after quoting this list, writes,[2] 'It is a curious position to find numbers of men of the artisan class subscribing to an expensive publication of this nature, and it would be interesting to know what inducement Chippendale offered to them. The cabinet-makers might profit by the opportunity this presented of copying Chippendale's designs, if they wished to, but it is difficult to see what benefit some of the others could derive from their subscriptions.' It is possible that the inducement was merely that of acquiring a copy of the *Director* at a reduced rate, although this seems unlikely. Possibly it was simply because they all shared an overwhelming interest in the *rococo* in all its manifestations.

The Nobility and Gentry would have subscribed for more readily understandable reasons. Perhaps, as in the case of the Earl of Northumberland, they were building and decorating at the time of the publication, or perhaps they were merely interested in everything that was new and *à la mode*. The lists includes five Dukes, a Marquess, five Earls, six Barons and five Baronets or Knights. Amongst these are the Duke of Hamilton, who was partly responsible for the formation of the famous collection at Hamilton Palace,[3] the Duke of Portland, who certainly bought two pier-glasses from Chippendale as is proved by the surviving accounts (see p. 117), and the Duke of Norfolk who probably bought the chair (Pl. 167) from Chippendale's, the design being taken straight from the third edition of the *Director*. The Duke of Beaufort, who was also a subscriber, almost certainly patronised Chippendale as examples in the *Director* style remain at Badminton.[4] The Chinese bedroom, which was described by Dr. Pococke[5] in 1754 as 'finished and furnished very elegantly in the Chinese manner', was filled with pieces in Chippendale's Chinese manner.[6] The Earl of Chesterfield, whose passion for the French rococo ornament

In 1758 he went into partnership with John Mayhew, fl. 1758–1810. See pp. 62–3.

Benjamin Parran, *cabinet-maker*, at The Golden Spread Eagle, Long Acre, fl. 1754–83. He was Benjamin Goodison's nephew and supplied the Crown from 1767–83.

James Rannie, *cabinet-maker*, in 1754 he became Thomas Chippendale's partner: died 1766.

George Seddon, *cabinet-maker*, London House, Aldersgate Street, 1727–1801. See pp. 152–4.

John Trotter, *cabinet-maker* (and *upholder*), 43, Frith Street, Soho. Upholder to George II, fl. 1755–92.

Thomas Whittle, *carver*, probably related to James Whittle. See pp. 141–2.

[1] There are designs for organ cases in the 3rd edition of the *Director*, pls. 103–106.

[2] This list is quoted from O. Bracket, *op. cit.*, p. 36.

[3] This famous collection was sold by Messrs. Christie, Manson and Woods Ltd. in 1882.

[4] Ill., *G.C-M.*, pls. 102, 104, 117, 129.

[5] Dr. R. Pococke, *Travels through England* (1754), published 1888–9, Vol. II, p. 31.

[6] This furniture has been sold but the bed (Plate C) and a commode (pl. 332) are now in the Victoria and Albert Museum: while a pair of etagères is in the Lady Lever Art Gallery (pl. 281) (one now on long loan to the Victoria and Albert Museum).

was so magnificently demonstrated by the decoration of Chesterfield House in Mayfair was another subscriber, as was the Countess of Shaftesbury who was responsible for ordering so much of the fine furniture in the rococo tradition remaining at St. Giles's House, Dorset.[1]

Another subscriber to the first edition was 'The Right Hon. Lord Montford', who was fifty-one years old at the time of publication and who lived at Holt Castle, Horseheath in Cambridgeshire. He was in the habit of leading a particularly dissolute and dissipated life and on 1st January, 1755, he committed suicide. The Castle and its entire contents were sold by his executors that same year to Lord Foley. These events would have had little bearing on the publication of Chippendale's *Director*, if two folio scrap books,[2] containing one hundred and eighty of Chippendale's original drawings, including nearly all of those for the plates of the first edition of the *Director*, had not been found in the collection of Lord Foley. There is no apparent reason why these designs should have been in the Foley collection, as there is no known link between the family and Chippendale; and Mr. A. G. Lewis has thus suggested to me that Lord Foley may have taken over the drawings from Lord Montford when he bought the contents of Holt Castle after the latter's death. Lord Montford who, it has been seen, was a subscriber to the *Director*, may have had these drawings in his possession as a security against money that he had lent to Chippendale in order that he might publish the first edition of the *Director*. It is strongly stressed here that this is only put forward as a possible theory, but, if Lord Montford was indeed Chippendale's backer, a great deal of speculation as to how Chippendale managed to finance the publication would be solved.[3] It has been suggested elsewhere[4] that James Rannie, who became Chippendale's partner in 1754,[5] may have given the firm financial backing, but it is unlikely that he would have done so before he became a partner in the business. All that can at present be said is that Chippendale must almost certainly have needed a backer, or even several, and Lord Montford's name is put forward as a possible candidate.

The list of subscribers is followed by rules for the drawing of the five Orders of Architecture, 'Tuscan, Dorick, Ionick Corinthian and Composite', and further 'rules to draw . . . in perspective'. These are later complemented by plates with explanatory illustrations. Chippendale claims to have a knowledge of the rules of perspective and states that without them a clear understanding of his designs will be impossible. It is of interest to note in this connection that Sheraton, writing in 1791 in his *Cabinet-Makers and Upholsterer's Drawing-Book*, says, 'It may be remarked to his [Chippendale's] credit that, although he has not given us the rules for drawing in perspective himself, yet he is sensible of their importance and use in designing.' Of course, Chippendale had, in fact, *in the first edition*, given the rules and Sheraton must have been referring to the *third edition*, where this section was omitted when he wrote the above.

Chippendale's reasons for including the rules are fully given in his preface when he

[1] See p. 119.
[2] Now in the Metropolitan Museum, New York.
[3] I am indebted to Mr. A. G. Lewis for suggesting this theory to me.
[4] Sir Ambrose Heal, *The London Furniture Makers*, London, 1953, p. 147.
[5] A lease was issued to Chippendale and Rannie in August 1754, for Nos. 60 and 61, St. Martin's Lane — Middlesex Register.

writes, 'Of all the Arts which are either improved or ornamented by Architecture, that of CABINET-MAKING is not only the most useful and ornamental, but capable of receiving as great assistance from it as any whatever. I have therefore prefixed to the following designs a short explanation of the five Orders. Without an acquaintance with this science, and some knowledge of the rules of Perspective, the Cabinet-maker cannot make the designs of his work intelligible, nor shew, in a little compass, the whole conduct and effect of the piece. These, therefore, ought to be carefully studied by everyone who would excel in this branch, since they are the very soul and basis of his Art.'

These rules are followed by descriptive notes to the plates which, if studied with care, yield much valuable information. Great stress is laid on the question of proportion and on this point intricate calculations and detailed instructions are often given. Little reference is made to types of wood, and it is obvious that a high proportion of the furniture was to be gilded or japanned. Thus in referring to *A China Case*, plate 109, he writes, 'The design must be executed by the hands of an ingenious workman, and when neatly japann'd will appear very beautiful.' He recommended that sofas and screens should be gilded, as should mirror-frames and girandoles. Mahogany is never mentioned, and one is reminded by this that many of the finest pieces of furniture made during this period were, in fact, produced in other kinds of exotic and rare woods which often resemble mahogany, although they were actually of even rarer species. Novelty was of paramount importance to the smart and rich at this time, and this explains not only the constant demand for new and outrageous designs, but also the eagerness of customers to have their furniture made of even more exotic and unusual kinds of timber.

Chippendale was not shy of praising his own designs. For instance, in the notes, he refers to 'three-ribband-back chairs [cf. Pls. 172–7], which, if I may speak without vanity, are the best I have ever seen (or perhaps have been made)'. Again he mentions a china-case (cf. Pl. 265) as being 'not only the richest and most magnificent in the whole [Country], but perhaps in all Europe'. Referring to another design for a china-case, he writes, 'This design I have executed with great satisfaction to the purchaser.' It was patently not the custom to be modest during the middle of the eighteenth century.

It is clear that he utilised some of these designs prior to the publication of the first edition, as can be seen from his remarks in the note to plate 16 illustrating *ribband-back chairs*, which states that 'the Chair on the left hand has been executed from this design, which had an exellent effect. . . . I make no doubt but the other two will give the same content, if properly handled in the execution.' However, while discussing a Gothic design bookcase in the note to plate 75, he writes, 'This design is perhaps one of the best of its kind, and would give me great pleasure to see it executed.'

The *Director* contains one hundred and sixty-one plates.[1] Of those devoted to furniture, fifteen contain designs for chairs, two for sofas, six for beds, twenty-seven for commodes and tables, while the rest are allocated to brackets, bookcases, cabinets, candlestands, cornices, desks, girandoles, fire-screens, pier-glasses, shields, frets and Chinese railings. It will be noted that both carver's and joiner's pieces are included. The plates are dated 1753 and 1754, and the majority of them were engraved by Mathew Darly (see p. 52), whilst

[1] Two consecutive plates, for Chinese chairs and a Chinese *sopha*, are numbered 25 — the total number of plates being 161 inclusive.

T. and J. S. Müller were responsible for the remainder. As we have already noted on Lady Day, 1753, Chippendale had given up his house in Somerset (Northumberland) Court and Darly had taken it over. This can hardly have been a coincidence, but was probably an arrangement made so that Darly could settle down to engrave the plates for the *Director*.

It will be remembered that Chippendale, on the title page, describes the *Director* as 'Being a large collection of the most elegant and useful designs of household furniture in the *Gothic, Chinese* and *Modern* taste'. These then were the three stylistic trends on which he based his designs in the first edition. The *Modern* taste refers to the anglicised, and often incorrectly interpreted, version of the forms of the French *rococo* or *genre pittoresque*. This idiom has already been discussed on pp. 47–9, but nothing has so far been said about Chippendale's interpretation of it. Lock probably taught Chippendale how to handle the *French* or *Modern* style, and it has already been shown that his competent and self-assured interpretation of the rococo caught the essence of this lively idiom and shows that he must have made an intelligent study of the French originals. Amongst the 'Modern' designs in the *Director* are those for 'French elbow chairs' and 'French commode tables'.

The *Gothic* and *Chinese* tastes, on the other hand, form such an integral part of Chippendale's designs in the first edition, that some explanation as to how these two seemingly incompatible styles should have become fused together in so many of the *Director* designs seems necessary. It is important to realise, in this connection, that in the *Director*, and to most Englishmen of the period, that the Chinese and the Gothic tastes were merely different aspects or facets of the fantastic, the imaginary and the exotic which were thought to be the principal ingredients of the rococo. In a sense the Modern, the Gothic and the Chinese tastes were all manifestations of the same spirit — the spirit of the rococo; but, of course, both the Chinese and the Gothic tastes had their roots in the past.

The history of the Chinese taste, or chinoiserie, in Europe, goes back to the Middle Ages, but it was not until the seventeenth century that its influence began to be extensively felt in the applied Arts. Expansion of trade with the Far East had resulted in a craze for porcelain, lacquer and stuffs from China and Japan. In England this grew quickly after the Restoration and, in 1688, Stalker and Parker published their *Treatise of Japanning and Varnishing*. This resulted in a fashion for English *japanned* furniture in imitation of the original Oriental lacquer, and, by the beginning of the eighteenth century, the English had produced their own pseudo-Oriental style, which included a range of *chinoiserie* motives such as pagodas, mandarins, *ho-ho* birds with long beaks, and dragons. Edwards and Darly published their *New Book of Chinese Designs* in 1754 (see p. 52), which includes all of these ill-digested, quasi-Chinese motives. This was followed by the *Ladies Amusement or Whole Art of Japanning Made Easy*, which is based on Stalker and Parker's and Edwards' and Darly's respective publications, but had a new and lighter element perhaps introduced by the French draughtsman Jean Pillement, who contributed some of his first published designs to this book. It was published in circa 1760 and contains some fifteen hundred designs. It is filled with amusing advice, and ladies are cautioned against placing any 'exotic or preposterous object' in their design, if it is European, but 'with Indian or Chinese [compositions] greater liberties may be taken . . . for in these is often seen a Butterfly supporting an Elephant or things equally absurd . . .'. This then was the public image of the Chinese style around 1760.

THOMAS CHIPPENDALE (1718–79)

It has been pointed out by Mr. Ward-Jackson[1] that the English designers imitated directly a Chinese form of lattice-work which came to be known as 'Chinese railing' or 'Chinese paling'. The earliest engraved designs for it are included in William Halfpenny's *New Designs for Chinese Temples* which appeared in 1750. Later publications incorporating these forms were the *Director*, in all its editions, Edwards and Darly's *New Book of Chinese Designs* and *The Carpenter's Companion for Chinese Railings and Gates*, published by J. H. Morris and John Crunden in 1765. This lattice-work was frequently used on furniture, as pierced or openwork, or as blind-fret ornamentation (i.e. applied in relief, often in sunken panels), on the backs, seat-rails and legs of chairs, and on the angles, borders and galleries of case furniture.

The Gothic style was peculiar to England at this period and examples of furniture in this idiom are far rarer than are those in the Chinese taste. One should remember that the Gothic tradition had never entirely died out in this country, and that for ecclesiastical and university buildings Gothic was still the traditional and accepted style. Most of Wren's churches are a fusion of Gothic with baroque: his spires must have seemed most strange to Italian and French baroque architects. Thus many buildings had been erected in the traditional Gothic style throughout the seventeenth century and there were still a number of architects and masons well qualified to execute Gothic work during the early years of the eighteenth century. During the 1740's the style began to be admired and almost revered by sophisticated enthusiasts such as Sanderson Miller and Horace Walpole. This was, in fact, some seventy or eighty years before the style became fashionable on the Continent. Miller was an amateur architect and he designed many sham Gothic ruins and follies in the parks of his friends and clients, which did much to popularise the movement. Batty Langley (see p. 52) had been the first to publish designs for interiors in this style and in the Preface to his *Gothic Architecture Improved*, 1742, he recommended what he called the *Saxon* style for 'all parts of private buildings, and especially in Rooms of State, Dining Rooms, Parlours, Stair-cases, &c. And in Porticos, Umbrellos, Temples, and Pavillions in Gardens, Parks &c.'. This book contains no designs for furniture, but an early reference to chairs of Gothic design is found in a letter of 1749 to Sanderson Miller from his client, George Lyttelton of Hagley, who writes, 'I forget how many chairs you are wanting for the castle . . . but how can I bespeak them without the model you drew for them? You know they are not to be common chairs but in a Gothic form.'[2]

Horace Walpole was probably the most famous champion of the Gothic style and after he had bought his villa, Strawberry Hill, on the Thames at Twickenham, in 1747, he spent the next ten years in Gothicising and furnishing it. Walpole's experiments at Strawberry Hill were ruthlessly criticised by his friends and already, in 1750, some of them were saying that the Gothic had become so 'prevalent a craze as to be already unfashionable and middle class'.[3] Walpole was aided in his designs by Richard Bentley who 'employed Gothic because it licensed any extravagant invention'. In the nineteenth century Strawberry Hill sale catalogue is found the following entry: 'A truly splendid table in the Gothic Style, the top of Sicilian jasper of the rarest kind, on a black frame (the table was designed by

---

[1] *English Furniture Designs of the Eighteenth Century*, pp. 16–18, p. 42.
[2] L. Dickins and M. Stanton, *An Eighteenth Century Correspondence*, 1910, p. 159.
[3] R. W. Ketton-Cremer, *Horace Walpole*, p. 135.

Mr. Bentley and is perfectly unique).' This table may have been of similar design to an example at The Vyne, Hampshire (Pl. 148), which is *en suite* with a pier-glass, and was made for Walpole's close friend Anthony Chute in about 1755. In the same house, there is a curious girandole of Gothic idiom, which may also have associations with Walpole; it shows once again how the Gothic and the Chinese tastes could happily be intermingled at this stage, both being regarded as equally strange and unreal (Pl. 149). The 'Strawberry Room' from Lee Priory, Littlebourne, is illustrated in Pl. 150. This was built at this period by James Wyatt for a friend of Walpoles in emulation of Strawberry Hill — hence the name given to the room. Sir Roger Newdigate, 1719–1806, was yet another enthusiast for the Gothic style. He rebuilt Arbury in the Gothic taste, and employed William Hiorn, in about 1750, to remodel his library for him in this style. Arthur Devis painted him sitting at his desk in his Gothic library (Pl. 151).

A writer in *The World* in 1753 described the Gothic taste as virtually outmoded, deserted by fashion for the Chinese, though a few years ago everything had been Gothic: 'our home, our beds, our bookcases, and our couches were all copied from some parts or other of our old cathedrals'. He later admits, however, that some people 'still retain the last fashion, the Gothic'. One may, however, wonder whether a great number of people really adopted the Gothic style, in spite of this statement. Compared with the number of essays in Chinoiserie which survive from this period, Gothic works of art are not so common as all that. Could it be that the style was largely used, in the field of furniture, for more ephemeral purposes — for garden or summer-house furniture, for follies, and the like, where less robust materials were employed, so that little of this furniture has slipped through the fingers of Time? Or was the writer exaggerating?

It must anyway be remembered that Sir Roger Newdigate and Horace Walpole were amongst the innovators of the style, and the general public, who were still retaining 'the last fashion' in 1753, would have only become acquainted with it through published designs. The earliest pattern books to include designs for Gothic *furniture* were Darly's *A New Book of Chinese, Gothic and Modern Chairs*, 1750 and 1751 and Chippendale's first edition of the *Director* (1754). In many of these designs the Gothic motives are freely mixed with others in the Chinese and Modern styles, and, as Mr. Ward-Jackson writes:[1] 'these incongruous mixtures of style were typical of the age, and some of the plates in books like Halfpenny's *Chinese and Gothic Architecture properly ornamented* (1752) and Overs' *Architecture in the Gothic, Chinese and Modern Taste* (1758) are even stranger hotchpotches of Gothic, Chinese and baroque ingredients.' Chippendale included designs for Gothic tables, beds, library-tables, bookcases, cabinets and, above all, chairs. These designs for chairs, which are of quasi Gothic–Chinese inspiration, were taken-up and, in most cases, adapted by many cabinet-makers, and examples are illustrated in Pls. 152–7. A chair-back settee of similar tradition is in Pl. 158. A carved picture-frame (Pl. 159) of Gothic design is of great interest, as it was designed for the Gothic drawing-room of the Earl of Pomfret's house in Arlington Street which was built by Sanderson Miller in 1760. Horace Walpole also lived in Arlington Street and, describing a tempest in 1779, wrote: 'One of the stone Gothic towers at Lady Pomfret's house (now single-speech Hamilton's) in my street fell through the roof, and not a thought of it remains.' A pier-glass, a bird-cage

[1] See p. 87, n. 1.

and two other pieces of case furniture in the Gothic tradition are illustrated in Pls. 160–63, which demonstrate how the style was often used in the most incongruous way.

However the real vogue for the Gothic style was short-lived and little thought of it remained when the third edition of the *Director* was published in 1762.

Many pieces have survived from the third quarter of the eighteenth century which were either copied from, or directly inspired by, designs in Chippendale's *Director*. It is important to remember that the *Director* was heavily subscribed for by members of the cabinet-making and carvers' trades, both in London and throughout the provinces, and many of the country subscribers would not have hesitated to copy the designs in it freely. For this reason many of the extant pieces which are identical to the published designs — often known as *book pieces* — have, in fact, been made by a provincial or country cabinet-maker working from the *Director*. It is unlikely that a leading London firm would have exactly copied the designs published by a rival establishment, especially when executing a special commission for a client, since the customers of the London cabinet-makers were mostly aware of the latest trends of fashion and therefore demanded novelty above all : and if they failed to get it from one firm, there were plenty of others who would have been glad to supply what was needed.

Thus it can only be categorically stated that a piece of furniture was made by a certain cabinet-maker when the account relating to that piece of furniture, from the firm in question, is extant. However, if it is known from documentary evidence, in the form of ledger entries, letters or accounts, or (with certain reservations) from strong family tradition, that a certain cabinet-maker provided furniture for a house — as in the case of Chippendale at Wilton where there are several 'book pieces' remaining in the house — then it is fairly safe to attribute the pieces in question to the workshops of whoever published the designs — that is, of course, if the cabinet-maker, in question, had published designs.

It is not known how many copies Chippendale sold of the first edition, nor is it known whether he had sold them all by Saturday, 5th April, 1755. He, and James Rannie, who had become his partner sometime prior to August 1754,[1] suffered a very serious set-back on that day, for it was then that the fire broke out in their workshops (see p. 77). It has been suggested to the author by Mr. A. G. Lewis, that the remaining unsold copies of the first edition may have been consumed in this fire, which necessitated the reprint and subsequent issue of the second edition later in the year. Of course, if this is true, some copies of the first edition would have escaped the fire, as they were not only being sold 'at his (the author's) house in St. Martin's Lane', but also 'by T. Osborne, Book Seller, in Gray's-Inn; H. Piers, Bookseller, in Holborn; R. Sayer, Print-Seller, in Fleet Street; J. Swan, near Northumberland House, in the Strand; at Edinburgh, by Messrs. Hamilton and Balfour; and at Dublin, by Mr. John Smith, on the Blind Quay'. Various unsold copies would have been left over with these book-sellers. Moreover, the plates were presumably in Mathew Darly's safe-keeping in Chippendale's old house in Northumberland Court.

Anyway, whatever the reason may have been, a second edition was published in 1755. Apart from a few minor corrections in the numbering of the plates, and the changed date and edition number,[2] the second edition was no different from the first, although the name

---

[1] See p. 84, n. 5.   [2] *i.e.* MDCCLV and the 2nd edition.

of the printer 'J. Hakerborn, in Gerrard Street' was now inserted on the title page.

There may well have been several reprints of the second edition. There was certainly one; for, in the *British Chronicle* of 20th–22nd March, 1758,[1] the following advertisement appears:

> 'This day was published, Neatly engraved on 160 folio copper plates, Price 1l. 16s. and 2l. 2s. bound.
>
> THE GENTLEMAN AND CABINET-MAKERS DIRECTOR,
>
> comprehending a great variety of the most useful and elegant Designs of Household Furniture, in the Gothic, Chinese and Modern Taste, with Scals [Scales] and Directions for executing the most complicated Enrichments and Decorations of each Design. By *T. Chippendale of St. Martin's Lane, Cabinet-Maker*. Printed for the Author and Sold by *R. Sayer*, opposite *Fetter-Lane, Fleet Street*, and all Booksellers in *Great Britain and Ireland*.
>
> All commissions for Household Furniture, or Drawings thereof, sent to the Cabinet and Upholstery Warehouse, at the Chair in *St. Martin's Lane*, will be most punctually observed, and executed in the genteelest Taste, and on the most reasonable Terms, by the Public's most humble Servant's,   T. CHIPPENDALE and J. RANNIE.'

Several very interesting points arise from careful study of this advertisement.[2] First the printer has been changed yet again, and R. Sayer of Fleet Street has now been employed instead of J. Hackerborn, who had originally printed the second edition. In the first and second editions Sayer is only mentioned, at the foot of the title-page, in his capacity as an agent to sell the book. The second point of interest is that Chippendale claims that the *Director* may be obtained from 'All Booksellers in Great Britain and Ireland'. So Messrs. Hamilton and Balfour, in Edinburgh, and Mr. John Smith of the Blind Quay, in Dublin, can no longer have enjoyed a monopoly of the sales, as they had done in 1754. Sayer, who appears to have specialised in publications of this nature (p. 64, n. 1), was probably responsible for this wider distribution of the book, as he may have been in touch with all the principal book-sellers in the Kingdom. Thirdly, it is fascinating to see that Chippendale was, by this time, advertising the fact that he would send drawings of furniture to clients who sent him commissions for them to St. Martin's Lane. This is where Matthias Lock must have been so very useful to Chippendale (see p. 55). Finally it is interesting to see James Rannie's name, in addition to Chippendale's, at the foot of the advertisement. Rannie, an upholder by trade, had gone into partnership with Chippendale in 1754 and was probably responsible for the decorating and not the furniture-making side of the business.

It has already been recorded (see pp. 58–62) that Thomas Johnson published his *One Hundred and Fifty New Designs* in 1761, and that these designs had previously been issued in monthly parts with separate title-pages. Ince and Mayhew had taken-up Johnson's idea of publishing designs in monthly parts which were to be finally published as one bound volume. Thus on 13th July, 1759, they announced the publication of their designs in numbers (see p. 63). The sixteenth number was published seven months later, as is shown in the *Public Ledger*, and the designs were finally published in a bound volume in 1762 as the *Universal System of Household Furniture*. Mrs. Hayward, in drawing attention to the manner in which these rival designers and cabinet-makers were publishing their

---

[1] I am indebted to Mr. A. G. Lewis for drawing this advertisement to my attention.
[2] Hitherto unpublished.

designs in monthly issues, has pointed out how, at the height of the rococo period, between 1758 and 1763, it became a race between them as to who could publish first.[1] Chippendale, probably alarmed at the success of his rivals, joined the race in 1759, and in the *London Chronicle*, for 6th October of that year, he announced the publication of weekly sets of furniture designs on 'Four Folio Copper-plates, Price 1s.'. He maintained these weekly publications until 28th March, 1760, when he apologised for the delay of the appearance of the twenty-sixth number 'on account of his indifferent state of Health and to allow him Time for Executing of some new Designs'. It is not known whether he started to issue more sets of designs after his illness, or whether the twenty-fifth weekly issue was, in fact, the last to appear, before the third edition of the *Director* was published in its bound form early in 1762. It must also be remembered that, during this period, Chippendale was producing designs for the *Household Furniture in Genteel Taste for the year 1760* published by the Society of Upholsterers and Cabinet-Makers. His contribution to this publication has already been discussed on p. 70.

The third edition of the *Director* was published from St. Martin's Lane on 27th February, 1762. This was 'printed for the author and sold at his house, in St. Martin's Lane. Also by T. Becket and P. A. De Hondt, in the Strand.' No mention is made of the publisher, who may well have been Sayer again. The plates were engraved by M. Darly, T. and J. S. Müller, B. Clowes, I. Taylor, J. Hulett, W. Foster, and Hemerick Morris. The title-page is published in full in Appendix B, and it will be noted that it differs somewhat from that for the first edition (pp. 80–1). In the first edition Chippendale styles himself as *cabinet-maker*, while in the third, he has become *Cabinet-Maker and upholsterer*, which doubtless reflects the addition of James Rannie's *upholding and upholstering* activities to the business. Reference is no longer made to the Gothic and Chinese styles, which were already becoming outmoded, and the designs are merely described as being 'in the Most Fashionable Taste'. New subjects are included as being illustrated such as 'organ cases for private rooms, or churches . . . terms for busts, stands for china jars, and pedestals' and 'chimney pieces, and picture frames; stove-grates, boarders . . . chinese railing and brass-work, for furniture'.

The dedication to the Earl of Northumberland was retained in most copies, but in some rare copies[2] a dedication to Prince William Henry is found in its stead. This reads

> 'To His Royal Highness, Prince William Henry, ETC., ETC., ETC. May it please your Royal Highness, to take the following Work under Your Protection. Your Royal Highness's Ready Condescension to encourage whatever is Laudable and useful, in every Art and profession, emboldens the Author to lay it at your Royal Highness's Feet, as it gives him an opportunity of assuring your Royal Highness, that he is with the profoundest Respect.
>
> Your Royal Highness's, Most Obedient, Most
> Devoted and Most dutiful Servant   THOMAS CHIPPENDALE.'

It appears from study of the phrasing of this 'dedication', that Chippendale had not been granted the necessary permission to use Prince William Henry's name before he published the dedication. It seems that he had addressed his petition to the Prince 'to take the following work under Your Protection', in the published book itself, rather than in an

[1] Fully discussed in *Thomas Johnson and English Rococo*, pp. 28–31, 33–4.
[2] Including the French edition, see p. 93.

91

official letter sent prior to its publication. The Prince, or his advisers, may have told him that his entire behaviour over the matter was dubious, reprehensible and impertinent to say the least, and he was probably told to withdraw the page. After this 'try-on' had failed, he again included the dedication to the Earl of Northumberland, as in the first edition. All this suggests that Chippendale must have tried every other way to gain Royal patronage before embarking on such a ruse. If he could have gained the patronage of Prince William Henry, he would have made an entry into Royal circles, and would have had a chance to challenge the supremacy, in this lucrative field, of Vile and Cobb, the Royal cabinet-makers.

Chippendale, however, appears to have been loathe to take 'no for an answer', for six years later, in January 1768, we find him writing to Sir Rowland Winn of Nostell Priory and saying, 'I hope to perform better for the future but it was all owing to the great quantity of unexpected business which I did not know of nor could I refuse doing it as it was mostly for *the Royal Family*.' Sir Rowland had chided Chippendale in a letter for being so slow over his delivery dates, and the latter, as usual, was prevaricating and, at the same time, hinting at the importance of his Royal patronage. We do not know whether he was working for the King, or for another member of the Royal Family, but this letter, which is published here for the first time (Appendix H) is of the greatest importance as it proves that Chippendale did, in fact, work for the Crown — I am indebted to Mr. Peter Thornton and Mr. Stewart Johnson for pointing this letter out to me.

The number of plates was increased from one hundred and sixty-one to two hundred. Of these, ninety-five were retained from the first edition and one hundred and five new plates were added. Mr. Ward-Jackson, in discussing this subject, writes, 'Up to 12 alternative plates are found in some copies, numbered 25, 36, 45, 49, 67, 68, 153, 159, 167, 171, 179, 187. Number 68 is the same as number 47 in the first edition, while the other alternatives are mostly dated 1759 and 1760. The plates substituted for them in most copies, on the other hand, are all dated 1762, except two dated 1761 and one with no date. This suggests that the book was revised soon after the first printing and twelve more recent plates inserted in place of the earlier ones.'[1]

The perspective drawings were omitted but those illustrating the five Orders of Architecture were retained. New subjects illustrated include 'hall chairs, garden seats, shaving-tables, dressing-tables, basin-stands, cisterns, chandeliers, lanterns and overmantel mirrors'. The section in the first edition devoted to mirrors and girandoles was drastically revised, only one of the 1754 designs being retained. However, reviewed as a whole, the new plates reveal no radical change of style, although some of the fresh designs suggest that the engravings of the earlier French ornamentalists, such as Bérain, Marot and Toro, may have been consulted.[2] Mrs. Hayward suggests that Chippendale may have consulted designs in the Louis XIV style when he was working up the designs in the third edition. She is indeed correct when she writes, 'Trophies of arms, masks, mythological figures, bunches of fruit, putti and dolphins, all features which . . . did not appear in the first edition of the *Director*, were now used in the third edition with a feeling of Baroque panache.'[2]

The notes to the plates are similar in context to those in the first edition and, once again, are worthy of study. Thus the note to plate 39, a bedstead, starts 'A bed which has

[1] See p. 87, n. 1.　　[2] See p. 91, n. 1.

been made for the Earls of Dumfries and Morton'. Chippendale was working for the Earl of Dumfries at Dumfries House, Ayrshire, in 1759. His account to the Earl for that year is extant, and a bed in the Blue Bedroom in fact corresponds to plate 39 in the third edition. Again in the note concerning plate 46, 'a couch bed with a canopy', is written 'N.B. This Couch was made for an Alcove in Lord Pembroke's House at Whitehall.' Finally under plate 52, 'a design for a dressing table for a lady' (Pl. 166), the note informs us that 'Two Dressing Tables have been made of Rose-wood, from this design, which gave an entire Satisfaction'. The two dressing-tables referred to here can probably be related to two examples that were originally in the collections of the Duke of Manchester at Kimbolton Castle, Huntingdonshire (Pl. 164), and that of Lady Arniston (1706–98), mother of Henry, 1st Viscount Melville (Pl. 165).

In 1762 a French edition of the *Director* was also published under the title :

> *Le Guide du Tapissier, De l'Ébéniste et de tous ceux qui travaillent en meubles . . . un ample recueil de Desseins . . . troisième edition . . . augmentée . . . Londres . . . T. A. Becket and P. A. de Hondt 1762'*

Like Ince and Mayhew (see p. 64), Chippendale was obviously making serious efforts to break into the French and Continental markets. This is further corroborated by the statement that 'The description of the said Plates are printed also in French, for the Convenience of Foreigners', which was included in the following advertisement, published in the *British Chronicle*, 21st–23rd March, 1763[1] :

> 'This Day is published, Complete in One large Folio Volume, price 3l bound, the GENTLEMAN's and CABINET-MAKER's DIRECTOR. Containing 200 copper-plates, with 400 different and elegant Designs of the most curious Pieces of HOUSEHOLD FURNITURE, both useful and ornamental; with some Designs of Chimney-pieces, Organs, &c. &c. Gentlemen and Ladies have now an opportunity to gratify their Taste with Respect to Furniture, the Designs being both various and elegant. The Workman too may readily execute the same, as the Rules laid down are plain and easy.
>
> By THOMAS CHIPPENDALE, Cabinet-Maker and Upholsterer in *St. Martin's Lane*.
> ∴ Those who have bought the first Edition of this Book, may have the additional Plates separate, being 100 in Number, Price 1L. 16. bound. The Description of the said Plates are printed also in *French*, for the Convenience of Foreigners.
> Printed for the Author; and sold by *T. Becket* and Co. in the *Strand*.'

The price had increased from £2. 2. 0. in the 1758 advertisement for the first or second edition, to £3 in this advertisement. However, with thirty-nine extra plates, this seems a reasonable increase. It is interesting to read that it was possible 'for those who have bought the first Edition of this Book' to buy 'the additional Plates separate, being 100 in number', for £1. 16. *bound*.

Chippendale did, in fact, make a journey to France in 1768, which was five years after the publication of the advertisement in the *British Chronicle*. It has not, to date, been realised that he actually visited the Continent, although this has often been surmised; and this important fact has been established by the discovery of a hitherto unpublished letter amongst the Nostell Priory papers. This letter, which is quoted in full (Appendix G), was brought to my attention by Mr. Peter Thornton. Chippendale is apologising to Sir Row-

[1] See p. 90, n. 1.

land Winn for the dilatory way in which his firm has handled the delivery of a barometer (p. 115, Pl. 346) and some other pieces of furniture. He lays the blame for this 'neglect' on his foreman, whose wife and brother had just died, and then continues 'he [the foreman] not returning at ye time promised I left ye frame to be going forward till I returned (?) from *France*'. Much research remains to be undertaken on the whole complex question of Chippendale and his contemporaries' links with France and the Continent. However, by 1768, advanced French cabinet-makers had already started to adopt the neo-classical idiom and whatever influence this particular visit to France may have had on the work of Chippendale, it must presumably fall outside the scope of this present survey — for any new developments he may have noted would have been in the direction of classicism. It should, on the other hand, be recognised that he may well have visited France several times. There is no reason why he should not have done so. He had dealings with France on more than one occasion (see pp. 79, 93).

It is thought that Chippendale may have been working on the designs for a *fourth* edition of the *Director*, before he 'teamed-up' with Robert Adam in about 1766, in which year we find him furnishing rooms decorated by Adam at Nostell Priory. Amongst Chippendale's unpublished designs, there are certainly a number of pier-glasses which, stylistically, can be dated to a time after the publication of the third edition, in which the early Adam motives are grafted onto the rococo stock, and 'this hybrid character would have marked the fourth edition, had the plates for it been completed'.[1] It can, at any rate, be said that he was certainly still selling the third edition in March 1763, as can be seen from his advertisement in the *British Chronicle*.

Before discussing examples of pieces of furniture that may be related to designs in the various editions of the *Director*, it is necessary briefly to discuss the authorship of these designs. The first writers seriously to discuss this subject were Mr. Fiske Kimball and Miss Edna Donnell in *The Creators of the Chippendale Style*.[2] They put forward the theory that Chippendale was responsible for few, if any, of the designs in the *Director* and that these were mostly drawn by Lock and Copland — the former often being employed by Chippendale to draw special designs for private clients and the latter being responsible for the drawing of all the carver's pieces in the book.

The majority of the original drawings for the designs in the first edition of the *Director*, and many for the third edition, are in the Metropolitan Museum, New York. Until questioned by Kimball and Donnell,[2] these were all accepted as being by Chippendale. In the Victoria and Albert Museum, London, the 'Chippendale' material includes seventy-eight sheets of drawings and a folio scrap-book purchased in 1862/3 from George Lock, the grandson of Matthias Lock. In these, designs ascribed to Lock predominate, while other drawings, including seven designs for the third edition of the *Director*, have been attributed on stylistic grounds to Chippendale himself. In the same collection there are also one hundred and forty-four drawings purchased from a dealer in 1906, the majority of which are drawn by the same hand as those already ascribed to Chippendale.

[1] Quoted from Fiske Kimball and E. Donnell, 'The Creators of the Chippendale Style', *Metropolitan Museum Studies*, Vol. I, May 1929, p. 152. The unpublished designs concerned are in the Metropolitan Museum.

[2] Kimball and Donnell, *loc. cit.*, pp. 115–54.

The numerous examples of Lock's work amongst these drawings can be safely separated from the others on stylistic grounds. When this has been done, a considerable number remain, including fifteen original designs for the *Director*, all of which are drawn by the same hand. Many drawings in this group are captioned in ink by Chippendale and signed *T. Chippendale Invent. et delin.* This signature has always been accepted as authentic and resembles that of 1760 in the members' book of the Society of Arts.[1]

Copland collaborated with Lock in *A New Book of Ornaments*, published in 1752 (see p. 55). Kimball and Donnell contend that designs for this work have similarities with those in the *Director*. Unfortunately no known original drawing by Copland is extant and it is difficult to compare his engraved work with original sketches. There are also few furniture designs that can safely be attributed to him, although there are six plates in Manwaring's *Chair-Maker's Guide*, one of which is signed *Copland Fecit*, which are similar in many respects to those in *A New Book of Ornaments*. Thus it is reasonable to ascribe these latter designs, and not only the engravings, to Copland. These chair designs, however, have nothing in common with those in the *Director* and it is difficult to conclude that they were executed by the same hand.

Furthermore Chippendale himself, on more than one occasion, made it clear that he did, in fact, draw his own designs and in the preface to the *Director* writes: 'I frankly confess that in executing many of the drawings my pencil has but faintly copied out those images that my fancy suggested,' and also, in commenting on plate 3 in the first edition, he writes, 'I had a peculiar pleasure in re-touching and finishing this design'. Again in a letter written on 19th July, 1767, to Sir Rowland Winn he writes, 'As soon as I got to Mr. Lascelles and looked over the whole of ye house[2] I found that I should want many designs. I knowing that I had time enough I went to York to do them, but before I could get all don I was taken very ill of a Quinsey. . . .'[3]

Unless, therefore, it is supposed that Chippendale was a deceitful liar (of which some contemporary evidence would be bound to exist) in the light of his own evidence above, the matter would appear to require no further clarification. Thus it seems clear that Chippendale must have been responsible for the designs in the *Director* and that they were not the work of Copland. The latter may well have aided Chippendale in a subordinate capacity, but the theory that Copland was the inventor of the designs cannot be accepted.

B — THE DESIGNS

It has already been shown that many pieces of furniture have survived from the mid-eighteenth century which have been inspired by designs published in the three editions of Chippendale's famous publication. Both the first and the third editions start with designs for chairs, and there are twelve plates in the first, illustrating thirty-eight different chairs, and twenty-one plates in the third showing sixty chairs. It is therefore not surprising that many chairs stemming from these designs have survived. These can be divided into various

[1] Ibid., fig. 12.

[2] Harewood House, near Leeds.

[3] First published by R. W. Symonds in 'Chippendale Furniture at Nostell Priory', *Country Life*, 3 October 1952, p. 1028.

groups and the first, which is common to both editions, are those which usually have bowed top-rails and pierced, interlaced splats. In most examples, the chairs in this group are supported by elegant cabriole legs — although in 'country-made' examples these are often discarded in favour of legs of square section chamfered on the 'inside' edge. Four such chairs are illustrated in Pls. 167–71. The first (Pl. 167) is in the Duke of Norfolk's collection at Arundel Castle, Sussex, and corresponds closely to a plate in the third edition. It is further of interest to note that both the Duke and Duchess of Norfolk were subscribers to the first edition. Pl. 168 shows a fine example of a chair in which the design for its splat is based on another splat in the third edition. Related to this group, Pl. 169, from a set in the private Dining-Room at Nostell Priory, Yorkshire, was almost certainly made by Chippendale's firm as many fully documented pieces remain there and, furthermore, it is based on a *Director* design. They have square chamfered supports in place of the more elegant cabriole legs. A typical armchair in this style is shown in Pl. 170 and a rather more unusual single chair in Pl. 171. The splat is surmounted by tassels, the seat-rail carved with shells and foliage and the cabriole legs terminate in claw and ball feet. All these motives are more readily associated with the decade immediately prior to the publication of the first edition of the *Director*, when Chippendale was establishing himself in London.

Plate 16 in the first edition (Pl. 172) and plate 15 in the third each show the same three designs for 'Ribband Back Chairs'. In his note relating to these in the first edition, Chippendale describes them as being 'the best I have ever seen (or perhaps have ever been made)'. Examples of chairs and settees taken from these designs have survived and Pls. 173–5 are closely related to the *Director* designs (Pl. 172). An interesting adaptation of these designs is seen in Pls. 176–7 which shows a settee-bed of double chair-back form. This is *en suite* with six chairs and the set was acquired for Nostell Priory in 1883. It merges well with the documented examples from Chippendale's work-shops that are also at the house.

The next group consists of the so-called 'French' chairs. There are four plates illustrating eight designs for these in both the first and third editions. These designs were highly popular, as can be judged from the many surviving examples. They are often finely carved although Chippendale wrote that 'the carving may be lessened by an ingenious workman without detriment to the Chair'. They were usually covered in tapestry, needle-work or damask and the author, in his notes describing these, writes 'the ornaments on the backs and seats are in imitation of tapestry or needlework'. Plate 21 from the third edition is reproduced as Pl. 178 and two crisply carved examples in the full rococo taste are shown, their seats and backs covered in tapestry or needlework of chinoiserie design. The chair shown in Pl. 179, which is based on plate 22 in the *Director*, should be compared with these designs, as also should Pls. 180–6 which are all variations on the same theme. It is clear, from the different manners in which the designs have been interpreted, that these chairs are not all from the same workshop. Examples of 'French' chairs remain in Lord Pembroke's collection at Wilton House, Wiltshire, and are of exceptional interest as it is known, from surviving documents, that Chippendale supplied furniture for the house.[1] One of a pair of gilded chairs (Pl. 187) from the Double Cube Room closely resemble the

[1] See Anthony Coleridge, 'Chippendale at Wilton', *Apollo*, July 1964, pp. 4–11. Part of this article is quoted when discussing the Violin bookcase (Pls. 256–7).

design on plate 20 in the third edition of the *Director*, and so do the chairs in a set still in the Earl of Pembroke's private collection (Pl. 188). The needlework covers, worked with figures in exotic costumes, animals, urns and flowers, closely follow the designs suggested in the *Director*. Another form of 'French' chair, its plain upholstered back surmounted by a bowed top-rail, is illustrated in Pl. 189. This not uncommon type has often since the nineteenth century been called a 'Gainsborough' chair. This clearly also descends from a design in Chippendale's pattern-book.

Two plates showing six designs for 'Hall' chairs are included in the third edition. There is a set of nine (Pl. 190) in the Earl of Pembroke's collection which is related to one of these compositions. The pair of unusual hall chairs shown in Pl. 191 are also inspired by a design in the third edition.

The 'French' chairs are followed by designs for 'Gothick' chairs, and it is interesting to note that only three of the six designs in the first edition were retained in the third. However, by 1762, the Gothic craze was on the wane. Examples of seat-furniture in this tradition have already been illustrated in Pls. 152–8. These are followed by designs for 'Chinese' chairs and it is in fact often difficult to differentiate the 'Chinese' from the 'Gothick'. However the Chinese style seems to have retained its popularity and the nine designs for chairs in the first edition are all retained in the third. These all have open fretted backs and arms and, in some examples, the top-rails are carved with pagoda-like crestings (Pls. 192–6). The seat-rails and supports are often carved with fret decorations — either open or blind — while the legs occasionally take the form of single or cluster supports simulating bamboo (Pls. 192 and 193). This form of leg is not illustrated in the *Director*. However, seat-furniture in the Chinese tradition was not always so restrained, as can be judged from the exaggerated and bizarre carved detail on the chair in Pl. 197. This design has little in relationship with Chippendale's *Director* although he did use the dolphin toe on a 'French' chair (cf. Pl. 178 right).

Another example of this use of the dolphin mask is seen on a stool (Pl. 198), the carving on the seat-frame of which admirably portrays the English adaptation of the Gallic *rocaille*. It is strange that Chippendale omitted to include designs for stools in any edition of the *Director*, but he probably felt that any skilled chair-maker could adapt his designs for chairs to one for a stool. In this connection it is interesting to note that there is a pair of stools still at Wilton (Pl. 199) which is *en suite* with the armchairs shown in Pl. 187. The chair-maker, who was almost certainly in Chippendale's employ in this instance, must have merely adapted the design for the chairs to suit his purpose.

The plates showing designs for chairs are, as might be expected, followed by others illustrating designs for sofas, or 'sophas'. In the first edition, two plates are included showing 'Chinese Sophas' of exaggerated form standing beneath draped pagoda-like canopies. One of these is retained in the third edition but there are also others of a more conventional design. Plates 29 and 30 illustrate four examples with shaped top-rails and arms and with either cabriole or square-sectional supports. Two examples from Wilton are interesting in this connection, because they show how versatile Chippendale was as a designer and how he could adapt his designs to harmonise with existing, and often alien, schemes of decoration. Pl. 200 portrays his skill in designing a pair of settees for the Double Cube Room which blended with the original Kentian furniture already in it; while

Pl. 201 shows a settee in another of the State Apartments which is an admirable example of the transition between the rococo of the *Director* and the nascent neo-classical style of the mid 1760's (Pl. 367). Another settee, which has been attributed to Chippendale on stylistic grounds, is illustrated in Pl. 202 and this should be compared with plate 30 in the third edition of the *Director*. It formed part of a large and important set of seat furniture in the collection of the Earl of Shaftesbury at St. Giles's House, Dorset, and it has been traditionally held that Chippendale supplied much of the furniture to this house.[1] The fact that the Countess of Shaftesbury was also a subscriber to the first edition of the *Director* gives added weight to the tradition. A similar chair, in another collection, is illustrated in Pl. 203 : Pl. 204 shows a plainer example of the sofa in the same tradition which is part of a large set of seat-furniture (Pl. 341) from Lord Methuen's collection at Corsham Court, Wiltshire. It is known that John Cobb was supplying furniture to the house in 1772. On the other hand, there is a later entry concerning the firm of Chippendale and Haig in one of the Day Books although this does not concern the suite in question. This set of furniture may have, therefore, been made by Cobb, by Chippendale or by any of the other craftsmen retained by Paul Methuen. All that can with certainty be said is that it is of the highest quality and certainly stems from designs in the *Director* — perhaps Chippendale was, in fact, responsible for its fabrication. It should be added that some settees dating from this period are merely expanded chair designs. This is the case with the example in Pl. 205 which is derived from a design for a 'French' chair shown in plate 22 in the third edition of the *Director*, and is therefore related to the chair shown in Pl. 179.

Settees are followed by designs for bedsteads and the three editions include examples of 'Gothic, Canopy, Doom, Chinese, Couch and State Bedsteads'. The third edition also includes designs for 'Bed pillars and Cornices'. One of the most celebrated bedsteads extant from this period is the red and green japanned example now in the Victoria and Albert Museum, which was made to the order of the Duke of Beaufort for the Chinese Bedroom at Badminton House, Gloucestershire (Plate C). This room was described by Dr. Pococke in 1754[2] 'as finished and furnished very elegantly in the Chinese manner', and it is interesting to note that the date of his visit was the same as that of the publication of the first edition of the *Director*, suggesting that this furniture was made just before the book was published. The Duke of Beaufort was a subscriber to this edition and the bed is in fact very like that shown in plate 32 of the book. Pl. 207 illustrates a bedstead at Corsham Court which was made for Paul Methuen; and the finely carved posts take the form of *cluster-uprights* and resemble designs for 'Bed pillars' in the third edition.

Designs for 'Breakfast tables' are included in both the first and third editions (Pl. 208) and the examples illustrated in Pls. 209 and 210 are clearly related to these. These must have been popular innovations, as many have survived. A plate is also included in both editions showing two designs for 'China tables' — perhaps used for tea. Many examples of these are also extant and they can be ornamented with either plain or highly elaborate carved detail. An example carved with blind-fret ornamentation, from the Earl of Pembroke's collection, is shown in Pl. 212, while two others of more exaggerated design

[1] The archives at St. Giles's House are, at present, being sorted and it is hoped that some documentary evidence to support this tradition may be found.

[2] *Travels through England*, Vol. II, p. 31.

C. The 'Chippendale' bedstead from Badminton House. *The Victoria and Albert Museum.*
Photograph courtesy of Fratelli Fabbri Editori, Milan.

The commodes are followed by 'Writing tables' which, in the twentieth century, are used as card or tea-tables, depending on whether or not they have been lined with baize. They have folding tops and concertina gate-leg actions, and their friezes are often carved with Gothic or Chinese frets (Pls. 240–1). However, 'Writing-tables' of a rather more elaborate design are also illustrated: and in the notes to a plate (Pl. 242) which is common to all editions, Chippendale writes, 'This table has been made more than once from this design, and has a better appearance when made than in the drawing'. Two examples (Pls. 243–4) are included here, and it is interesting to note that there is a design in the third edition which has a built-up superstructure with drawers, pigeon-holes and shelves surmounting a base, similar to that in Pl. 244.

Chippendale next included designs for 'Library tables' and they are in the Gothic (Pl. 245), Chinese (Pl. 246) and French manner (Pls. 247–8). He writes that these tables 'frequently stand in the middle of a room, which requires both sides to be made useful'. The library table in the Gothic taste (Pl. 245) belonged to Single-Speech Hamilton, who bought the Earl of Promfret's house (Pl. 159) in Arlington Street, and it doubtless stood in the Gothic drawing-room which was built by Sanderson Miller in 1760. The unusual circular cusped motives on the pedestals stem from a design in the first edition. Pl. 247 shows Plate 57 from the first edition of the *Director*, and this is of the greatest importance as a library table (Pl. 248) made from this design was, until recently, in the Craven's collection at Coombe Abbey, Warwickshire. It is thought that Chippendale made furniture for William, 5th Baron Craven, and it is a fact that other pieces from his collection are in the *Director* manner. Chippendale, describing this piece, writes in his notes in the first edition 'A Library Table with all its dimensions fixed to the design. You have two different doors and terms. This table is intended to have circular doors at each corner, which may be made for convenience at pleasure.' The measurements correspond exactly with the Craven table which incorporates the right-hand pedestal design. Another important library table in the same tradition is illustrated in Pl. 249 and this was made by Chippendale's firm for Sir Rowland Winn in 1767 at a cost of £72. 10. 0. The entry in the account reads as follows: 'A large library table of very fine wood with doors on each side of the bottom part with drawers within on one side and partitions on the other, with terms to ditto carvd and ornamented with lions' heads and paws, with carved ovals in the pannls of the doors and the top covered with black leather, and the whole compleatly finished in the most elegant taste.' It is one of the finest pieces of case furniture that Chippendale's firm produced, and again is an interesting example of the transition between the late *Director* and neo-classical periods.

A large section is devoted to 'Library bookcases' in all editions (there are sixteen plates in the first edition and as many in the third, some being working drawings). The designs range from the Chinese and Gothic (Pls. 253–5) to the architectural (Pls. 250–2), which are more readily associated with the Burlingtonians but which must still have been in vogue during Chippendale's early creative years. The break-front bookcase illustrated in Pl. 250 was originally at Langley Park, Norfolk, a house which was built by Matthew Brettingham, senior, in 1740 for Sir William Beauchamp-Proctor, Bt. It has been confidently asserted that Chippendale's accounts for the furnishing of this house have been seen since the turn of the century,[1] and thus this bookcase may be one of Chippendale's

[1] Oliver Bracket, *op. cit.*, pp. 52–3.

earliest creations. If so, it shows him working — like the cabinet-makers discussed in Chapter I — in the Palladian-Kentian tradition in the years before the publication of the first edition of the *Director*. Seven plates in the first edition illustrate plain bookcases of architectural form in a very restrained style. A bookcase (Pl. 251) at Longford Castle, Wiltshire, in the Earl of Radnor's collection, is based on one of these. Pl. 252 illustrates a variant of the same design. Another (Pl. 253) at Nostell Priory, originally one of a pair[1] was almost certainly supplied by Chippendale's firm and it now stands on the South Staircase. It is related to plate 71 in the first edition or 97 in the third, although the design of its pediment and the panelling of the lower doors have been simplified. Another example (Pl. 254) in the Lady Lever Art Gallery, Port Sunlight, is in the full Gothic tradition and its design is taken from the central section of yet another plate in the third edition (Pl. 255). It is interesting to see a piece that has been so faithfully copied from a design.

Bookcases were sometimes made in sets for Libraries, as has already been seen at Althorp, p. 51, n. 3, and, without doubt, one of the finest of these sets is at Wilton (Pls. 256–8). This consists of the celebrated 'Violin' bookcase (Pls. 256–7) and a pair of break-front bookcases (Pl. 258) *en suite*. The authors of *Georgian Cabinet-Makers*[2] describe the violin bookcase as 'a superlative specimen of the maker's *Director* period', and how right they are! The musical trophy, suspended from the swan-neck pediment, is very similar to that on the left-hand bottom door on the 'Library bookcase' which is illustrated as plate 92 in the third edition. Chippendale's note states that 'the trusses, pilasters and drops of flowers are pretty ornaments, as well as those on the pediment, and on the bottom doors, but all of them may be omitted if required'. Probably the most unusual feature on the 'Violin' bookcase is the carved rococo oval suspended from the musical trophy in the upper section of the central glass door; the design for this has been lifted straight from a bookcase also given in the third edition.[3]

Six designs for 'Chamber Organs' are then included in the third edition and plate 105 (Pl. 259) shows the design from which an organ (Pl. 260), now in the Victoria and Albert Museum, was taken. Organs made from Chippendale's designs are rare, although an example in the Gothic tradition in the Dulwich College Chapel, erected in 1760, has triple arcaded spirettes which have affinities with *Director* examples.[4] Another organ with a *Director* inspired case may be seen at St. Peter's Church, Winchcombe, Gloucestershire.

All editions then include designs for 'Desks and Bookcases', which are now called 'Bureau-bookcases'. Some of these are highly elaborate and again there are examples in the 'French, Chinese and Gothic' tastes. These are followed by 'Dressing Chests and Bookcases' and an example at Nostell Priory, which almost certainly emanated from Chippendale's workshops, is similar to a design in the third edition, although it has been pruned of its chinoiserie and rococo enrichments. An allied class are the 'Ladies Writing Tables and Bookcases' for which the *Director* provides several designs and Pls. 262 and

[1] The pair sold Sotheby's, 31 January 1964, lot 287. From the collections of Sir Berkeley (later Lord) Moynihan and Dr. Carlton Oldfield of Harewood.

[2] Ralph Edwards and Margaret Jourdain.

[3] See p. 96, n. 1.

[4] Cf. *Director*, 3rd edition, plate 104, right.

263 are somewhat free adaptations of these, while their fretted upper sections being inspired by designs for 'China Cases' which are discussed below. The former was ordered by Sir Rowland Winn for Nostell Priory and is in a sense an English version of the *bonheur-du-jour* then so fashionable in France. The latter (Pl. 263) is now in the Temple Newsam House collections.

In the third edition, Chippendale then goes on to provide some elaborate designs for 'Toylet Tables', and these are, in reality, 'Dressing-tables', with heavily garlanded drapes and curtains supported by winged *putti* and mounted with satyr masks.

The last important class of case-furniture in all three editions is that which deals with 'Cabinets, Cloths Chests and Presses, China Cases and Hanging and China Shelves'. The plates illustrating 'Cabinets' range from plain unadorned examples to elaborate confections in the Chinese and Gothic manner. Other designs are included for 'China Cases' which are, in fact, adaptations of those entitled 'Cabinets'. These plates will, therefore, be discussed together. Pl. 264 illustrates a plate in the first edition, republished in the third, about which Chippendale notes that this 'China Case I have executed with great satisfaction to the purchaser'. An example (Pl. 265) is in the L. David Collection, Copenhagen, which was, without doubt, inspired by the *Director* design (cf. Pl. 264).[1] Another plate in the first edition shows a design for a 'China Case' from which the example from the Earl of Lichfield's collection at Shugborough Hall, Stafford, was taken (Pl. 266). This 'China Case', or bookcase, is very similar to the design, about which Chippendale comments that 'I have executed this design, and it looks much better than in the drawing'. Other display and china cabinets based on Chippendale's Chinese and Gothic traditions are illustrated in Pls. 267 to 272.

A highly important japanned 'pagoda' cabinet (Colour Plate A) stands on the Grand Staircase at Uppark, Sussex. It is japanned in black and gold and the central pagoda and two of the drawers below are veneered with panels of Chinese lacquer. The cabinet is centred by an open shrine with steps leading to a mirror-backed niche (Pl. 273) of pagoda form which surmounts and flanks twelve drawers and three hinged panels. Seven of these drawers are japanned and are decorated with applied arcading and Chinese fret decoration — the upper two are mounted with carved ivory medallions with busts of Homer and Brutus. Six others are inset with Florentine *pietre dure* panels depicting birds amidst flowers and bouquets knotted with ribbon-ties. It is almost certain that the cabinet was specially commissioned by Sir Matthew Fetherstonhaugh, Bart., who was redecorating Uppark at this period, and he probably instructed the cabinet-maker to incorporate the Florentine hardstone panels and the ivory medallions in its decoration. It is not known, unfortunately, who the cabinet-maker can have been, although Sir Matthew recorded payments to Hallett, Cobb and Vile in his account book in 1754, 1764 and 1765, respectively. Another 'pagoda' cabinet, based on *Director* designs, is illustrated in Plate 420.

All editions include designs for 'Cloths Presses' and 'Commode Cloths Presses'. The latter being rather more elaborate versions of the former, the drawers below the two doors being of serpentine or bombé form — and are, in fact, designed as a chest of drawers surmounted by hanging sections enclosed by twin doors. A fine example of a 'Commode Cloths Press' from Temple Newsam House, Leeds, is shown in Pl. 274 which is related to

[1] See J. F. Hayward, 'A China case attributed to Thomas Chippendale', *Connoisseur*, June 1962.

plate 131 in the third edition and plate 104 in the first. Another example taken from a *Director* design is in the collection of Mr. Frederick Poke at Wimbledon. A more simple version of a 'Cloths Press', given in the third edition, is at Paxton House, Berwickshire,[1] (Pl. 276). It was delivered in 1774 at a cost of £12. 12. 0. and was invoiced by Chippendale in his extant account as 'a large mahogany cloaths press with folding doors, fine wood, sliding shelves lined with marble paper and baize aprons . . .'. The design had been altered little since 1754 when it first appeared in the *Director*.

The designs for 'China Cases' are followed by others 'For Shelfs for Books & etc.' (Pl. 277), 'Hanging Shelves' (Pls. 278–80), 'Shelves for China' (Pls. 281–3) and 'China Shelves' (Pl. 284). Some rare examples of 'what-nots' or étagères (Pls. 285–6) with Chinese open-fret sides should be mentioned at this point as, although they are not illustrated in the *Director*, their designs stem from those depicting 'Chinese Railings'.

Twelve designs for 'Candle Stands', or *torchères*, are included in the first edition and seventeen in the third, Pl. 287 showing plate 144 from the latter. These intricate creations were made by specialist carvers and were then, if they were carved in mahogany, left in an undecorated state, while, if they were in a softwood, they were then passed over to the gilders, japanners or decorators to be embellished. One of a pair of 'candle stands' is illustrated in Pl. 288; they were probably delivered by Thomas Chippendale to the 2nd Duke of Atholl for Blair Castle in May 1758. An account from his firm remains at Blair Castle for 'a pair of large candlestands neatly carved and painted white . . . £7. 7. 0.', and it is probable that this entry refers to one of the pairs in the Large Drawing-Room, even if they have lost their original white colour and are now a burnished gold.[2] Two other examples in gilt (Pls. 289 and 290) clearly derive from the designs in plate 145 in the third edition. Pl. 291 shows a pair that are japanned in black and gold, and it should be remembered that many examples that are now japanned or gilded were originally merely painted. However many pairs were made in mahogany (Pls. 292–4) and rely for their decoration purely on the carved work. Chippendale, in his note to plate 123 in the first edition, writes, 'Three designs for stands, intended for carving, and nothing of directions can be said concerning them, as their being well executed depends on the judgment of the workman.' Pl. 292 illustrates a candlestand with a fretted hexagonal top which is very like the design in plate 120 in the first edition. A very different example of much plainer form (Pl. 293) was delivered by Chippendale to Paxton House, Berwickshire, in 1774 at a cost of £3. 6. 0. the pair.[1] A candlestand of slightly later date (Pl. 294) may also be attributed to Chippendale's workshop, as it is in the collection of the Earl of Pembroke at Wilton House, Salisbury, and it has already been shown that Chippendale had strong connections with this family and house.[3]

The third edition alone then devotes a plate to 'Terms for Busto's & etc.' and another to 'Stands for China Jars'. The former are of classical design with *rocaille* ornamentation grafted on to their plain surfaces, and the latter are in the full 'French' *Director* tradition, their scrolled outlines carved with *putti*, urns and foliage. These in turn are followed

---

[1] See p. 99, n. 1.

[2] See Anthony Coleridge, 'Chippendale, *The Director*, and some Cabinet-makers at Blair Castle', *Connoisseur*, December 1960, fig. 12.

[3] See p. 96, n. 1.

(again only in the third edition) by designs for 'Pedestals' and 'Cisterns', the latter being envisaged as shells and baskets, and also by 'Lanthorns for Halls or Staircases' and 'Chandeliers for Halls & etc.'. The lanthorn illustrated as Pl. 295 is taken straight from a design in the third edition, while Pl. 296, which shows an example in mahogany and not gilt, can also be related to examples in the same plate (153). Three chandeliers in carved giltwood are here shown as Pls. 297–9. The last is in the State Dining-Room at St. Giles's House, Dorset — a house which has a strong link with Chippendale, as Lady Shaftesbury, it will be remembered, described as 'a liberal encourager of the arts and sciences' was a subscriber to the first edition.

All editions then illustrate designs for 'Fire Screens', some of tripod form and others of horse or cheval form. The former have tripod stands which are often of a highly carved and intricate form (Pls. 300–2). These are also known as 'banner' or 'pole' screens, as their panels or banners may be adjusted on the poles or uprights. The latter type has dual, splayed-end supports, each with four legs — hence the *horse* (Pl. 303). A variant of these designs is seen in the screen illustrated in Pl. 304, its two panels lined in Chinese wallpaper. The panels were filled with a variety of fabrics including tapestry (the panels on Pls. 300 and 301 may both have come from the Fulham workshops), needlework, silk and damask, the needlework often being worked by members of the purchaser's family.

Designs for 'Tea Chests', or tea-caddies,[1] and 'China Trays', the latter often with Chinese open-fret borders are then included. 'Brackets for Busts . . . for Bustos' and 'for Marble Shelves' are the next important group to be discussed. They are naturally all carvers' pieces and the designs vary considerably and are highly naturalistic. Two examples are illustrated here (Pls. 305–6) and they are clearly connected with designs in the third edition. All editions then include patterns for 'Clock Cases' and 'Table Clock Cases', and Pl. 307 shows a clock-case of typical *Director* design. The table clock-cases are carved in the Gothic and Chinese manners and the third edition has a plate showing designs for cartel, or hanging clocks, and for bracket clocks, both of French rococo inspiration.

The final section devoted to carvers' pieces is of the greatest importance as it covers pier-glasses, overmantels and girandoles. The first edition starts with 'Cornices for Beds or Windows' and some of these may have been consulted when the pelmets were designed for the State Rooms at Wilton House, Salisbury.[2] These are followed by four designs for 'Gerandoles' but, in the third edition, these are supplemented by eight others, Pl. 308 showing five of them. Such confections were highly popular during this period: five examples are illustrated in Pls. 309–13, the last being taken from the bottom left-hand example in plate 177 in the third edition (Pl. 308). Two other 'gerandoles', or brackets, are shown (Pls. 314–15), both of which are from houses with which Chippendale's name has been linked — the former from St. Giles's house and the latter from Harewood House.

The designs for 'Pier Glass Frames' offer a wide range of variety and they must have been highly popular, judging from the number of surviving examples and also from the number of designs which are given included in the *Director* — there being seven plates in the first edition and ten in the third, the latter having many more designs to each plate.

---

[1] An example of a tea-chest, or caddy, stemming from a *Director* design, 1st edition plate 129, 3rd edition, plate 149A, is in the collection of Judge Irwin Untermyer, *English Furniture catalogue*, fig. 371, plate 323.

[2] See p. 96, n. 1.

Illustrated here are two glasses in this style, one (Pl. 316) from Crichel, Dorset, where it is thought that Chippendale was probably employed — the house being rebuilt by Sir William Napier after a fire in 1742 — the other from nearby St. Giles's House (Pl. 317). A third glass in the Royal Collection (Pl. 318) also incorporates *ho-ho* birds in the intricate design of its carved frame, and so does a mirror in Boston (Pl. 319). An oval version is shown in Pl. 320. An overmantel glass of rather different form, with tri-partite plates, is illustrated in Pl. 321, while one of a splendid pair of pier-glasses from the Double Cube Room at Wilton[1] is seen in Pl. 322. The latter is gold and white and its cornice incorporates the Pembroke wyvern. Its design is not based on one of those for pier-glasses in the *Director*, but rather on those for 'Picture Frames' in the third edition. Preceding the designs for picture frames are several for 'Frames for Marble Slabs', or console tables. Some of these are of highly intricate and exaggerated form, incorporating Chinese figures on staircases and in pagodas, obelisks, fantastic birds, musical trophies, playful amorini and leaping dolphins.

These are followed, in the third edition, by designs for chimney-pieces which incorporate those for overmantels and grates. A piece of this type, from Stone Easton, near Bath, is illustrated in Pl. 323 and another from the Royal Collection is shown in Pl. 324. Both of these are also influenced by the designs of Thomas Johnson. However a more interesting example (Pl. 325) was recently sold by Christie's from Linton Park, near Maidstone,[2] the design for one of the supporting figures of the chimney-piece and a plate in the third edition of the *Director* being inspired by a common source (cf. Pl. 326).

Finally, designs for 'Shields for Pediments' are included in all editions, and the third edition shows two plates filled with designs for 'Stove Grates'.

No mention is made of Chinese mirror or glass pictures but, as many of these are contained in carved frames of the highest quality and of most intricate design in the *Director* idiom, five examples are included (Pls. 327–31). All editions end with plates showing designs for 'Frets' and 'Chinese Railings' and the third edition has two additional plates of 'Designs of Borders for Damask and Paper Hangings'.

PART III   HIS CLIENTS

We have traced the career of Thomas Chippendale. We have studied the publication and the contents of the three editions of his great work, *The Gentleman and Cabinetmaker's Director*. It now remains to discuss his clients, or rather those of them, who are known to us. These, as far as is possible, are listed alphabetically under the names of their houses and, broadly speaking, only pieces of furniture in the *Director* tradition are discussed. It is inevitable, however, that the designs for some of them are already showing signs of neo-classicism, as it is almost impossible, during the 1760's, to separate Chippendale's work

[1] See p. 96, n. 1.
[2] 2 October, 1961 — previously at Clumber, Worksop and sold from there in 1938.

in the rococo taste from that in the early neo-classical idiom. Many examples illustrate the transition between the two and some of these are illustrated and discussed here. I have drawn freely from Mr. Ralph Edwards' and the late Miss Margaret Jourdain's research into Chippendale's clients, which is published in *Georgian Cabinet-Makers*, and I have found this work an invaluable guide while writing this chapter. Furthermore Mr. Clifford Musgrave's *Adam and Hepplewhite Furniture* should be studied in close conjunction with this section, as the work in the neo-classical style, which Chippendale carried out for many of his clients, is fully discussed there. Recent research has, however, brought to light some hitherto unrecorded clients of Chippendale's firm, and these are briefly alluded to in the list, notwithstanding the fact that their style should strictly exclude them from a work that is primarily concerned with furniture in the rococo taste.

ALNWICK, NORTHUMBERLAND

It has already been shown (p. 81) that the first edition of the *Director* was dedicated by Chippendale to the Earl of Northumberland, who was created Duke in 1766, and whose name is also among the list of subscribers to the book. On 9th February, 1752, Matthias Lock, who was at that time probably in Chippendale's employ, noted on the reverse of the leaf of a diary '. . . to table Ld. Northumb'ld' (see p. 54). The Earl, with the extensive building programme that he had entered into at the time (p. 81), must have been an obvious target for Chippendale and, although no documentary evidence has yet been found, several pieces remain at Alnwick which are in the *Director* tradition. The backs of twelve gilt armchairs in the Music Room are similar to those on plate 23 in the third edition, and there are pier-glasses and girandoles in the castle which may also have been inspired by *Director* designs.

AMPTON HALL, SUFFOLK

James Calthorpe (1699–1788), who was Deputy Lieutenant of Suffolk in 1727, Gentleman Usher Quarter Waiter in Ordinary in 1731 and Yeoman of the Removing Wardrobe in 1742, inherited Ampton Hall in 1736. His manuscript notebook dealing with the rebuilding and redecorating of Ampton Hall and of his London house in Pall Mall, was, at the time of writing, in the trade.[1] On 13th March, 1758, there is an important entry to the effect that 'Mr. Chippendale is to be with me Tuesday Evening at 9'. This probably refers to the furnishing of his London house although Chippendale may well also have advised on the decoration of Ampton.

ARUNDEL, SUSSEX

The names of both the Duke and Duchess of Norfolk are listed as being subscribers to the first edition of the *Director*, and a chair at Arundel (Pl. 167) corresponds closely to a

---

[1] B. Weinreb Ltd. — *Furniture Catalogue*, 1965, no. 48 : my notes on James Calthorpe are based on this entry.

plate in the third edition (see p. 96). Moreover one of a pair of commodes with ormolu mounts (Pl. 234) which are also in the *Director* tradition, are known to have been made for Norfolk House, London.

BADMINTON HOUSE, GLOUCESTERSHIRE

Charles Noel, fourth Duke of Beaufort, was also a subscriber to the *Director* and, although once again there is no documentary evidence of Chippendale's connection with this great house, many 'book pieces' are to be found in the collection there. A mahogany chest of drawers on a carved giltwood stand[1] has its stand based on a design for a clothes press (plate 101) in the first edition. A fine giltwood frame for a portrait of Admiral Boscawen by Reynolds, is also in the *Director* tradition. Moreover a library table, with carved lion-mask and ring-terminals, has affinities with the famous example which was supplied by Chippendale to Nostell Priory in 1767 (cf. Pl. 249).

The lacquered bedstead (Pl. C) from the celebrated Chinese Bedroom has already been described (see p. 98), and it will be remembered that Dr. Pococke in 1754 described the room as 'finished and furnished very elegantly in the Chinese manner'.[2] The bedstead, with some of the other furniture from this room, was sold in 1921[3] and amongst it was a set of four japanned china stands, their pagoda tops hung with bells. One of a pair of these, now in the Lady Lever Art Gallery, is illustrated as Pl. 281. A commode (Pl. 332) from the same room is now in the Victoria and Albert Museum, where it stands near the bed from the same room, and by one of the china stands which has recently been placed there on loan from the Lady Lever Art Gallery. Another commode (Pl. 333) of slightly later date but of different provenance, has its top drawer fitted as a dressing-table. Furthermore a rectangular japanned knee-hole dressing-table from the same bedroom is illustrated in the *Dictionary of English Furniture*.[4]

Two other commodes (Pls. 334 and 335) should be compared with that shown in Pl. 333. Their cast and chased ormolu mounts and feet are of a quality that, once again, compare most favourably with their French counterparts. Pl. 336 illustrates one of a pair of commodes at St. Giles's House (see p. 119). These have their drawers and tops veneered with panels of Chinese 'Coromandel' lacquer which have probably been cut from a screen. Its sides are of English japan-work imitating Oriental lacquer. This affords an interesting example of how the two different processes were utilised to decorate the same piece of furniture — a common practice during the eighteenth century, both in England and France. A fine, and probably unique, set of *four* commodes of such combined work is at Uppark in Sussex (colour plate B and Pl. 337).

[1] This and the two pieces mentioned in the next sentences are ill., *G.C-M.*, p. 176, pl. 104: p. 187, pl. 129: p. 175, pl. 102.
[2] See p. 98, n. 2.
[3] Christie, Manson and Woods Ltd., 30 June 1921.
[4] 2nd edition, Vol. III, p. 227, fig. 10.

SIR ROBERT BURDETT OF BRAMCOTE, WARWICKSHIRE

Chippendale is mentioned in the household accounts of Sir Robert Burdett,[1] and there are two entries as follows :

'1766 Feb. 17 . . . to Mr. Chippendale
Cabbinet Makers for chairs for the Country[2] . . .   £37–4–0
'1758 Feb. 4 . . . to Mr. Chippendale
on account of furniture at Colemark[3] Upholsterers, Saint Martin's Lane,
London . . .   £100.'

BLAIR CASTLE, PERTHSHIRE

There is one account extant in the Blair Castle archives, dated 8th May, 1758, from Rannie and Chippendale to the second Duke of Atholl. It reads :

'To a Firescreen of fine french Tapestry wt a neat mahogany Pillar and Claw . . .   £3. –. –.'
A Pair of large Candlestands neatly carvd. and painted white . . .   £7. 7. 7.'

It is now impossible to recognise the firescreen although there are three examples of such screens in the Castle, but it has been possible, on the other hand, to relate the description of the pair of candlestands in the account to those illustrated in Pl. 288. There are, in fact, two pairs of these candlestands, or *torchères*, in the Large Drawing-Room at Blair Castle and they could be almost reconstructed from those illustrated in plates 144 and 145 of the third edition of the *Director*.[4]

There are also some carved giltwood wall-brackets in the *Director* style in the State Rooms, and a set of mahogany stools on crossed supports which are in a similar tradition to the set in Christ Church Library, Oxford.

JAMES BULLER OF DOWNES, DEVON, AND MORVAL, CORNWALL

An account, dated 29th January, 1757, from Rannie and Chippendale to James Buller Esquire is in the Cornwall County Record Office.[5] James Buller, who died in 1765, was, from 1754 until his death, Member of Parliament for the County of Cornwall. He owned various properties in Devon and Cornwall, and the account which is quoted below may

---

[1] Berkshire Record Office.
[2] The Burdett's seat at Foremark, Derbyshire.
[3] Unrecorded upholsterer.
[4] See Anthony Coleridge, 'Chippendale, The Director, and some Cabinet-makers at Blair Castle', *Connoisseur*, December 1960, pp. 255–6.
[5] Collection of Buller papers deposited at Cornwall County Record Office by Major R. R. B. Kitson of Morval — I am indebted to the County Archivist, Mr. P. L. Hull, for drawing my attention to this account.

either refer to furniture for one of these or, more probably, to some which he had ordered for his London house.

'A mahogany Cloaths press w^t sliding shelves . . .	£6. 6. 0.
Bayes tops tacks etc. . . .	£0. 10. 0.
A neat mahogany Nursing Chair w^t carved knees . . . }	£1. 10. 0.
Stuffed seat Check case etc. . . .	
Mending a mahogany Breakfast table . . .	£0. 5. 0.'

CARLISLE HOUSE, SOHO SQUARE

Carlisle House, Soho Square, was owned by an Italian singer named Madame Cornelys. During the third quarter of the eighteenth century this remarkable woman gave a series of lavish and extravagant entertainments in this house for which her guests were charged an entrance fee. The house was furnished at great expense and there are many references to it in the literature of the time.[1] Teresa Cornelys was bankrupted in 1772 and her bankruptcy was announced in the *London Gazette* for 3rd to 7th November of that year. Proceedings taken in the Court of Bankruptcy during the following year show that Thomas Chippendale, being one of the principal creditors, together with three others, James Cullen,[2] *cabinet-maker*, Samuel Spencer, *jeweller*, and Augustus Lesage, *goldsmith*, were appointed as assignees of the Estate. They, together with a few of the other creditors, appear to have acted in a highly improper way as they arranged for the house, together with all its contents, to be offered by auction in one lot, without first consulting the remaining creditors. Furthermore, they arranged for Samuel Spencer's son-in-law to bid on their joint behalf for the estate, which he did, securing it for £10,200, being the only bidder at the sale. The other creditors, who claimed that they had been excluded from the sale — amongst other complaints they stated that catalogues were sold at 'the enormous price of five shillings' — petitioned the Court that the assignees had acted improperly and that the sale should be made void. The proceedings in the Court of Bankruptcy are quoted verbatim in *Thomas Chippendale* by Mr. Oliver Bracket[3] and two important facts emerge from careful study of them. First, it appears that Chippendale, and Haig, who was also a creditor, were far from scrupulous in their business dealings; and secondly, as they were major creditors, it is more than probable that they supplied much of the fine furniture to Madame Cornelys for Carlisle House — the furniture being valued independently after her bankruptcy at £10,000.

THE LIBRARY, CHRIST CHURCH, OXFORD

There is an entry in the building accounts of Christ Church Library, Oxford, for 21st July, 1764, which reads as follows:

[1] Fanny Burney in her diary in 1770: Samuel Curwen in 1780 — *Journal and letters, 1864.*

[2] James Cullen, of 56 Greek Street, Soho, was an important cabinet-maker who supplied fine furniture to Hopetoun House, West Lothian, and to Blair Castle, Perthshire, during the third quarter of the eighteenth century (see pp. 160–69).

[3] Appendix VI, pp. 138–41 — taken from *Record Office Bankruptcy Court Order Books.*

'Mr. Chippendale's Bill for stools for the Library . . .   £38. 15. 0.
For carriage of the stools from London . . .   £0. 18. 6.'[1]

The number of the stools is not mentioned but it is reasonable to suppose that there were twelve or more.[2] There is a set of twenty-six mahogany stools (Pl. 338) in the Library, some of which may be of later date, although the older ones can probably be related to this entry. It will be remembered that there is a set of similar stools in the Duke of Atholl's collection at Blair Castle. It is interesting to note that Chippendale charged £8. 8. 0. for '4 . . . mahogany stools . . . of fine wood . . . with scro'l Heads . . . and neat Carv'd Roses' for Mersham Hatch in 1767 (see Appendix C).

COOMBE ABBEY, WARWICKSHIRE

Until recently[3] a superb library table (Pl. 248), based on a *Director* design (Pl. 247) was at Coombe Abbey (see p. 100). This may well have been made by Chippendale's firm for William, 5th Lord Craven (1705–69). Other pieces in the *Director* tradition were at Coombe Abbey and amongst these was a *bonheur-du-jour* in the French taste (Pl. 339). Although Chippendale does not include designs for *bonheurs-du-jour* in the *Director*, the quality of this example, with its finely contrasted mahogany veneers and open-fret gallery, is entirely consonant with the output and high standard of his workshops. Another desk of this general type, but larger, is illustrated as Pl. 340. This too is very much in the *Director* idiom, and would seem to confirm that Chippendale produced furniture of this class.

CORSHAM COURT, WILTSHIRE [In the Eighteenth Century *Corsham House*]

There is no documentary evidence in the form of accounts or ledger-entries to prove that Chippendale provided furniture for Mr. Paul Methuen at Corsham House although his rivals Vile and Cobb (see pp. 33–4), Thomas Johnson and George Cole (see p. 60) were certainly employed by Methuen. There is, in fact, an entry from Chippendale and Haig of a much later date, but it has no bearing on the considerable amount of furniture in the *Director* style which remains in the house. Amongst these pieces are the following which, although they are closely connected with Chippendale's style, cannot be definitely associated with him and thus added to his proven *oeuvre* :

A set of mahogany seat-furniture comprising :

  30 armchairs (Pl. 341)
  4 settees (Pl. 204)
  two stools
  a winged armchair.

[1] Discussed and illustrated by W. G. Hiscock, *Christ Church Miscellany*, 1946, pl. 59, and *Country Life*, 5 January 1945.
[2] I am indebted to Mr. H. J. R. Wing, of Christ Church Library, for this information.
[3] Sold at Sotheby's, 1 December 1961, Lot 162.

A mahogany four-poster bedstead (Pl. 207).
Eight window seats.
A pair of mahogany side-tables with porphyry tops set in ormolu surrounds (Pl. 216).
A pair of mahogany serpentine chests of drawers.

The large set is discussed on page 98. It is remarkable because it appears to be upholstered in the original damask material. The nailing of this is noteworthy.

CRICHEL, DORSET

Crichel was rebuilt by Sir William Napier in 1742 after a disastrous fire, and important interior alterations and decoration took place during the opening years of George III's reign — that is, during the 1760's. Examples of pier-glasses, overmantels and girandoles in the *Director* manner remain in the house. A pair of pier-glasses (Pl. 316) is based on plate 143 in the first edition of the *Director*. The only difference from the design is that the Crichel examples have a youth and not a mandarin placed on the crestings under the pagoda canopies. A chimney-mirror,[1] or overmantel, follows a design in the third edition, and so does a pair of girandoles in the Boudoir (respectively plates 182 and 178).

DUMFRIES HOUSE, AYRSHIRE

Two accounts, dated 1759 and 1766, are extant from Chippendale and Rannie for furniture supplied to Dumfries House, which was built for the Earl of Dumfries by the Adam brothers at the early date of 1754 — the year Robert Adam set off on his epoch-making tour to Italy and the Dalmatian coast. Amongst the entries in these accounts are :

'Rosewood bookcase with rich carved and gilt ornaments on the top and doors. . . .
A mahogany frame for a tapestry fire-screen. . . .
A mahogany pillar and claw richly carved. . . .
A pair of carved and gilt girandoles. . . .
A mahogany library table of very fine wood, fitted with a writing drawer at one end, with a double rising slide. . . .
A neat mahogany clothes press with cedar shelves and one drawer at the bottom. . . .

The bookcase and girandoles are illustrated in *Georgian Cabinet-Makers* (Figs. 92 and 122). An important bedstead in the Blue Bedroom is similar to plate 39 in the third edition of the *Director*, and Chippendale, in his notes to the plates, actually states that this had been made for the Earls of Dumfries and Morton.

HAREWOOD HOUSE, YORKSHIRE

The marquetry case-furniture in the neo-classical style which was supplied by Chippendale's firm to Edwin Lascelles, later Lord Harewood, is among the finest that was designed

[1] Ill., *G.C-M.*, p. 182, pl. 121 : identified by Fiske Kimball, *Metropolitan Museum Studies*, Vol. II, Part 1, November 1929.

and made in this country during the eighteenth century. It is fully discussed by Mr. Clifford Musgrave in his *Adam and Hepplewhite Furniture* and is illustrated in all major reference books on the subject.[1] These important pieces are therefore beyond the scope of this book.

There are, however, a few pieces in Chippendale's earlier *Director* style at Harewood House, near Leeds, and there are others in Chippendale's transitional style illustrating the change between the rococo and neo-classic. Robert Adam had been called in to supersede the Yorkshire architect, John Carr, and he had completed the work by 1771, the first stone having been laid in 1759. Adam's drawings for the interior range in date from 1765 to as late as 1779.[2] There are many accounts extant from Chippendale and Haig which are dated between 1772 and 1775; they total £6,326. The firm, however, must have been employed at Harewood prior to 1772 as the first entry on the account for that year reads, 'To a bill delivered . . . £3,024. 19. 3.'. This was a large sum and no doubt represented the work of several years. In the house a certain amount of furniture survives which may well have formed part of this earlier group of Chippendale pieces.

A pair of giltwood girandoles in the high rococo manner are illustrated in Pl. 315 and one of a pair of green japanned bedside-cupboards are shown in Pl. 342. These are reminiscent of some of the pieces of similarly decorated bedroom furniture that Chippendale is thought to have delivered to Nostell Priory (see p. 116), which, incidently, is not so far from Harewood. Two examples from sets of chairs are also shown here as they admirably represent Chippendale's transitional phase. The first (Pl. 343) has retained the cartouche-shaped back, serpentine seat-rail and cabriole legs of some of the later *Director* examples, and on to this *quasi-rococo* framework, typical neo-classical decorative details have been grafted. The second example (Pl. 344) has only retained the serpentine seat-rail, scrolled down-curved arms and back legs of the *Director* period.

It should be briefly noted here that there is no evidence to support the commonly quoted theory that Chippendale made the furniture at Harewood to Robert Adam's designs.[3] While discussing this Mrs. Eileen Harris writes:[4] '. . . there are no designs or bills from Adam, as there are from Chippendale, to associate him with any part of the furnishing of the house. His authorship can also be ruled out on stylistic grounds. The choice and handling of ornament, the shape of the parts, and the general proportioning of the major Harewood pieces are typical of Chippendale, but markedly different from any authenticated Adam design. . . .' The relationship between Adam and Chippendale has also been discussed at length in Mr. Musgrave's book in this series, *Adam and Hepplewhite Furniture*, where the same conclusion is reached.

[1] *G.C-M.*; Oliver Bracket, *op. cit.*; *D.E.F.*, etc.
[2] 'Harewood House', *Country Life*, 4 July 1914.
[3] This theory was first discredited by R. W. Symonds in 'Adam and Chippendale: A Myth Exploded', *Country Life Annual* (1958), pp. 53–6. Some of Chippendale's accounts are quoted in this article: others in Oliver Bracket, Appendix IV, pp. 131–3.
[4] *The Furniture of Robert Adam*, 1963, p. 27.

DAVID GARRICK AND CHIPPENDALE

Chippendale, Haig & Co. furnished David Garrick's London house, No. 5 Adelphi Terrace, between 1771 and 1772. The accounts[1] are now in the Victoria and Albert Museum, and they are of exceptional interest as they are drawn up room by room, thus indicating the manner in which each room was furnished. However, as the dates of the accounts suggest, the furniture and furnishings were in the neo-classical style and are, thus once again, beyond the scope of this book.

Garrick also had a country villa at Hampton-on-Thames and it is thought that some of the furniture[2] in this house may have been provided by Chippendale's firm. A pair of pinewood wardrobes, a bed, and some chairs of mock bamboo, all painted with green *chinoiseries* combined with simple neo-classical decoration, come from this villa and are now in the Victoria and Albert Museum.[3] The bed has Indian painted hangings. Mrs. Garrick had great difficulty getting these through the customs.

KIMBOLTON CASTLE, HUNTINGDONSHIRE

There was formerly in the collection of the Duke of Manchester at Kimbolton Castle, a dressing-table (Pl. 164) which was made from a design in the third edition of the *Director* (Pl. 166).[4] Chippendale writes the following in his note on this plate:

> 'A design of a dressing table for a lady: the drawer above the recess hath all the conveniences for dressing, and the top of it is a dressing glass, which comes forward with folding hinges. On each side is a cupboard with glass doors, which may be either transparent or silvered, and in the inside drawers or pigeon-holes. Two dressing tables have been made of rosewood from this design, which gave an entire satisfaction.'

The Kimbolton dressing-table is probably one of the two examples referred to by Chippendale, the other[5] (Pl. 165), now in the Lady Lever Art Gallery, having been made for Lady Arniston (1706–98) (see p. 93).

KENWOOD, MIDDLESEX

Thomas Chippendale is briefly alluded to in the archives preserved at Kenwood House, a house built for the Earl of Mansfield by Robert Adam. His connection with the furnishing of this house has already been discussed (see pp. 56–7), when he is seen, in 1769, in the character of a dealer in mirror-glass plates.

[1] Quoted in Oliver Bracket, *op. cit.*, Appendix III, pp. 122–30.
[2] Sold by auction, 22 June 1864.
[3] Ill., *Georgian Furniture*, Victoria and Albert Museum, 1951, pl. 171, and Oliver Bracket, *op. cit.*, pl. 57.
[4] First identified in *D.E.F.*, 1st edition, Vol. III, p. 219, Fig. 13.
[5] Sold Christie, Manson and Woods Ltd., 6 July 1916.

LANGLEY PARK, NORFOLK

The building of Langley Park was started in 1740 by the architect Matthew Brettingham, Senior.[1] In 1924, while discussing the furnishing of this house, the late Oliver Bracket wrote,[2] 'It is confidently asserted that Chippendale's bills for furnishing this house exist and have been seen within recent years, although for the moment they cannot be found.' It cannot, therefore, be confidently asserted that Chippendale provided furniture for this house although the family tradition is strong. It is now unlikely that proof will ever be forthcoming in the form of the original accounts, as the contents of the house have been sold and dispersed. There were, in the house, important pieces of furniture in the *pre-Director* style which must have been made between 1740 and 1750. One of these (Pl. 250) is a mahogany bookcase of architectural form which, in design, still adheres to the strict dictates of Palladianism.[3] There were also examples in the *Director* manner and, amongst these, were a pair of giltwood brackets (Pl. 305), one of which, carved with a satyr's mask, is based on a plate in the third edition of the *Director*. Another example in the same tradition from this house was a cabinet with a pagoda top,[4] the doors and sides being applied with hardstones (Pl. 270).

LANSDOWNE HOUSE, LONDON

Lansdowne House, which was situated on the present site of the Lansdowne Club, off Berkeley Square, was the London House of The Earl of Shelburne. There is a note in the Shelburne papers, amongst a list of payments made to various artists and craftsmen, which reads as follows:

'Thos. Chippendale 1770. £200 & balance, 1772, £228.'[5]

MERSHAM-LE-HATCH, KENT

Accounts[6] from Chippendale's firm for the furnishing of Mersham-le-Hatch for Sir Edward Knatchbull cover the period from 1767 to 1778. Although these ten years fall beyond the scope of this book, extracts from the 1767 account are quoted in Appendix C as they are typical of bills from Chippendale's firm. The later accounts largely refer to upholstery and repairs. Some of the furniture from the bedrooms still survives; it is simple in character and utilitarian in design.

The correspondence from Chippendale and Haig to Sir Edward Knatchbull also survives[6]

[1] 'Neale, in his *Views of Seats*, states that it was begun about 1740 for Mr. Recorder Berney of Norwich and finished by George Proctor (who bought the estate in 1742) and Sir William Beauchamp-Proctor, his nephew and heir' — quoted from *G.C-M.*, p. 68.
[2] Oliver Bracket, *op. cit.*, p. 53.
[3] Other examples from the same decade are illustrated in Oliver Bracket, *op. cit.*, pls. 10, 12, 22, 33.
[4] Ill., *Country Life*, 31 March 1928, p. 469, Fig. 5.
[5] Oliver Bracket, *op. cit.*, p. 78.
[6] Lent by Lord Brabourne to the Kent Archives, Maidstone: Published in Oliver Bracket, *op. cit.*, Appendices II and V.

and some of these letters are quoted in Appendix D. They illustrate how Chippendale was often acutely short of money,[1] as his clients were not infrequently dilatory in the extreme in settling his accounts. They also show the manner in which the furniture was delivered to clients in the country, and to what great lengths Chippendale and Haig went in sending designs, quotations and estimates to their clients.[2]

LORD MELBOURNE'S HOUSE IN PICCADILLY, LONDON

Lord Melbourne's house was on the site of the Albany. It has already been shown (p. 79) how, in 1773, Chippendale designed tables and pier-glasses for this house which was being built by Sir William Chambers for Lord Melbourne. Nothing more is known about this commission or its fruits, at present.

NOSTELL PRIORY, YORKSHIRE

Chippendale was employed by Sir Rowland Winn, the fourth baronet (1739–85), to provide furniture for Nostell Priory. His extant accounts are dated between 1766 and 1770 and there was a balance owing two years later.[3] Extracts from these accounts are quoted in Appendix E. Examples from the Nostell Priory collection have been published in all major books on the subject and they range in design from pieces in the *Director* tradition, through Chippendale's 'transitional' phase to the neo-classical. Examples from the *Director* phase include a breakfront bookcase with foliated Gothic glazing bars (Pl. 253 discussed on p. 101), which may be the one referred to in the account of 23rd June, 1766, and described as 'a very large mahogany bookcase with glass door and pediment top . . . £38'. An unusual mahogany writing-table with open-fretted upper section (Pl. 262), a pair of hanging shelves (Pl. 279), each with a Baron's coronet as finial, a commode with ormolu mounts (Pl. 235), and a knee-hole cabinet (Pl. 261) with a mirror-panelled door above are also in the *Director* tradition. Pl. 169 illustrates one from a set of seven dining-chairs in the private dining-room with typical foliated top-rails and pierced interlaced splats, while Pl. 345 shows an upholstered chair which may have been supplied by Chippendale's firm for one of the bedrooms. If this is the case, as seems probable, the last item is a reminder that Chippendale was perfectly willing to supply simple and straight-forward furniture, when necessary. All the same, is it too much to recognise in this plain chair a certain elegance of line that may reflect its origin in a far from humble stable? A barometer (Pl. 346) — the movement by Justin Vulliamy — which was supplied in 1769 at a cost of £25 and was invoiced as 'To a very neat case for a barometer made of fine tulip and other woods and very rich carvd ornaments Gilt in Burnish gold and plate glass in the doors', is already ornamented with neo-classical motives, and this should be compared with

[1] A letter, dated January 1770, requesting settlement of a bill states, 'It is a time of year when money is much wanted for Credit'. Quoted from Oliver Bracket, *op. cit.*, p. 25.

[2] See H. Avrey Tipping, 'Letters and Accounts relating to Mersham-le-Hatch', *Country Life*, Vol. LV, 12 April 1924.

[3] Extracts from these accounts are published in Oliver Bracket, *op. cit.*, Appendix I, pp. 111–16.

the two other barometers shown in Pls. 347 and 348, where the cases are carved with *rocaille* decoration, although they are not, of course, attributed to Chippendale. Three years later, in 1770, there is a further entry for 'altering the ornaments of the Barometer frame and gilding in Burnish Gold . . . £1. 3. 0.'.

In the accounts for 1769 there is an entry relating to the hanging of Chinese wall-paper. The green japanned bedroom furniture which complements the wall-paper was probably supplied by Chippendale's firm. The State Bedroom contains a green japanned bedstead and a dressing-table *en suite* (Pl. 349) and these, with a similarly decorated wardrobe (Pl. 350) and commode (Pl. 351) from the same house should be compared with the bedside-cupboards at Harewood (cf. 342). All these pieces were at Nostell by 1771 when Chippendale drew up a list of the furniture that he had supplied to the house so far.

There are two magnificent commodes (Pls. 352 and 353) of 'transitional' design in the State Rooms, either of which could be the piece referred to in Chippendale's entry for 1770, 'A large antique commode very curiously inlaid with various fine woods. With folding doors and drawers within and very rich chased brass ornaments complete . . . £40.' Other pieces in the 'transitional' style at Nostell are a lady's writing-table with incorporated rising fire-screen (Pl. 354), a pembroke-table, the drawer inlaid as a backgammon table (Pl. 355), a wardrobe (Pl. 275) and a set of mahogany framed open-armchairs (Pl. 356). The celebrated library-table (Pl. 249) which was delivered in 1767 at a cost of £72. 10. 0. has already been discussed (see p. 100), but Pl. 357 shows a picture painted by an unknown artist of Sir Rowland and Lady Winn standing in the Library at Nostell by this library table. An interesting point worth noting about this painting is that it shows the table still in its light, reddish and raw-looking state, before assiduous polishing and the passage of time had given it the handsome dark patina it now displays. The stand for the bust of Venus and the draped chair may also have come from Chippendale's establishment.

Finally a pair of giltwood *torchères* (Pl. 358), a pair of mahogany serving-tables (Pl. 359) and a wall medal-cabinet (Pl. 360), all neo-classical designs, are shown here, as examples from the many pieces that Chippendale provided for this house in that taste, although this phase falls, as we have said, beyond the scope of this book.

Study of the accounts for Nostell Priory (see Appendix E) show how diverse were the pieces that Chippendale's firm could provide, *e.g.* :

'A mahogany case for a monkey. . . .
A large strong wainscot mangle. . . .'

They also illustrate the importance of the 'upholding', or decorating and upholstering, side of the business, with the hanging of curtains, papering of walls and laying of carpets. It is interesting to note that 5s. was charged for 'writing 2 Inventories of his furniture'.

PAXTON HOUSE, BERWICK-ON-TWEED

Chippendale & Haig were making furniture for Ninian Home of Paxton House during the 1770's and one account which covers the period from 14th March to 6th August, 1774, survives to prove this. Most of the surviving examples that can be related to the descriptions in this account are in the neo-classical tradition,[1] but some are still in the late rococo or transitional vein. Thus a pair of *torchères* (Pl. 293) was invoiced at £3. 6. 0. and a pair of open hanging bookshelves cost 15s. each (Pl. 280). The designs for their fretted open ends are based on plate 192 in the third edition of the *Director*. A wardrobe (Pl. 275) and two gentlemen's dressing-tables (Pls. 220 and 221) already show signs of neo-classicism. One of the latter (Pl. 221) was described as 'a large size shaving table . . . with a bottle and basin compleat', and cost £7. 7. 0., while the other (Pl. 220) as 'a mahogany dressing-table with folding top, boxes, bottles, a glass and compleat', and cost £5. 18. 0. Both seem to have been inspired by a design for 'a shaving table' (Pl. 219) published as plate 54 in the third edition.

Chippendale's work at Paxton is of interest because it illustrates the fact that he often made furniture of utilitarian and plain form. This is particularly well exemplified by a bedside commode (Pl. 361), which cost £2. 12. 6., and the chest of drawers (Pl. 362) which was invoiced at £6. 16. 4. Finally a backgammon board (Pl. 363) is illustrated which cost £4. 14. 6. 'with ivory men, boxes and dice compleat'. It should be compared with the pembroke table in the Tapestry Room at Nostell Priory (cf. Pl. 355) which has its drawer inlaid as a backgammon board and which retains its original ivory and ebony men : these are very similar to those at Paxton.

THE DUKE OF PORTLAND

Oliver Bracket, in *Thomas Chippendale*, publishes an account, dated 1766, from Chippendale to the Duke of Portland. It refers to a pair of pier-glasses and the Duke, who was one of the original subscribers to the *Director*, may have either bought them for Welbeck Abbey, in Nottinghamshire, or for his London house. The account reads as follows :

'His Grace the Duke of Portland . . . Dr.   To Thos. Chippendale.
1766
Oct. 28 To two very large oval glasses with rich carved frames Gilt in
    burnished Gold with 3 branches for candles to each and brass pans and
    Nosselles to Ditto.   48. —. —.
    Repairing Do. & cleaning the Gilding and fixing up at your house   10. —.

                      £48. 10. —.

Received February 16th, 1767 of His Grace the Duke of Portland by T. Hutchinson the above contents in full of all Demands. £48.

                    Thos. Chippendale.'

Here is an instance of a customer settling his account fairly promptly. It has been suggested, without supporting evidence, that two pier-glasses, now in the Victoria and Albert Museum (nos. W2387 and W2388–1855) which were purchased at the Bernal Sale, 1855, could be those discussed above.

---

[1] See Anthony Coleridge, 'Chippendale, Interior-Decorator and House-Furnisher', *Apollo*, April 1963, where his work at Paxton is fully discussed.

THOMAS CHIPPENDALE (1718–79)

RAYNHAM HALL, NORFOLK

It is thought without definite proof, however, that Chippendale provided furniture to Raynham Hall for Captain Townshend, M.P., during the 1750's. A celebrated commode[1] (Pl. 236), which was originally in the house,[2] is based on a plate in the first edition of the *Director* (Pl. 233), which Chippendale describes as a 'French Commode Table'. Another commode, which was based on the adjacent plate in the same edition, was sold at the same time,[2] and it is illustrated by Oliver Bracket.[3] Other examples of furniture in the *Director* tradition from Raynham Hall survive. A pair of chairs (Pl. 203) and a side-table (Pl. 364) are now in the collection of Mr. Robert Cooke of Athelhampton, Dorset.

ROUSHAM, OXFORDSHIRE

Chippendale was employed at Rousham by Sir Charles Cottrell, nephew and heir of Lieut.-General James Dormer (1679–1741),[4] as is shown by an entry in the Day Book for the library dated 1764. This reads :

| 'By Chippondel upholsterer | £14, 4. 6. |
| By do | 11. 5. 0.' |

Unfortunately no accounts from his firm survive to show what he provided, although the fact that Chippendale is here referred to as an upholsterer rather suggests that the work was connected with decoration and soft furnishings, and not with furniture in the generally accepted meaning of the term.

SALTRAM HOUSE, DEVON

Mr. Peter Thornton has kindly drawn to my attention the fact that some pieces of mahogany bedroom furniture in Chippendale's plain and more restrained *Director* tradition remain at Saltram House, near Plymouth. Included amongst these are a serpentine-shaped dressing-commode, with carved console angles and intricately cast and chased handles; an unusual shaving-table; a small bedside commode with galleried top and doors surmounting drawers in the serpentine front; and two fine bedsteads.

There are, unfortunately, no invoices or receipts extant at Saltram, but Mr. Nigel Neatby, the Curator, has searched the account books covering a part of John Parker's expenditure from 1770 to 1772 — the Parkers were the owners of Saltram. Payments to Chippendale from the cash account for those years are listed below and they may well refer to some of the pieces described above :

'1771
20th May.	Chippendale's Bill	..	..	..	..	..	£120. 0. 0.
1772							
15th April	To Chippendale upon Acct.	..	..	..	..	£50. 0. 0.

[1] Fully discussed by H. Cescinsky in *Raynham Hall and its Furniture*, Burlington, June 1921.

[2] Sold Sotheby's, 24 June 1921 — sold Christie's, H. H. Mülliner Collection, 1924 — William Randolph Hearst Collection, Christie's, May, 1939 — now in Philadelphia Museum of Art.

[3] Oliver Bracket, *op. cit.*, pl. 38.

[4] He had employed his friend William Kent to carry out additions and alterations.

| 15th June | To Chippendale beside a Draft on Mr. Radcliffe for £50 in part of his Bill .. | .. | .. | .. | .. | .. | £52. 10. 0. |
| 30th June | To Chippendale .. | .. | .. | .. | .. | .. | £2. 10. 0.' |

SANDON HALL, STAFFORD

Nathanial Ryder, first Baron Harrowby,[1] of Sandon Hall employed Chippendale's firm, as can be seen from entries in the Steward's book. An entry was made on 24th May, 1766,[2] which reads, 'To Chippendale for mahog. dining table . . . £13. 13. 6d.', while twelve chairs were supplied eleven years later in 1777.[3]

ST. GILES'S HOUSE, DORSET

The archives at St. Giles's House are, as yet, largely unexamined and it is to be hoped that they may yield up a clue as to who provided the fine examples of rococo furniture in the collection. The refurnishing of the house was carried out by the fourth Earl of Shaftesbury and his first wife[4] during the mid-eighteenth century. The Countess was a subscriber to the first edition of the *Director* and it is therefore reasonable to suppose that Chippendale may have been employed to supply some of the furniture.[5] Pieces in the *Director* tradition include pier-glasses (Pl. 317), picture-frames, a chandelier (Pl. 299), wall brackets (Pl. 314) and pier-tables (Pl. 365). A settee from a large and important set of seat-furniture is illustrated here as Pl. 202, and one from a set of eight hall chairs in padouk-wood (Pl. 366) has affinities with plate 17 right in the third edition of the *Director*. A pair of commodes veneered in 'coromandel' lacquer have finely cast and chased ormolu handles and lockplates, and are clearly of this period (Pl. 336).

Mrs. Hayward has pointed out to me, with good reason, that some of the rococo pieces at St. Giles's (e.g. Pls. 314, 317, 365) are probably based on designs of Thomas Johnson —animals, especially of a domestic breed, being a favourite decorative detail of his.

TEMPLE NEWSAM HOUSE, YORKSHIRE

An account[6] from Chippendale and Haig's firm is extant for furniture provided by them for Temple Newsam House, near Leeds, to the order of the ninth Viscount Irwin. It reads :

[1] Created Baron 1776.
[2] Harrowby MS. ledger No. 330.
[3] Oliver Bracket, *op. cit.*, p. 16.
[4] Lady Susannah Noel, died 1758.
[5] For further information on the furniture at St. Giles's see :
'St. Giles's House, Dorset', *Country Life*, Vol. XXXVII, 13 and 20 March 1915.
R. C. Lines, 'My House at St. Giles's', *Connoisseur*, October 1959; 'St. Giles's House', *Antique Collector*, August 1962.
R. W. Symonds, 'Rococo at St. Giles's House', *Antique Collector*, December 1955; 'St. Giles's House', *Antique Collector*, August 1962.
[6] I am indebted to Mr. Christopher Gilbert, assistant Keeper at Temple Newsam House, for giving me a transcription of this account.

'The Right Honble Lord Irwin — Dr.

To Chippendale Haig & Co.

1774

Feby 10th.

	£.	s.	d.
To a Hexagon Table of very fine yellow sattin wood on a neat pillar & claw	4.	14.	6.
A Pole Glass on a mahogany frame		7.	6.

June 7th.

To a mahogany Travelling Strong Box with private partitions, drawer etc compleat   2. 18. 0.

           £8. 0. 0

1775 May 17th.

Rec'd the contents in full for Chippendale Haig & Co.

         John Leareth.'[1]

WILTON HOUSE, WILTSHIRE

Unfortunately none of the accounts for the work that Thomas Chippendale's firm carried out at Wilton have survived and the only documentary evidence that remains to prove that such work was in fact done is in the form of receipts from Chippendale to the Earl of Pembroke. These range in date from 1763 to 1791 but only the earlier ones concern us here.[2] These, in abbreviated form, are as follows:

'Received 24 Sepr. 1763 of the Rt. Hoble the Earl of Pembroke by the hands of Mr. John Lambe, the sum of £100 on account for Partner and self . . . (signed) Thomas Chippendale'
'Rec.d 29 Feby 1764 . . . the sum of £97. 11. 0 on account for the use of Messrs. Chippendale & Co. (signed) Tho. Haig.'
'Recd. 11 Janry 1766 . . . by the hands of Anthony Sayer Esquire the sum of £100 on account for partner and self (signed) Thos. Chippendale.'
'Recd. 21 June 1770 . . . the sum of £460–5–0 being in full for bonds now delivered up with interest thereon to this day and is in full of all demands due from His Lordship to ye partnership estate of Thos. Chippendale and the late James Rannie (signed) Thos. Haig, acting executor of the late Mr. James Rannie.'

A banker's draft is also preserved in the archives at Wilton which reads:

'Sir, Pay to Messrs. Chippendale and Co. the sum of £243 in full of an account settled with them this day and all demands upon my account to the 31st March, 1773 [signed] Pembroke [and to] John Lambe Esq.'

It can therefore be seen that the tenth Earl of Pembroke spent substantial sums at Chippendale's between 1763 and 1773. There is a further link between Chippendale and the Pembroke family, for in a note referring to a 'couch bed', illustrated as plate 46 in the third edition of the *Director*, he states that 'this couch was made for an alcove in Lord Pembroke's House in Whitehall'. It is therefore reasonable to suppose that many of the pieces in the *Director* tradition at Wilton actually emanated from Chippendale's workshops.

The most important of these is the celebrated 'violin' bookcase (Pls. 256–7), decorative

[1] Temple Newsam Papers at Leeds Reference Library — Ref. TN/EA 12/5.
[2] See Anthony Coleridge, 'Chippendale at Wilton', *Apollo*, July 1964.

details in which are based on plates 87 and 92 in the third edition of the *Director*. Two other bookcases (Pl. 258), which are in the same room, are *en suite* with it. A pair of walnut side-tables (Pl. 215), which have their friezes and supports carved with blind-fret ornamentation, are also based on *Director* designs, as are a silver-table (Pl. 212), a *torchère* (Pl. 294) and a set of hall-chairs (Pl. 310). A set of six open-armchairs and eight single chairs (Pl. 188) are similar to designs for 'French chairs' in the third edition of the *Director* as we have already seen. A pair of giltwood armchairs (Pl. 187) and a pair of stools *en suite* (Pl. 199) are also in the full *Director* tradition. However a pair of pier-glasses in what appears to be the Kentian idiom (Pl. 322), their swan-neck pediments centred by the Pembroke Wyvern, may have been designed and made by Chippendale's firm to harmonise with the existing rather ponderous furniture in the Double Cube Room. The same may be the case with the settees shown in Pl. 200. These too look, at first glance, as if they were made under the aegis of William Kent, but the *Rocailles* in the aprons, and the curious cartileginous forms at the ends of the crestings indicate that these in fact belong to the rococo period — and thus they may be the work of Chippendale.

THE MARQUESS OF ZETLAND, MOOR PARK AND 19 ARLINGTON STREET

It has for many years been thought that Samuel Norman made the chair which is illustrated in Pl. 367.[1] This is part of a suite of giltwood seat furniture believed to have been made by Norman to the designs of Robert Adam, who was advising Sir Lawrence Dundas, Bart., on the alterations to, and redecoration of, his London house, 19 Arlington Street, and of one of his country houses, Moor Park, Hertfordshire. The basis for this assumption is the same as that which was used to suggest that Norman also made the suite of seat-furniture, covered in Gobelin's tapestry woven by Neilson in Paris that was at Moor Park, which Mr. and Mrs. John Harris have now discovered[2] was in fact supplied by the, otherwise, unknown cabinet-makers, Fell and Turton (see p. 143). The importance of Mr. and Mrs. Harris's recent discovery of the Dundas furnishing accounts at Aske, in the North Riding of Yorkshire — the Seat of the Marquess of Zetland, the direct descendant of Sir Lawrence Dundas — was further magnified when an account from Chippendale's firm was found amongst them.

This account, extracts from which are quoted in Appendix F, was presented to Sir Lawrence by 'Thomas Chippendale and the Executor of James Rannie', for work carried out between July 1763 and January 1766, and it was settled, for the sum of £1,123. 1. 6., on 1st August, 1766. Rannie had died earlier in 1766 and his share in the business was still being wound-up by Chippendale and his executor. Although the account is long and detailed, there is no indication of whether the furniture described in it was destined for Moor Park or Arlington Street. In addition to many pieces, which were obviously of the highest quality, 'two very large mahogany bookcase(s)', at £80[3] and £73 (Pl. 257), and 'a large Mahogany Library Table of exceeding fine wood and rich carv'd ornaments to

[1] *G.C-M.*, p. 61.

[2] I am much indebted to the Marquess of Zetland and to Mr. and Mrs. John Harris for their permission to publish extracts from the Dundas furniture accounts.

[3] The larger of these two bookcases has recently been rediscovered and, at the time of writing, was in the stock of R. L. Harrington Ltd. Ill. in *Apollo*, September, 1967, p. 200, fig. 20.

match the Bookcases', at £37, are included. One of the bookcases and the library table are at Aske, the Marquess of Zetland's house, near Richmond in Yorkshire. An unusual item, which cost £13, was for '2 large French Arm Chairs and a Stool made to Join together . . .' (*a chaise-longue*), and it is interesting to read that Chippendale was prepared to supply such mundane pieces as 'A neat Mahogany Linen Airer, at 12s., a Mahogany Teatray with a neat cut Rim', at £1. 4. 0., 'a Black Inkstand dish with Cutt Bottles', at 10s. 6d., and 'a large Goulty Cradle complete for 2 legs' for £2. 5. 0. The latter was a kind of foot-rest for supporting a leg crippled with gout. He also refers to a table of 'Guadalupe Wood' and another table 'border'd with Pidgeonwood'.

A suite of '10 Large French armchairs . . . and 3 very large Rich Sofas to Match' (see Appendix F) is invoiced towards the end of the account at a cost of £130 for the chairs and £105 for the sofas. This suite can be related to 'A set of ten Chippendale giltwood armchairs and three settees' which were catalogued by Christie's as lot 70 in their sale of tapestries and furniture, removed from 19 Arlington Street, on 26th April, 1934. One of the settees is illustrated in Percy Macquoid's *The Age of Mahogany* as figure 196.

However Chippendale also supplied Sir Lawrence with another suite of giltwood seat-furniture which was obviously more grandiose in conception, as the cost per piece was higher. The discovery of the fact that this set was, in fact, made by Chippendale and not by Norman, as previously hazarded, is also of supreme importance because Adam's design for one of the sofas is extant. It has thus, at last, been conclusively proved that Thomas Chippendale did on occasion work from designs provided by Robert Adam.

The entry, invoiced on 9th July, 1765, is as follows :

	£	s.	d.
'To 8 large Arm Chairs exceeding Richly Carv'd in the Antick manner and Gilt in oil Gold Stuff'd and cover'd with your own Damask — and strong castors on the feet	160	–	–
8 leather cases to ditto lin'd with Flannel	8	8	–
8 crimson Check cases to Ditto . . .	6	–	–
4 large Sofas exceeding Rich to match the chairs	216.	–	–
4 leather covers to Ditto lin'd with flannel	12.	12.	–
4 Cheque cases to Ditto . . .	7	4.	–.'

The sofas were executed from a design of Adam's, dated 1764,[1] and are recorded in his bill of charges for Arlington Street, 18th July, 1765, 'To a Design of sopha chairs for the Salon £5.'.[2] The dates fit admirably. Adam made the design in 1764 and sent in his account for it in July 1765. Chippendale, who had spent about a year working on the suite, from the time that Adam had given him the design, also invoiced it in July 1765. It was obviously an order of the highest importance as the chairs were 'exceeding Richly carv'd and Gilt in oil Gold' — the sofas also being described as 'Exceeding Rich'. Each chair cost £20 and each sofa £54, whilst Chippendale only charged £13 for a chair and £35 for a sofa in the other suite, which are also described as 'Large French Arm Chairs very Richly carv'd and gilt.' Perhaps the difference of the quality in the carving and gilding is explained by the choice of the adjectives *exceeding* and *very*. The chairs are also described as being

---

[1] Soane, Vol. 17, no. 74.

[2] A. T. Bolton, *The Architecture of Robert and James Adam*, London, 1922, Vol. II, p. 345.

'carv'd in the Antick Manner' which refers to the classical sphinxes, anthemions and arabesques carved on the giltwood top-rails and seat-rails of the suite (Pl. 367). It must be remembered that 1765 was an early date for the use of neo-classical motives in this country and Chippendale would have been eager to point this out to his client. The chairs are further described as being 'cover'd with your own Damask' which Dundas must have supplied to Chippendale. Dundas did, in fact, buy damask from Neilson in Paris in 1769, and he may well have had the suite recovered with it four years after it was supplied to him. Finally it will be noticed that the *strong castors* are still on the feet.

The chairs were admired by Lady Shelburne in March 1768, when she writes in her diary, recording a visit to Lady Charlotte Dundas in Arlington Street, 'I had vast pleasure in seeing a house, which I had so much admired, and improved as much as possible. The apartment for company is up one pair of stairs, the Great Room is now hung with red damask, and with a few very large and capital pictures, with very noble glasses between the piers, and *Gilt chairs.*'

The suite remained at Arlington Street until 1934, when Christie's sold four armchairs and a sofa from it.[1] These passed through the collection of Mr. Ronald Tree to that of Mrs. Derek Fitzgerald, one chair going to the Victoria and Albert Museum. The remainder was then sold again in 1963. Four chairs and three sofas, which were not included in the 1934 sale, being retained by the family, still remain at Aske.

APPENDIX A

The Preface from the first edition of Chippendale's *Director*, 1754:

Of all the Arts which are either improved or ornamented by Architecture, that of Cabinet-Making is not only the most useful and ornamental, but capable of receiving as great assistance from it as any whatever. I have therefore prefixed to the following designs a short explanation of the five Orders. Without an acquaintance with this science, and some knowledge of the rules of Perspective, the Cabinet-maker cannot make the designs of his work intelligible, nor show, in a little compass, the whole conduct and effect of the piece. These, therefore, ought to be carefully studied by every one who would excel in this branch, since they are the very soul and basis of his art.

The Title-Page has already called the following work, The *Gentleman and Cabinet-Maker's Director*, as being calculated to assist the one in the choice, and the other in the execution of the designs; which are so contrived, that if no one drawing should singly answer the Gentlemen's taste, there will yet be found a variety of hints sufficient to construct a new one.

I have been encouraged to begin and carry on this work not only (as the puff in the play-bill says) by persons of distinction, but of eminent taste for performances of this sort; who have, upon many occasions, signified some surprise and regret, that an art capable of so much perfection and refinement, should be executed with so little propriety and elegance. How far the following sheets may remove a complaint which I am afraid is not altogether groundless, the judicious reader will determine: I hope, however, the novelty, as well as the usefulness of the performance, will make some atonement for its faults and imperfections. I am sensible there are too many to be found in it; for I frankly confess, my pencil has but faintly copied out

---

[1] 26 April 1934, lot 26.

those images that my fancy suggested; and had they not been published till I could have pronounced them perfect, perhaps they had never seen the light. Nevertheless, I was not upon that account afraid to let them go abroad, for I have been told that the greatest masters of every other art have laboured under the same difficulty.

A late writer of distinguished taste and abilities, speaking of the delicacy of every author of genius with respect to his own performances, observes, that he has the continued mortification to find himself incapable of taking entire possession of that ideal beauty that warms and fills his imagination.

Never, says he (in a quotation from Tully) was any thing more beautiful than the Venus of Apelles, or the Jove of Phidias, yet were they by no means equal to those high notions of beauty which animated the geniuses of those wonderful artists. The case is the same in all arts where taste and imagination are concerned; and I am persuaded that he who can survey his own works with entire satisfaction and complacency, will hardly ever find the world of the same favourable opinion with himself.

I am not afraid of the fate an author usually meets with in his first appearance, from a set of critics who are never wanting to show their wit and malice on the performances of others : I shall repay their censures with contempt. Let them unmolested deal out their pointless abuse, and convince the world they neither have good nature to commend, judgment to correct, nor skill to execute what they find fault with.

The correction of the judicious and impartial I shall always receive with diffidence in my own abilities and respect to theirs. But tho' the following designs were more perfect than my fondness for my own offspring could ever suppose them, I should yet be far from expecting the united approbation of All those whose sentiments have an undoubted claim to be regarded; for a thousand accidental circumstances may concur in dividing the opinions of the most improved judges, and the most unprejudiced will find it difficult to disengage himself from a partial affection to some particular beauties, of which the general course of his studies, or the peculiar cast of his temper may have rendered him most sensible. The mind, when pronouncing judgment upon any work of taste and genius, is apt to decide on its merit according as those circumstances which she most admires either prevail or are deficient. Thus, for instance (says the ingenious author before quoted) the excellency of the *Roman* Masters in painting consists in beauty of *design*, nobleness of attitude, and delicacy of expression, but the charms of good colouring are wanting. On the contrary, the *Venetian* School is said to have neglected *design* a little too much, but at the same time has been more attentive to the grace and harmony of well-disposed *lights* and *shades*. Now it will be admitted by all admirers of this noble art, that no composition of the pencil can be perfect, where either of these qualities are absent; yet the most accomplished judge may be so particularly struck with one or other of these excellencies, in preference to the rest, as to be influenced in his censure or applause of the whole tablature, by the predominancy or deficiency of his favourite beauty. Something of this kind, tho' the following sheets had all the perfection of human composition, would no doubt subject them in many things to the censure of the most approved judges whose applause I should esteem my greatest honour, and whose correction I shall ever be proud to improve by.

Upon the whole, I have here given no design but what may be executed with advantage by the hands of a skillful workman, tho' some of the profession have been diligent enough to represent them (especially those after the Gothic and Chinese manner) as so many specious drawings, impossible to be work'd off by any mechanic whatsoever. I will not scruple to attribute this to malice, ignorance and inability : and I am confident that I can convince all Noblemen, Gentlemen, or others, who will honour me with their commands, that every design in the book can be improved, both in beauty and enrichment, in the execution of it, by

Their Most Obedient Servant.

St. Martin's Lane
March 3, 1754.

Thomas Chippendale.

APPENDIX B

Facsimile title-page from the third edition of Chippendale's *Director*, 1762 :

THE

GENTLEMAN and CABINET-MAKER's

DIRECTOR:

Being a large COLLECTION of the

Moſt ELEGANT and USEFUL DESIGNS

OF

HOUSEHOLD FURNITURE,

In the Moſt FASHIONABLE TASTE.

Including a great VARIETY of

CHAIRS, SOFAS, BEDS, and COUCHES; CHINA-TABLES, DRESSING-TABLES, SHAVING-TABLES, BASON-STANDS, and TEAKETTLE-STANDS; FRAMES for MARBLE-SLABS, BUREAU-DRESSING-TABLES, and COMMODES; WRITING-TABLES, and LIBRARY-TABLES; LIBRARY-BOOK-CASES, ORGAN-CASES for private Rooms, or Churches, DESKS, and BOOK-CASES; DRESSING and WRITING-TABLES with BOOK-CASES, TOILETS, CABINETS, and CLOATHS-PRESSES; CHINA-CASES, CHINA-SHELVES, and BOOK-SHELVES; CANDLE-STANDS, TERMS for BUSTS, STANDS for CHINA JARS, and PEDESTALS; CISTERNS for WATER, LANTHORNS, and CHANDELIERS; FIRE-SCREENS, BRACKETS, and CLOCK-CASES; PIER-GLASSES, and TABLE-FRAMES; GIRANDOLES, CHIMNEY-PIECES, and PICTURE-FRAMES; STOVE-GRATES, BOARDERS, FRETS, CHINESE-RAILING, and BRASS-WORK, for Furniture.

AND OTHER

ORNAMENTS.

TO WHICH IS PREFIXED,

A Short EXPLANATION of the Five ORDERS of ARCHITECTURE;

WITH

Proper DIRECTIONS for executing the moſt difficult Pieces, the Mouldings being exhibited at large, and the Dimenſions of each DESIGN ſpecified.

The Whole comprehended in TWO HUNDRED COPPER-PLATES, neatly engraved.

Calculated to improve and refine the preſent TASTE, and ſuited to the Fancy and Circumſtances of Perſons in all Degrees of Life.

By THOMAS CHIPPENDALE,

CABINET-MAKER and UPHOLSTERER, in St. Martin's Lane, London.

THE THIRD EDITION.

LONDON:

Printed for the AUTHOR, and ſold at his Houſe, in St. Martin's Lane; Alſo by T. BECKET and P. A. DE HONDT, in the Strand.

MDCCLXII.

APPENDIX C

Extracts from Chippendale's accounts for furnishing Mersham-le-Hatch: (lent by Lord Brabourne to the Kent Archives, Maidstone.)

'*Sir Edward Knatchbull, Bart.*   Dr.
                                      To Thomas Chippendale.

1767
Oct. 14.   *DINING PARLOUR*

To a large Mahogany sideboard Table of very fine wood with neat feet & carv'd Moldings.	£12.	12.	0.
To 10 Mahogany Chairs with neat Open Carv'd Backs the seats stuff'd over the rails, cover'd with Crimson Haircloth & Brass nail'd.	25.	0.	0.
To 2 long Stools for the windows with scro'l Heads and stuff'd & Cover'd to Match the Chairs.	9.	9.	0.
To a Very large Oval Glass in a Very rich Carv'd frame partly Gilt & Glass Borders . . .	46.	0.	0.
To a Very large Gerandole richly Carv'd & part Gilt with looking Glass in the Back & three Branches with Brass leaf Nozels . . .	22.	0.	0.

HALL.

To 2 very large neat Mahogany stools with scro'l Heads of fine wood & neat Carv'd Roses & other ornaments	14.	14.	0.
To 4 smaller Mahogany stools without heads and Made to Match the large stools	8.	8.	0.

(Ill. *G.C-M.* p. 179, pl. 113.)

ANTI ROOM.

To sewing silk thread tape & Making 2 Drapery window Curtains of Blue Damask		1.	4.	0.
Braid Brass rings & Plumbets		0.	6.	0.
63 yds. Supperfine Blue Mix'd damask @ 7/–		22.	1.	0.
49¼ yds. Supperfine Tammy to line		13.	10.	0.
60 Yds. Lace	/4.	1.	0.	0.
55 Yds. Line	/2.	0.	9.	2.
12 Mixed Tassels	2/6	1.	10.	0.
2 Pulley laths & 8 Brass Cloakpins		0.	9.	0.
2 Rich Carv'd Cornices cover'd with Damask & laced — 6½ yds. damask		8.	0.	0.

ALCOVE BEDCHAMBER

To large Dome Bedsteads with Mahogany feet Posts a sacking bottom and Castors & very rich Carv'd Cornices & Vases Japann'd Blue & White.		26.	0.	0.
Thread tape & Making a Cotton furniture for ditto to draw in drapery & lin'd.		2.	18.	0.
Braid Brass rings & Plumbets		0.	7.	6.
64¾ Yds. Cotton @ 4/–		12.	19.	0.
35½ Yds. Lining 1/6		2.	13.	3.

8½ *Yds. Buckram*	*1/2*	*£0.*	*9. 11.*
108 *Yds. Lace*	*/2.*	*0. 18. 0.*
39 *Yds. Line*	*/2.*	*0. 6. 6.*
5 *Yds. Hessians*	*1/2.*	*0. 5. 10.*

SUNDRIES

To Making new Backs & feet for 3 Japann'd Glass frames 2 new Glasses &   *2. 15. 0.*
silvering one your own.

To 6 Mahogany dressing frames for your own Glass new silvering the Glasses &   *2. 5. 0.'*
a large Glass with a Compas Top in a Mahogany frame.

APPENDIX D

Letters from Chippendale's firm to Sir Edward Knatchbull relating to the furnishing of Mersham-le-Hatch, Kent (1770–1778): (lent by Lord Brabourne to the Kent Archives, Maidstone.)

1.   Sir Edward

I Received your letter of 11th Inst and am much obligd to you for your sending to me; The £150 will be of great service to me, which is the best way to send I know not, if any person at Ashford could give a draft payable to me or order at sight, it could be the best and reedist way of sending it. If that cannot be done perhaps your Banker will pay it if you desire him, you remitting the money by the first opportunity, I do not think it safe to remit it in Bank Notes, as the Mails are so often rob'd, I should be greatly obliged to you if you would do it as fast as possible.

Octr 15th 1770.   I remain
St. Martin's Lane.   With due Respect
                          Your Honours
20 Octo'r 1770.   Most obedt and
Remitted Chippendale   Most Hble Servt.
£150 on this letter.   Tho. Chippendale.

                                   London, 7th May 1773

2.   Sir Edward,

Your Chairs, Glasses, Table, &c. is all ready to be sent away, but as Lady Knatchbull seemed to want 4 larger Chairs — what we call Barjairs, they must be made & in the meantime We must send her Ladyship patterns for the needlework which will be Very large, consequently will take some time in working, We should rather recommend 2 large Barjairs as We think it would be of more propriety in one room — as the Chairs can only at present be finished in Linnen We should be glad to know what kind of Covers you would please to have for them Serge is most commonly used but as the room is hung with India paper, perhaps you might Chuse some sort of Cotton — Suppose a green Stripe Cotton which at this is fashionable — You will please to favour us with Your orders which shall be duly attended to & much oblige

You will please to   Sir Edwd.
observe there is no   Yr. most obedt. Hble. Servts.
Chairs made, How many   Chippendale Haig & Co.
you would chuse to have
sent.

THOMAS CHIPPENDALE (1718–79)

London 19th May 1773

3. Sir Edward

We Receiv'd your favour of the 11th Inst. The Chairs & Stools is stuff'd in Canvas & loose Covers made out(?) of Green stripe Cotton, which will be a sort of finish at present & be very necessary when cover'd with needlework the 10 Chairs, 3 Stools, 2 Glasses, Marble table & frame in 3 Close & 4 open Cases were carefully packd up & put on board the Kent, John Sherwood Martin (Jones or Raymen not being up) this Day, which We hope will come safe to hand and be approv'd of

We are
Sr. Edwd.
Your most obedt. hble. Servts.
Chippendale, Haig & Co.

4. Sir,

We have this Evening forwarded by the Canterbury Coach two different designs of Glasses and frames No. 1 fills the pier in width, is 99 Inches long by 58 inches wide, but wants a small head Glass to make it out in height, as you will see by the ornamt. sketched over that piece of Glass, the very lowest price will be £170 Each, We have two other Glasses long enough without any head plate, they will come to £180 Each and which size we have often sold for 200 Guineas.

No. 2 is a smaller Glass as you will see by the sketch not filling the Pier either in width or height, the 96 Inches by 53. the Price £155 Each, but the last mentioned Glasses of £180 according to their size are the Cheapest as well as most suitable for your Room. As to frames No. 1 will cost about 28 £. No. 2 about 36 £ but either may be slighted and made for less —

You have likewise a design for an Axminster Carpet to Correspond with your Ceiling to go into the Bow and at equal distances from the plinth all round the Room, the Expense of it will be according to their best Price about £100 They will have a painting to make of it at large and the Colours to dye on purpose, but if you Chuse to have it made square, like your other Carpet it will be proportionably less in price and if you or Lady Knatchbull chuses any alterations in any of the Colours, by describing it properly, it may be done.

Along with them you have a sketch of a Very handsome Gerandole with Glass in the Back for your choice and if all or any of the above designs meet with your & My Lady's Approbation we shall be happy in being favoured with your Orders.

We are Sir
Your most Obedient
and obliged humble Servt.
Chippendale Haig & Co.

St. Martin's Lane.

23 June 1778.

In the Case with the designs we have sent 4 Spring Barrels which we had to repair.

(It is interesting to see that Chippendale was sending designs for the Axminster carpet and not Robert Adam who had designed the ceiling — Author's note.)

APPENDIX E

Extract from Chippendale's accounts for furnishing Nostell Priory (in the Nostell Priory Archives).

1766

June 21. 'To a very large mahogany Library Table covered with black leather and a writing drawer: doublt spring and tumbler locks to ditto. coverd with green cloth. £12. 0. 0.

    A mahogany elbow chair coverd with black leather and brass naild 3. 10. 0.

    4 Mahogany backstools to match. 8. 16. 0.

June 23. A mahogany case for papers to stand on a frame with pidgeon holes, drawers, and divisions for books etc. 13. 10. 0.

    A Lady's commode writing table made of tulip and rosewood with a slider coverd with green cloth. 5. 14. 0.

June 24. To a pair of very neat mahogany dining tables made of fine wood to join together 11. 0. 0.

    A mahogany Lady'(s) secretary made of very fine wood, a bookcase at top, pannelld doors with pidgeon holes and drawers in the uper case and a scrowl pediment 25. 0. 0.

    A mahogany pillar and claw table with a square top 1. 17. 0.

    A mahogany pembroke table, with writing drawer 3. 10. 0.

    Repairing and cleaning furniture 4. 10. 0.

June 27. 12 Rush bottom chairs 1. 10. 0.

    8 plain yolk back chairs 2. 4. 0.

June 24. A mahogany house for a monkey 18. 0.

    (cf. p. 26, Vile's entry in Royal Accounts 1761–2, "Two mahogany houses for a Turkey Monkey.")

1767

June 25. Writing 2 Inventories of his furniture 5. 0. 0.

To a very neat mahogany Cabinet with drawers and a medall case, with a glass door to ditto elegantly ornamented with carvd work and made to fit into the recess of a blanck door 38. 10. 0.

    (see Pl. 360)

1768.

Jan. 20. To a large strong wainscot mangle made to go by a Wheel and Pinion complete 14. 0. 0.

1769

Nov. 17. Papering up a bed and fixing up all the Window Curtains and laying down Carpets 1. 8. 0.

Dec. 15. Taking down furniture Glasses pictures etc. and moving sundry goods 10. 6. 0.

Dec. 22. Taking down the paper of the Bed Chamber and repairing the wainscot Paper paste and hanging the Room with your India paper upon canvas 3. 10. 0.'

(Fuller extracts from these accounts are published by Oliver Bracket in *Thomas Chippendale,* Appendix I, pp. 111–116.)

APPENDIX F

Extracts from the account presented to Sir Lawrence Dundas, Bart., by Thomas Chippendale and the Executor of James Rannie for work carried out between July 1763 and January 1766, totalling £1,123. 1. 6., settled 1st August, 1766 (lent by the Marquess of Zetland to the North Riding Record Office, Northallerton, Yorkshire)

1763

'Augᵗ. 13.   *A large mah. Cloathes press in two parts with folding doors and sliding shelves cover'd with Marble paper and bayes aprons . . .*   £10. 0. 0.

Septʳ· 12.   *2 large Mahogany Terms of fine wood with crystal Globes neatly fitted up with brass and crystal shades supported by brass ribs and fixed to the Globes and Jappan'd lamps to Ditto complete . . .*   15. 15. 0.

Novʳ· 18.   *A Neat Mahogany Linen airer . . .*   12. 0.

1764

Janry. 20.   *To a very large Mahogany Bookcase of fine wood with a scrol pediment top and Rich folding doors glaz'd with plate Glass in the upper part and Cupboards with folding doors of very fine wood in the under part*   80. 0. 0.

Febʳy· 24.   *2 large French Arm Chairs and a Stool made to Join together stuff'd in Linen, and Crimson check cases and 2 Bolsters for the Chairs and Mahogany posts to screw at Top and a Throw over Crimson Check furniture and Castors on the feet . . .*   13. 0. 0.

   To a very neat work Table of Guadalupe wood with a Hexagon top and a carv'd pillar and Claws . . .   3. 13. 6.

Apʳ· 18.   *A Mahogany Chest of drawers with a Desk drawer and Bookcase with a Scrol Pediment top and Looking Glass*   26. 0. 0.

May 11.   *A Neat Mahogany dressing Table of very fine wood with a folding top and looking Glass boxes bottles etc. . . .*   7. 7. 0.

May 21.   *A very neat Mahogany Ladys Secretary with a fine cutt Bookshelf on the Top and a Neat fret round the desk drawer*   10. 10. 0.
   [now at Aske, near Richmond, Yorkshire — the upper section has been altered]

Augᵗ· 16.   *A large Mahogany Bookcase same scrol as before the upper doors Glaz'd with Croun Glass . . .*   73. 0. 0.

Augᵗ· 17.   *A very neat Mahogany Teabox with 2 wood Cannisters lin'd with Lead . . .*   2. 2. 0.

1765

Feby· 21.   *A large 8 leg Mahogany table border'd with Pidgeonwood . . .*   2. 10. 0.

May 21.   *12 very large best Red stain'd chairs wᵗ· Sweep backs . . .*   4. 4. 0.

Septʳ· 16.   *2 fine Hexagon Teaboards in Shape with Cutt rims . . .*   4. 4. 0.

Octr. 14.	A Mahogany Tea tray with a neat cut Rim . . .	£1. 4. 0.
,, ,,	A Round Teaboard with a plain rim	0. 9. 0.
Octr. 22.	A large Goulty Cradle complete for 2 legs . . .	2. 5. 0.
Octr. 28.	2 large Mahogany pole screens cover'd w^t India pict. . . .	2. 4. 0.
,, ,,	2 very Neat Mahogany folding Firescreens cover'd w^t. fine India pictures and Cutt fretts at Bottom . . .	5. 10. 0.
Novr. 6.	A large Mahogany Breakfast Table of fine Wood w^t a Drawer and a Shelf underneath	3. 8. 0.
Novr 6.	A Black Inkstand dish with Cutt Bottles for D^o . . .	0. 10. 6.
,, ,,	To a Tent frame for Needlework with brass work complete . . .	4. 10. 0.
,, ,,	A large walnut Gouty Cradle with 2 legs w^t a wooden horse . . .	2. 2. 0.
,, ,,	A large Mahogany Library Table of exceeding fine wood and rich carv'd ornaments to match the Bookcases, the top cover'd with supperfine green cloth and Strong Castors . . .	3. 7. 0.
1766		
Janry 20.	*To 10 Large French Arm Chairs very richly carv'd and gilt in Burnish'd Gold Stuff'd and cover'd with his Damask, and brass nail'd, Strong Castors on the feet	130. 0. 0.
,, ,,	10 large Down cushions for Ditto . . .	10. 10. 0.
,, ,,	*3 very large Rich Sofas to Match the Chairs . . .	105. 0. 0.
,, ,,	3 large Down Cushions for the seats	9. 15. 0.
Janry. 20.	6 Splat Back Chairs painted the seats stuff'd o'er the rails in Best Linen and Cushions for the Backs . . .	7. 16. 0.
,, ,,	A large Couch with 2 heads painted and stuff'd in Best Linen . . .	4. 15. 0.'

*This suite was sold by Christie, Manson and Woods Ltd. as Lot 70 on 26 April, 1934, in the sale of the Marquess of Zetland's tapestries, furniture, etc. removed from 19 Arlington Street. It is now in the collection of the Earl of Rosse at Birr Castle, Offaly, Ireland.

Ill. P. Macquoid, *The History of English Furniture — The Age of Mahogany*, 1906, p. 216, fig. 196.

M. Girouard, 'Birr Castle, Co. Offaly — II', pp. 469–70, pls. 3, 4, *Country Life*, CXXXVII.

APPENDIX G

Letter from Thomas Chippendale to Sir Rowland Winn (in the Nostell Priory Archives)

'Sr Rowland

I am Extreamly sorry that you are so Much displeased about ye Berometer frame and the Other things I do assure your Honour and with the greatest Certainty that all the Neglect is Owing to My foreman's inatention to my Business for his wife dyed about a year ago and after that his Broather died and what with the death and some law that he has had Concerning the death of his wife and Broather I can very safely aver for the truth that I have lost above four thousand pounds by him upon ye whole besides disobliging My Customers. when I had Got ye Orders about ye Berometer frame he went into yorkshire and promised to be back again in a very short time but on ye Contrary he Stayd six (?) week he not returning at ye time promised I left ye frame to be going forward till I returned from france (?) And I

Expected that it was nigh finished but to my great surprise there was nothing don to it this is nothing but yᵉ truth and if your Honour would be so kind as to permit me to Make it I shall Esteem it a very perticular favour and as to any other part of your Business should be so happy to Continue in it Shall be still more diligent for yᵉ future

Sᵗ Martins
lane Octʳ 22
1768

I am with due respect your Humle Serᵗ

Thos Chippendale'

APPENDIX H

Letter from Thomas Chippendale to Sir Rowland Winn (in the Nostell Priory Archives) :

'Sʳ Rowland

Yours of the 7th Inst I received and in Answer to it I have to inform your Honour that the Library Chairs, Green Lutestring Curtains and Sunblinds are finished, and all the picture frames are Carved and now Gilding, they would have been finished by this time had not the frost come on so very severe. I shall send the Chairs, Curtains and Sunblinds by Fridays Waggon, and I think the picture frames the week following and the yellow Morcan (?) Cornices and bedposts at the same time. I am Sʳ Rowland greatly obliged to you for giving me so much time to finish the remainder of your kind order. I hope to perform better for the future but it was all owing to the great quantity of unexpected business which I did not know of nor could I refuse doing it as it was mostly for the Royal Family.

I have one favour to beg of your Honour tho' I am really ashamed to ask one, which is if you could spare me a little Cash it would be the greatest Service immaginable at this time as I have many large Accounts to Settle and money seems very Short. I need not good Sir explain myself any further as you know my necessity.

London Jany. 11th
1768

I remain with due respect
your honours most obedt.
and most hbˡᵉ Servᵗ.

Thos. Chippendale'

CHAPTER IV

Some Leading Cabinet-Makers Working in the *Director* Tradition

In the first chapter, we dealt with the principal London cabinet-makers who were active in the 1740's — when the rococo period opens and before the publication of Chippendale's *Director* which, as it were, provided the blue-print on which the second wave of so much English rococo furniture was modelled. The designs and work of Chippendale and the other English furniture designers of the period were discussed in Chapters II and III. It now remains to consider the work of some of the many important cabinet-makers who practised in 'the *Director* Style', but who did not publish designs of their own. Their activities mainly fall within the third quarter of the eighteenth century. It is, of course, only their work in the rococo idiom which principally concerns us here: their work in the neo-classical style is discussed by Mr. Clifford Musgrave in his *Adam and Hepplewhite Furniture*, in this series.

BENJAMIN GOODISON
Fl. about 1727–67

Benjamin Goodison had his premises at the sign of The Golden Spread Eagle, Long Acre, from 1727 to 1767, as can be seen from advertisements and other notices in contemporary newspapers. He was one of the leading cabinet-makers of his day and is primarily remembered for his work in the rather heavy Kentian style that was in vogue prior to, and also during the early formative years of, the English rococo style. Most of it, therefore, does not concern us here. He supplied fine furniture in this tradition to Viscount Folkestone for Longford Castle, Wiltshire, between 1737 and 1747.[1] A pair of pedestals in mahogany and parcel-gilt, which are headed by carved busts of Hercules supporting Ionic capitals, of about 1740 and also at Longford, which are attributed to him,[2] are from the same stable as a set[3] which he made for Hampton Court Palace between 1731 and 1733. These again are in the same tradition as a set of four, and also a pair, which, until recently, were in the Earl of Harrington's Collection at Elvaston Castle, Derby.[4] It has already been shown that Goodison was employed by the Crown at Hampton Court Palace and he was, in

[1] Discussed *G.C-M.*, p. 45, and ill. pls. 42, 44–5.
[2] Mr. Peter Thornton has pointed out that these are after the drawing by Vardy (ill. Ward-Jackson, *English Furniture Designs of the Eighteenth Century*, p. 41) in the R.I.B.A.
[3] Ill. *G.C-M.*, pl. 43.
[4] Sotheby's, 8 November 1963, Lots 166, 167. Another almost identical pair was also sold.

fact, supplying furniture to the Royal Palaces between 1727 and 1767. In about 1735 he had probably supplied a mahogany case for an organ and mechanical harpsichord (Pl. 15) to Kensington Palace for the Queen's Gallery, which was altered to a cabinet by William Vile in 1763 (see p. 23). He also supplied other important pieces of furniture to Hampton Court and Kensington Palaces,[1] and between 1729 and 1759 was supplying furniture for the Prince of Wales's apartments at St. James's Palace. It was recorded that between 1758 and 1759 he charged £16. 16. 0. for 'A mahogany commode chest of drawers, ornamented with carving and wrought brass handles to do, and lifting handles' for the Prince of Wales's Dining-Room at St. James's.

The fourth Earl of Cardigan employed Goodison at Deene Park, Northamptonshire, and at Dover House in London, between 1739 and 1745. Thus in January 1741 he supplied 'a carved and gilt dolphin table frame to match another', and in the same year, on 7th February, 'A new glass to a chimney frame and painting the frame white and fixing the glass with an allowance for your old glass by which above 2 pounds a looser — £2. 2s.'[2] Goodison was also patronised by Sarah, Duchess of Marlborough, 'who employed him in her many houses'.[3]

However, it is the work at Holkham, Norfolk, that he executed for Thomas Coke, first Earl of Leicester, that chiefly falls into our period. The authors of *Georgian Cabinet-Makers*, while discussing his work at Holkham write, 'Attached to a bill for tables, stands, and a picture frame is a letter from Benjamin Goodison which says "The Table[5] for the Drawing Room is in forwardness, but I thout your Lordship wo'd not chuse to have it finisht till the chairs and other furniture was done for it". . . . He also supplied the brass-work on the great porphyry sideboard at Holkham,[6] and in 1740 charges an unexpectedly large sum "for the use of three chandelier Branch to burn lights in the Greenhouse on Mr. Coke's birthday".' In the *Holkham Weekly Departmental Accounts* for the week ending 11th June, 1757, are the following entries :[7]

'Mr. Goodison for a mahog. table press carv'd and Gilt with wire doors for ye Gallery . . .	£14. 16. 0.
Do 2 card table to do . . .	12. 10. 0.
Do for 4 carved and Gilt branches for candles . . .	12. 16. 0.
Do for a Gilt frame to ye Picture of Coriolanus	74. 0. 0.'

There is a mahogany table press (Pls. 368 and 369) at Holkham, in the Countess of Leicester's Drawing-Room, which is indeed 'carv'd and gilt with wire doors'. Its sides have the applied ovals with four foliated scrolls (Pl. 369) that have generally become associated with the name of William Vile (see p. 23), ever since it was discovered that Vile was responsible for the furniture made for Queen Charlotte, which has applied panels of this type. There is also a knee-hole writing- or dressing-table (Pl. 370) in the same

[1] *G.C-M.*, pp. 45–6.

[2] MS. account book of the 4th Earl of Cardigan — *G.C-M.*, p. 45, note 3.

[3] Earl Spencer, *Country Life*, 13 March 1942, p. 517. [4] Ralph Edwards and Margaret Jourdain, pp. 44–5.

[5] This table, which has similar brass enrichments to that on the porphyry sideboard, is still standing in its original position.

[6] John Vardy's (see pp. 50–1) design for a leg and part of the frieze, showing details of the ormoulu metal-gilt mounts, is in the R.I.B.A. Library (9416): it is annotated 'a Table at Holkham Porfery Leg orniments Brass Guilt.' The frieze enrichments are identical to those on the table illustrated in Pl. 74 (cf.).

[7] See Anthony Coleridge, 'Some Mid-Georgian Cabinet-Makers at Holkham', *Apollo*, February 1964.

room, which has many features similar to those of the table press (Pl. 368) and, although there is no mention of it in the *Departmental Accounts*, it also may have been supplied by Goodison's firm. It is stressed, however, that these two pieces are only *attributed* to Goodison, as the description of the table press is not sufficiently explicit or detailed to relate it definitely to the example illustrated in Pl. 368.

Goodison also provided, at the same time, '2 card tables for ye Gallery'. One of several pairs of card-tables of about this period at Holkham is illustrated here (Pl. 371).[1] Their foliate scrolled toes are again typical of what has come to be known as Vile's style, and are very similar to those on Queen Charlotte's work-table (cf. Pl. 17). However an entry from Goodison in the March 1756 *Departmental Accounts* proves, almost beyond doubt, that these were in fact supplied by him. They are invoiced as 'two mahogany card tables with white Frett workt round the tops and frames and ye feet ornamented with carveing and gilding. . .'. The description fits exactly.

He was also probably responsible for supplying some of the important giltwood-framed case and seat furniture at Holkham and amongst this is a chair (Pl. 380) from a large set of seat furniture.

Goodison died in 1767 and his will, dated 29th May, 1765, was proved in December of that year. He left real estate in the parish of St. George's, Hanover Square, to 'his dear son Benjamin Goodison', who also inherited his household effects and £8,000. An equal sum was divided amongst members of his family and charity. He was succeeded by his nephew and partner, Benjamin Parran, who, apparently with Benjamin *junior*, carried on the business until 1783. Parran was supplying inexpensive furniture to the Crown from 1767 when a 'Mahogany Writing Table with 3 drawers in the fframe' was delivered by him. That Benjamin *Junior* must, for a short period, have gone into partnership with Benjamin Parran is indicated by the fact that, in 1769, the Duke of Newcastle received an account for furniture from Messrs. Goodison and Parran. In 1783 Parran went into partnership with William Gates, until the following year when he formed a partnership with John Russell.

GILES GRENDEY
1693–1780

Giles Grendey is another eminent cabinet-maker, an important section of whose career falls outside the scope of this book. His workshop and private address were in part of an old house, called Aylesbury House, in St. John's Square, Clerkenwell. We learn from the newspapers that, in 1731, a serious fire had broken out there and that Grendey had suffered a great loss. Among the 'rich and valuable goods' that were burnt was 'an easy chair of such rich and curious workmanship that he had refused 500 guineas for it, it being intended 'tis said, to be purchas'd by a person of quality who design'd it as a present to a German Prince'.[2] He also lost in this fire furniture worth a thousand pounds which he 'had pack'd

---

[1] A pair of fine tables of very similar design are in the collection of D. Szeben Esq. A table with similar inlay is in the C. D. Rotch Bequest at the Victoria and Albert Museum.
[2] Cited by R. W. Symonds, *Apollo*, December 1935, p. 337, and *G.C-M.*, p. 48.

for Exportation against the Morning'. This allusion to his export trade is illuminating and should be compared with Ince and Mayhew's efforts (pp. 62–7) to attract it. Further evidence of Grendey's trade with the Continent is supplied by a suite of red and gold japanned seat-furniture which was in Spain, until 1935, in the Castle of Lazcano in the collection of the Duke of Infantado. It consists of a day-bed, in the Victoria and Albert Museum, six armchairs and twenty single chairs. One of the single chairs (Pl. 372), in the Metropolitan Museum, as is the case with some of the others in the set, has Grendey's trade label stuck under the seat-rail which reads, 'Giles Grendey, St. John's Square, Clerkenwell, London, Makes and Sells all Sorts Tables, Glasses etc.' Other pieces of scarlet lacquer furniture that may be attributed to him are extant,[1] amongst which is a bureau-cabinet, of about 1745, bearing Grendey's label in a drawer.[2]

Another piece bearing his label is a mahogany cabinet with two mirror-panelled doors above surmounting a cupboard with folding doors below.[3] Its unusual carved apron-piece has been compared by the late R. W. Symonds with two side-tables and a low wardrobe which have very similar carving on their aprons.[3] Furthermore, he has pointed out that both the cabinet and the wardrobe have two doors in their upper section of double serpentine shape carved with egg and tongue mouldings. He also illustrates another mahogany wardrobe,[4] bearing Grendey's label and dateable to about 1745, with similar double serpentine scrolled panels to those on the japanned bureau-cabinet referred to above. It has thus been shown from study of three pieces of his case-furniture, all bearing his labels, that Grendey favoured the use of panels of this unusual shape — at least during one phase in his career. A low wardrobe, or clothes-press, in the Victoria and Albert Museum, which has similar panels may thus also be attributed to him (Pl. 373), and so may a bureau-cabinet in the Museum of Fine Arts, Boston (Pl. 374). Another interesting piece (Pl. 375) in scarlet and gilt lacquer bears the trade label of Giles Grendey.[5]

Giles Grendey was employed at Longford Castle, Wiltshire, and there is a note in the accounts[6] of a payment of £68 to 'Grendey, chair-maker'.[7] The chair illustrated in Pl. 376, which is one of a set bought for Longford by the first Lord Folkestone, may be one of the pieces for which Grendey was paid £68. A finely carved mahogany centre-table in the same tradition is illustrated in Pl. 377. Grendey also worked for Sir Richard Hoare of Barn Elms between the years of 1732 and 1739,[8] as is shown by bills and signed receipts which are extant.

Little is known of Grendey's work in the rococo style although there is small doubt that he was working throughout the period, for he was elected Master of the Joiners' Company in 1766, after having been on the Livery since 1729. The late R. W. Symonds, discussing this subject, writes,[3] 'It is recorded in the Company's Minute Book that the clerk was instructed to write to Grendey telling him that his better attendances in the duties of his office was expected, and that, unless he was present at the next Court, "such methods will be taken as shall be adjudged proper, which 'tis hoped he will prevent as the same will be equally disagreeable to the Court as to himself".' Symonds continues, 'A possible explana-

---

[1] See *G.C-M.*, p. 48. [2] Idem and pl. 50.
[3] Ill. R. W. Symonds, 'In Search of Giles Grendey', *Country Life*, 30 November 1951, p. 1792, pl. 1.
[4] Idem., pl. 5. [5] The trade label is stuck inside the top drawer. [6] 1739.
[7] *Country Life*, 19 December 1931. [8] See *G.C-M.*, p. 47.

tion of the lack of Grendey's furniture after 1745 is that owing to the flourishing state of his trade he found it unnecessary (and, perhaps, a little undignified) to mark his wares with a printed label. This was not a custom with the best makers.' However he certainly appears to have labelled his export wares, and, perhaps for the home market, he only labelled his ready made wares sold from his shop and not his bespoken orders.

Giles Grendey made his will in 1775 and added a codicil in 1779, just after he had retired to Palmer's Green from Clerkenwell. Encircling his new house he had 'a Coach House, Stable building and ground . . . lately purchased . . . and which I have since converted into five cottages'.[1] He appears to have left the cabinet-making business only to start dabbling in real estate.

WILLIAM BRADSHAW, GEORGE SMITH BRADSHAW AND PAUL SAUNDERS
Fl. about 1736–72

William Bradshaw, whose address is unrecorded, was employed by important and influential clients during the middle period of George II's reign. Lord Stanhope paid him £1,200 in 1736,[2] and it is thought that he was responsible for the gilt seat- and case-furniture at Chevening, in Kent, which has the knees carved with masks.[3] He is also recorded as working for the fourth Earl of Cardigan in 1741.[4] In 1738 the first Earl of Bristol noted in his diary[5] 'Paid William Bradshaw, Upholder, for ye Table, bed, and lining ye needlework carpet £3. 5s.' and in 1745 he was paid £10. 10. 0. by the third Earl of Marchmont.[6] He provided a tapestry carpet for Longford Castle in 1737 and was paid by Lord Folkestone in 1750 for hanging a Brussels tapestry.[7]

It is not known whether George Smith Bradshaw was related to William Bradshaw, but it is recorded in the *London Directories* of the period that the former had premises in Dean Street, Soho, from 1760–84, and in Crown Court, Soho, from 1769–93.[8] He is listed[9] as providing furniture for 'the House and Appartments belonging to the Admiralty Office usually inhabited by the first Lord' between 1764 and 1774.

He went into partnership for one year, 1756, with Paul Saunders, a tapestry-weaver, in Greek Street, Soho. The partnership was short-lived, for in the *London Gazette*, 26th–30th October, for that year, it was announced that 'the partnership between Messrs. Bradshaw

---

[1] Quoted from *G.C-M.*, p. 48.

[2] *English Houses, Early Georgian*, ed. H. A. Tipping, 1921.

[3] Ill. *G.C-M.*, pls. 52–4.

[4] Account Book in the possession of the Hon. Mrs. E. Pleydell-Bouverie.

[5] Diary of the 1st Earl of Bristol, p. 156.

[6] MS. account book in the Victoria and Albert Museum — the note under the heading *Old Bills* and to *Wm. Bradshaw Upholsterer*.

[7] *G.C-M.*, p. 51 — I am indebted to the authors of this book for much of the information on William and George Smith Bradshaw published here.

[8] It is suggested in Ambrose Heal's *London Furniture Makers* that these two addresses may apply to the same premises although Crown Court led off Princes Street and not Dean Street.

[9] Contingent Accounts, Chief Clerk, Admiralty.

and Saunders, upholders and Cabinet-Makers, being dissolved the 15th of this Instant October; we beg leave to inform the Nobility and Gentry who for the future we may have the Honour to serve, that the Business will continue to be carried on as usual by Mr. Bradshaw in Greek Street, Soho, and Mr. Saunders in Soho Square, and the corner of Sutton Street, on our own and seperate Accounts. And whoever has any Demands on the said Partnership are advised forthwith to bring their Accounts to Mr. Mayhew[1] at Mr. Bradshaw's.' During that year (1756) they had delivered tapestries and a quantity of upholstery work to Holkham, Norfolk, and the accounts are made out to George Smith Bradshaw and Paul Saunders jointly.

However they are receipted by Paul Saunders alone 'for self and partner', and in the *Holkham Weekly Departmental Accounts* for the week ending 11th June, 1757, are the following entries :[2]

'Mr. Saunders for 10 Elbow chairs with carved and gilt frames and covd. cut blue Turkey leather . . .	£74. 0. 4.
Do. for 2 large sophas ditto	41. 18. 0.
Do. 12 chairs, mahog. frames Gilt and stuffd.	39. 10. 3.'

This set of seat furniture can still be recognised and there are at Holkham six armchairs (Pl. 378), nine single chairs and two sofas in the Statue Gallery and Tribunes. The single chairs (Pl. 379) are not, in fact, *en suite* with the armchairs, and sofas, but they are so alike in design, colouring and execution that they are probably the chairs referred to as having been delivered by Saunders.

Saunders also delivered a variety of other items to Holkham during this period, 1757-9, and there are entries in the *Departmental Accounts* for the following :

'Week ending		
June 11, 1757.	Mr. Saunders blue serge for lining Tammy, silk line and all for ye Statue Gallery	£26. 10. 10
	Do for 6 lanthorns	1. 10. 0
	Do for a man 16 days at Holkham	2. 16. 0
	Do for ye expences of his horses.	5. 6. 0
	Do for Caffoy paper and work in Russell St.[3]	8. 0. 2
	Do for 15 Ells, 7 stick, and 12 Ell stick of Fine Tapestry for ye State Bedchamber at 3 £ 10 sh. per Ell.	54. 5. 0
	Do for ye modell of ye State bed	13. 2. 0
July 2, 1757.	Mr. Saunders for 12 card table chairs	4. 4. 6
July 15, 1758	Mr. Saunders, Upholr, for paper hanging	8. 10. 2
	Do for a mahog. tea board, and a mah. pail	2. 14. 0.'

These entries are of great interest as they illustrate the fact that Saunders was an 'upholsterer', and, or 'upholder', in addition to being a 'cabinet-maker' and 'tapestry weaver'. This side of the business was always extremely important and we thus read of Saunders providing wall-hangings, wall-paper, carpets, bed linen and also, of course, tapestries. Three tapestries in the Green State Bedroom, which depict a pilgrimage to

[1] John Mayhew who went into partnership with William Ince in 1759 (see pp. 62-7).

[2] Quoted from Anthony Coleridge, 'Some Mid-Georgian Cabinet-Makers at Holkham', *Apollo*, February 1964.

[3] The Earl's London House, Thanet House, was in Russell Street on a site adjoining the British Museum's.

Mecca were woven by Saunders' weavers at his Soho looms and one is signed 'Paul Saunders of Soho'.

The second important entry in the Holkham Departmental Accounts is the one referring to :

'Do [Saunders] Ye modell of ye State bed . . .   £13. 2. 0.'

In Lady Leicester's inventory of 'the furniture that she bought at her own expense for compleating the Furnishing of Holkham from June 1759 to June 1769',[1] the following pieces are itemised immediately after the description of the 'Mecca' tapestry panel which we know to have been delivered by Saunders :

'Fringe binding Embroidery Coronets velvet ermine 3 mattresses a feather bed 3 pillows and bolster.	£76. 4. 0.
Sarsnet, sattin and lutestring	14. 2. 0.
Pullies, castors, pillars and a brass rod	9. 11. 0.
Screws and silk	5. 12. 0.
Carpet round the bed	4. 16. 0.
Canvass paper nails Lines and other materials	37. 17. 8.
Shammy skins and other Materials.	4. 16. 0.
3 cornices for the curtains	8. 10. 0.
166 yds. of green stuf for case curtains and covers	15. 0. 0.
Upholsterers work	37. 13. 8.'

It is not unreasonable to suppose that the above description, which clearly refers to a State Bed, was copied *verbatim* from the account of the cabinet-maker who made the bed, straight into the inventory when it was prepared for the Countess. Since we know that Saunders supplied the tapestry for the refurnishing of the room, it seems likely that he was also responsible for the other alterations and additions to the room. This supposition is further strengthened when it is remembered that his model for a State Bed was invoiced in the *Departmental Accounts* on the same day as was his panel of 'Mecca' tapestry. The Green State Bedroom, or Tapestry Bedroom, contains a tester bedstead covered in contemporary cut velvet which is probably the bed in question. Its scrolled canopy is centred by cartouches emblazoned in gilt with the Leicester 'L's and the pelmets for the velvet curtains are *en suite* with it. In the inventory quoted above the '3 cornices for the curtains' cost £8. 10. 0. The fact that the description of the cornices is included with that of the bed is an indication that they were all made for the same room. It can thus be said that this bedstead is, almost certainly, the one described in the inventory above and that it was therefore probably supplied by Saunders. The fact that it must have been rather 'old-fashioned' in style can perhaps be explained by the taste of the elderly Countess.

In 1756, as has already been seen, Paul Saunders set up business on his own account in Sutton Street, Soho.[2] From 1763 to 1768 he was at Great Queen Street, Lincoln's Inn Fields and in 1770 he moved to Great Russell Street, Bloomsbury.[3] Two years later, in 1772, he

---

[1] The Earl died in 1759 and his widow spent £3,096. 5. 8. on completing the furnishing of the house during the subsequent ten years.

[2] In *The British Chronicle*, under *Promotions*, on September 30, 1757, is found the following announcement: 'Mr. Paul Saunders, of Sutton Street, Soho, is appointed Tapestry Maker to his Majesty, and on Thursday was sworn into office.' I am indebted to Mr. Alex Lewis for drawing my attention to the above.

[3] By 1770 he had become a member of the Court of Assistants of the Upholders' Company — Guildhall Library, MS. 7142, vol. I, Register of apprentices, p. 203.

appears to have formed a partnership with a certain Bracken, in Charlotte Street, Bloomsbury, for, until 1790, the firm of *Paul Saunders and Bracken* is recorded at that address in the *London Directories*. In his will he left the lease of his 'dwelling house, work shops, warehouses and premises' in trust to his wife Anne, his son Hugh and his 'worthy friend' Theodosius Forest, of York Buildings, St. Martin in the Fields.

JAMES WHITTLE AND SAMUEL NORMAN
Fl. about 1742–65

James Whittle, carver and gilder, of King Street, Covent Garden, is first recorded in 1742 when he supplied the Earl of Cardigan with some carved giltwood pier-glasses and side tables.[1] A pair of these was invoiced as 'two rich tables like the Duke of Montagu's with Boy's heads'.[2] He retained his King Street premises until 1761.[3] However, there is an advertisement in the *General Evening Post*, 1758, which states that James Whittle, Samuel Norman and John Mayhew,[4] after forming a partnership, 'having purchased the lease of the late Mr. West's[5] house and warehouse in King Street, beg leave to acquaint the Nobility, Gentry and others that they continue to carry on the Upholstery and Cabinet as well as the Carving and Gilding Businesses in all their branches . . .'.

Mayhew left the partnership in 1759 and immediately formed another with John Ince, as was announced in the *Public Advertiser* of 27th January for that year : the activities of that partnership have already been discussed (pp. 62–7). Samuel Norman, on the other hand, who was a cabinet-maker and carver, seems to have been the dominant member of the earlier partnership as, with the exception of the Holkham pier-glasses discussed below, no further record of Whittle seems to have come down to us after the advertisement announcing the firm's establishment in 1758. This may be accounted for by a serious fire which broke out in the following year in the King Street premises and, which was reported thus in *Public Advertiser* of 24th December, 1759; 'Yesterday morning, about four o'clock, a terrible Fire broke out at Mr. Norman's (late Mr. West's), an eminent Cabinet-maker Carver and Gilder in King Street, Covent Garden, which entirely consumed that house.' It will be noted that only Norman's name is mentioned here. However, Samuel Norman seems to have carried on and set up by himself in Soho Square where he remained until at least 1765. In Mortimer's *Universal Director* for 1763, he is described as 'Sculptor and carver to their Majesties, and Surveyor of the curious Carvings in Windsor Castle',[6] and his address is given as Soho Square. In one of his accounts for work carried out for Woburn Abbey in 1760, his address is given as 'The Royal Tapestry Manufactury, Soho Square'.

It has already been shown that the partners were specialist carvers and gilders and it is therefore not surprising to read that Matthew Brettingham, junior, ascribes[7] the pier-glass

[1] MS. account book of the Earl of Cardigan in the collection of the Hon. Mrs. E. Pleydell-Bouverie.
[2] *G.C-M.*, p. 104.   [3] *London Furniture Makers* — contemporary sources.
[4] See Ince and Mayhew (pp. 62–3).
[5] John West, an eminent cabinet-maker, had died in 1758.
[6] To date no record of any work carried out by him for the Crown appears to have been published.
[7] *The Plans, Elevations and Sections of Holkham House in Norfolk* (1773), *2nd Edition:* Much of the following text has already been published by the author in 'Some Mid-Georgian Cabinet-Makers at Holkham', *Apollo*, February 1964.

(Pl. 381) in the Drawing-Room at Holkham to Whittle.[1] The Brettinghams' book can be taken as a primary source, since father and son were so closely connected with the building of the house and thus the statement that there is 'a magnificent Pier-glass, the frame by Whittle' can be accepted without reservation. There is, in the adjoining Saloon, an even finer set of pier-glasses and console tables (Pl. 382) which has, at one time,[2] been ascribed to a certain 'Pugh'. However as, to date, no primary evidence in the form of accounts or ledger entries have been found to back this statement, and as no carver of this name is known, it is reasonable to suppose that this statement may be unfounded — or perhaps Pugh was merely an artisan who hung the pier-glasses or carried out some such unskilled task. The suite is so masterly in conception and design and so highly finished in its detail and execution that it is unthinkable that it could have been produced anywhere other than in one of the leading London workshops. If Whittle and Norman produced the superb pier-glass in the Drawing-Room (Pl. 381) then it seems conceivable that they also made the set of four in the adjoining Saloon (Pl. 382). The latter, which are more fully in the rococo tradition, each also have four candle sconces.[3] The console tables (Pl. 382) were almost certainly made *en suite* with them, as can be seen by the similarity of the unusual shells and scrolled foliage which appear on both.

It is tantalising that Whittle's accounts for these sets have not, to date, been discovered, but they must have been very similar to those which the same firm presented to the Duke of Bedford for pier-glasses which they had also been making for Woburn Abbey. Thus on 13th September, 1760, Samuel Norman presented the following account[2] to the Duke of Bedford for a pair of pier-glasses (Pl. 384) which now hang in the Blue Drawing-Room:

'September 13, 1760.

William Norman for 2 large glass frames in burnished gold	£229. 0. 0.
For a plate of glass	183. 5. 0.
	412. 5. 0.'

William Norman, whose name is mentioned in this account, was probably a relative and member of the firm but the guarantee that accompanied the account was signed by Samuel Norman himself.[4] The account was thought to be excessively high by the Duke and thus another firm was asked to give an independent valuation:[5]

'The two large glass frames in burnished gold	£229. 0. 0.
One large plate to ditto 76 × 44 supposed to be ready for delivery in town	167. 10. 0.
Risk of such plate if sent to the country and carriage of ditto thither	15. 15. 0.
	412. 5. 0.

Signed { Thomas Woodin
Paul Saunders.'

[1] One of a pair, the other being in the South Dining-Room.

[2] See C. W. James, *Chief Justice Coke, His Family and Descendants at Holkham*, 1929.

[3] In Benjamin Goodison's account of March 1756 to the Earl of Leicester are invoiced 'four branches for candles carved and gilt in Burnisht gold with an iron stem through ditto and wrot brass panns and nossils and brass plates and sockets to let into the stem for the Branches to fix and move in, all at £3. 4. 0. each. . . .' This entry may well refer to the above.

[4] See G. Scott-Thomson, *Family Background*, 1949, pp. 67–8, 74–8.

[5] *G.C-M.*, p. 60.

It is interesting to note that Paul Saunders was called in as one of the arbitrators and it appears that he must have been a good friend of Norman and Whittle's as he did not reduce their account — they probably already knew each other well, having met at Holkham or elsewhere. However, Samuel Norman was not given such preferential treatment over a pier-glass, which has now disappeared, but which he delivered to the State Bedchamber at Woburn. In this instance Messrs. Robert Hyde and Charles Smith,[1] were called in as arbitrators, and they reduced the account[2] by £20:

'1759
For making and carving that exceeding large and grand oval frame, with eagles, a shield and rich "swaggs", festoons of flowers twisting round, Flora's head, top and rich flowers curiously finished and gilt in burnish gold complete .... £97. 10. 0.
For a plate of best glass to ditto 49 × 38 complete .... £65. 3. 0.'

Another fine pair of pier-glasses by Norman and Whittle, their oval frames surmounted by Ceres and flanked by female figures with dolphins' tails, are hanging in the State Dining-Room.[2]

It has thus been shown that Messrs. Norman and Whittle were carvers and gilders of the highest dexterity, but it is important to remember that they were also cabinet-makers and upholsterers, and we thus read that they also provided for Woburn 'a grand state bed', 14 Virginia walnut chairs, 'a large grand sofa, French shap'd, richly carved and partly gilt and varnished' and also lengths of damask and silk hangings and cartridge paper. The walnut chairs, which were described as 'fourteen neat carved Virginia Walnut chairs partly gilt . . . upholstered and covered with your Grace's silk damask', and the State bedstead, which was not rehung but was trimmed with 150 yards of 'the best blue Belladine silk crape fringe . . .' at a cost of about £160, can, with a high degree of certainty, still be recognised in the Abbey.[3]

A pier-glass in the Victoria and Albert Museum (Pl. 385) has been attributed to Norman and Whittle on stylistic grounds, and the shell at the base should be compared with those on the Holkham examples (cf. 382).

It has for long[4] been thought that Norman was associated with Robert Adam over the furnishing and refurbishing of Sir Lawrence Dundas's houses at 19 Arlington Street and Moor Park in Hertfordshire.[5] Mrs. Harris,[6] writing to her son, the first Earl of Malmesbury, on 20th August, 1763, says that she had spent the whole morning with him [Norman], 'partly at Whitehall and partly at his warehouse, and had given what are, for us, I think, large orders, though not so great as those of Sir Lawrence Dundas, who has ordered furniture from Norman's to the amount of ten thousand.' On the evidence alone of this contemporary reference to Norman, it has become the custom to attribute all the

---

[1] Robert Hyde was a chair-maker of Maiden Lane, Covent Garden; Charles Smith, Cabinet-Maker, of Marshall Street, Carnaby Market, sold his premises to Ince and Mayhew in January 1759 — He then moved to Portugal Street and in 1763 was one of William Vile's two executors.
[2] See p. 141, n. 4.
[3] First published by Ralph Edwards in 'Patrons of Taste and Sensibility, English Furniture of the Eighteenth Century, Woburn Abbey', *Apollo*, December 1965.
[4] *G.C-M.*, p. 61.   [5] He also owned Aske near Richmond, Yorkshire.
[6] *Letters of the First Earl of Malmesbury, 1745–1820*, Vol. I (1870), p. 94.

furniture of this date, which has survived from Arlington Street and Moor Park, to Norman's firm.[1] Thus the large suite of giltwood framed seat-furniture in the neo-classical style, which was covered in Gobelin's tapestry from Neilson's atelier, has been thought to have been carved by Norman for the Tapestry Room at Moor Park. The suite, when it was included in Christie's sale of the Marquess of Zetland's[2] furniture from Arlington Street in 1934 — after the Moor Park sale in 1784 the suite and the tapestries had been moved to the Ballroom in 19 Arlington Street — consisted of:

a pair of settees (Pl. 386)
10 armchairs
2 pairs of firescreens
a pair of window seats
2 stools

It was, therefore, an exciting moment when Mr. and Mrs. John Harris discovered, in 1965, the original account for this suite in the Zetland archives[3] at Aske in North Yorkshire, the Marquess of Zetland's country house. It was not presented by Norman, whose accounts were also found there, but by the partners Samuel Fell and William Turton, who are, to date, unrecorded. It is dated 1771, and is one of several accounts from this firm for work carried out at Arlington Street and Moor Park between 1766 and 1771. It reads:

	£	s.	d.
'To 2 sophas carved and gilt in Burnished gold. Stuff'd with Best curl'd hair and fine linnen . . . . £25 each	50	—	—
To covering do with your Tapistrey, used Brass naills sewing silk fine Durant for the back Backs tax etc.	1	10	—
To 2 stools carved and gilt in Burnished gold stuff'd with best curled hair and fine linnen . . . . £8 each	16	—	—
To covering Do with your Tapistrey used sewing silk fine Durant for the ends tax etc.		14	—
To 6 elbow chairs carv'd and gilt in Burnished gold stuff'd in Best curl'd hair and fine linnen . . . . £10 each	60	—	—
To Covering do with your Tapistray used sewing silk fine Durant for the Backs tax etc.	2	8	—.'

The words *To covering Do with your Tapistray* are of the greatest importance as they obviously refer to the covers that had been woven for Sir Lawrence by Neilson at the Gobelin's. The fact that there were four armchairs, four firescreens and two stools additional to the suite, when it was sold in 1934 than when it was supplied in 1771, can probably be explained by the fact that the extra pieces were ordered shortly after the suite had been delivered, perhaps to utilise some extra pieces of the tapestry. It has already been

---

[1] *G.C-M.*, p. 61.
[2] Lawrence Dundas created Baronet 1762 — Baron Dundas 1794, Earl of Zetland 1838.
[3] Zetland furniture accounts now lent to the North Riding Record Office, Northallerton, Yorks. Reproduced by kind permission of the Marquess of Zetland and Mr. and Mrs. John Harris who discovered these important accounts and brought them to my notice.

shown (p. 122) that another important suite, that was always thought to have been made by Norman to Adam's designs,[1] was in fact supplied by Chippendale in 1765 (Pl. 367).

Samuel Norman did, however, provide much important furniture for Sir Lawrence, as can be seen from study of a bound, sixteen page folio notebook which was also recently discovered at Aske. Mrs. Harris, in her letter,[2] had been exaggerating when she said that Dundas had spent ten thousand pounds with Norman, but it appears that Norman's account was contested by his client as being exorbitantly high, as was the case with the Duke of Bedford's (pp. 141–2), and the dispute seems to have been taken to Court. The notebook contains a detailed inventory of all the work that Norman carried out for Dundas, and of all the furniture that he supplied to him, at Moor Park, Arlington Street and Aske. After the last entry the following is to be read :

'The several Articles in the beforegoing Account have been examined and are valued at the sum of one Thousand, Six Hundred and Eighty pounds one shilling by us

/signed/ Tho⁸ Chippendale
G. S. Bradshaw[3]
Th. Mayhew

The Entire Gilding of the Gallery valued and Settled by Mr. Richard Brown, Mr. Samuel Haworth and Mr. William Almond at the sum of Seven Hundred Thirty pounds, and to which they answer as witness their hands.

/signed/Willm Almond
Richd Brown
Saml Haworth.'

These two sums total to £2,410. 1. 0. On a loose sheet of paper, which was found tucked into the notebook, is written the following :

'Money Paid Saml Norman from Mr. Drum^d,[4] and Geo. Colebrooks books

From Colebrook 26 Nov. 1763			£200
From Mess. Drum^ds 16 Aug. 1763			200
From D⁰	14 Aug.	64	600
From D⁰	2 Aug.	66	300
From D⁰	17 Octo.	66	100
P^d by Adams	7 Sep.	64	200
P^d by Lady Dundas	17 Aug.	63	200
P^d by Porter			100
			————
			1,900
. . . to Mr. Pearce			500
Ditto Paid into Court			300
			————
			2,700
			2,410
			————
			290'

[1] See p. 143, n. 1.   [2] See p. 142, n. 6.
[3] George Smith Bradshaw, see pp. 137–8.   [4] Mr. Drummond, founder of Drummond's Bank.

This appears to be Sir Lawrence's, or his steward's, summary of the payments made to Norman between August 1763 and October 1766. By the latter date Sir Lawrence obviously felt that he had been overcharged, and payments ceased. Norman then probably took an action against him and Dundas was ordered to pay the £300 into the Court, pending arbitration as to the value of the work to be decided by other leading members of the trade. Chippendale, Bradshaw and Mayhew were appointed to value the furniture and furnishings, and Almond, Brown and Haworth the cost of gilding the Gallery. Their finding was that the total value of the work was £2,410. 1. 0., and Dundas was therefore entitled to the return of £290 from the £300 that he had lodged with the Court, as his total payments to Norman and to the Court had been £2,700. Details of some of the entries in the inventory are given in Appendix A.

A fine carved mahogany commode (Pl. 383), in the full *Director* style, can almost certainly be related to '2 very large and neat Mahogany Commodes Extra fine Wood Best Lox Large lifting handles at the Ends Complete', which Norman provided for Aske, between 1763 and 1766 and which still remain there.

Samuel Norman must, indeed, have been a leading member of his trade to have counted so many of the great amongst his clients. It would appear that he, Cole, John Linnell, Lock, Johnson, Cullen, France and Bradburn, Chippendale, and Ince and Mayhew must all have been serious rivals.

JOHN BRADBURN, AND WILLIAM AND EDWARD FRANCE
Fl. about 1764–1803

John Bradburn (or Bradbourne), Cabinet-maker, was established in Hemings Row, St. Martin's Lane, in 1764, where he remained until 1767 when, from the London Polling Lists, it is seen that he had moved to Long Acre to a house which subsequently became No. 8. He appears to have been employed by Vile and Cobb, for, 'in William Vile's will, dated August 24, 1763, he is bequeathed twenty pounds. In a codicil (dated November 9, 1764) Vile states that his "meaning" was that the bequest applied only to a "servant" at the time of his (Vile's) death. This reference doubtless relates to the establishment of Bradburn in independent business in about 1764.'[1] On Vile's retirement from his post of Royal Cabinet-Maker in 1764, probably on account of ill-health, Bradburn was appointed as his successor (see Chapter I). Whether this was on Vile's recommendation is not known. Bradburn retained this post until he retired in 1776.

In 1766 he supplied for the Queen's House (later Buckingham House) a 'very grand organ case' which was carved with a 'variety of ornaments, viz. Satyr Boys, musical instruments, Drapery for Curtains, foliage, Palms, festoons of husks', for which he charged £156 for the carving alone.[1] In the following year for the 'Queen's Library' in the new 'North Wing', he delivered 'an extraordinary neat mahogany round table' costing

[1] Quoted from *G.C-M.*, p. 61.

£71.[1] In the same year he provided for the 'Nursery at the Queen's House', for £10. 15. 0., 'A Neat Chamber Horse . . . to carry 4 children at once, with a mahogany frame and spring seat covered all round with morocco leather . . . with 4 handles . . . and made to turn on a swivel, and 4 footboards made to fall down occasionally for the Conveniency of carrying it through any doorway,' — a truly ingenious piece. In the same year, 1767, for the apartment of Mrs. Kroms, the Princess Royal's governess, he supplied furniture 'all to match' including 'a good mahogany Cloaths Press' for £19, and 'a very large Mohogany Beaufet . . .'. He was also busy during the following year when he altered cabinets and presses to fit recesses in the Mathematical Room or Gallery, and he delivered 'a neat mahogany piece of work for papers in His Majesty's New Dressing Room'. In 1770 he invoiced a neat mahogany case with glass doors 'for India figures dressed in the habit of the country' for which he charged £7. 7. 0. This was made for the apartments of the nurses for the Royal children and was presumably intended to house some of the children's toys.

In 1774 he supplied for the Princess Royal, then aged eight, 'A neat mahogany Secretary with drawers in front, and a writing drawer lined with fine cloth, made to draw forward, with drawers and pidgeon holes, and an inkstand made to take out, with cut bottles and silvered tops to do: a neat bookcase at top with looking glass doors, and mahogany panels within-side to preserve the glass, good locks to the whole and two keys to pass, one marked P.R., the other L.F.C., and a carved scrowl pediment top to ditto bookcase' all at a cost of £20. This fine piece of furniture is illustrated in Pl. 387. Four years previously, in 1770, he had delivered the low serpentine-shaped cabinet illustrated in Pl. 388. He charged £84. 10. 0. for it and invoiced it as 'A neat Mohogany press for Linnen with 4 wood doors (and 4 ditto at top) the pannels cross banded, and Roses in the Corners of the Framing, the whole inside groov'd like a Book Case, the Mohogany sliding shelves in do, (a fret work Ballustrade on the Top of the 2 wings with carved ornaments and carved patulae on the pedestals, on handsome dentide Cornish to the middle part) and a carv'd Gudroon moulding to the Surbace, with 6 extra good guarded Tumbler Locks and 2 Dutch bow'd keys to pass to'. These descriptions would in no way disgrace a twentieth-century auctioneer's catalogue and much can be learnt from careful study of the terms in use by the trade at the time. A mahogany cabinet in the same tradition (Pl. 389) has recently been in the market and it is interesting to be able to compare the two examples.

During 1765 and 1766 Bradburn had made the case for an important astronomical clock with four dials, which had been supplied to George III by Eardley Norton in 1765 at the high cost of £1,178. Bradburn's first entry in the Lord Chamberlain's accounts relating to the clock-case, for which he charged £35. 15. 0., reads, 'A very rich antique carved and burnished gilt bracket [case] for a clock in His Majesty's Dressing Room. The top cornice very richly carved with a very neat mosaick work border round ditto . . . and Flowers pierced through, and the ground pannelled and enriched with a small ogee; the front part and the sides enriched with an Antique Foliage leaf which speads at each end to support a demi Lion and Unicorn, the whole very rich and completely finished.' Finally an octagonal card table, the top covered in needlework, which Bradburn invoiced in 1767 as a

---

[1] Information relating to Bradburn's work for the Crown, especially at Buckingham House, is taken from H. Clifford-Smith, *Buckingham Palace*, 1930.

CABINET-MAKERS WORKING IN THE *DIRECTOR* TRADITION

'mahogany octagon pillar and claw table neatly carved . . . needlework in being', has been recognised at Kew Palace.[1]

John Bradburn, however, did not only work for the Crown. In July 1764, we find him with a partner, William France, employed by Sir Lawrence Dundas, Bart., at his London house, 19 Arlington Street, and at Moor Park, his house in Hertfordshire (see also under S. Norman, pp. 142–5). Robert Adam was advising Sir Lawrence on both these important projects. Bradburn must have formed this partnership with France between 3rd May and 13th July of that year, because two accounts[2] are extant from William France to Sir Lawrence for work carried out at Arlington Street and Moor Park which are still invoiced by William France alone. They are dated 16th April and 3rd May respectively. A third account, dated 13th July, on the other hand, is headed 'to Wm France and Jno Bradburn'. This is further born out by the wording of a synopsis of the three accounts which is as follows :

'D^r . . . Sir Lawrence Dundas Bart., with William France . . .C^r

1764			£	s.	d.
April	To Household Furniture for the house in Arlington Street as per acco^nt of Particulars — No. 1.		263	5	6¾
,,	To Household Furniture for Moorpark as per acco^nt of Particulars — No. 2		847	16	8
,,	To ditto furnish'd to Arlington Street and Moorpark as per acco^nt of Particulars — No. 3		990	12	11½
			2,101	15	2¼.'

The *Particulars* of the three accounts referred to in the above are in detailed form and are contained in three bound manuscript note books.[2] Some of the entries are listed in Appendix B and many of them refer to *Upholders'* or *Upholsterers'* work.

Two important entries are included in account no. 3 relating to a pair of console tables :

1765		£	s.	d.
Jany 12th	For a Circular Frame, for a Marble Table, richly carv'd with rams heads, at Top, and Husks falling down the 3 shaped Legs, and gilt in burnished gold and puting up the above.	37	10	–
	For cutting the Carpett in the blue drawing Room, to fitt the Pedestal of the above Table.		1	6
Decr 30th	For a circular Frame for a Marble Table, Richly Carved with Rams heads, and husks falling, as the one in the Blue drawing Room, and putting up D^o Screws etc.	37	10	0.'

These tables were executed from a design of Robert Adam's,[3] dated 1765, and the design is described in Adam's account of 18th July, 1765, as '. . . a Table Frame for Long Room next the Eating Parlour £5. 5. 0.'. It has therefore been shown that France and Bradburn were, in this instance, working from one of Adam's designs. The tables (Pl. 393) were sold by Christie's in April 1934 when they offered some of the furniture from 19 Arlington Street. A pair of giltwood-framed girandoles,[4] which now hang on the gallery

---

[1] *G.C-M.*, p. 62, pl. 87.

[2] See p. 143, n. 3.

[3] Ill. *Apollo*, September 1967, p. 214, fig. 2.

[4] *Ibid.*, p. 217, fig. 4.

walls at Aske, near Richmond in Yorkshire, the Marquess of Zetland's seat, may be related to the pair which France and Bradburn made for Arlington Street in 1764 for £56. 12. 0., and which they invoiced as '2 elegant carved Girandoles with a large plate of Glass, and 3 lights in each to shew in the Glass, festoons, and drops of husks falling from Different parts all gilt in burnished gold'.

William France, who is recorded as working for George III at Buckingham House as early as 1765, was an important cabinet-maker, and his partnership with Bradburn, which has not hitherto been recorded, must have been mutually beneficial to both parties. In March 1765, they were both employed by John Chute, Horace Walpole's friend, at the Vyne, near Basingstoke in Hampshire. This business was probably introduced by Bradburn, as Vile and Cobb had been supplying furniture to the Vyne in 1752–3 (see p. 27 and p. 43) for Anthony Chute, John's brother, and it would be reasonable to suppose that they recommended their late pupil and assistant to John Chute. It is also possible that Bradburn may have been working there for Vile in 1752 and, as a result of this, established himself in the eyes of the Chutes as the inheritor of his Master's mantle.[1]

France and Bradburn's accounts[2] for The Vyne are bound in a paper book without a cover, the front of which has been annotated in 1884 as follows 'the bill must have been chiefly for the London House in Charles Street, but the hangings and mirrors were probably moved to the Vyne'. This statement should have been elaborated as there are certain pieces at the Vyne which can be related to their descriptions in the bills. Perhaps the most important of these is a set of mahogany seat furniture consisting of five settees, six open armchairs and seven single chairs (Pl. 390). The mahogany frames are carved with blind fret ornamentation, foliage and rosettes and the seat rails and chamfered supports are united by scrolled brackets.[1] Some of the set are invoiced as :

'For a very large sopha with mahoy carved feet, and brackets, on stout castors stuffed in canvas, and best curled hair compleatly with 3 large cushions and bolsters	£13. 16. 0.
For covering the sopha above with your own damask, the 3 large cushions and 2 bolsters seperate corder'd . . .	2. 3. 0.
For 2 more sophas of a smaller size	13. 10. 0.
For 8 armed chairs with mahoy feet and brackets on castors . . .	36. 0. 0.'

France and Bradburn also supplied a fine pair of semi-circular side-tables (Pl. 391) which cost £11 the pair, the account reading 'for 2 mahoy half circle sidebord tables with gudroon edges and carved fronts'. Four oak hall chairs also remain in the Ante-Room to the Chapel; these have pierced vase-shaped splats painted with the Chute crest, and can be related to the partners' entry in their account, 'for 6 wainsc't hall chairs made very stout with open backs . . . at £15. 4. 10.'.[3] Finally, it is interesting to see that they were prepared to provide 'a shed in the yard for hens' — an eighteenth-century cabinet-maker had to be a jack-of-all-trades!

---

[1] Bradburn and France's work at the Vyne was discussed by the author in '18th Century Furniture at The Vyne', *Country Life*, 25 July 1963 — Some of the text is quoted here, and I am grateful for permission to do this.

[2] Accounts loaned to the Hampshire record office by Captain A. V. Chute.

[3] Coleridge, '18th Century Furniture at The Vyne', *loc. cit.*, pl. 7.

Bradburn appears to have retired in 1777 and William Gates was appointed Cabinet-Maker to the Crown in his place, in July of that year. In his will, of 19th August, 1780, Bradburn is described as of 'the parish of Wandsworth . . . gentleman'.[1]

There are certain discrepancies over the date of William France's death. The Dundas accounts are all clearly signed by William France, and witnessed, on 3rd January, 1767. In France and Bradburn's accounts for work carried out at The Vyne between 1765 and 1767, on the other hand, the first page of their long account is headed 'John Chute Esqr. . . . To John Bradburne and the Executors of the late Mr. Wm. France'. However, in his account to Lord Mansfield,[2] covering the period of 11th November, 1768, to 4th December, 1770, the last page is headed (as is the first), 'The Right Honble. Lord Mansfield . . . To Wm. France'. It is, however, receipted, 'Received March 4th 1771 of the Right Honble. Lord Mansfield the full contents of this Bill and all Demands for Mr. France . . .pr. Mr. Edwd France.' It would appear from the wording of the receipt that Edward France, who was presumably a relation of William's, perhaps his son, had signed it in his father's absence, and it is here suggested that William may have died earlier on, that is, between his receipting of the Dundas accounts in January 1767 and the presentation of the Chute accounts later in the year, in which case it would seem that Edward carried on the business in William's name, until he went into partnership with Samuel Beckwith. The earliest reference to this later partnership, to my knowledge, is given in the list of cabinet-makers at the end of *Sheraton's Drawing Book*, 1791, where they are listed as 'France and Beckwith'. The latter is mentioned in the Royal accounts, for he also worked for the Crown, as early as 1784. It is thus suggested that William France died during 1767 and that much of the furniture that has hitherto been attributed to him was, in fact, made by Edward France, who, for some years, carried on business under William's name.

The account from William France's firm to the Earl of Mansfield is long, and most of the entries are for furniture in the neo-classical style, often made to Robert Adam's design, which are beyond the scope of this book.[3] However some of the furniture is in the *Director* style, and a reading stand (Pl. 392) for which he charged £6. 14. 0. on 4th December, 1770, could be dated stylistically to nearer 1760. Its carved tripod support and scrolled feet are similar to a design for 'Reading or Music Desks' in Ince and Mayhew's *The Universal System of Household Furniture*, 1759–62, pl. 26.[4] The reading stand is invoiced in France's account as 'For the Library at Kenwood — For a large Mahogany Reading Stand on a stout Pillar and Claw, with a screw nutt, work'd very true, capable of screwing to rise 10 inches if required, the whole of very Good mahogany, and the pillar and claw richly carv'd'.[5] A pair of firescreens, in a rather ponderous version of the rococo style, cost £11. 16. 0. and were also delivered for the Library in 1770. They are invoiced as '2 very

---

[1] *G.C-M.*, p. 62.

[2] In The Victoria and Albert Museum.

[3] See the Appendix, *G.C-M.*, p. 119, for extracts from France's account to the Earl of Mansfield, headed 'The underwritten articles are what I perform'd from Mr. Adam's designs'. See also C. Musgrave, *Adam and Hepplewhite Furniture*, 1965, pp. 78, 116.

[4] P. Ward-Jackson, *English Furniture Designs of the Eighteenth Century*, pl. 156.

[5] I am indebted to the late Mr. Alister Campbell and Miss Elizabeth Johnston, late Curator and the Assistant Curator of the Iveagh Bequest, Kenwood, for typescripts of these France accounts.

elegant screens richly carved and Gilded on 2 Mahogany poles, with Pine Apples at the Top Gilded and the pillars and claws richly carv'd and Gilded, as also the ornaments round the Screen Parts very perfectly carv'd in Good shapes and well Gilded . . . at £5. 18. each. . . . Covering the Screen Parts with White Cloth and fine Elephant Paper & Your own India-Damask after, and papering up the Damask carefully to defend from Gold, size & etc. . . . 11/6.' One of these is illustrated in *the Dictionary of English Furniture*, Vol. III, figure 22, p. 63. The remainder of the account, apart from the entries relating to furniture of neo-classical design, largely refers to curtains and bedding, which would have been supplied by the upholsterer's department in the firm.

It has already been shown (pp. 56–7) how France provided the frames for the pier-glasses in the Library, which he had carved to Adam's designs and which were to hold the mirror-plates imported by Thomas Chippendale from Paris. Lord Mansfield had paid France £170, on 25th August, 1769, by a draft on Messrs. Hoare and Co. 'to be paid to Thos. Chippendale on account of an agreement enter'd into by him with Robert Adam Esqr. and in case the said Mr. Chippendale shall not within three months deliver all ye Glass pursuant to his Agreement in good Condition, I do engage that the said Mr. Chippendale shall upon Demand repay ye said sum of £170. 0. 0. or in Case of any neglect on his part, I hereby promise to pay ye Same to his Lordship' — signed Wm. France. The glass was safely delivered and the younger Thomas Chippendale and Mr. France signed the receipt.

Beckwith and France continued to supply fine furniture to the Crown and other influential clients, such as the Earl of Verulam, from their premises at No. 101, St. Martin's Lane, throughout the neo-classical period — indeed until 1803.[1]

WILLIAM LINNELL AND JOHN LINNELL
Fl. about 1730–63

It is not known whether the Linnell, whose name is amongst the members of the Academy of Painting and Sculpture established in St. Martin's Lane in 1720,[2] and who was described as being an excellent carver in wood,[3] is identical with William Linnell, carver, cabinet-maker and upholsterer of No. 28 Berkeley Square. William Linnell appears to have opened his premises in Berkeley Square in about 1730, and it was from this address that he sent accounts to Sir Richard Hoare of Barn Elms, dated between 1739 and 1752. These total to nearly £1,100, and include, in 1739, such entries as 12s. 'ffor Carving a Large flower for ye bed', and £8. 10. 0. 'ffor carving ye two Large Drops of fruit and flowers betwene ye windows'. In the same year he charged £13. 12. 0. 'ffor makinge and Carving a pair of half length picture frams very neatly Carvd with a Venus

---

[1] For details of this later period see *G.C-M.*, p. 82.
[2] *G.C-M.*, pp. 75, 78.
[3] W. H. Pyne, *Wine and Walnuts*, 1824, Vol. I, p. 77.

head and feathers at top and foulidge on each side, foulidge at Bottom and a Duble french shell in ye middle drops of frute and flowers all down ye sides . . . & Kea frett in ye sandinge'.[1]

Sir William Lea of Hartwell must have been one of Linnell's clients for in May 1754, he is recorded as having 'Paid Linnell for a glass and frame for ye back parlour and a picture for ye chimney in ye fore parlour and 3 brackets, £62. 2. 0.'.[1] Mrs. Montagu, while decorating a Chinese room in Hill Street in 1752, wrote to her cousin, Gilbert West, as follows : 'If Mr. Linnell designs to gild the bird he sent me in a drawing . . . it will look like the sign of an eagle at a laceman's door. If japanned in proper colours, it will resemble a bird only in colour, for in shape it is like a horse.' Later in the year, in another letter, she is disturbed by Linnell's high costs and ends, '. . . . if you will proceed in spite of my sad and woeful example, I cannot help it'.[1]

Most of his work for Sir Richard Hoare was of a carved nature, but, between 1749 and 1758, in a series of accounts to Mr. William Drake of Shardeloes in Buckinghamshire, he charges for work relating to all branches of the cabinet-making trade.[2] There are eight different accounts extant, all from William Linnel to 'The Hon[ble.] Wm. Drake Esq.' with the exception of the last which is from 'Mary Linnell Administeratrix of Wm. Linnell'. The last entry on this account is dated 11th February, 1763, which must be the year in which William died. He is still listed as 'William Linnell, carver in Mortimer's *Universal Director* which appeared in that very year, so he must have died shortly after its publication. In fact he probably died in March or April as, in *The Public Advertiser* for May 1763, there is a notice stating that his 'large and genuine stock in trade at his late House and Ware rooms in Berkeley Square' was to be auctioned. It consisted of 'magnificent large Pier and other glasses, large library bookcases and writing tables, elegant carved Terms, Brackets and girandoles, Hall and other Lanthorns, Large Sienna, Derbyshire and Italian marble tables, mahogany chairs and settees, Dressing, Dining and card tables, commodes, Clothes Presses and a variety of other cabinet work in mahogany etc.'[1]

His accounts to William Drake include 'pier and other glasses'. Thus on 13th March, 1749, he charged Drake £10. 0. 0. for '2 ovall glass frames. Comp[l] : fix[d] : up & painted'. Pier-glasses for the Drawing-Room cost £41. 4. 6. and he charged £10. 10. 0. for 'carving and Japanning a pr. of figures for D[o].'. 'Woodwork for 4 Picture frame[s]' cost £10. 0. 0. and 'carving and Gilding of same . . . £80. 0. 0.'. He also provided drawings for his frames as can be seen from an entry to '6 Half Length picture frame[s] comp[t]. [accompanied] by Drawing at £5. 10. 0. . . . £33. 0. 0.' He appears to have hired out marble tables, as he charged 1/6 for '2 mon. [month] Marble table' and a further £1. 5. 0.' for new pollishing of table'. Somebody must have damaged it very seriously. In the same year '136 yds. $\frac{1}{2}$ of Carpett at 5/6' cost £36. 19. 9., and £2. 5. 0. was charged 'to Painting 6 Hall Chairs w[t] ye Crest etc.'. In October 1754 'a 4 post Doom Canopy bedstead on Castor[s] with vase at Cornor' was invoiced for £18. 6. 9. : 'a thick check mattress' costing £2. 2. 0. and a 'Holland quilt to D[o].' £1. 16. 6. In the following December he delivered to Shardeloes '2 mahoy elbow chairs on castors ye same Coverd

---

[1] See p. 150, n. 2.
[2] Buckinghamshire Record Office D/DR/5/31 and 34.

with Damask . . . guilded & Duble burnish^d. nails . . .' at a cost of £7. 15. 6. However he had not been paid by November 1761, for the account for that year opens with the entry 'Due on Bills Deliver'd . . . £19. 6. 1½.'. This was his last account, presented by Mary Linnell, after his death.

It was probably settled soon after its presentation, because John Linnell (pp. 68–9), William's 'natural and lawful son',[1] who carried on the business from Berkeley Square after the auction, began to provide furniture and upholstery for Shardeloes in the same year. John's account had risen to £1,056 by the end of 1768, and Drake, thinking that he had been over-charged, ordered a cabinet-maker named Wicksted to make an independent valuation of the items that Linnell had supplied. While discussing the question of this arbitration, the authors of *Georgian Cabinet-Makers*[2] write 'in a letter from Linnell to Drake in that year [1768] he begs for a settlement and speaks of the great loss he had suffered by his foreman's mistake "in the expense of the man coming down, the materials wasted and Damask spoiled which I shall allow you for the same at cost". "I flatter myself," he continues, "you will not be offended at my requesting you'll take this into consideration and that your settling this account at this juncture (as I am in great need of money) will in some measure eleveate [sic] the loss I shall sustain." ' Mr. Drake appears to have expected unlimited credit from the craftsmen whom he patronised. John Linnell's designs have already been discussed (pp. 68–9), and the remainder of his career, he died in 1796, is beyond the scope of this book.

An account from John Linnell to Lord Harrowby, dated 1762, is recorded as a ledger entry and it reads, 'To Linnel for a mahogany bottle stand and a dumb-waiter . . . £4. 0. 0.'.[3]

GEORGE SEDDON

1727–1801

George Seddon, who was a cabinet-maker of the greatest importance, and also a businessman of the highest acumen, had a full and active career which spanned the second half of the eighteenth century. The busiest, or at any rate the more fully documented, years of his business life — 1770–1800 — largely fall beyond the period covered by this book. These notes should, therefore, be read in conjunction with the description of his life in *Georgian Cabinet-Makers*,[4] and with what Mr. Musgrave has to say about Seddon in his book on Adam and Hepplewhite in the present series.

George Seddon, who was born in 1727, was the son of John Seddon of Blakelea in Lancashire. He was apprenticed in 1743 to a certain G. Clemapon, a cabinet-maker of Mugwell Street, Cripplegate, and a premium of £16 was paid for his indenture — a moderate

---

[1] See P. A. Kirkham, 'The Careers of William and John Linnell', *Journal of the Furniture History Society*, vol. iii, 1967 — important new information is published here, including a list of many of their clients.
[2] *G.C-M.*, p. 77.
[3] Letter no. 330, Harrowby MS. : This reference was kindly supplied to me by Mr. Geoffrey Beard.
[4] *G.C-M.*, p. 79.

premium at the time. He set up in business on his own account in about 1760[1-3] at London House in Aldersgate Street. He was a subscriber to the first edition of Thomas Chippendale's *Director* which was published in 1754. In the *Annual Register* for 1768 there appears the following notice : 'A dreadful fire burnt down London House, formerley the residence of the Bishops of London, now occupied by Mr. Seddon, one of the most eminent of cabinet-makers of London. The damage is computed at £20,000'. There is another interesting description of London House and its history after it had been purchased by Seddon in *Londinium Redivivum*[2] — poor Seddon seems to have been a 'bad fire risk'. 'In 1749 Parliament granted permission to Bishop Sherlock and his successors, to convey the premises for 40 years, on a building lease, or to demise or sell the place, for the benefit of the See. It was divided into tenements and warehouses before that time; and in or about 1768,[3] Mr. Seddon, the eminent cabinet-maker obtained possession. The family have witnessed three dreadful instances of domestic calamity in London House, and all by fire. The first consumed the whole of the premises and stock, which were uninsured. Mr. Seddon rebuilt the house, on a place convenient and elegant; but it was burnt a second time in 1783 when a great number of adjoining buildings were destroyed. The third, and I sincerely hope the last, conflagration, happened within the present most respectable London House; which for . . . simplicity, and the beautiful specimens of mechanic art, contained in the warerooms, deserved particular notice from the stranger, whose sympathy must be excited by the recollection that Miss Seddon's cloaths accidently caught fire, by which melancholy casualty she was burnt to death.'

Seddon must have been successful at an early age for, taking Thomas Seddon's view,[1] he could have only been in business for eighteen years at the time of the fire, and more likely only for about eight,[3] and yet, at this time, 1768, his stock was valued at £20,000. It was apparently uninsured, but, undeterred, he rebuilt his premises, only to suffer the second fire in 1783. Three years later, however, his business was operating at full capacity once again, for it is fully described in the diary[4] of a young German lady, Sophie von la Roche, who visited his warehouse in 1786. This is quoted in full because, although it describes the state of his business some twenty years later than the period generally covered by this book, it is one of the most illuminating descriptions of a cabinet-maker's premises penned during the eighteenth century. 'We drove first to Mr. Seddon's. . . . He employs four hundred apprentices (journeymen and apprentices) on any work connected with the making of household furniture — joiners, carvers, gilders, mirror-workers, upholsterers, girdlers — who mould the bronze into graceful patterns — and locksmiths. All these are housed in a building with six wings. In the basement mirrors are cast and cut. Some other department contains nothing but chairs, sofas and stools of every description, some quite simple, others exquisitely carved and made of all varieties of wood,

---

[1] In *Memoir of Thomas Seddon*, the artist, a great grandson of George; the date of his start in independent business is given as about 1750.

[2] J. P. Malcolm, *Londinium Redivivum*, 4V, 1803–7, 11, 1803, p. 544

[3] There is an obvious discrepancy here between the date given by Thomas Seddon (n. 1.), about 1750, and the date of 1763 quoted by J. P. Malcolm, *op. cit.* The earliest recorded entry relating to Seddon in the *London Directories*, is for 1763 when his address is given as No. 158, Aldersgate Street. It is suggested here that a date somewhere between the two may be the correct one.

[4] *Sophie in London* (1788), translated from the German by Clare Williams, 1933, pp. 173–5.

and one large room is full up with all the finished articles in this line, while others are occupied by writing tables, cupboards, chests of drawers, charmingly fashioned desks, chests both large and small, work- and toilet-tables in all manner of wood and patterns, from the simplest and cheapest to the most elegant and expensive.' Sophie von la Roche described Seddon as a man 'with an understanding of the requirements of the needy and luxurious, knowing how to satisfy them from the products of nature and the artistry of manufacture'. She also asserts 'that he is for ever creating new forms'.[1]

One of these 'new forms' is probably referred to in the wording on the firm's trade label which was found on a rather ordinary piece of late eighteenth-century furniture. It reads : 'Blackstone : Some account of the different uses of this piece of furniture, containing trays for papers, drawings, prints, bills, letters etc. and serving as a table etc. (called a Croft, from the gentleman who first directed them to be made for the papers of his dictionary, as a portable desk is called a Blackstone). Manufactured and sold by Messrs. Seddon, Sons and Shackleton, Aldersgate Street, London.'[2]

George Seddon took his son-in-law into the business in 1790 and the firm became Seddon, Sons and Shackleton — his sons George and Thomas had joined him at an earlier date. George Seddon, senior, who had been elected to the livery of the Joiners Company in 1757, was master in 1795. He died in his house at Hampstead in 1801.[3]

An unpublished account from George Seddon to a Mr. Charles Long, which is in the Ipswich and East Suffolk Record Office, is quoted here as accounts from his firm, at this early date, 1766, are rare :

'Charles Long Esq.

Bt. of Geo Seddon

		£	s	d
1766				
June 10th	1 large Mahogany Sideboard fine Wood	4	10	0
	Matt & battening		3	0
		£4	13	0

Rec^d then the contents in full for Mr Seddon

S. Oldfield.'

THE FIRM OF GILLOW OF LANCASTER
During the period circa *1730-70*

This celebrated firm was founded by Robert Gillow (1703–73) in about 1730, after he had been made free of the Borough of Lancaster in 1727. Robert's eldest son, Richard, was taken into partnership in 1757, and in 1776 another son, also named Robert, went to London in order to run the branch of the firm at 176 Oxford Road (now Street). In 1790

[1] See p. 152, n. 3.　　　[2] Discussed by Sir Ambrose Heal, *Country Life*, 17 January 1947.
[3] Sir Ambrose Heal, 'The Firm of Seddon', *Country Life*, 20 January 1934; and Ralph Edwards, 'A Great Georgian Cabinet-Maker', *Country Life*, October 21, 1933.

the firm was styled *Robert Gillows and Company* and in 1811 *G. and R. Gillow and Company*. A few years later, in 1817, the family of Gillow ceased to be connected with the firm, which is, of course, still trading under the name of *Waring and Gillow*. As in the case of George Seddon's firm, the majority of the extant examples of furniture made by the firm of Gillow date from after the period under discussion in this book. This applied also to many of the references to the firm in the literature of the period. Therefore, once again, these notes should be read in conjunction with *Georgian Cabinet-Makers*.[1] It should be mentioned here that it was the custom of the firm to stamp its products *Gillows, Lancaster*, and thus many pieces have been recognised. The majority of these, however, date from the neo-classical and Regency periods.

The firm's *Cost Books* have been retained from an early date and often, during the latter half of the eighteenth century, the clerk, who kept these books, inserted a sketch of the piece that he was invoicing on the appropriate page. As the headquarters of the firm was in Lancaster, many of its important clients are found to be from the North. Amongst these were The Earl of Strafford at Wentworth Castle; Sir Henry Hoghton; Mr. Fawkes of Farnley Hall, Yorkshire; The Earl of Derby; John Christian of Workington Hall, Cumberland; and the Duke of Atholl, who, between 1805 and 1807, bought furniture for Castle Mona, Isle of Man, and for Dunkeld House, Perthshire.[2] However, they also had many clients in the South, doubtless served by the Oxford Street branch of the firm, and amongst these was Mrs. Piozzi, who, after her marriage in 1784, employed Gillow's firm to refurnish Streatham Park 'in modern style, supremely elegant, but not expensive'.[3] Another client must have been Lord Clifford of Ugbrooke Park, Chudleigh, Devon, who, in about 1765, bought the bookcase illustrated in Pl. 394, which is stamped by the firm. It is a superb example of its type and has many details similar to those in examples illustrated in the third edition of the *Director* (1762). At the same time the two flanking doors in the lower section are decorated with oval panels clasped by scrolls of acanthus — a feature so often thought to identify the work of William Vile (cf. Pls. 3, 9, 12, 13).

Robert Gillow also had an eye for foreign markets and 'among the list of goods exported by Robert Gillow and other merchants to Riga in 1742 are a mahogany dressing chest and a *snap table*'.[4] The firm also had a considerable trade with the West Indies, and, in 1748, Robert Gillow writes to a correspondent with reference to a shipment to those Islands[4] that he 'should esteem it a particular favour if you can engage any orders in my wooden way'.[5] The firm's furniture was at first sent to London by sea and these shipments are rather significantly listed in the firm's books under the heading 'Adventure to London'.[4] Robert Gillow had always been in close touch with the London trade, and in about 1765 the premises in Oxford Street were erected. In a letter of 1760[5] Gillow asked for 'Chippendale's additional number' — presumably in reference to the second edition of the *Director*, and in another letter he reminds his cousin James Gillow that 'a few sketches of fashionable and other things would be very acceptable'.[4]

---

[1] *G.C-M.*, pp. 84–6.
[2] Anthony Coleridge, 'The Firm of Gillow and Co. at Blair Castle', *Connoisseur*, October 1964.
[3] *G.C-M.*, p. 85.
[4] Quoted *G.C-M.*, pp. 84–5.
[5] Gillow Letter Books.

Robert Gillow, who died in 1773, is thus shown as another *master* cabinet-maker, who, as with Chippendale and Seddon, combined business acumen, technical ability and, most important of all, boundless drive and energy.[1]

WILLIAM MASTERS
fl. 1740–60

William Masters[2] styles himself on his billhead (Pl. 395), *Upholder, Appraiser and Undertaker* and his premises, in 1749, were at 'The Golden Fleece, Coventry Street, Piccadilly' A William Masters is recorded[3] as having premises in Princes Street off Wardour Street, in the same year, and it is probable that both entries refer to the same man who may well have had two places of business. It is also interesting to note that a Charles Masters, according to the records of one of the Insurance Companies, was at the sign of 'The Eagle and Child' at Ditch Side, near Holborn Bridge in 1725. If this was a relation it would seem that the Masters family, as was so often the case, were practising as cabinet-makers and upholders for several generations.

At the time of writing only one of William Masters' clients has been discovered, but he must have had many more, if the volume of work that he carried out for the Duke of Atholl at Blair Castle is a fair indication of the scale of business that he was able to undertake and successfully carry out. Twenty bills are preserved at Blair Castle, Perthshire, from Masters to the second Duke of Atholl.[4] Masters was chiefly responsible for the refurnishing and decoration of the State Rooms at Blair Castle, or Atholl House as it was then called. The accounts cover the period 1740–60 and total about £4,700, a substantial sum largely accounted for by soft furnishings like curtains, carpets and linen.

Some of the entries in his first account (Pl. 395) illustrate the care with which furniture was packed for transportation and how high high the charges were for freight and packing :

'To 12 large packing cases . . .   £11. 3. 9.
To labour in packing up the above goods . . .   £0. 14. 0
To battons used for the inside of the cases to secure the goods   £0. 4. 0 '

We are lucky in being able to recognise, with a reasonable degree of certainty, some of Masters' work. For instance, in the Entrance Hall of the Castle is a mahogany hall table (Pl. 396) which supports an impressive granite slab. This can probably be related to Masters' account of 10th May, 1749, which refers to 'a large mahogany frame for a slab with shaped feet and a leaf on the knees . . . £2. 15. 0.'. There is also a set of twelve oak hall chairs, in the same room, with waisted backs and shaped seats and supports (Pl. 397)

---

[1] For further literature on the firm of Gillow see : 'A Record of Two Centuries, 1901'; Gillow B. Shaw, 'Gillows of Lancaster', *Country Life*, Vol. 102, 1947, p. 430; C. Musgrave, *Adam and Hepplewhite Furniture*, London, 1966.

[2] *London Furniture Makers*, p. 113.

[3] The notes here on William Masters are based on an article by the author, entitled 'William Masters and Some Early Eighteenth Century Furniture at Blair Castle', published in the *Connoisseur*, October 1963.

[4] Succeeded in 1724 and died in 1764.

which were delivered by Masters in 1751. They were painted in colour with the Atholl crests, motto and Ducal coronet in 1752 by a certain Sam Cobb, who was paid for his work in 1759. His account, which totalled £4. 10. 0., is worded as follows: 'for painting one dos of hall chairs with crests, coronetts, gartars and stars 7/6d. each.'.

An octagonal mahogany tea-table (Pl. 398), which was made by Masters in 1755, is of unusual design and the legs of its open tripod-shaped support are carved at the knees with acanthus foliage. Masters charged £3 on 20th February, 1756, for '2 mahogany candle-stands with openwork tops and fluted pillows ribb'd . . .' and these also still remain in the Castle (Pl. 399). They are extremely elegant, with fretted octagonal tops, and the unusual combination of fluting and spiral-and-baluster turning that has been employed on their stems is noteworthy.

A pair of dumb-waiters in the State Dining-Room (Pl. 400) cost £4. 4. 0. and Masters invoiced them in his account of 4th April, 1753, as 'to 2 mahogany dumb waiters, the bottom boards 30"'. There is also a heavy mahogany rectangular side-table in the Tapestry Room (Pl. 401), the frieze of which is carved with a key-fret pattern, much in the tradition of the 'sideboard tables' shown in plates 56–9 of the third edition of Chippendale's *Director*, 1762.

There are finally four chests of drawers in the Castle (Pl. 402), which form a set, and each contains four drawers — the top one divided into compartments in the usual way and with a baize-lined slide. There is an entry in Masters' account of February 1756, which may well apply to one, or indeed all, of these chests. It reads 'to a mahogany commode with furniture drawer framed back and the best wrought brass work, 3'6" wide . . . £8. 10. 0.' Other pieces in the Castle can also be attributed to Masters,[1] and amongst them are a large set of mahogany framed seat-furniture, both chairs and stools, which are carved with blind-fret ornamentation. It has thus been shown that Masters was capable of producing furniture of a high and uniform quality and, with his upholding and interior decorating business as a second string to his bow, he must have been looked upon as a man of substance by friends and rivals alike.

GEORGE SANDEMAN OF PERTH
1724-1803

George Sandeman, cabinet-maker (Pl. 403), was born in 1724,[2] and on 27th June, 1747, he joined the Wrights Incorporation of Perth as an apprentice wright. He married in 1747 Jane Duncan of 'Seaside', probably in the village of Errol, and two years later in 1749 we find him in London at the age of twenty-five.[3] During this time he was presumably gaining

[1] See p. 156, n. 3.

[2] These notes were first published in the *Connoisseur* by the author in an article entitled 'George Sandeman of Perth: Cabinet-Maker', March 1960.

[3] Sandeman's letters are in the possession of Mr. Robert Waterston.

experience with one of the leading London cabinet-makers after having completed his apprenticeship in Scotland. Anyway, this visit to London, of however short or long a duration, was of vital importance to him, because he returned to Scotland imbued with the fine traditions of the leading craftsmanship of the time. He died, in 1803, at Perth.[1]

Very little more is known of his life, but some interesting sidelights are thrown on his character by his letters to his daughter, Katharine.[2] In a letter of 11th April, 1789, he complains about dull trade and intends to draw in his horns. He continues, 'I am determined not to meddle with the country business except at Dupplin,[3] being not only near at hand but of certain payment within the year.' He then continues by saying that he is thinking of selling up his business and dividing the proceeds amongst his family, but he is dissuaded from this by his wife who thinks it will be injurious to his health. He was obviously, therefore, still in trade when he was an old man.

He had six children, and David George, of Springfield,[4] Perth, the eldest son, born in 1757, may have inherited the family home. No other mention of an estate belonging to George Sandeman has yet been traced, but family tradition claims that he had business premises in Perth and a country house and saw-mill outside the city. According to *Penny's Traditions of Perth* he was, in 1784, 'at the head of his trade and was a most industrious cabinet maker, very different from the prevalent type of wright. He possessed property in the Watergate[5] . . . and also had a saw-mill on Annaty-burn,[4] opposite the white dyke, and enjoyed the patronage of many of the country gentlemen and genteel families in the town.'[6]

Apart from a set of laburnumwood chairs,[7] at present the only known examples of his work are at Blair Castle in Perthshire. These are of special interest because they are veneered with small strips of broomwood which have been cut from the common broom. Obviously, on account of the size and nature of these bushes, the strips of veneer are extremely small, but this apparent drawback has been cleverly utilised, because the dark grained strips of veneer, not unlike zebra wood in colour, have been laid to form attractive geometric patterns.

It is fortunate that two of George Sandeman's original accounts have been preserved.[8] One of these, dated 1770, enumerates furniture of a normal nature such as a gilt pier-glass, three mahogany chests of drawers and six mahogany basin stands, and also some billiard masts and cues.[9] The other, dated 1758, is for a bureau bookcase (Pl. 404) veneered in broomwood which James Murray,[10] to whom it was delivered, endorsed on the outer face of the bill as a 'Plantaginet Cabinet'. This was doubtless so named because the broom is

---

[1] The *Scots Magazine*, Vol. LXV, p. 363; May 1803, under *Deaths* — 'At Perth, Mr. George Sandeman, aged 79. His relict and he were married 56 years nearly.'

[2] See p. 157, n. 3.

[3] Dupplin Castle, Perthshire, was the seat of the Earls of Kinnoull.

[4] As Annaty-burn runs through Scone, a few miles from Perth, it is possible that Springfield, which is also in Scone, may have been his home.

[5] The Watergate is one of the oldest streets in the centre of Perth.

[6] I am indebted to Mr. A. S. Tait, A.L.A., Perth City Librarian, for much of the above information.

[7] In the collection of his descendant, Mr. Robert Waterston of Edinburgh.

[8] Blair Castle archives.

[9] None of these can now be identified.

[10] James Murray, 1734–94, was the son of Lord George Murray, the famous Jacobite General.

sometimes called the *planta genista* — and was incidentally the badge of the House of Plantagenet. The broom is also the badge of the Murrays and this explains why the Dukes of Atholl, whose family name is Murray, commissioned Sandeman to make furniture in this unusual wood. The bureau interior (Pl. 405) is lined with mahogany and the pigeon-holes are centred by a mirror-glass panel painted with flowers which is *en suite* with two others hanging elsewhere in the Castle. The account for the bureau-bookcase, dated 26th September, 1758, which is of extreme interest, is reproduced in detail below.

'Note of prime coast of a Desk and Bookcase veneered with Broom for The Hon. John Murray Esquire —

To David Stewart, 64 days at 1/4	£4.	5. 4.
To Andrew Anderson, 42 days at 1/2.	2.	9. 7.
To Andrew Bissett, 39 days at 1/2.	2.	5. 6.
To James Drummond, 16 days at 12d.	—	16. 0.
To John Crerar, 34½ days at 12d.	1.	14. 6.
To James Shoolbread, 15 days at 10d.	—	12. 6.

$$\text{£12. 3. 5.}$$

To locks, brasses, hinges, etc.	1.	5. 6.
To Sundries green cloath	—	12. 6.
To Glew 8/2, Oil 10d., fir and rushes 3/6	—	12. 6.
To Sundries wainscot	1.	19. 6.
To Fir 4/4, Walnuttree 9/6	—	13. 9.
To Mahogany 4/2, 2 glasses 3/6	—	9. 8.
To Sundries 2d., and etc. 4d.	—	— 6.

$$\text{£17. 12. 9.}$$

To 2 packing cases and packing	1.	3. 9.

$$\text{£18. 15. 8.}$$

To glazing	—	15. —

$$\text{£19. 10. 8.}$$

Atholl House, 26th September 1758'

It is probable that the other pieces of Broomwood furniture at Blair Castle, for which the bills are no longer extant, were also delivered by Sandeman, as it hardly seems credible that there should have been more than one craftsman making furniture in such an unusual medium at the same time and place.

The other pieces include a medal cabinet (Pl. 406) veneered in broomwood and of Palladian inspiration. It is fashioned as a Roman Temple with Ionic columns and has a cube tesselated pavement and starred ceiling. The facade pulls forward on runners to reveal a mahogany interior with tiers of numerous small drawers lined with baize. The pediment is surmounted by three small seventeenth-century ivory statuettes, probably of Venus, Neptune and a Satyr; these may have come from a Renaissance cabinet and were probably given to Sandeman to incorporate in his work. The account for this is lost, but there is a bill from James Cullen, dated 1771, in the sum of £1. 19. 6. for 'polishing and repairing and fixing a new lock and key to a Temple Cabinet', so it must have been delivered prior to that date.

Another account for 5s. 6d. was sent in the same year by John McInnes for 'repairs to four Broom card tables, and a fire screen, glazing and etc.'. Two of the four card tables remain and are of rectagular form with square tapered legs and block feet, they probably date from between 1760 to 1770. The pole screen has also survived, although extensively restored, and from its carved tripod support can be dated to about 1750.

The collection is completed by a set of four small circular tables, 17½″ diameter, which are banded in rosewood and have the triangular cusped platforms of the Regency period. As Sandemand died in 1803, they must have been almost his last achievement, unless his firm completed them after his death, or one of his competitors was commissioned to use this strange wood.

JAMES CULLEN

By careful study of the archives[1] at Hopetoun House, West Lothian, the seat of the Marquess of Linlithgow, it has been possible to resurrect from obscurity another mid-eighteenth-century cabinet-maker of the first flight, who must have rivalled in importance Chippendale, Vile and Cobb, Ince and Mayhew and the other leading firms of the period. Only three references to James Cullen have been published prior to the writing of this chapter, and two of these show that he had few scruples as a business man.

The earliest of these references is in the form of an account[2] from Cullen to the third Duke of Atholl. This account, dated 1770–1, totalled £116. 16. 0. and included entries for :

'2 Elegant Pier Glass frames Carv'd & gilt in Burnish'd Gold, with 3 light
Branches for the above mention'd Plates. . . . . £44. –. –.
4 Carv'd Settees, with Chinese Backs, a frett & Carv'd ornaments Round
Yᵉ frames . . . . [price illegible]
2 Elbow Chairs to match the above. . . . . 7. 7. –.'

Unfortunately none of these pieces appears to have survived at Blair Castle, the Highland stronghold of the Dukes of Atholl. Cullen's name is next found, together with that of John Cobb's, in connection with the alleged charges brought by a committee of cabinet-makers in June 1772 against Count Pignatelli, the Neapolitan Minister, and the Venetian Resident, Baron Berlindis.[3] The cabinet-makers claimed that these two gentlemen were making use of their diplomatic privileges in order to smuggle Continental

[1] Hopetoun House archives retained at Hopetoun House, West Lothian — I am deeply indebted to Mr. Basil Skinner of the Scottish National Portrait Gallery for all the help that he has given me relating to the study of these accounts.
[2] Blair Castle Archives, Blair Atholl, Perthshire.
[3] This case has already been discussed relating to Cobb (p. 32).

furniture into this country, without the payment of Customs' dues, and were then trying to sell these pieces to the public by placing them amongst the stock of certain cabinet-makers, the most eminent of whom were Cullen and Cobb. Petitions were made to the House of Commons and in May 1773 a special committee was appointed by the House to inquire into these allegations. This whole fascinating subject, together with the evidence and findings of the Committee, is fully discussed by Mr. Geoffrey Wills in his recent article *Furniture-Smuggling in Eighteenth-Century London*.[1] Cullen and Cobb come out of the affair in a poor light, and it appears that they were trying to sell these pieces for the two Continental diplomats on a commission basis. Lastly, in 1773, we find Cullen appointed as one of the assignees, together with Thomas Chippendale, Samuel Spencer and Augustus Lesage,[2] of the house and chattels of the bankrupt, Teresa Cornelys (see p. 109). She had run into financial difficulties over her management of Carlisle House, Soho Square, which for some years had been a centre of the London social season. Mr. Wills, whilst discussing this subject, writes:[1] 'In March 1773 all four of them (the assignees) conspired to buy the house and contents in a single lot, instead of selling each item separately. The matter was brought to the notice of the Court of Bankruptcy, but the complaint was dismissed, and in spite of the fact that the affair appears somewhat shady it was apparently in good legal order.'[3]

James Cullen was an important cabinet-maker who counted the great amongst his clients — for in addition to the Duke of Atholl, he also worked for the Duke of Abercorn, the Earl of Waldegrave, Mr. Lauderdale, and, of course, the Earl of Hopetoun. He was also associated in business deals, admittedly of an unsavoury nature, with Thomas Chippendale and John Cobb. The *London Directory* records that James Cullen, 'Upholder and Cabinet-maker', had premises at 56 Greek Street, Soho, from 1765–79. Whether he was trading from these premises in 1755, when he is first mentioned in the Hopetoun archives is not known.

John Hope had bought the estate in 1678, and Sir William Bruce, the distinguished Scottish architect, had built the house for his son, Charles, between 1699 and 1703. Twenty years later the Earl engaged William Adam to enlarge Bruce's house. In 1753 William Adam's son, the more famous Robert, took over from him and completed the work. It was two years after this, in 1755, that James Cullen first figures in the Hopetoun accounts. He apparently made the long journey north in order to advise his client on certain architectural details in the State Appartments, and on how much damask he would need for the 'Grand Appartments'. He made a memo, dated 1st February, 1755, giving details of his suggestions in answer to the points raised by the Earl, or by Robert Adam, relating to the siting of the tables and pier-glasses for the 'New Dining Roome and Drawing Roome'. It is interesting that Cullen should have travelled to Scotland to see the rooms in which his pier-glasses and tables were to be placed before the internal architectural details had been completed. It appears that every detail had to be carefully considered on the site by client, architect and cabinet-maker alike. Cullen's memorandum runs as follows:

[1] *Apollo*, August 1965.   [2] Jewellers and Goldsmiths.
[3] The proceedings in the Court of Bankruptcy are printed by Oliver Brackett, *Thomas Chippendale*, n.d. (1930), pp. 138–41.

'New Dining Roome.

> 2 peers [pier-glassess] 5′0½″ between the architraves of the Windows — surbace 3′1⅛″ high. To be square in front.
>
> The tables in my humble opinion should be the height of the surbace — 4′9″ long, 2′6″ broad.

New Drawing Roome.

> 4 peers 4′11″ between the avilos of the windows. The Surbace 3′2″ high. To be shaped in front. The tables about 4′7″ long, from 2′ to 2′6″ broad & as high as the surbace. I think the tables should be little more than 4′ long or about it and 2′ or little more broad.'

During the same visit Cullen made an estimate as to how much damask would be needed to cover the walls in the Drawing-Room, the Bed-Chamber and the Dressing-Room, and how much would be needed to make the curtains for, and cover the furniture in, these rooms. Work was doubtless put in hand when he returned to London, and a pair of pier-glasses (Pl. 407) and side-tables (Pl. 408), which are now in what has been named 'The Yellow Drawing Room', were probably made as a result of the measurements and recommendations that he had made for the 'New Dining Roome'. The pier-glasses are in the full rococo tradition, and the candle-branches, which are of later date, are an unusual addition. The tables, on the other hand, although they are carved with blind-fret and other rococo ornamentation, still retain certain features of an almost Kentian character.

Cullen apparently returned again to Hopetoun in 1758, in order to advise the Earl as to what new furniture he would need for the State Appartments. Thus on 17th July he made an inventory which is annotated on the outer face 'Mr. Cullen's Memo of Furniture to be made, 1758, for the appartments'. It is interesting that no mention is made of the Dining-Room in this inventory, and the answer probably lies in the fact that the nature of the furniture for this room had already been settled during Cullen's first visit. As this inventory is important, it is recorded here in some detail :

> 'Drawing Roome.
>
> 2 large sofa(s) with low seats on Castors
> 6 small chairs
> 8 elbow ch^rs.
> 4 glasses in Burnished Gold frames with concealed Socketts for Branches
> 4 Table frames in Burnished Gold
> 5 Spring W^w Blinds
>
> Bed^rm.
>
> Bedstead &^c
> 2 glasses (the plates my L^ds. Own being in the House packt up in a box)
> 2 commodes
> 2 night tables
> Bed Carpett
> 2 foot stools
> 8 Single chairs
> An easy chair
> A Table with a drawer

Dressing Roome.

    A Dressing Table for Toilet
    A couch, 2 chairs & 2 stools
    A fly Table

Green Dam^{sk} Bed Ch^r.

    A mahog^y Beds^{d.}

Waiting Roome

    A cabinett for China
    A Tea Table & Tray.'

From careful study of this list, it can be seen that Cullen was in a position to provide a wide variety of articles for a great house; and that he did in fact provide many important pieces for Hopetoun will become evident from the letters quoted below. It is only regretted that his accounts for this work have not survived; for, if they had, it would doubtless be possible to relate many of the pieces mentioned in his preliminary inventory to extant pieces in the house. However, it is now only possible to do this in the instances where a sketch or letter relating to individual pieces has survived.

The '2 large sofas' (Pl. 409) and '6 small chairs . . . [and] 8 elbow ch^{rs}' (Pl. 410) can probably be related to those now in the Red Drawing-Room, but the '4 glasses in Burnished Gold frames with concealed socketts for Branches', which are also mentioned in Cullen's inventory for the *Drawing Roome*, can be identified with greater certainty. It has already been pointed out that the Earl must have been an exacting client and that Cullen was expected by him to attend to every detail relating to his commissions. It is therefore not surprising to find that the designs for the drawing-room glasses were returned to Cullen as being unsuitable, on at least one occasion. It will be remembered that Cullen took measurements for these glasses during his first visit, in 1755 – his design for them had still not been approved by May 1766, as can be seen from the following letter :

'My Lord

    With this you will *again* receive the design for your drawing room glass which I have endeavoured to Estimate but cannot do it exactly tho' with the assistance of a very Eminent carver and Gilder — the plate must be much wider in an oval than in a square glass — which greatly increases the value — to this scale the plate will be 43 inches by 36 inches, & I believe about six Inches wider than the great plates of the dining room glasses.

    This will cost me (glass book price) £31 10 0
26/– per f^{t.} is the allowed profit on manufactured glass but if your Lordship will run the risk of Fractures . . . 10/– per ft.   3 3 0
or 5/– per ft. — if I do not advance the money which is allways paid for before the Glass house will deliver it.

    The frame Carved in the best manner & well gilt in burnished Gold will at least come to 40 Guineas   £42 0 0

    A small plate of mirror for the Top   7 0

         £77 0 0

I should not say much in favour of the design yet cannot forbear assuring your Lordship that it has been much admired for its Singularity & the Species of Ornament it is composed of . . .

(signed) J^as Cullen,
London, May 22nd. 1766.'

Three important points are raised by this letter. First Cullen writes 'you will again receive the design' — obviously one or more had already been rejected. Secondly, he cannot estimate the cost without 'the assistance of a Very Eminent Carver and Gilder'. In a letter of 1768 to the Earl, Cullen refers, while discussing the State bedstead (Pl. 413), to a 'Mr Norman'. This must be a reference to the celebrated cabinet-maker and carver, Samuel Norman (see pp. 140–5), who worked for the Duke of Bedford at Woburn, Sir Laurence Dundas at Moor Park and 19 Arlington Street, and for the Earl of Leicester at Holkham. Thirdly, it is interesting to see how the cost of the plate glass was arrived at, and that a reduction was offered by the Glass House if the client would bear 'the risk of Fractures'.

On the basis of the above evidence, it is more than likely that Samuel Norman provided the frames 'carved in the best manner & well gilt in burnished Gold' for these glasses, which now hang between the windows in the Red Drawing-Room at Hopetoun (Pl. 411). The plates are in fact oval and they each have 'a small plate of mirror for the Top' as the letter describes it. Cullen wrote that the design 'has been much admired for its Singularity', and this is hardly surprising when it is remembered that his accompanying letter was dated 1766. This was only four years after Chippendale had published the third edition of the *Director*, and yet the glasses are almost entirely neo-classical in form and decorative detail. A highly gifted designer, who had already fully grasped the new neo-classic idiom, must have produced this design. In 1769 Matthias Lock published *A New Book of Pier-Frames, Ovals, Gerandoles, Tables & etc.* . . . which reproduces designs in the full neo-classic tradition. It has for long been thought that he left Chippendale's employ after the publication of the third edition of the *Director* in 1762, and he must have been working on these neo-classical designs during the last years of his life — as we have seen he probably died in 1770 — after he had severed his connection with Chippendale, if, in fact, he ever did so. It would obviously have been outrageous to couple Lock's name with the design on such slender grounds, if a scrap of paper had not been found amongst Cullen's letters in the Hopetoun archives, inscribed with the following words,

'The Enclosed Drawings are valuable being designed and drawn by the famous Mr Matt Lock recently deceased who was reputed the best Draftsman in that way that had ever been in England.'

It is not clear from the wording whether this note was attached by the Earl to a bundle of Lock's earlier drawings, after the designer's death, or whether, as is more likely, Cullen sent some of Lock's last drawings to the Earl, shortly after Lock's death in 1770, and accompanied them with the note. However, if this was the case, it is strange that Cullen should not have written a letter to the Earl in the place of this rather vague note. It will now probably never be known who wrote those words, but their discovery is of the greatest importance, as they not only show in what high esteem Lock was held by his contemporaries, but they prove that he was producing designs that were being sent, probably by James Cullen, to Lord Hopetoun at this date. It is therefore suggested that these pier-glasses (Pl. 411) were supplied by James Cullen and that their frames were probably carved and gilded by Samuel Norman to a design of Matthias Lock's.

The '4 Table frames in Burnished Gold', which Cullen noted as being necessary for the Drawing-Room in his 1758 inventory, no longer stand below their pier-glasses in the Red Drawing-Room. A pair of console tables (Pl. 412), which are now in the Entrance Hall, and two others, *en suite*, in the private apartments, may, however, just possibly be those in question; although, being in the full rococo tradition, they would have appeared rather incongruous in relation to the almost neo-classical pier-glasses (Pl. 411). As can be seen they are inferior in conception and carving, as well.

The next important piece to be discussed is the State Bedstead (Pl. 413). It is first mentioned in the correspondence between Cullen and Lord Hopetoun in a letter dated 18th January, 1768. Cullen writes :

> 'My Lord,
>   Herewith I enclose your Lordship the two small drawings for the State Bed which are just come to my hands, — One shows the End of the Bed with the feet posts supporting the Doom, Cornices & Vauses, allso shews the carved HeadBoard or Bolster piece with the gilt Ornaments above it surrounded with drapery : the other shows the Ornaments & drapery where the inside head Vallens commonly are, & a Section of the inside of Doom with the coves and gilt Embellishments [Pl. 414].
>   All the Ornaments colloured yellow are in the Bed carved & gilt in burnished Gold. — The Fringes are the richest for silk that I ever saw being worth about 19s. p.yd. — & amount to nigh 80 £ — The Woodwork of the Bedstd. — the Doom & Cornice & — all abt the Bed cost Mr Norman about 80 £ as his Clark this Day assured me. . . .'

We have already discussed Norman's connection with Cullen. Unfortunately the two drawings have not survived, but the letter is of importance, as it shows that Cullen was prepared to act as a middleman. He had obviously been instructed to find a grand and imposing State Bedstead by his client and, rather than make one in his own workshops — if, indeed, he was capable of doing so — he goes to Samuel Norman, the celebrated carver and gilder of Soho Square, who, it appears, had a bedstead of the right kind in stock. The procuring of this bedstead was obviously a commission of the highest importance to Cullen and in going to Norman he was employing the help of the most skilled carver and gilder in the trade, a man who was described in Mortimer's *Universal Director* (1763) as 'Sculptor and Carver to their Majesties, and Surveyor of the Curious Carvings in Windsor Castle'. The Earl obviously approved of the sketches, for on 2nd February Cullen writes again,

> 'My Lord Hopetoun makes me very happy by acquainting me of the approbation the design of the State Bed has met with at Hopetoun and the probability of its height answers the Bed Chr. . . . We have finally concluded the bargain last week (Wednesday 27th) . . . all the packages and cases are included as they have luckily been preserved, but there is not one article of the bedding. . . .'

This letter is interesting as it suggests that Norman had the bedstead in stock, either because it had, for some reason, been returned by a client or bought at a sale — 'the packages and cases . . . have luckily been preserved, but there is not one article of the bedding'.

The mystery is solved by Cullen in a third letter, dated 25th February, in which he writes:

> 'I have just got the Bed intirely packed up with very great care & all mark'd according to my Ld Hopes directions. . . . — I am sorry it has suffer'd much by the curious examiners at the *Sale*. Mr. Hope has paid the £230.'

The last extant document relating to the bedstead is an

> 'Invoice of Goods ship'd on board the King George, Captn Marshill, belonging to the Right Honble the Earl of Hoptoun, June the 28th 1768 — viz.
>
> No. 1. A case containing . . . all the Curtains, Vallens, Bases, the Doom, 2 inside Cornices, 4 gilt vauses and all the small Ornaments and Leaves — the head Board and head Ornaments, two corner Ornaments and 2 Counterpanes — a large wrapper and a coverled to pack the whole — all belonging to the State Bed —
> No. 2. A Case containing . . . 3 outside cornices, two inside Do., 2 carv'd and gilt capitals for the feet posts belonging to the State Bed 2 Blanketts etc. to pack Do —
> No. 3. A Case containing . . . The carv'd and gilt feet posts of the Bed and polish'd Rod . . .'

The greatest care was taken by Cullen in the selection, purchase, packing and delivery of this bedstead, and part of his success as a businessman can be attributed to the great lengths to which he went to cater to the whims, foibles and tastes of his clients.

Cullen continued his letter of 25th February, 1768, by writing:

> 'Herewith are the designs for the Commodes in the Grand Bedch^r. one of which is intended to introduce different collourd woods which with good brasses has an Effect that is generally approved here — at the top is one long drawer & the Bottom is two presses that have their doors in the End pannells — I have made some very fine ones of this kind for Ld Walgrave that are on Castors to turn round & the doors are behind — these in grand appartments are more intended to furnish & adorn than for real use — .'

One of the designs that Cullen enclosed has survived (Pl. 415), although the drawing that he selected has not survived, as Lord Hopetoun probably returned it to Cullen when he had made his choice. The pair of commodes that Cullen made from this lost design are illustrated as Pl. 416. It appears that Lord Hopetoun chose the design which was intended 'to introduce different collourd woods which with good brasses has an effect that is generally approved here' — and the commodes do indeed have one long drawer at the top while the doors *are* in the sides. The metal-gilt escutcheons, mounts and handles are highly distinctive in form and execution and it is sad that no commodes of this design remain in the Earl of Waldegrave's collection at Chewton House, near Bath.[1]

Cullen finishes this long letter by discussing a toilet table. His description is included here as it again illustrates the great importance that he obviously attached to detail, and also illustrates how complicated the upholsterer's side of the trade had become by this date.

---

[1] I am indebted to my colleague, Mr. John Critchley, for this information.

'The Toilet Table is mark'd rather too narrow as the dressing room is scarce broad enough — the petticoat be some brocaded silk or crimson silk dam^k. fringed at Bottom, the Top covr'd with Marseils or other fine Quilting made to the shape. The shade and outside petticoat is generally the finest sheer muslin (striped) or wrought & edged with flounced or puckerd lace in which they mix narrow and broad Ribbons according to the fancy of the owner or performer. The Scarf over the Glass should be twice as long as the length from the Top of the Glass as it Stands in its place from the Table to the ground & half a yard more & when the Scarf is doubled the middle half yard makes the hood. . . .'

There are several designs in the *Director* showing dressing-tables draped like this, and many readers will know the painting by Zoffany which shows Queen Charlotte seated in front of her dressing-table which is completely swathed in tiers of lace with ribbons.

A design for a curious pier-glass (Pl. 417) is amongst the Hopetoun archives, and it appears that Lord Hopetoun approved the design and ordered it to be executed, as it is annotated 'The frame order'd to be executed according to this design 23rd Jan, 1767'. The elaborate design with its figures, banners and trophies is not unlike some of those published by Chippendale in the third edition of the *Director*, 1762 (plates CLXX, CLXXI and CLXXIII). If a pier-glass was, in fact, made exactly to this design, it has not survived, but two unusual and very important examples in a somewhat similar tradition are in the private apartments at Hopetoun (Pls. 418 and 419). The use in this country of engraved mirrored plates (Pl. 418) is extremely rare and must have been inspired by some Venetian prototype. The giltwood dolphins and entwined serpents incorporated in the frame of Pl. 419 are vigorously portrayed.

It has already been seen that in 1755 James Cullen was advising the Earl on the amount of damask that he would need for the 'Grand Apartments'. His calculations were as follows :

'Damask for all the Drawing Room . . . 434 yds. 3 ft.
   walls, curtains, 16 elb. chairs, 2 sofas.

Damask for all the BedChamber . . . 855 yds. 2 ft. 1 inch.
   walls, curtains, 4 small chairs, 2 elb. chairs, 2 stools, Bed and Counterpane.

Damask for all the Dressing Room . . . 134 yds. 2 ft. 4 inches.
   walls, curtains, 6 small chairs and a couch.'

It appears that the damask was not purchased and hung until 1766, and Cullen's letters to the Earl relating to its purchase and delivery, which are of the greatest importance, are quoted here in some detail. They show that Cullen, during this transaction as well, had few scruples over outwitting the Customs and Excise.

Cullen first writes to the Earl on the subject of the damask on 4th February, 1766, in the following words :

'My Lord. —
   If you have not furnish'd yourself with the crimson silk damask for the grand appartment I have an opportunity of getting a quantity for you now much below the markett price. There is about 800 yds & has been offerd me at 13/6 per yard. It was brought from abroad by a Nobleman who is going back & at present has not use for it. He has also a quantity of yellow at 12/– per yard. . . .'

The letter is annotated thus by the Earl or his secretary '12 Feby, 1766, Answered desiring him to secure the Damask'. This Cullen hastened to do and, on 14th July, he writes,

'Yesterday morning I got notice of 6 pieces of the Silk Dam^sk being arrived & in the Evening received two of them — very good & correspondent with the pattron [pattern] & agreem^t. —

These two pieces contain 167 yrds. —

They promise to deliver the other four pieces this Night or tomorrow Night. — which will be about half our Quantity. For the remainder we must have a little patience 'till a proper Opportunity occurs which I expect will be soon. The late Act in favour of the English Weavers has passed since our Contract & rendered the fulfilling of it extremely difficult & expensive. — the Bargain was one Thous^d yards for 600 £ & a compliment [commission] to himself — to be paid on delivery.

Already I have advanced him some for Expenses Etc. — & Expect he will demand payment for the 500 yards directly as they seeme needy — & absolutely can sell it now for above 15/- per *yard* to the Mercers directly.

By next post I hope to be able to give your L^dShip some further Satisfactory acc^t. of this Matter. . . .'

Cullen then writes again on 22nd July, probably in answer to a letter from the Earl inquiring as to how he proposed to avoid paying the very high Customs' dues which should have been levied on the damask. It will be remembered that Cullen agreed to buy the damask in February at 12s. 6d. a yard, and that by September its market value had *shot-up* on account of the very high import duties that were being levied resulting from an Act of Parliament passed during the summer, to try and protect the English silk weavers.[1] Cullen's ingenuity in evading the Customs is admirably portrayed in his reply to the Earl — he writes :

'I am extremely happy in finding your Lordship's determination correspondent with my own opinion & do assure you that your order has relieved me from the greatest anxiety altho. I had deposited them [the pieces of damask] myself where I thought them impossible to be found by our Fielding's Rascals [Henry Fielding, the celebrated magistrate and author].

I had great apprehensions of Danger by sending them directed to my House subject to Excise officers, as every Grocer is, and therefore have took the liberty to send them yesterday to the Newcastle Waggon, viz.

6 pieces . . . 510 yards mark'd {Messrs. B. Williamson / Lawn Market, Edinburgh

Bertram and Williamson are Linnen Factors & my Friends. It would be right for the Hopton Carrier to give Mr Williamson notice of my having sent a Bundle for you to his Care — they will be at Edin^h. about the 6th of August.

I thought of packing in a dry cask but that piece of Cunning might cause it to be searched for Teas, & if in a flatt case as Marble Slabbs or Glasses, directed to Miss H — might expose it to the like fate from the Curious, this determined me to pack them in Straw in a pack shut corded like Manchester Goods [cotton?] & directed to peoples who deals in such.

I beg your Lordship will not consider my disobeying your Commands as impertinence but rather as proof how much and how earnestly I wish to be worthy of your Lordship's services. . . . Mr Hope has enabled me to pay the man £250 which is above £50 short.

[1] The whole question of the clandestine importation of foreign silks and the measures introduced to protect the Spitalfields silk industry are discussed by Mr. Peter Thornton in *Baroque and Rococo silks*, London, 1965.

I have a large house to furnish in Northamptonshire where I must go soon & having promised my Ld Abbercorn to be with him at Duddiston this Summer I propose to go on for Edin^h. & expect to be there about the middle of August & to gratyfy myself once more with the Honour of being under your Lordship's Roof at Hopetoun. . . .'

Cullen probably travelled north to Hopetoun during August, calling on Lord Abercorn and his Northamptonshire client on the way, and was back in London by 2nd September, for on that day he writes again to the Earl :

'On my arrival here I found the remainder of your silk, it had been here fourteen days & the man nigh forty times for payment being under a necessity of returning the money by the person who brought it & waiting in Town for that only, obliged me to apply to Mr Hope who immediately discharged the whole debt & has my Receipt. — Saturday last I packed & forwarded it as before & wish it may come safe to Hopetoun. — the necessary man's gratuity is yet unpaid & at your option — I have paid portridge's & packages . . . 15/– which is the whole expenses —'

The crimson damask still covers the furniture and walls in the Red Drawing-Room and the State Bedroom and the window and bed curtains are also made from it. The Yellow Drawing-Room, and the seat-furniture in it, is likewise covered with the yellow damask which cost 12s. a yard, rather than the 12s. 6d. a yard charged for the crimson damask.[1]

James Cullen, therefore, emerges as a cabinet-maker and business-man of considerable importance and acumen, who did not hesitate to employ the help of the leading specialists, such as Lock and Norman, when the commission was of sufficient importance. His insistence on the highest standards of workmanship and his close attention to his client's every wish must have been instrumental in his undoubted success, while his rather dubious morals were probably no worse than those of many of his rivals and contemporaries.[2]

APPENDIX A

Extracts from the inventory prepared for the purpose of an arbitration as to the value of the work carried out by Samuel Norman, between 1763 and 1766, for Sir Lawrence Dundas, Bart., for his houses — 19 Arlington Street, Moor Park, Hertfordshire, and Aske, North Yorkshire (lent by the Marquess of Zetland to the North Riding Record Office, Northallerton, Yorks.) :

'*For Moor Park*

Library

6 Very neat mahogany Chairs richly carv'd seats stuff'd and cover'd Blue Spanish leather Brass nail'd compleat Brackets Richly carv'd.

A Very large neat Mahog^y Library Steps made to turn down to appear like a Stool, Very

---

[1] It should be stated that the Earl made several substantial purchases of furnishing materials direct from some of the leading silk mercers, as well — not all the deals were as shady as this.

[2] I am deeply indebted to the Marquess of Linlithgow and to his factor Mr. J. N. Douglas-Menzies, for their help to me during the preparation of this section. Much of it has already been published in the *Connoisseur*, in an article by the author entitled 'James Cullen, cabinet-maker, at Hopetoun House'.

Richly carv'd the top stuff'd and cover'd in Blue Spanish Leather Brass nail'd compleat wt. Brackets richly carv'd.

A neat letter case for the Postman to carry letters in.

Crimson Drawing Room

2 large sunshades painted Green and to draw up wt. tape.

Making and Carving 10 very rich Elbow Chairs Gilt complete in the best Burnish'd Gold and Varnish'd 5 times over stuff'd with best curl'd hair in fine linen on Castors.

A very large Grand Pier frame Richly and Elegantly Carv'd and Gilt in Burnish'd Gold with Glasses to ditto complete.

Rich Antique Lamps Elegantly Carv'd with Antique pillars Canopy Shades with wreath of Laurell the ornaments in the Vetruvian Taste all of fine Brass work double water Gilt Complete.

Mr. Dundas's Dressing Room

222 feet neat Gadroon Border Carv'd in Wood and Richly Gilt in Burnish'd Gold.

Kitchen

2 neat and Large Plate Racks made in a particular manner.

A Neat Wainscot Excercising Horse seat and Back Stuff'd and cover'd with Blue Spanish Leather and Brass-Nail'd with a loose Cushion to ditto complete.

For Ask Hall

2 Very large and neat Mahogany Commodes Extra fine Wood Best Lox Large lifting handles at the Ends Complete.

A Very Neat Mahogany Cabinet on a frame made to draw out on Rollers Curious Locks and Black Ebony Moldings.

For Arlington Street

The Bedchamber Closet

A neat Mahogany Low Chest of drawers fine wood, Good Lox.

Drawing Room, Ground Floor

A neat Italian Picture frame with spandrels richly Carv'd and Gilt in Burnish'd Gold Complete.

2 neat Mahogany oval Cisterns w^t Rich brass Ornaments and Stands to ditto Complete.

A Very Curious Mahogany Teabox with inside lin'd w^t lead Top cover to d^o lin'd w^t Green Velvet and Mahogany Canisters.'

APPENDIX B

Extracts from William France's (accounts 1 and 2) and William France's and John Bradburn's accounts (account 3) to Sir Lawrence Dundas, Bart., for work carried out by them at 19 Arlington

Street and Moor Park, Hertfordshire, between 1764 and 1767 (lent by the Marquess of Zetland to the North Riding Record Office, Northallerton, Yorks.) :

'May 1764 (Account 1 for Arlington House)	For 6 Bell lamps blown to a particular size and shape fixed to the window side of the Arcade by very stout brass scroles richly ornamented, and supporters to strengthen D⁰ and fluted double Canopies gilt in burnish'd gold with pine apples at the top, the upper Canopy raised from the Bottom ones by brass scrowls inrich'd and strong double brass Ornaments reversed to defend the top of the Lamps from wavering, and Burners for oyl in brass with 2 lights carved to the Drawing . . . £9/6 each	£55. 16. 0.
June	For 2 elegant carved Girandoles with a large plate of Glass, and 3 lights in each to shew in the Glass, festoons, and drops of husks falling from Different parts all gilt in burnished Gold at £28. 6. 0. each	56. 12. 0.
(Account 2 for Moor Park) May	For a large oval pier glass with Glass Boarders all round D⁰., and a beautiful Scrole Boarder gilt over the Glass Boarders, and on the outside of the Boarders an elegant frame rich, and well carved, and gilt in burnished Gold, and a double and Knott to tye up D⁰ under the Cornices with strong canvass, Backhold fasts, screws etc. [one of a pair, invoiced later]	59. 12. 0.
June	For a good wainscott 4 post Bedstead on strong treble wheel castors, a strong lath[?] Bottom to D⁰ webbed, and Mahoᵞ stout footposts richly carved, with a rich carved Bottom with twisted foldages to D⁰ . . .	12. 18. 0.
November (Account 3 for Arlington House and Moor Park)	For making hangings of your own Crimson Genoa Damask to fit the 2 large Rooms Compleat, and putting up the whole, and moving Tressels and Scaffolding, as the Bussiness required, without which assistance Rooms so large and so high could not be hung without the greatest Difficulty and large expence . . .	28. 16. 0.
December	For a Mahogany Secretaire for My Ladie's Dressing Room . . .	8. 10. 0.
1765 May	For 6 Stout Wainscot Blind Frames, prepared as those in Town, and 6 framed Back boards, and holdfasts for puting up D⁰, for the 6 Glass's in the large Room at Moor Park, backboards cover'd with flannel and . . .	59. 10. 0.
July	For hanging with Canvas, and paper, the long Room at Moor Park, and finishing the whole with a border round Glasses and all	22. 7. 0.
July	For 4 Men putting up all the paintings in the Ceiling at Moor Park and fitting to the different Shaped Compartments, Paste and Pins Needle points . . .	21. 10. 0.
October	For 185 yds, of large Crimson silk Line at 2/9 p. yᵈ . . .	25. 8. 9.
,,	For 72 large crimson Silk tassels to D⁰ at 5/9 . . .	20. 14. 0.
December	For 3 large Cornices, with a carved Moulding Top, and Bottom, and a Rich folding Ornament in the flatt, laid on Damask, all very well carv'd and Gilt in Burnish'd Gold . . .	24. 15. 0.'

171

Notes to the Illustrations

AUTHOR'S NOTES

(*a*) The '*Literature*' and '*Exhibitions*' listed in the *Notes To Illustrations* are not claimed to be definitive.

(*b*) The word *inlaid* is used throughout in the sense of a marquetry of woods, wood, brass, ivory, horn etc. inlaid into a veneered or solid wooden surface.

ABBREVIATIONS

D.E.F. stands for *The Dictionary of English Furniture*, 3 vols., revised edition by Ralph Edwards, *Country Life*, 1954, unless an accompanying date denotes the 1924–7 edition, *Country Life*, by Percy Macquoid and Ralph Edwards.

G.C-M. stands for *Georgian Cabinet-Makers*, by Ralph Edwards and Margaret Jourdian, a new and revised edition, *Country Life*, 1955.

English Furniture Designs of the Eighteenth Century was written by P. Ward-Jackson and published by H.M.S.O. in 1953 — only the title is referred to in the text.

COLOUR PLATES

A. A rare black and gold lacquered and japanned 'pagoda' cabinet inlaid with ivory and *pietre dure*. It was ordered by Sir Mathew Fetherstonhaugh, Bt., for his house, Uppark in Sussex. It should be compared with pls. 134 and 135 in the third edition of the *Director* (1762), and with pls. 48 and 49 in *Ince and Mayhew's Universal System of Household Furniture* (1762). It is japanned in black and gold and the central pagoda and two of the drawers below are veneered with panels of Chinese lacquer. The two upper drawers are mounted with carved ivory bust medallions of Homer and Brutus. Six other drawers are inset with Florentine *pietre dure* panels depicting birds amidst flowers and bouquets knotted with ribbon-ties. The cabinet was almost certainly a special commission by Sir Mathew, and he probably instructed the cabinet-maker to incorporate the Florentine hardstone panels and the ivory medallions in its decoration. He had doubtless brought these when he was in Italy between 1750 and 1752 (see Pl. 273 for a detail of the interior).

    Lit: Anthony Coleridge, 'Georgian Cabinet-Makers at Uppark, Sussex — Part II', *Connoisseur*, November, 1967.

    Loc: Uppark, Sussex.

B. One of a set of four japanned and lacquered commodes — two pairs forming a set of four — the doors, tops and side panels decorated with Chinese figures on terraces and in gardens, in shades of gilt. The angles, toes and borders, on the example illustrated here, are in carved foliated giltwood which is an unusual refinement. The set was probably ordered by Sir Mathew Fetherstonhaugh, Bt., for his house, Uppark, near Petersfield, Sussex (see also Pl. 337).

> Lit: Anthony Coleridge, 'Georgian Cabinet-Makers at Uppark, Sussex — Part I', *Connoisseur*, October, 1967.
>
> Loc: Uppark, Sussex.

C. A japanned bedstead made for the Chinese bedroom at Badminton House for the fourth Duke of Beaufort, perhaps by Chippendale's firm: the Chinese bedroom was already furnished '. . . in the Chinese manner' by 1754: cf. the *Director*, 1st edition, pl. 32. Until a few years ago, the bed was black and gold, but a recent cleaning revealed the original bright red and green japanning with chinoiseries. The original bed-hangings are missing, but new ones following the proposals given in the *Director* have now been provided.

> Lit: *D.E.F.*, I, p. 64, fig. 51.
>
> *G.C-M.*, p. 173, fig. 98.
>
> Oliver Bracket, *Thomas Chippendale*, London, 1930, pl. 24.
>
> Ralph Edwards, *Georgian Furniture*, London, 1951, fig. 6.
>
> Loc: The Victoria and Albert Museum.

MONOCHROME PLATES

1. A mahogany library writing-table:
   Possibly designed by William Kent for the 3rd Earl of Burlington for Chiswick House, about 1730, and perhaps one of William Vile's earliest creations.
   > Lit: *D.E.F.*, III, pp. 244, 249, pl. IX.
   >
   > Exhib: Royal Academy of Arts, *English Taste in the Eighteenth Century*, 1955–56, Cat. No. 76.
   >
   > Loc: Chatsworth House, Derbyshire.

2. A mahogany library writing-table with marble top:
   Adapted to form a pair at a later date, with two commodes and a buffet *en suite*, from Rokeby Hall, Yorkshire. Perhaps made by Vile for Sir Thomas Robinson in the early 1740's.
   > Lit: *D.E.F.*, Vol. III, p. 249, fig. 12, p. 245.
   >
   > *G.C-M.*, p. 59.
   >
   > Exhib: Victoria and Albert Museum, 1954, 'Queen Mary's Treasures', *Guide*, p. 8.
   >
   > Musée des Arts Décoratifs, Paris, 1959, *Le Siècle de L'Élégance*, Cat. No. 56.
   >
   > Loc: The Royal Collection.

3. A mahogany library writing-table:
   Perhaps made by Vile for Ashburnham Place, Kent.
   > Lit: *D.E.F.*, Vol. III, fig. 21, p. 249.
   >
   > C. Hussey, 'Ashburnham Place (Part II)', *Country Life*, 23 April, 1959, and 'A Library table by William Vile', *Connoisseur*, December 1957, p. 257.
   >
   > Loc: The Victoria and Albert Museum.

4. A mahogany writing-table with folding top:
   > Sale: Parke-Bernet Galleries Inc., New York, Walter P. Chrysler Jr. sale, 7 May, 1960, Lot 535.
   >
   > Loc: Private Collection.

5. A mahogany commode with lion mask-and-ring handles — typical of Vile's early style.
   > Loc: Private Collection.

6. An engraved metal-gilt escutcheon on Pl. 5 above.

7. One of a pair of commodes with lifting tops and false drawers :
   Attributed to Vile.
   Lit :   *D.E.F.*, II, p. 112, fig. 4, p. 109.
            G.C-M., pp. 53–4, fig. 55, p. 148.
   Exhib : Royal Academy of Arts, *English Taste in the Eighteenth Century*, 1955–56, Cat.
            No. 144.
   Loc :   Goodwood House, Sussex.

8. A mahogany knee-hole writing-table :
   Coll :   Sir James Horlick.
   Sale :   Walter P. Chrysler Jr., 30 April, 1960, Lot 249 (cf. 4 above).
   Loc :   Private Collection.

9. A mahogany commode :
   Attributed to Vile.
   From the Earl of Shaftesbury's collection at St. Giles's House, Dorset.
   Sale :   Christie's, 27 March, 1952, Lot 75.
   Loc :   The Victoria and Albert Museum.

10. A commode, about 1750 :
    Its pair was in the collection of the late H.R.H. Princess Mary at Harewood House, nr.
    Leeds.
    Coll :   Col. H. H. Mülliner.
    Lit :   Y. Hackenbroch (Ed.), *English Furniture in the Collection of Irwin Untermyer*,
             London, 1958, fig. 324, pl. 282.
    Loc :   The Metropolitan Museum of Art.

11. A mahogany cabinet or press :
    Its decorative details show many of the characteristics of Vile's accepted style.
    Sale :   Christie's, 16 November, 1955.
    Coll :   The late Howard Reed.
    Lit :   *D.E.F.*, II, fig. 23, p. 166.
             G.C-M., fig. 58, p. 149.
    Loc :   The Metropolitan Museum of Art.

12. Queen Charlotte's jewel-cabinet.
    Made by Vile and Cobb in 1761 (see account p. 23).
    Coll :   Marquess of Cambridge.
    Lit :   H. Clifford-Smith, *Buckingham Palace*, London, 1931, pp. 73–4.
             D.E.F., I, p. 186, figs. 44, 45, pp. 154–5.
             G.C-M., p. 53, figs. 62, 63, p. 152.
             E. H. Pinto, 'The furniture of William Vile and John Cobb', *Antiques*, January
             1959.
    Exhib : Royal Academy of Arts, *English Taste in the Eighteenth Century*, 1955–56, Cat.
             No. 214.
             The Queen's Gallery, Buckingham Palace — 1962. *Treasures from the Royal
             Collection*, Cat. No. 43.
    Loc :   The Royal Collection.

13. A mahogany bureau-cabinet :
    Made by William Vile for Queen Charlotte's Apartments at St. James's in 1761 (see
    account, p. 23).
    Lit :   H. Clifford-Smith, *Buckingham Palace*, London, 1931, pp. 73, 278, pls. 62, 63.
             D.E.F., I, p. 148, figs. 54, 55, p. 146.
             G.C-M., p. 53, fig. 60, p. 151.

Exhib: Royal Academy of Arts, *English Taste in the Eighteenth Century*, 1955–56, Cat. No. 114.

Loc: The Royal Collection.

14. A mahogany bookcase:

Made by William Vile and John Cobb for Queen Charlotte in 1762 (see account p. 23).

Lit: H. Clifford-Smith, *Buckingham Palace*, London, 1931, pp. 78, 278–9, pl. 66.

D.E.F., I, Frontis.

G.C-M., p. 53.

Exhib: Royal Academy of Arts, *English Taste in the Eighteenth Century*, 1955–56, Cat. No. 196.

Loc: The Royal Collection.

15. A mahogany cabinet:

Altered into a cabinet by Vile in 1763: originally made as a case for an organ and mechanical harpsichord, probably by Benjamin Goodison, in about 1735.

Lit: H. Clifford-Smith, *Buckingham Palace*, London, 1931, p. 78, pl. 69.

Loc: The Royal Collection.

16. A mahogany dwarf-cabinet:

One of a set of nine made to contain organ rolls and attributed to Vile.

Lit: H. Clifford-Smith, *Buckingham Palace*, London, 1931, pp. 78–9, pls. 67–8.

D.E.F., II, p. 168, fig. 23, p. 166.

G.C-M., p. 53, pl. 67, p. 155.

Exhib: Musée des Arts Décoratifs, Paris, 1959, *Le Siècle de L'Élégance*, Cat. No. 48.

Loc: The Royal Collection.

17. A mahogany work-table:

Made by William Vile for Queen Charlotte in 1763 (see account p. 24).

Lit: H. Clifford-Smith, *Buckingham Palace*, London, 1931, p. 78, pl. 64.

D.E.F., III, p. 321, fig. 3, p. 320.

G.C-M., pl. 65, p. 154.

Exhib: Royal Academy of Arts, *English Taste in the Eighteenth Century*, 1955–56, Cat. No. 137.

Loc: The Royal Collection.

18. A mahogany knee-hole writing-table:

One of a pair, in the style of Vile.

Loc: Holyrood Palace, Edinburgh.

19. A mahogany knee-hole writing-table:

One of a pair, in the style of Vile.

Lit: H. Clifford-Smith, 'Two hundred years of the Mansion House, London, and some of its furniture', *Connoisseur*, December 1952.

Loc: The Mansion House, London.

20. A mahogany knee-hole writing-table:

Inscribed David Wright, Lancaster, 17 August, 1751.

Loc: The Victoria and Albert Museum.

21. One of a pair of mahogany medal-cabinets:

Adapted, in 1761, by Vile for George III from *His Majesty's Grand Medal Case*.

The pair, which passed into the collection of the second Duke of Wellington at Stratfield Saye House, Hampshire, has now been split — one being in the Victoria and Albert Museum and the other in the Metropolitan Museum of Art.

Lit: *D.E.F.*, Vol. I, p. 187, fig. 48.

G.C-M., p. 54, pl. 61, p. 151.

M. Jourdain, 'A pair of Royal Medal Cabinets', *Country Life*, 1949, Vol. 105, p. 983.

D. Shrub, 'The Vile Problem', *Victoria and Albert Museum Bulletin*, October 1965, No. 4.

Loc: The Victoria and Albert Museum.

22. A mahogany medal-cabinet in three stages:

Colls: Lord Kenyon, The Duke of Leeds, Mrs. Hannah Gubby.

Lit: Y. Hackenbroch (Ed.), *English Furniture in the Collection of Irwin Untermyer*, figs. 287–9, pl. 246–8, p. 59.

Loc: The Irwin Untermyer Collection, New York.

23. A mahogany *bonheur-du-jour* in the French taste:

Traditionally held to have been made by Vile and Cobb for George III, when Prince of Wales, and given to the Countess of Pembroke.

Loc: Private Collection.

24. An engraving after a painting by Henry Singleton of the marriage of the Duke and Duchess of York in 1791 in the Saloon at Buckingham House.

The chandeliers, which can be clearly seen, are probably those referred to in Vile's account of 1764 (see Appendix A, pp. 44–5).

Lit: H. Clifford-Smith, 'Attributions to William Vile', *Country Life*, 4 November, 1954.

25. A carved giltwood cabinet-stand:

The stand attributed to Vile's firm, as they probably repaired the cabinet in 1752.

Lit: Anthony Coleridge, 'Eighteenth Century Furniture at the Vyne', *Country Life*, 25 July, 1963.

Loc: The Vyne, Hampshire.

26. An Oriental lacquer casket on carved giltwood stand:

The stand perhaps made by Vile for Lord Folkestone at Longford Castle.

Lit: *D.E.F.*, I, p. 111, fig. 28.

Exhib: The Royal Academy of Arts, *English Taste in the Eighteenth Century*, 1955–56, Cat. No. 225.

Loc: Longford Castle, Wiltshire.

27. One of a set of four mahogany chairs:

Vile and Cobb made these for Anthony Chute at the Vyne, Basingstoke, in 1753 at a cost of 19s. each.

Lit: Anthony Coleridge, 'Eighteenth Century Furniture at the Vyne', *Country Life*, 25 July, 1963.

Loc: The Vyne, Hampshire.

28. One of a set of seven mahogany stools:

There were originally eight at the Vyne, and Vile and Cobb charged Anthony Chute £3. 12. 0. for each of them.

Lit: Coleridge, 'The Vyne', *loc. cit.*

Loc: The Vyne, Hampshire.

29. One of a pair of chair-back settees in the Gothic taste:

Thought to have been made by Vile for Richard Chauncey, for Edgecote in Northamptonshire.

Loc: Private Collection.

30. A carved and gilt chest with lacquer top:

Probably made by Vile for the first Lord Folkestone — Vile's name is first mentioned in the Longford Castle accounts in 1760.

Lit: *D.E.F.*, II, pp. 24–5, fig. 49.

G.C-M., p. 52, pl. 66, p. 154.

Exhib: Royal Academy of Arts, *English Taste in the Eighteenth Century*, Cat. No. 186.

Loc: Longford Castle, Wiltshire.

31. A carved mahogany stand with fretted panels :
    Probably made by Vile for the first Lord Folkestone for Longford Castle.
    Lit :   *D.E.F.*, III, p. 164, fig. 1.
              G.C-M., p. 52, pl. 68, p. 155.
    Loc :   Longford Castle, Wiltshire.

32. An olivewood veneered commode with carved and gilt enrichments, the top inset with a Chinese black lacquer panel :
    Originally in St. Giles's House, Dorset, and possibly supplied by Vile.
    Lit :   *G.C-M.*, pl. 57, p. 149.
    Sale :   Christie's, 23 October, 1953, Lot 101.
    Loc :   The Fitzwilliam Museum, Cambridge.

33. A mahogany bookcase :
    In the manner of William Vile (perhaps some alterations) :
    Lit :   *D.E.F.*, I, p. 188, fig. 49, p. 185.
              G.C-M., pl. 59, p. 150.
    Exhib : Royal Academy of Arts, *English Taste in the Eighteenth Century*, 1955–56, Cat. No. 149.
    Loc :   The Victoria and Albert Museum.

34. A mahogany bookcase :
    In the manner of Vile and said to have come from Charlemont House, Dublin.
    Exhib : Royal Academy of Arts, *English Taste in the Eighteenth Century*, Cat. No. 167.
    Loc :   Collection of Lord Rockley.

35. A mahogany bookcase :
    In the manner of Vile.
    Loc :   The Victoria and Albert Museum.

36. A mahogany bureau-bookcase inlaid with engraved brass :
    It is of unusual design and its execution and finish are of the highest standard.
    Lit :   Anthony Coleridge, 'Some Furniture in the Collection of the Earl of Mansfield', *Connoisseur*, April 1966.
    Loc :   Scone Palace, Perthshire.

37. A goldfish bowl on a mahogany stand :
    Attributed to Vile.
    Lit :   'A goldfish bowl and stand by William Vile', *Connoisseur*, June 1960.
    Loc :   Private Collection.

38. A mahogany armchair, one of a set of eight :
    Made by Cobb for the sixth Earl of Coventry in 1764 for Croome Court in Worcestershire — the splats carved by Sefferin Alken.
    Lit :   Clifford Musgrave, *Adam and Hepplewhite Furniture*, 1966, pl. 58.
    Loc :   Cannon Hall, Cawthorne, Barnsley, Yorkshire.

39. An inlaid commode with simulated marble top :
    Made by Cobb for Mr. Paul Methuen in 1772.
    Lit :   *G.C-M.*, p. 56, pl. 71, p. 156.
              O. Bracket, 'Documented Furniture at Corsham', *Country Life*, 28 November, 1936.
              R. Edwards, 'Two Commodes by John Cobb', *Country Life*, 22 May, 1937.
    Exhib : Burlington Fine Arts Club, Winter 1938, No. 4.
              Royal Academy of Arts, *English Taste in the Eighteenth Century*, 1955–56, Cat. No. 361.
    Loc :   Corsham Court, Wiltshire.

40. A pair of satinwood pedestals and marble vases :

The pedestals made by Cobb for Mr. Paul Methuen in 1772, the vases made two years later.

    Lit: *D.E.F.*, III, p. 160, fig. 8.

            G.C-M., p. 56, pl. 73, p. 157.

    Exhib: Burlington Fine Arts Club, Winter 1938, No. 5.

            Royal Academy of Arts, *English Taste in the Eighteenth Century*, 1955–56, Cat. No. 360.

    Loc: Corsham Court, Wiltshire.

41. An inlaid commode in the style of Cobb:

    From the first Baron Tweedmouth's Collection, Guisachan House, Beauly, Inverness.

    Lit: The companion commode, in the Victoria and Albert Museum (W30 — 1937) illustrated:

            D.E.F., II, pl. 111, p. 118.

            G.C-M., pl. 70, p. 156.

            H. H. Mülliner, *Decorative Arts in England*, London, N.D. fig. 53.

    Exhib: Frank Partridge Ltd., Winter Exhibition 1964.

    Loc: Private Collection.

42. Detail showing top of 41.

43. An inlaid commode:

    Some of the inlaid decoration is in the manner of Cobb.

    Lit: *D.E.F.*, II, p. 117, fig. 19.

    Loc: The Metropolitan Museum of Art.

44. The top of a commode which is almost a pair to 43.

    Colls: Sir Anthony de Rothschild, Aston Clinton, Bucks.

            First Viscount Leverhulme, The Hill, Hampstead, London.

    Sale: Lillian S. Whitmarsh, Coll., Parke-Bernet Galleries Inc., 7 April 1961, lot 181.

    Loc: Private Collection.

45. An inlaid commode:

    From the collection of R. Olaf Hambro, Linton Park, near Maidstone.

    Sale: Christie's, 2 October, 1961, Lot 110, cf. with 43.

    Loc: Private Collection.

46. One of a pair of inlaid commodes:

    These, and a similar pair, are all at West Wycombe Park, Buckinghamshire.

    Lit: *Connoisseur Year Book*, 1953.

    Exhib: Christie's, *Treasures from National Trust Houses*, 1958, Cat. No. 36.

    Loc: West Wycombe Park, Buckinghamshire.

47. An inlaid commode with marble top:

    Compare the unusual linear striping of the veneers with 46.

    Loc: Private Collection.

48. An inlaid commode:

    From the Earl of Shaftesbury's collection at St. Giles's House, Dorset.

    Sale: Christie's, 12 May, 1955, Lot 108.

    Lit: James Parker, 'Rococo and formal order in English Furniture', *Metropolitan Museum of Art Bulletin*, January 1957, pp. 134–7.

    Loc: The Metropolitan Museum of Art.

49. An inlaid *bureau-de-dame*:

    The fall-flap inlaid with the arms of Walpole impaling Waldegrave. The detached floral sprays knotted with ribbon-ties are much in the style of Pierre Langlois (see pp. 35–8).

    Loc: Chewton House, Somerset.

50. A marquetry inlaid commode, enriched with finely cast and chased ormolu, which was made by Langlois for Woburn Abbey — note the unusual arrangement of the central door flanked

by four drawers. The Bedford accounts include the following receipt made out to the third Duke: 'Received December 18th 1760 of his Grace the Duke of Bedford by Richard Branson seventy eight pounds eight shillings . . . for a large inlaid commode table. . . .'

    Lit: G. Scott Thomson, *Family Background*, 1949, p. 53.

             Ralph Edwards, 'Patrons of taste and Sensibility, English Furniture of the Eighteenth Century, Woburn Abbey', *Apollo*, December 1965.

    Loc: Woburn Abbey, Bedfordshire.

51. One of a pair of very similar commodes which were almost certainly made by Langlois for Sir Lawrence Dundas — probably either for Moor Park, Surrey, or 19 Arlington Street: cf. 50.

    Lit: Anthony Coleridge, 'Dundas and some Rococo Cabinet-Makers', *Apollo*, September, 1967.

    Loc: Aske, Richmond, Yorkshire.

52. A kingwood commode inlaid with marquetry and with fine ormolu mounts — the panel on the top is inlaid with architectural scenes in marquetry, patently by another hand. The carcase of the top drawer is signed 'Daniel Langlois' — probably a specialist in ormolu and gilding, who was apprenticed to 'Dominic Jean of St. Pancras Water Gilder'.

    The design, execution and ornamentation of this commode is very similar to a pair attributed to Pierre Langlois at Woburn Abbey — the Woburn pair have scagliola tops made by Lambertus Christianus Gori of Florence in 1763.

    Lit: *The Journal of the Furniture History Society*, Vol. 1, 1965. The Woburn commodes are illustrated and discussed by Ralph Edwards, 'Patrons of Taste and Sensibility, English Furniture of the Eighteenth Century, Woburn Abbey', *Apollo*, December 1965.

    Loc: The Fitzwilliam Museum, Cambridge.

53. The signature, in pencil, on the carcase of the top drawer of the above: the relationship between Daniel and Pierre Langlois has not yet been established.

54. One of a pair of inlaid commodes:

    Probably made by Langlois for John Chute of the Vyne.

    The drawers have been vertically divided at a later date.

    Lit: Anthony Coleridge, 'Eighteenth Century Furniture at the Vyne', *Country Life*, 25 July 1963.

    Loc: The Vyne, Hampshire.

55. An inlaid commode:

    Made by Langlois in 1764 for the seventh Earl of Coventry for Croome Court.

    Lit: James Parker, 'Croome Court, The Architecture and Furniture', *Metropolitan Museum of Art Bulletin*, November 1959, pp. 90–1.

    Loc: The Metropolitan Museum of Art.

56. An inlaid commode attributed to Langlois:

    One of a pair:

    Lit: G. F. Laking, *Windsor Castle Furniture*, n.d. p. 77.

    Loc: The Royal Collection.

57. A kingwood commode, one of a set of four: the top inlaid with a basket of flowers in engraved brass and signed G. M. Dutton: at the time of writing Messrs. Mallett and Son Ltd had an identical example in stock.

    Lit: G. F. Laking, *Windsor Castle Furniture*, p. 75.

    Exhib: The Queen's Gallery, Buckingham Palace — 1962, *Treasures from the Royal Collection*, Cat. No. 9.

    Loc: The Royal Collection.

58. A mahogany commode in the French style:

    Lit: G. F. Laking, *Windsor Castle Furniture*, p. 76.

    Loc: The Royal Collection.

59. One of a pair of giltwood and inlaid side-tables :
> In the Style of Langlois and made for Audley End, Essex. In fact delivered by Gordon and
> Taitt (see p. 51) in 1771 at a cost of £46. 16. 0. (see p. 38, n. 5).
> Lit : J. D. Williams, *Audley End*, Chelmsford, 1966, p. 61.
> Exhib : The Royal Academy of Arts, *English Taste in the Eighteenth Century*, Cat. No.
> 411.
> Loc : Audley End, Essex.

60. A cabinet-on-stand, made of mahogany with gilt brass mounts and engraved brass inlay : Note
the fine female-mask knee-mounts in cast and gilt brass : it dates from about 1735–40. On
stylistic grounds it can be said that this was probably made in the workshops of John Channon
in St. Martin's Lane. The hinge and plates are engraved with the maker's emblem, *a ram
pendant from entwined snakes.*
> Lit : John Hayward, 'English Brass-inlaid Furniture', *Victoria and Albert Museum
> Bulletin*, January 1965, Vol. 1, no. 1, fig. 1.
> Loc : The Victoria and Albert Museum.

61. A mahogany library-desk, cross-banded in rosewood and with cast and gilt brass mounts of
exceptional quality. This desk, one of the finest surviving pieces of English furniture,
originally stood back-to-back with a second desk (sold Sotheby's, 12 February 1965) forming
a library table. This desk, according to a family tradition of a later owner, was at Fonthill
Abbey, but it cannot be recognised in the catalogue of William Beckford's collection. It dates
from about 1740–45. Probably made in the workshops of John Channon.
> Lit : Hayward, 'Brass-inlaid Furniture', *loc. cit.*, Fig. 5.
> R. W. Symonds, 'A Magnificent Dressing Table', *Country Life*, 16 February
> 1965.
> Exhib : Musée des Arts Décoratifs, Paris, 1959, *Le Siècle de L'Élégance*, cat. no. 75.
> Loc : The Victoria and Albert Museum.

62. Details of 61, showing the high quality of the mounts.

63. A mahogany commode, probably by John Channon, with identical handle, angle and toe
mounts to those on a very similar commode at Temple Newsam House, Nr. Leeds (described
by R. W. Symonds, 'An English Commode of rare design and quality'. *Leeds Art Calendar*,
Vol. 12, no. 39, Spring 1938).
> Lit : *The Antique Collector*, August 1962, p. 165.
> Loc : The Fitzwilliam Museum.

64. An inlaid mahogany writing-cabinet with gilded brass mounts of the highest quality and
inlaid with engraved brasswork (cf. the mounts with those on Pls. 61 and 63). Probably made
in the workshops of John Channon.
> Lit : *D.E.F.*, I, p. 144, fig. 45, p. 140.
> R. W. Symonds, 'Furniture of the Nobility', *Country Life*, 7 May 1948.
> R. W. Symonds, 'A George II Writing Cabinet', *Country Life*, 13 January 1950.
> R. W. Symonds, 'Rediscovering old Furniture', *Country Life*, 18 October 1956.
> Exhib : The Royal Academy of Arts, *English Taste in the Eighteenth Century*, cat. no. 180.
> Sale : Christie's, 30 June 1949, lot 130.
> Loc : Private Collection.

65. One of a pair of rosewood bookcases inlaid with engraved brass designs : the dolphin feet (cf.
those supporting the library desk Pl. 61) and the floral swags are in gilded wood instead of
gilt bronze. The strong flavour of Continental Baroque in their design is marked. The bookcases were made for Sir William Courtenay of Powderham Castle, near Exeter, by John
Channon in 1740. They are both signed and dated 'J. Channon 1740'. on brass plaques set in
the middle of the door frames at the bottom (Pl. 66). The Payment of £50. 'part on account'
to John Channon on 29 April 1741, which is recorded in the Account Books of Sir William
Courtenay, presumably refers to these bookcases.

Lit: John Hayward, 'The Channon family of Exeter and London, CHAIR AND CABINET MAKERS', *Victoria and Albert Museum Bulletin*, April 1966, Vol. 11, No. 2, fig. 1.

Mark Girouard, 'Powderham Castle', *Country Life*, 4, 11, 18, July 1963.

Loc: Powderham Castle, Near Exeter, Devon.

66. A medal or specimen-cabinet, which may be said on stylistic grounds to have been almost certainly made by John Channon about 1740–50 : cf. Pls. 60 and 64.

Lit: Hayward, 'Channon', *loc. cit.*, fig. 4.

Loc: The City Art Gallery, Bristol.

67. A carved mahogany open-armchair covered in tapestry, which can perhaps be related to the entry in the *Holkam Weekly Departmental Accounts*, March 1738 — 'Mr. Hallett for a pattern chair for Holkam . . . £3. 5. 0.'. However, on April 15, £2. 5. 0. was paid to Hallett 'in exchange of a pattern chair which he received £3. 5. 0. for. . .'. These entries are somewhat obscure.

Lit: *D.E.F.*, I, fig. 122, p. 265.

Anthony Coleridge, 'Some Mid-Georgian Cabinet-Makers at Holkham', *Apollo*, February 1964.

Anthony Coleridge, 'A Reappraisal of William Hallett', *Journal of the Furniture History Society*, Vol. 1, 1965.

Loc: Holkham House, Norfolk.

68. A mahogany cabinet of architectural design, which can perhaps be related to the entry in Sir Mathew Fetherstonhaugh's account book (retained at Uppark), dated 27 March 1754, 'Pd. Mr. Hallett for a cabinet . . . £43. 5. 6.'.

Lit: Anthony Coleridge, 'Georgian Cabinet-Makers at Uppark — Part II', *Connoisseur*, November, 1967.

Coleridge, 'William Hallett', *loc. cit.*

Loc: Uppark, Sussex.

69. A mahogany cabinet of Kentian tradition, which is signed in pencil on the carcase of the base with the words 'William Hallett 1763 Long Acre'. Stylistically this piece is more readily datable to the early 1740's.

Lit: Coleridge, 'William Hallett', *loc. cit.*

Loc: Private Collection.

70. A detail of 69 above.

71. The inscription on the base of 69 above.

72. A mahogany architectural bookcase in the Kentian tradition and in the manner associated with Hallett's work — cf. the key-pattern design carved on the frieze with 70 above.

Lit: Coleridge, 'William Hallett', *loc. cit.*

Loc: Private Collection.

73. One of a pair of mahogany side-chairs :

Inspired by a design of Gaetano Brunetti in *Sixty Different Sorts of Ornaments*, published 1736.

Lit: *English Furniture Designs of the Eighteenth Century*, p. 35, pl. 29.

Loc: Private Collection.

74. A drawing for two tables and pier-glasses designed by John Vardy for the Great Dining-Room and Parlour at Spencer House. See p. 134, n. 6.

(Iolo Williams Gift, 1962–7–14–68.)

Loc: British Museum, Print Room.

75. A drawing for a table and pier-glass designed by John Vardy for the Little Dining-Room at Spencer House — signed and dated 1758.

(Iolo Williams Gift, 1962–7–14–67.)

Loc: British Museum, Print Room.

76. A giltwood framed pier-glass probably designed for Spencer House by John Vardy in about 1758. The frame may have been carved by Vardy's brother, Thomas. The over-carved acanthus fronds are typical of Vardy's style, cf. 78, 79 and 80 below.
    Loc: Althorp, Northamptonshire.

77. A design for a pier-glass and table drawn by John Vardy in 1761 for the Duke of Bolton. The frieze of the table bears the Duke's arms — three swords in pile. The drawing G4/4² (R.I.B.A., Sir Banister Fletcher Library Drawings Collection) is inscribed 'Probably for Grosvenor Square, 1761'. A pair of tables made from this design are in the collection of Lord Bolton at Bolton Hall, Yorkshire.
    Lit: Anthony Coleridge, 'John Vardy and the Hackwood Suite', *Connoisseur*, January 1962, p. 17, pl. 8.
    Loc: R.I.B.A., London.

78. A design for a pier-glass and table drawn by John Vardy, about 1745 — R.I.B.A., Sir Banister Fletcher Library, Drawings Collection, G4/8.
    Lit: *English Furniture Designs of the Eighteenth Century*, p. 37, pl. 43.
            Coleridge, 'John Vardy', *loc. cit.*
    Loc: R.I.B.A., London.

{ 79. One of a pair of giltwood pier-glasses and tables made for the third or fourth Duke of Bolton
{ 80. for Hackwood Park, Basingstoke, after John Vardy's design, cf. 78 above.
    Lit: Coleridge, 'John Vardy', *loc. cit.*, pp. 12–14.
    Loc: Hackwood Park, Hampshire.

81. A giltwood and metal hexagonal hall-lantern designed by John Vardy for the hall of Spencer House, Green Park.
    Loc: Althorp, Northamptonshire.

82. One of a set of twenty-three mahogany single chairs — some with pierced stretchers — made for Spencer House, probably after designs by Vardy, perhaps by the cabinet-makers William and John Gordon.
    Loc: Althorp, Northamptonshire.

83. One of a set of twelve hall-chairs, the seat-rails carved with bucrania, as is the frieze in the hall at Spencer House, where they stood, which was designed by Vardy in 1758. The set was repaired by Gordon and Taitt in 1772.
    Lit: *D.E.F.*, I, fig. 2, p. 316.
    Loc: Althorp, Northamptonshire.

84. One of a suite of two settees, two armchairs, eight single chairs and a library table which were made for Spencer House, perhaps by William and John Gordon.
    Loc: Althorp, Northamptonshire.

85. One of a set of five chairs and three stools from Spencer House attributed to William and John Gordon.
    Loc: Althorp, Northamptonshire.

86. One of a set of six chairs and two settees for which John Gordon charged the second Duke of Atholl £36. 10. 0. in 1753.
    Lit: Anthony Coleridge, 'Chippendale, The Director and some Cabinet-makers at Blair Castle', *Connoisseur*, December 1960, pp. 252–3.
    Loc: Blair Castle, Perthshire.

87. One of a set of eight chairs for which John Gordon charged the second Duke of Atholl £14 in 1756. They are upholstered with floral needlework panels worked by Jean Drummond, second wife of James, second Duke of Atholl. In Gordon's account they are described as '8 mahogany chairs, carv'd frames in fish scales, with a french foot and carv'd leaf upon the toe'. cf. the toes of Pl. 85.
    Lit: Coleridge, 'Chippendale, The Director . . .', *loc. cit.*
    Loc: Blair Castle, Perthshire.

88. A pair of carved mahogany open-armchairs from a set of eight armchairs and two settees: cf. the scale carving and toes with 87. This set originated from Ditton Park, Thames Ditton, Surrey, belonging to Lord Montagu of Beaulieu and later the Duke of Buccleuch. The set originally contained 24 chairs.

    Lit: H. Cescinsky, *English Furniture of the Eighteenth Century, 1910*, Vol. II, fig. 392.

    Sale: Parke-Bernet Galleries Inc. — New York, Walter P. Chrysler, Jr. collection: Lots 520–5, 7 May 1960.

    Loc: Private Collection.

89. A mahogany side-table with marble top:

    After a design published by William Jones, pl. 32 *The Gentlemens or Builders Companion*, 1739, and Batty and Thomas Langley, pl. 143 *The City and Country Builder's and Workman's Treasury of Designs*, 1740, plagiarised from Nicolas Pineau's *Nouveaux Desseins de Pieds de Tables*.

    Lit: *D.E.F.*, III, fig. 48, p. 291.

    Jones's design illustrated in *English Furniture Designs of the Eighteenth Century*, pl. 23.

    Loc: The Victoria and Albert Museum.

90. An annotated working sketch for a console table drawn by Matthias Lock in about 1745:

    A table, now in the Victoria and Albert Museum from the collection of the late Mrs. Rhodes of Thorpe Underwood Hall, Yorkshire, was made from this drawing for Earl Poulett for Hinton House, Hinton St. George, Somerset.

    Lit: The table, together with other pieces from the same source, is discussed by J. F. Hayward, 'Furniture designed and carved by Matthias Lock for Hinton House, Somerset', *Connoisseur*, December 1960, pp. 284–6.

    The design, in the George Lock Collection, Victoria and Albert Museum, 2602, is illustrated in *English Furniture Designs of the Eighteenth Century*, pl. 61.

    Loc: The Victoria and Albert Museum.

91. A giltwood and bronzed pier-glass after a design by Matthias Lock:

    Lock's annotated working sketch is in the George Lock collection (see Pl. 90).

    Lit: J. F. Hayward, 'Furniture designed and carved by Matthias Lock', *loc. cit.*

    Loc: The Victoria and Albert Museum.

92. A design for a pier-glass from Lock's *Six Sconces*, 1744.

    Lit: *English Furniture Designs of the Eighteenth Century*, pl. 51.

    Loc: The Victoria and Albert Museum.

93. An annotated working sketch for a side-table drawn by Matthias Lock: George Lock Collection, Victoria and Albert Museum, 2610.

    One example was bought by Earl Poulett, another is in the Earl of Dartmouth's Collection.

    Lit: Anthony Coleridge, 'Furniture in the Collection of Viscount and Viscountess Lewisham, *Connoisseur*, November 1962.

    Loc: The Victoria and Albert Museum.

94. A carved giltwood side-table attributed to Matthias Lock:

    After the design in Pl. 93 above. Another version was made for Earl Poulett and is still at Hinton House, Somerset. The mirror is late seventeenth century.

    Lit: Coleridge, 'Lewisham', *loc. cit.*

    J. F. Hayward, 'Furniture designed and carved by Matthias Lock', *loc. cit.*

    Loc: Private Collection.

95. A design for a side-table by Matthias Lock:

    The apron is carved with a mask of Hercules draped with the pelt of the Nemean lion: George Lock Collection, Victoria and Albert Museum, 2848–98.

Lit: *English Furniture Designs of the Eighteenth Century*, pl. 48.
Loc: The Victoria and Albert Museum.

96. A painted and giltwood side-table from Hamilton Palace, Lanarkshire.
 After the design in Pl. 95.
 Loc: The Metropolitan Museum.

97. A painted side-table of similar design.
 Lit: Anthony Coleridge, 'John Hodson and Some Cabinet-Makers at Blair Castle', *Connoisseur*, April 1963.
 Loc: Blair Castle, Perthshire.

98. A giltwood pier-glass in the tradition of Matthias Lock: cf. 91 above.
 Loc: Temple Newsam House, Yorkshire.

99. A giltwood console-table attributed to Thomas Johnson:
 Inspired by Johnson's design pl. 2 of *Twelve Gerondoles*, 1755, incorporating Francis Barlow's design, *Aesop's Fables* No. XI: The Wolf in Sheep's Clothing, 1687:
 Lit: Helena Hayward, *Thomas Johnson and English Rococo*, pls. 138, 188.
 Sale: Sotheby's, 10 April 1964, Lot 187 — From the collection of the seventh Earl of Dartmouth, Patshull House, Wolverhampton.
 Loc: Private Collection.

100. One of a set of four pier-glasses for which George Cole charged the Duke of Atholl £56 each in 1763. Probably designed and carved by Thomas Johnson.
 Lit: Anthony Coleridge, 'Chippendale, The Director and Some Cabinet-Makers at Blair Castle', *Connoisseur*, December 1960, pp. 254–5.
 Thomas Johnson and English Rococo, pp. 36–7.
 Loc: Blair Castle, Perthshire.

101. Carved detail of a squirrel eating a nut from the base of the pier-glass in Pl. 100:
 The estimate as well as the account from Cole's firm for these pier-glasses are still extant — Blair Castle Archives.
 Lit: Coleridge, 'Chippendale, The Director', *loc. cit.*
 Loc: Blair Castle, Perthshire.

102. Carved detail of a satyr mask on one of three console-tables made by Cole *en suite* with the Blair Castle pier-glasses (Pl. 100).
 The tables cost £43 each and the bill for them is dated 28 February 1763.
 Lit: Coleridge, 'Chippendale, The Director', *loc. cit.*
 Loc: Blair Castle, Perthshire.

103. A giltwood-framed overmantle-glass, now in the Assembly Rooms at York, to which it was presented by the York Georgian Society: it is based on a design for a *Glass Frame*, pl. 5, in Thomas Johnson's *Collection of Designs* (1758).
 Lit: Helena Hayward, 'Thomas Johnson and Rococo Carving', *Connoisseur Year Book*, 1964.
 Loc: Assembly Rooms, York.

104. One of a pair of oval pier-glasses at Corsham Court, Wiltshire:
 These may have been sold to Paul Methuen for Corsham House by George Cole and carved and designed by Thomas Johnson. Cole was paid substantial sums for work carried out for Corsham in 1761 and 1763.
 Lit: *D.E.F.*, II, fig. 89, p. 344.
 Helena Hayward, *Thomas Johnson and English Rococo*, pp. 36–7.
 Fiske Kimball and Edna Donnell, 'The Creators of the Chippendale Style', *Metropolitan Museum Studies*, II, Nov. 1929, p. 44, figs. 9–10.
 G.C.-M., p. 57, pl. 75.
 O. Bracket, *Thomas Chippendale*, pl. XLIV.
 Loc: Corsham Court, Wiltshire.

105. A design by Thomas Johnson, the inspiration for the Corsham pier-glasses (104 above):
   Published in Thomas Johnson's *Collection of Designs*, 1758, p. 10, left, and re-published by him in *One Hundred and Fifty New Designs*, 1761, p. 55, left.
   Lit: As for Pl. 104.

106. One of a pair of giltwood pier-glasses, also made for Paul Methuen, at Corsham Court:
   Similar in form to 104 above and also inspired by the design shown in Pl. 105.
   Lit: As for Pl. 104.

107. A pair of candlestands, or *torchères*, and a pair of girandoles made for Hagley Hall, Worcestershire, after designs by Thomas Johnson: (cf. Pls. 108 and 110).
   The candlestands, a pair from a set of four, the others at Temple Newsam House, Leeds, and the Victoria and Albert Museum.
   Lit: *D.E.F.*, Vol. III, p. 151, fig. 21.
       G.C-M., pp. 57–8, pl. 77.
       Fiske Kimball and Edna Donnell, 'The Creators of the Chippendale Style', *Metropolitan Museum Studies*, II, November 1929, p. 56, figs. 15–17.
       O. Bracket, *Thomas Chippendale*, 1930, pl. XLVII.
       M. Jourdain, 'Furniture at Hagley Hall', *Apollo*, Vol. LI, January 1950, p. 9, fig. 4.
       R. Edwards, *Georgian Furniture*, No. 86, p.11.
       Thomas Johnson and English Rococo, pp. 39–40.
   Exhib: Musée des Arts Décoratifs, Paris, 1959, *Le Siècle De L'Élégance*, Cat. No. 58, pl. 33.
   The torchères.
   Lit: *G.C-M.*, p. 57, pl. 76.
       Kimball and Donnell, 'The Creators of the Chippendale Style', *loc. cit.*, figs. 13–14, etc.
   Loc: The Philadelphia Museum of Art.

108. A design by Thomas Johnson from which the Hagley Hall girandoles were copied: (cf. Pl. 107).
   Published in Thomas Johnson's *Collections of Designs*, 1758, pl. 48, right, and re-published by him in *One Hundred and Fifty New Designs*, 1761, pl. 52, right.
   Lit: As for Pl. 107.

109. One of a pair of giltwood girandoles in Thomas Johnson's tradition:
   It is thought that these may have come from Hagley Hall, Worcestershire. Another pair of girandoles from Hagley Hall is illustrated in *G.C-M.*, pl. 74 and attributed to Johnson.
   Sale: Sotheby's, 5 July 1963, Lot 161 — From the collection of Mrs. Derek Fitz-Gerald, Heathfield Park, Sussex.
   Loc: Private Collection.

110. A design by Thomas Johnson from which the Hagley Hall candlestands, or *torchères*, were copied: (cf. Pl. 107).
   Published in Thomas Johnson's *Collections of Designs*, 1758, pl. 13, right, and re-published by him in *One Hundred and Fifty New Designs*, 1761, pl. 39, right.
   Lit: As for Pl. 107.

111. A giltwood mirror, from Brinkburn Priory, Northumberland, in Thomas Johnson's tradition:
   Cf. pl. 32, right, *Collection of Designs*, 1758.
   Lit: *Thomas Johnson and English Rococo*, p. 40.
       Leeds Art Calendar, No. 32–3, p. 27.
       Leeds Art Calendar, No. 38, p. 21.
   Loc: Temple Newsam House, Leeds.

112. A giltwood girandole after a design by Thomas Johnson:
    Cf. pl. 4, *Twelve Gerondoles*, 1755.
    Lit: The design is published in *Thomas Johnson and English Rococo*, pl. 140.
    Loc: Private Collection.

113. A pair of giltwood girandoles in the tradition of Thomas Johnson, the design inspired by one of Aesop's Fables:
    These are rather heavier and more massive in design than Johnson's usual work — perhaps made by another carver utilising an unpublished Johnson design.
    Lit: P. MacQuoid, *English Furniture . . . in the Lady Lever Art Gallery*, No. 147, pl. 41.
    Exhib: Royal Academy of Arts, *English Taste in the Eighteenth Century*, 1955–56, Cat. No. 166.
              Musée des Arts Décoratifs, Paris, 1959, *Le Siècle de L'Élégance*, Cat. No. 59.
    Loc: Lady Lever Art Gallery, Cheshire.

114. A pair of giltwood girandoles probably after a design by Matthias Lock:
    These have until recently (see *Thomas Johnson and English Rococo*, p. 40, note 69) been attributed to Johnson (*G.C-M.*, pp. 57–8). They are probably, however, inspired by a Lock design that was never engraved but which is now in the George Lock Collection, Victoria and Albert Museum (No. 2550, published in *English Furniture Designs of the Eighteenth Century*, Fig. 58).
    Lit: *op. cit., G.C-M.*
              Thomas Johnson and English Rococo.
              English Furniture Designs of the Eighteenth Century.
    Lenygon, *Decoration in England* (1640–1760), Fig. 349.
    Loc: Temple Newsam House, Yorkshire.

115. A design by Ince and Mayhew for three *Claw Tables*: Published pl. 13, *The Universal System of Household Furniture*, 1762.
    Chippendale did not include designs for *claw tables* in his *Director*.

116. A design by Ince and Mayhew for *two corner shelves or encoineurs*: published, pl. 47, *The Universal System of Household Furniture*, 1759–62.
    The central motif in the back of a hall-seat (cf. Pl. 125) may have been inspired by the tracery decoration on the door of the left-hand example.
    Lit: Ill. *English Furniture Designs of the Eighteenth Century*, pl. 152.

117. One of a set of six armchairs and two settees in carved giltwood covered in the original Gobelins tapestry:
    Made by Ince and Mayhew for the Earl of Coventry for Croome Court in 1769. The chairs cost £77. 8. 0. and the settees £56. 10. 0. The Earl had ordered the covers, which match the set of tapestries woven to his specifications for the room, from the atelier of Jacques Neilson at the Gobelins in August 1764.
    Lit: James Parker, 'The Architecture and Furniture at Croome Court', and Edith A. Standen, 'The Tapestries at Croome Court', *Metropolitan Museum of Art Bulletin*, November 1959, pp. 89, 108.
              Eileen Harris, 'Robert Adam and the Gobelins', *Apollo*, April 1962.
              Clifford Musgrave, *Adam and Hepplewhite*, 1966, pl. 63.
    Loc: The Metropolitan Museum of Art.

118. A carved giltwood side-table probably made by Ince and Mayhew for Lord Coventry between 1763 and 1765: It supports a black marble slab inlaid with specimen marbles and coloured stones (see p. 66, n. 2 for wording of account), made by John Wildsmith in 1759 for £46. 3. 0.
    Lit: Parker, 'The Architecture and Furniture at Croome Court', *loc. cit.*, pp. 89–90.
    Loc: The Metropolitan Museum of Art.

119. A pair of commodes of neo-classical design delivered to Croome Court by Ince and Mayhew in 1761. Their account is extant in the Croome Court Archives. Made by Ince and Mayhew perhaps to designs by Robert Adam in the early neo-classical style.

      Lit: Clifford Musgrave, *Adam and Hepplewhite*, 1966, pl. 119.

      Exhib: *The Adam Style in Furniture*, The Iveagh Bequest, Kenwood, 1964, cat. no. 6.

      Loc: Kenwood House, Middlesex.

120. A mahogany break-front bookcase, about 1760, bearing the trade label of Ince and Mayhew. The trade label (see text, p. 63, n. 5), is illustrated in select facsimile version of *The Universal System* . . . with introduction by Ralph Edwards — Tiranti, 1960. Ince and Mayhew include designs for *Bookcases for Recesses* in the *Universal System* (cf. Pl. 121).

      Lit: *D.E.F.*, I, fig. 54, p. 191.

              G.C-M., p. 73, pl. 161.

              Furniture Designs of the Eighteenth Century, p. 50.

              Universal System of Household Furniture, Tiranti off-print, 1960.

      Loc: The Museum of Decorative Arts, Copenhagen.

121. A design by Ince and Mayhew for *Bookcases for Recesses*: published pl. 19, right, *The Universal System of Household Furniture*, 1759–62: cf. 120 above.

122. One of a pair of carved giltwood pier-glasses attributed to Ince and Mayhew: (cf. Pl. 123 which shows a design from *The Universal System* . . .).

      Loc: The Metropolitan Museum of Art.

123. A design by Ince and Mayhew for a *chimney-piece*: published, pl. 85, *The Universal System of Household Furniture*, 1759–62: cf. 122 and 124.

124. A pair of giltwood wall-brackets in the tradition of Ince and Mayhew: (cf. Pl. 123).

      Exhib: Temple Newsam House, Leeds, 1951, *Thomas Chippendale*, Cat. No. 67.

      Loc: Private Collection.

125. A mahogany hall-seat, about 1750. The unusual design of tracery in the centre of the back has affinities with Ince and Mayhew's design for *encoineurs* (cf. Pl. 116).

      Lit: M. Harris and Sons, *Catalogue of Old English Furniture*, p. 314, pl. 11.

      Sale: Parke-Bernet Galleries Inc., 29–30 April 1960, Lot 131 — Walter P. Chrysler Jr., collection.

      Loc: Private Collection.

126. A mahogany open-armchair, about 1760, the rear seat-rail stamped I.M.: cf. the design of the splat with an Ince and Mayhew design for one of four *Parlour Chairs*, pl. 9 of the *Universal System*. . . .

      Loc: Private Collection.

127. A design drawn by John Linnell for a side-table: Victoria and Albert Museum E.237–1929. This appears to derive from a design for a table decorated with dragons composed by François Cuvilliés — Ill. *English Furniture Designs of the Eighteenth Century*, pl. 354.

      Lit: *English Furniture Designs of the Eighteenth Century*, pl. 193.

      Loc: The Victoria and Albert Museum.

128. A chimney-glass for one of the bedrooms at Osterley Park, Middlesex — the chimney-piece is a replacement. Designed by John Linnell (cf. Pl. 129), and carved in his workshops at 28 Berkeley Square. Extant documents prove that Linnell was supplying furniture to Mr. Child for Osterley from 1767 onwards.

      Lit: *G.C-M.*, p. 77, pl. 165.

      Loc: The Victoria and Albert Museum (Osterley Park House).

129. The design by John Linnell for the chimney-glass, shown in Pl. 128. Victoria and Albert Museum, E.281–1929.

      Lit: *G.C-M.*, p. 77, pl. 154.

              English Furniture Designs of the Eighteenth Century, pl. 194.

      Loc: The Victoria and Albert Museum.

130. A design by John Linnell for a console-table and pier-glass, about 1760 — pen and ink and watercolour. Victoria and Albert Museum, E.247–1929.
> Lit: *English Furniture Designs of the Eighteenth Century*, pl. 199.

131. A carved giltwood-framed sofa after designs by John Linnell and Robert Adam: A similar sofa was made after John Linnell's design (Victoria and Albert Museum, E.129–1929) for Kedleston Hall, Derbyshire. Robert Adam also executed a similar design in 1762 (Sir John Soane's Museum, Adam, Vol. 17, No. 69).
> Lit: The Kedleston sofa is illustrated:
> *Bolton*, Vol. II, p. 292.
> *D.E.F.*, III, fig. 57, p. 96.
> *G.C-M.*, pl. 163.
> Loc: The Philadelphia Museum of Art.

132. A carved mahogany armchair, the back similar to a design in Robert Manwaring's *The Chair-Maker's Friend*, 1765 (cf. Pl. 133), from Bramshill, Hampshire.
> Lit: *D.E.F.*, I, fig. 185, p. 285.
> Loc: The Metropolitan Museum of Art.

133. A design by Robert Manwaring from which the back of the chair, shown in Pl. 132, may have been taken: published pl. 10, right, in *The Chair-Maker's Friend*, 1765.

134. One of a set of four mahogany armchairs, from a larger set, the back inset with the crest of the Lane family: (cf. Pls. 132 and 133).
> Lit: Leeds Art Calendar, No. 46–7, pp. 18–19.
> Loc: Temple Newsam House, Yorkshire.

135. A carved mahogany open-armchair — for the design see 136 below.
> Loc: The Victoria and Albert Museum, London.

136. A design by Robert Manwaring from *The Chair-Maker's Friend*, 1765: published as pl. 13, right. The examples shown in Pls. 135 and 137 appear to have been inspired by this design.

137. A carved mahogany open-armchair: its design stems from pl. 13 in Manwaring's *The Chair-Maker's Friend*, cf. 136.
> Loc: Scone Palace, Perthshire.

138. A carved mahogany side-chair from a set of eighteen. Four armchairs with panelled seats and similar backs are also extant. Originally in the Summer Dining-Room at Stowe, Buckinghamshire.
> Sale: Christie's, 28 May 1964, Lot 70, pl. 10.
> Loc: Private Collection.

139. A mahogany armchair and a single chair from a set of six single and two armchairs: their design is based on that for a *Gothick Chair* published as pl. 14, right, in Manwaring's *The Chair-Maker's Friend*.
> Loc: Private Collection.

140. One of a set of twenty-six dining-chairs at Stourhead House, Wiltshire — four with arms: Twelve in walnut and parcel-gilt and fourteen in mahogany.
> Traditionally held to have been made by Chippendale (Chippendale, the younger, was employed there between 1795 and 1820), but probably stemming from Mathew Darly's designs, published 1750–51, and plagiarised by Manwaring.
> Lit: 'Stourhead Wiltshire', *Country Life*, LXXXVIII, pp. 608, 638.
> Loc: Stourhead House, Wiltshire.

141. One of a set of single chairs in Virginia walnut with similar backs (cf. Pl. 140). This design is not uncommon.
> Loc: Private Collection.

142. A mahogany single chair: the back similar to a design for *Parlour Chairs* published by Manwaring, as pl. 41, in his *The Chair-Maker's Guide*, 1766, but probably designed by Mathew Darly: (cf. the latter's designs in *A New Book of Chinese, Gothic and Modern Chairs*, 1750–51).

Lit: *D.E.F.*, I, fig. 177, p. 282.
English Furniture Designs of the Eighteenth Century, pls. 46, 47 and 180.
Loc: The Victoria and Albert Museum.

143. Two designs for *Rural Chairs for Summer houses* from *The Chair-Maker's Friend*, 1765: Published as pl. 26 (cf. Pl. 144).
Lit: Ill. *English Furniture Designs of the Eighteenth Century*, pl. 177.

144. One from a set of rural chairs after Robert Manwaring's design, cf. 143.
Loc: The Victoria and Albert Museum.

145. Two chairs and a table of a type similar to the forms shown in Pls. 143 and 144.
Loc: Private Collection.

146. A mahogany dolls' house of Palladian design, about 1740:
Family tradition holds that this was made by Thomas Chippendale before he left Yorkshire for London. There is, however, no documentary evidence to back this supposition.
Loc: Nostell Priory, Yorkshire.

147. A section of a contemporary map of London showing Chippendale's premises in St. Martin's Lane, Nos. 60 and 61. William Hallett was at 71, and Vile and Cobb were next door on the corner of the Lane and Long Acre.

148. A black decorated and gilt carved wood console-table, with pier-glass *en suite*, in the Gothic tradition, about 1755.
These were made for Horace Walpole's friend, Anthony Chute, for the Vyne, Hampshire: they may be similar in design to 'A truly splendid table in the Gothic style, the top of Sicilian jasper of the rarest kind, on a black frame (the table was designed by Mr. [Richard] Bentley and is perfectly unique)' — Strawberry Hill Sale Catalogue.
Loc: The Vyne, Hampshire.

149. A circular girandole of similar date and design to 148.
Loc: The Vyne, Hampshire.

150. The 'Strawberry Room' from Lee Priory, Littlebourne, Kent, built in the Gothic manner by James Wyatt, 1782–90, for Thomas Barrett (1744–1803) in emulation of the house of his friend, Horace Walpole, at Strawberry Hill. Note the three pieces of Gothic furniture. The table is in the style of Ince and Mayhew, while the pole-screen and left-hand chair appear to owe much to Chippendale's *Director*.
Loc: The Victoria and Albert Museum.

151. A portrait by Arthur Devis (1708–87) of Sir Roger Newdigate in his Gothic Library.
Sir Roger Newdigate (1719–1806), 5th Bt. M.P. rebuilt Arbury in the Gothic style. The remodelling of the library in the Gothic style was carried out by William Hiorn from about 1750 onwards.
Lit: S. H. Paviere, *The Devis Family of Painters*, Leigh-on-Sea, 1950, p. 52, No. 110.
Exhib: Royal Academy of Arts, *English Taste in the Eighteenth Century*, 1955–56, Cat. No. 305.
Loc: Private Collection.

152. One of a set of painted chairs in the Gothic taste from the Chapel at Audley End, Essex, about 1750–55. Cf. a very similar chair designed by Adam for Alnwick Castle, Northumberland (Ill. Clifford Musgrave, *Adam and Hepplewhite Furniture*, 1966, fig. 56).
Exhib: Royal Academy, *op. cit.*, Cat. No. 301.
Loc: Audley End, Essex.

153. One of a pair of green and gold decorated softwood armchairs in the Gothic tradition, made for the Orangery or Pavilion at Stonor Park, Henley-on-Thames.
Lit: *D.E.F.*, I, p. 283, fig. 182.
Exhib: Royal Academy, *op. cit.*, Cat. No. 306.
Loc: Stonor Park, Oxfordshire.

154. One of a set of mahogany armchairs and a settee, in the Gothic taste, the embroidery covers worked by Lady Newdigate, mother of Sir Roger who 'Gothicised' Arbury: see Pl. 151.
      Exhib: Royal Academy, *op. cit.*, Cat. No. 267.
      Loc: Private Collection.

155. The Master's Chair of the Joiners' Company carved in 1754 by Edward Newman — [Liveryman, 1720, Court of Assistants 1730, Master 1749].
      The cost of this 'proper Handsome Masters Chair', for the Court Parlour was £27. 6. 0.
      Lit: *D.E.F.*, I, p. 283, fig. 181.
              G.C-M., p. 101, p. 237, fig. 225.
      Loc: The Victoria and Albert Museum.

156. An unusual open-armchair in the Gothic taste, of a somewhat rustic conception.
      Loc: Private Collection.

157. A 'Windsor chair' of Gothic design in turned and cut-out yew, and shaped mahogany — mid-eighteenth century.
      Lit: *D.E.F.*, I, fig. 2, p. 319.
              Ralph Edwards, *English Chairs*, London, 1951, fig. 79.
      Loc: The Victoria and Albert Museum.

158. An oak twin chair-back settee, one of a pair with 3 chairs *en suite* — from Kirtlington Park.
      Loc: The Museum of Fine Arts, Boston.

159. A portrait of the Earl and Countess of Pomfret by Thomas Bardwell (d. about 1780): its Gothic frame was designed for the drawing-room of the Pomfret's house in Arlington Street which was Gothicised by Sanderson Miller in 1760.
      Lit: Mrs. Poole, *Catalogue of Oxford Portraits*, Oxford, 1912, Vol. 1, p. 188, No. 456.
      Exhib: Royal Academy of Arts, *English Taste in the Eighteenth Century*, 1955–56, Cat. No. 270.
      Loc: The Ashmolean Museum, Oxford.

160. A giltwood and ebonised wall-glass in the mixed Gothic and Chinese taste, which also has rococo ornamentation.
      Loc: Private Collection.

161. A mahogany aviary inlaid with brass, about 1750:
      Lit: *D.E.F.*, 1924, Vol. I, p. 60, fig. 5.
      Exhib: *Loan Exhibition of Antique Bird Cages*, Cooper Union Museum of Arts and Decoration, New York.
      Loc: Private Collection.

162. A carved mahogany display-cabinet in the full Gothic tradition.
      Loc: The Victoria and Albert Museum.

163. A mahogany clothes-press with carved and applied Gothic ornamentation:
      Lit: Yvonne Hackenbroch (Ed.), *English Furniture in the Collection of Irwin Untermyer*, London, 1958, figs. 318, 319, pls. 276, 277.
              A similar example ill. Constance Simon, *English Furniture Designers of the Eighteenth Century*, London, 1905, fig. 18.
      Loc: The Irwin Untermyer Collection, New York.

164. A dressing-table, based on a *Director* design (cf. Pl. 166) originally from Kimbolton Castle, Huntingdonshire, and from the collection of the Duke of Manchester.
      Lit: *D.E.F.*, III, fig. 14, p. 228.
              G.C-M., p. 172, fig. 97.
      Exhib: Victoria and Albert Museum, 1962, *International Art Treasures Exhibition*, Cat. No. 91.
      Loc: Private Collection.

165. A rosewood dressing-table made for Lady Arniston (1706–98), mother of Henry, first Viscount Melville. Like that shown in Pl. 164, this may also have been made by Chippendale.

Lit: O. Bracket, *Thomas Chippendale*, London, 1930, pl. 39.

P. Macquoid, *English Furniture, Tapestry and Needlework . . . in the Lady Lever Art Gallery*, No. 201, pl. 57.

Exhib: Musée des Arts Décoratifs, Paris, 1959, *Le Siècle de L'Élégance*, Cat. No. 49, pls. 22–3.

Loc: The Lady Lever Art Gallery, Cheshire.

166. Plate from the third edition of the *Director*, pl. 52 — 'A design for a dressing-table for a lady.' The notes in the foreword inform us that 'Two Dressing Tables have been made of Rose-wood, from this design, which gave an entire satisfaction'. The dressing-tables in question may possibly be those shown in Pls. 164 and 165.

167. A mahogany dining-chair, the splat closely following pl. 14, in the third edition of the *Director*. The Duke and Duchess of Norfolk were subscribers to the first edition.

Lit: *D.E.F.*, I, p. 280, fig. 172, p. 282.

G.C-M., p. 177, fig. 106.

Exhib: Royal Academy of Arts, *English Taste in the Eighteenth Century*, 1955–56, Cat. No. 142.

Loc: Arundel Castle, Sussex.

168. One of a set of mahogany dining-chairs of *Director* design, the splat closely following pl. 10 in the third edition of the *Director*.

Loc: Private Collection.

169. One of a set of mahogany dining-chairs from the Private Dining-Room at Nostell Priory, Nr. Wakefield, Yorkshire — almost certainly made by Thomas Chippendale.

Exhib: Temple Newsam House, Leeds, 1951, *Thomas Chippendale*, Cat. No. 30.

Loc: Nostell Priory, Yorkshire.

170. A mahogany open-armchair of *Director* design — a fine example of its kind.

Loc: Private Collection.

171. A single chair of unusual design, the splat carved with tassels. The overall-carving suggests a country origin, and the chair probably dates from the decade prior to the publication of the *Director*, as is shown by its rather ponderous and *retardé* design. It is interesting to note that Chippendale does not include an example of the 'claw and ball' foot in the *Director*.

Loc: Private Collection.

172. Plate 16 from the first edition of the *Director* showing three designs for 'Ribband Back Chairs'. In his notes Chippendale describes these as being 'the best I have ever seen (or perhaps have ever been made)'.

173. A mahogany 'ribband back chair' from a set of four: cf. Pl. 172 above.

Lit: Ralph Edwards, *English Chairs*, London, 1950, pl. 73.

Loc: The Victoria and Albert Museum.

174. A mahogany chair-back settee of 'ribband back' design.

Loc: The Victoria and Albert Museum.

175. One of a set of four mahogany 'ribband back chairs'.

Loc: The Metropolitan Museum.

176. and 177. A mahogany chair-back settee of 'ribband back' design converting to form a day-bed. Although this example, which is *en suite* with six chairs, is at Nostell Priory, it is not original to the house; it was acquired in 1883.

Lit: chair — *D.E.F.*, I, p. 281, fig. 173.

settee — *G.C-M.*, p. 174, fig. 99.

Exhib: Temple Newsam House, Leeds, 1951, *Thomas Chippendale*, Cat. No. 29.

Loc: Nostell Priory, Yorkshire.

178. Plate 21 from the third edition of the *Director*, where they are described as 'French Chairs'.

179. A carved mahogany framed 'French Chair' — designs for these only appear in the third edition of the *Director*:

> The design of this chair closely corresponds with pl. 22 in the third edition. The upholstery of the back of this and some of the other chairs in this class is fixed to an inner framing which is inserted from the back into the carved frame.

> Lit: *D.E.F.*, I, p. 288, fig. 198.
> *G.C-M.*, p. 178, fig. 110.
> Ralph Edwards, *English Chairs*, London, 1950, pl. 74.

> Loc: The Victoria and Albert Museum.

180. One of a pair of mahogany 'French Chairs' covered with tapestry, which was perhaps made at the Fulham workshops.

> Loc: The Museum of Fine Arts, Boston.

181. A carved mahogany-framed open-armchair of *Director* design.

> Loc: The Victoria and Albert Museum, C. D. Rotch Bequest.

182. One of a set of four carved mahogany-framed armchairs in the French taste, covered in Beauvais tapestry. Originally purchased by Peregrine Bertie, third Duke of Ancaster, in about 1760, for Grimthorpe Castle, Lincs.

> Lit: Yvonne Hackenbroch (Ed.), *English Furniture in the Collection of Irwin Untermyer*, London, 1958, figs. 143–7, pls. 116–20.

> Loc: The Irwin Untermyer Collection, New York.

183. A mahogany-framed armchair carved with the crest of the Marquess of Abergavenny and covered in what appears to be the original needlework which is thought to be of French origin.

> Lit: *Op. cit.* Figs. 131–2, pls. 104–5.

> Loc: The Irwin Untermyer Collection, New York.

184. A similar armchair.

> Loc: Private Collection.

185. A pair of similar armchairs, covered in tapestry, from a set of twelve — traditionally held to have been supplied by Chippendale, in collaboration with Sir William Chambers, to Walcot House for Clive of India.

> Loc: Private Collection.

186. A similar armchair covered in what may be Fulham tapestry, from one of the Committee Rooms in the House of Lords.

> This chair is described in the sale catalogue of the Fulham factory, 30 April 1755.

> Lit: Oliver Bracket, *Encyclopaedia of English Furniture*, 1927, p. 212.
> Oliver Bracket and H. Clifford Smith, *English Furniture Illustrated*, 1950, pl. 153.
> H. H. Mülliner, *The Decorative Arts in England*, 1660–1780, fig. 186.

> Exhib: Burlington Fine Arts Club, London, 1920.
> Chippendale Furniture Exhibition for St. Luke's Hospital, New York, 1929.
> Art Treasures Exhibition, Parke-Bernet Galleries, New York, 1955, No. 226.

> Loc: Private Collection.

187. One of a pair of giltwood framed 'French Chairs' at Wilton House, Wiltshire, which were probably provided by Chippendale's firm.

> Lit: Anthony Coleridge, 'Chippendale at Wilton', *Apollo*, July 1964.

> Loc: Wilton House, Wiltshire.

188. One of a set of six open-armchairs and eight single chairs, covered in what may well be the original needlework, and probably supplied by Chippendale for Wilton: they are similar to a design in pl. 20 in the third edition of the *Director*.

> Lit: Coleridge, 'Chippendale at Wilton', *loc. cit.*

> Loc: Wilton House, Wiltshire.

189. A mahogany-framed open-armchair of *Director* design.
    Loc: Private Collection.

190. One of a set of mahogany hall-chairs, painted with the Pembroke heraldic devices, which was probably supplied by Chippendale for Wilton House: Their design is related to a chair shown on pl. 17 in the third edition of the *Director*.
    Lit: Coleridge, 'Chippendale at Wilton', *loc. cit.*
    Loc: Wilton House, Wiltshire.

191. A pair of unusual hall chairs, also based on pl. 17 in the third edition of the *Director*.
    Loc: Private Collection.

192. A mahogany armchair based on pl. 27 in the third edition of the *Director* where such pieces are called 'Chinese Chairs'.
    Loc: The Metropolitan Museum of Art.

193. A mahogany twin chair-back settee, its design incorporating Chinese and Gothic motives.
    Loc: Private Collection.

194. A carved mahogany single-chair, the back based on pl. 24 in the first edition of the *Director*.
    Lit: Ralph Edwards, *English Chairs*, London, 1950, pl. 75.
    Loc: The Victoria and Albert Museum.

195. One of a pair of mahogany settees in the Chinese taste covered in contemporary needlework.
    Lit: *D.E.F.*, III, fig. 32, p. 84.
    Exhib: Royal Academy of Arts, 1955–56, *English Taste in the Eighteenth Century*, Cat. No. 227.
    Loc: Private Collection.

196. A mahogany single chair of Chinese design, one of a set of four with a settee *en suite*: their design based on pl. 28 in the third edition of the *Director*.
    Lit: P. Macquoid, *English Furniture, Tapestry and Needlework . . . in the Lady Lever Art Gallery*, London, 1928, No. 157, pl. 47, No. 158, pl. 48.
            Yvonne Hackenbroch (Ed.), *English Furniture in the Collection of Irwin Untermyer*, London, 1958, fig. 148, pl. 121.
    Exhib: Musée des Arts Décoratifs, Paris, 1959, *Le Siècle D'Élégance*, Cat. No. 65, pl. 26.
    Loc: The Lady Lever Art Gallery, Cheshire.

197. A mahogany armchair, from a set of seven, grotesquely carved with chinoiserie motives and on dolphin feet.
    Lit: P. Macquoid, *Lady Lever Art Gallery, op. cit.*, No. 155, pl. 47.
    Exhib: The Royal Academy of Arts, 1955–56, *English Taste in the Eighteenth Century*, Cat. No. 179.
            Musée des Arts Décoratifs, *Le Siècle D'Élégance*, Cat. No. 71, pl. 29.
    Loc: The Lady Lever Art Gallery, Cheshire. (One is on loan to the Victoria and Albert Museum [1966].)

198. A carved mahogany stool based on a *chair* design in pl. 20 in the first edition of the *Director*: Designs for *stools* are not included in the *Director*: note the dolphin feet, a refinement sometimes found on seat-furniture at this period.
    Lit: *D.E.F.*, III, fig. 51, p. 178.
    Loc: The Victoria and Albert Museum.

199. One of a pair of giltwood stools at Wilton House *en suite* with the 'French Chairs' (Pl. 187), which were probably supplied by Chippendale.
    Lit: Coleridge, 'Chippendale at Wilton', *loc. cit.*
    Loc: Wilton House, Wiltshire.

200. One of a pair of giltwood settees, probably made by Chippendale's firm to harmonise with the existing furniture of Kentian design in the Double Cube Room at Wilton — their top-rails carved with coronets.

Lit :   Coleridge, 'Chippendale at Wilton', *loc. cit.*
Loc :   Wilton House, Wiltshire.

201. A giltwood-framed settee at Wilton probably supplied by Chippendale — its essentially scrolling framework is carved with neo-classical husks, garlands and anthemions : a good example of the transitional phase between the rococo and neo-classical styles.

Lit :   Coleridge, 'Chippendale at Wilton', *loc. cit.*
Loc :   Wilton House, Wiltshire.

202. A mahogany framed settee from a large set of seat-furniture, the major part of which is still in the collection of the Earl of Shaftesbury at St. Giles's House, Dorset. cf. pl. 30, the third edition of the *Director*.

Lit :   *D.E.F.*, III, fig. 54, p. 94.
           O. Bracket, *Thomas Chippendale*, London, 1930, pl. 21.
           R. C. Lines, 'My House at St. Giles's', *Connoisseur*, October 1959, pl. 12.
           'St. Giles's House', *Antique Collector*, August 1762, p. 145.
           'St. Giles's House, Dorset', *Country Life*, 13 March 1915.
Exhib : A pair of chairs from the set, The Royal Academy of Arts, 1955–56, *English Taste in the Eighteenth Century*, Cat. No. 194.
Sale :   4 armchairs and a settee from this set were sold at Christie's, 24 November 1966, lots 122, 123. Other pieces from the same set have been sold at Christie's on the following dates : 23 June, 1949 — 2 chairs; 3 May, 1951 — 3 chairs; 23 October, 1953 — 4 chairs and 1 settee.
Loc :   Private Collection.

203. A mahogany chair of similar design to the settee shown in Pl. 202. One of a pair. These were originally at Raynham Hall, Norfolk and were made for Captain Townshend, M.P. — perhaps by Chippendale's firm.

Loc :   Private Collection.

204. A mahogany framed settee from a large set, comprising : thirty armchairs (see Pl. 341), four settees, two stools and a winged armchair at Corsham. The maker has not been identified but accounts for other furniture from Cobb, and Chippendale and Haig, are extant in the Corsham Court archives. This set still has its original silk damask coverings. Note the wavy line of huge brass-headed nails.

Lit :   A stool from this set is ill.
           Oliver Bracket, *Thomas Chippendale*, London, 1930, pl. 20.
           A settee, ill. *D.E.F.*, III, p. 94, fig. 54.
Loc :   Corsham Court, Wiltshire.

205. A carved mahogany framed settee, its design derived from pl. 22, dated 1759, in the third edition of the *Director* — 'A French Chair' (cf. Pl. 179).

Loc :   The Metropolitan Museum of Art.

206. A mahogany bedstead with honeysuckle antefixae, about 1770.

Lit :   Anthony Coleridge, 'Dundas and some Rococo Cabinet-Makers, *Apollo*, September 1967.
Loc :   Aske Hall, near Richmond, Yorkshire.

207. A mahogany-framed bedstead, the 'cluster column' posts are similar to some designs for 'Bed Pillars' in pl. 34 of the third edition of the *Director* : see note on Pl. 204 above. However it is not certain whether Chippendale made this bed, although there is a very similar, although simpler, example at Saltram House, Devon, where Chippendale's firm was employed. The silk damask hangings are original.

Lit :   *D.E.F.*, I, p. 64, fig. 49.
Loc :   Corsham Court, Wiltshire.

194

208. Plate 53 from the third edition of the *Director* where they are described as 'Breakfast Tables'.

209. A mahogany breakfast-table that is presumably based on a *Director* design (cf. Pl. 208).
- Lit: Anthony Coleridge, 'English Furniture in the Duke of Argyll's collection', *Connoisseur*, March 1965.
- Loc: Inveraray Castle, Argyll.

210. A mahogany breakfast-table based on a *Director* design (cf. Pl. 208).
- Loc: Private Collection.

211. A mahogany breakfast-table (cf. Pls. 208–210).
- Lit: Anthony Coleridge, 'Some Furniture in the Collection of the Earl of Mansfield', *Connoisseur*, April 1966.
- Loc: Scone Palace, Perthshire.

212. A mahogany china, or silver, table based on pl. 51 in the third edition of the *Director*. Probably part of the furniture that Chippendale is thought to have made for Wilton.
- Lit: Coleridge, 'Chippendale at Wilton', *loc. cit.*
- Loc: Wilton House, Wiltshire.

213. A 'China Table' of elaborate design with finely carved detail, in the *Director* style.
- Loc: Private Collection.

214. A 'China Table' of restrained form with foliated cross stretcher, all in the *Director* style.
- Loc: Private Collection.

215. A walnut 'Sideboard Table', one of a pair, the rectangular top inset with a granite slab: Its design based on pl. 57 in the third edition of the *Director* — probably supplied by Chippendale for Wilton.
- Lit: Coleridge, 'Chippendale at Wilton', *loc. cit.*
- Loc: Wilton House, Wiltshire.

216. One of a pair of mahogany sideboard-tables, their tops inset with porphyry slabs within ormolu borders. Possibly by Chippendale (see note to Pl. 204) — [possibly adapted].
- Lit: Oliver Bracket, *Thomas Chippendale*, London, 1924, pl. 31.
- Loc: Corsham Court, Wiltshire.

217. A sideboard-table based on pl. 60 in the third edition of the *Director*.
- Loc: The Victoria and Albert Museum.

218. One of a pair of mahogany side-tables in the Gothic taste with shaped Convent-Siena marble tops: there are three grotesque faces along the front edge.
- Lit: P. Macquoid, *English Furniture, Tapestry and Needlework . . . in the Lady Lever Art Gallery*, London, 1928, No. 234, pl. 62.
- Exhib: The Royal Academy of Arts, 1955–56, *English Taste in the Eighteenth Century*, Cat. No. 308.
- Loc: The Lady Lever Art Gallery, Cheshire (one on long loan to the Victoria and Albert Museum).

219. Plate 54 for the third edition of the *Director*, showing what are there called 'Shaving Tables'.

220. A mahogany shaving-table or, as it is described in Chippendale's account of 1774 to Ninian Home of Paxton, Berwick-on-Tweed, 'A mahogany dressing table with folding top, boxes, bottles, a glass and compleat'. It cost £5. 18. 0.; cf. Pl. 219 above.
- Lit: Anthony Coleridge, 'Chippendale, Interior-Decorator and House-Furnisher', *Apollo*, April 1963.
- Loc: Paxton House, Berwick-on-Tweed.

221. 'A large size shaving table . . . with a bottle and basin compleat' — Chippendale accounts at Paxton, cf. 220: It cost £7. 7. 0. A similar shaving-table is at Saltram House, Devon (see pp. 118–9).
- Lit: Coleridge, 'Chippendale, Interior-Decorator', *loc. cit.*
- Loc: Paxton House, Berwick-on-Tweed.

222. A mahogany 'Bason Stand' based on pl. 50 in the third edition of the *Director*. Such pieces are sometimes known as 'Wig Stands', when they usually have a small drawer in an undertier (probably adapted).
    Loc :   The Victoria and Albert Museum.

223. A basin-stand with carved, Gothic design trellis-work.
    Loc :   Private Collection.

224. A mahogany 'teakettle Stand', or wine-table, which is one of many extant examples : Chippendale, however, only includes one design in the third edition of the *Director* (pl. 55), although Ince and Mayhew in *The Universal System*, 1762, include seven alternate designs (pls. 13 and 14).
    Loc :   The Victoria and Albert Museum.

225. A carved mahogany tripod-table.
    Exhib : Royal Academy of Arts, 1955–56, *English Taste in the Eighteenth Century*, Cat. No. 192.
    Loc :   Private Collection.

226. A tea-table with finely carved pie-crust border. Tables of this design, although not included in the *Director*, are not uncommon.
    Exhib : Royal Academy of Arts, 1955–56, *English Taste in the Eighteenth Century*, Cat. No. 213.
    Brighton Art Gallery, 1956.
    Loc :   Private Collection.

227. A 'dumb-waiter', its tripod support of *Director* design : defined by Sheraton in his *Cabinet Dictionary* (1803) as 'a useful piece of furniture, to serve in some respects the place of a waiter, whence it is so named'. Miss Mary Hamilton in her diary, 1784, writes 'we had dumb waiters so our conversation was not under any restraint by ye Servants being in ye room' (*D.E.F.*, II, p. 226). Chippendale does not include designs for dumb-waiters in the *Director*.
    Loc :   Private Collection.

228. A dumb-waiter in the *Director* taste, of mahogany with parcel-gilt details. Note the curious way in which the legs are scrolled in three dimensions.
    Loc :   Private Collection.

229. A design for two 'Buroe Tables', dated 1753, from the first edition of the *Director* : they are called 'Buroe Dressing Tables' in the third edition.

230. A mahogany 'buroe table', the canted, satinwood veneered angles decorated with applied carvings, surmounted by the Crewe crest : 'out of a ducal coronet . . . a lion's jamb erect . . .' — originally from Madeley Manor, nr. Stoke-on-Trent.
    Lit :   *Leeds Arts Calendar*, Vol. 6, No. 21, p. 6–7.
    Antique Collector, August 1953, p. 138.
    Illustrated London News, 15 May 1954, p. 792.
    Loc :   Temple Newsam House, Yorkshire.

231. A bureau-table of unusual design with gilded enrichments. The small garlands below the capitals at the corners suggest a rather late date for this piece.
    Loc :   Private Collection.

232. A bureau-table in the Chinese taste — the bow-fronted banks of drawers are probably inspired by designs for bow windows : Miss Hackenbroch writes, 'This unusually compact type of design may have determined the shape of contemporary American block-fronted desks.'
    Lit :   Yvonne Hackenbroch (Ed.), *English Furniture in the Collection of Irwin Untermyer*, London, 1958, fig. 276, pl. 237.
    T. H. Ormsbee, *Prime Antiques and their Current Prices*, New York, 1947, p. 113, right.
    Loc :   The Irwin Untermyer Collection, New York.

233. Plate 65 from the third edition of the *Director*, where this class of furniture is named a 'French Commode Table' (cf. Pls. 237–8).

234. One of a pair of mahogany commodes made for the Duke of Norfolk for Norfolk House, London — both the Duke and Duchess of Norfolk were subscribers to the first edition of the *Director*.
    Exhib : The Victoria and Albert Museum, *International Art Treasures Exhibition*, 1962, pl. 100.
    Loc :   Private Collection.

235. A mahogany commode with ormolu enrichments now in the Private Dining-Room at Nostell Priory, and probably supplied by Chippendale's firm to Sir Rowland Winn.
    Loc :   Nostell Priory, Yorkshire.

236. A carved mahogany commode based on pl. 44 in the first edition of the *Director* — repeated in the third edition, pl. 65, cf. Pl. 237 : Originally made for Captain Townshend M.P. of Raynham Hall, Norfolk — perhaps by Chippendale's firm.
    Lit :   *D.E.F.*, II, p. 112, fig. 6.
            G.C-M., p. 174, fig. 100.
            Oliver Bracket, *Thomas Chippendale*, London, 1930, pl. 37.
            H. H. Mülliner, *Decorative Arts in England*, 1924, fig. 13.
            Discussed by H. Cescinsky, *The Burlington Magazine*, June 1921.
            Antiques, Vol. XLV, March 1944, p. 112.
    Loc :   The Philadelphia Museum of Art.

237. A commode of very similar design to that shown in Pl. 236.
    Loc :   On loan to the City of Birmingham Art Gallery.

238. A commode, its design based on pl. 44 in the third edition of the *Director*.
    Loc :   Private Collection.

239. A detail from a mahogany commode of *Director* design showing the high quality of the carved foliated enrichments on the angles and of the giltmetal *rococo* mounts. The outward scrolled volute at the top of the angles is a characteristic feature of Chippendale's designs. This becomes an outward scrolled capital surmounting a pilaster in the neo-classical phase (cf. Pl. 249 below, and see C. Musgrave, *Adam and Hepplewhite Furniture*, London, 1966). An intermediate stage is shown in Pl. 247.
    Loc :   Private Collection.

240. A carved mahogany 'Writing Table', the name given to such tables in the *Director* — pl. 73, third edition : Nowadays they are called 'card' or 'tea-tables', depending on whether or not they have baize-lined interiors.
    Loc :   Private Collection.

241. A 'Writing Table' of Gothic design and serpentine form.
    Loc :   Private Collection.

242. Plate 76 from the third edition of the *Director*. Chippendale, in his notes, writes, 'This table has been made more than once from this design, and has a better appearance when made than the drawing.'

243. A mahogany 'writing table' based on pls. 75 and 76 in the third edition of the *Director* (see Pl. 242).
    Loc :   Private Collection.

244. Another example.
    Lit :   *D.E.F.*, III, p. 248, fig. 18.
            G.C-M., p. 176, pl. 103.
    Exhib : Temple Newsam House, Leeds 1951, *Thomas Chippendale*, Cat. No. 104.
    Loc :   Private Collection.

245. A mahogany desk, or library table, of Gothic design — the unusual circular cusped motives on the pedestals are based on pl. 58 in the first edition of the *Director*. It was made for 'Single-Speech Hamilton', probably for his Gothic drawing-room in Arlington Street, which was designed by Sanderson Millar in 1760.

  Exhib : Temple Newsam House, Leeds, 1951, *Thomas Chippendale*, Cat. No. 114.
  Loc :   Temple Newsam House, Yorkshire.

246. An unusual mahogany pedestal-desk in two sections with hinged supports.

  Lit :   Anthony Coleridge, 'Some Furniture in the Collection of the Earl of Mansfield', *Connoisseur*, April 1966.
  Loc :   Scone Palace, Perthshire.

247. Plate 83 from the third edition of the *Director*, and Pl. 57 from the first edition.

248. A mahogany library-table, probably supplied by Chippendale's firm, made for the fifth Baron Craven of Coombe Abbey, Warwickshire : its design corresponds to pl. 83 in the third edition of the *Director* (cf. Pl. 247). The measurements correspond exactly.

  Lit :   *G.C-M.*, p. 65.
          Oliver Bracket, *Thomas Chippendale*, London, 1930, pl. 35.
          H. Avrey Tipping, *English Homes*, period VI, Vol. I, p. 169, pl. 225.
          Munro Bell, *Chippendale, Sheraton, Hepplewhite*, p. 54.
          T. A. Strange, *English Furniture*, London, N.D., p. 138.
  Exhib : The Victoria and Albert Museum, *International Art Treasures Exhibition*, 1962, pl. 90.
  Loc :   Private Collection.

249. A detail of the famous carved mahogany library-table, supplied by Thomas Chippendale to Sir Rowland Winn in 1767 for the library at Nostell Priory, at a cost of £72. 10. 0.

  Lit :   *D.E.F.*, III, p. 251, fig. 24.
          G.C-M., p. 167, pl. 90.
          Oliver Bracket, *Thomas Chippendale*, London, 1930, pl. 36.
          C. Musgrave, *Adam and Hepplewhite Furniture*, London, 1966, pl. 166.
  Exhib : Temple Newsam House, Leeds, 1951, *Thomas Chippendale*, Cat. No. 21.
  Loc :   Nostell Priory, Yorkshire.

250. A mahogany break-front bookcase, the upper section with mirror-panelled doors — originally at Langley Park, Nr. Norwich, Norfolk, where Chippendale is supposed to have been employed : this bookcase was probably made about ten years prior to the publication of the first edition of the *Director*.

  Lit :   Oliver Bracket, *Thomas Chippendale*, London, 1930, pl. 11.
  Loc :   Private Collection.

251. A break-front bookcase based on pl. 62 in the first edition of the *Director*. Compared with that shown in Pl. 250, the Baroque flavour has now largely been lost.

  Lit :   *D.E.F.*, I, p. 85, fig. 17.
          G.C-M., p. 171, pl. 96.
  Loc :   Longford Castle, Wiltshire.

252. A break-front bookcase, illustrating a variant of the same design as that shown in Pl. 251.

  Loc :   Private Collection.

253. A break-front bookcase, originally one of a pair at Nostell Priory, based on pl. 71 in the first edition of the *Director* : probably supplied by Chippendale's firm, and perhaps the example described in Chippendale's account of 23 June 1766, as 'A very large mahogany bookcase with a glass door and pediment top . . . £38.' A similar bookcase is at Newby Hall, Yorkshire, where Chippendale was also employed (see Harewood Archives; Steward's letter-book, 1763–92, p. 289).

  Loc :   Nostell Priory, Yorkshire.

254. A bookcase, based on the design shown in Pl. 255.
> Lit: P. Macquoid, *English Furniture, Tapestry and Needlework . . . in the Lady Lever Art Gallery*, London, 1928, pl. 443.
> R. Fastnedge, 'A Chippendale Gothic bookcase in the Lady Lever Art Gallery', *Apollo*, October 1960.
> Loc: The Lady Lever Art Gallery, Cheshire.

255. Plate 75 from the third edition of the *Director*.

256. The celebrated 'Violin' bookcase at Wilton House, Wiltshire, probably supplied by Chippendale: Receipts dated between 1763 and 1791, are preserved at Wilton from Chippendale's firm to the Earl of Pembroke; cf. the design for the carved rococo oval with that in pl. 87 of the third edition of the *Director*.
> Lit: *D.E.F.*, I, p. 86, fig. 19.
> *G.C-M.*, p. 168, pl. 91.
> Anthony Coleridge, 'Chippendale at Wilton', *Apollo*, July 1964.
> R. W. Luff, 'Two Chippendale Bookcases', *The Antique Collector*, August 1962.
> Loc: Wilton House, Wiltshire.

257. A mahogany break-front bookcase which was supplied by Chippendale to Sir Lawrence Dundas in August 1764 at a cost of £73. He invoiced it as 'A very large Mahogany Bookcase same scrol as before the upper doors Glaz'd with Crown Glass'. Its design is based on pl. 92 in the *Director*.
> Lit: Anthony Coleridge, 'Sir Lawrence Dundas and Chippendale', *Apollo*, September, 1967.
> Loc: Aske Hall, Near Richmond, Yorkshire.

258. One of a pair of mahogany break-front bookcases, *en suite*, with the 'Violin' bookcase, shown in Pl. 256.
> Lit: Coleridge, 'Chippendale at Wilton', *loc. cit.*
> Loc: Wilton House, Wiltshire.

259. Plate 105 from the third edition of the *Director* — 'Chamber Organs' made after Chippendale's designs are rare.

260. A mahogany chamber-organ based on the design in Pl. 259 above — from Polebarn House, Trowbridge. Only the façade now survives; the mechanism has apparently disappeared.
> Lit: *D.E.F.*, II, p. 381, fig. 22.
> Ralph Edwards, *Georgian Furniture*, London, 1947, fig. 132.
> *A Catalogue of Musical Instruments in the Victoria and Albert Museum*, Vol. I, 1967.
> Loc: The Victoria and Albert Museum.

261. A mahogany 'Dressing Chest and Bookcase' based on pl. 114 in the third edition of the *Director*: probably supplied by Chippendale to Sir Rowland Winn for Nostell Priory.
> Exhib: Temple Newsam House, Leeds, 1951, *Thomas Chippendale*, Cat. No. 26.
> Loc: Nostell Priory, Yorkshire.

262. An unusual mahogany writing-table with fretted upper section, probably supplied by Chippendale to Sir Rowland Winn.
> Loc: Nostell Priory, Yorkshire.

263. A writing-table of similar design to that shown in Pl. 262, the 'pull-out', writing-drawer and supports entirely decorated with blind-fret ornamentation.
> Loc: Temple Newsam House, Yorkshire.

264. Plate 108 in the first edition of the *Director*, republished as pl. 133 in the third: Chippendale, in his notes on these 'China Cases', writes 'this design I have executed with great satisfaction to the purchaser'.

265. A mahogany and parcel-gilt 'China Case' based on the design shown in Pl. 264.
    Lit: J. F. Hayward, 'A China Case attributed to Thomas Chippendale', *Connoisseur*, June 1962.
    Loc: The L. David Collection, Copenhagen.

266. A mahogany 'China Case' based on pl. 106 in the first edition of the *Director*.
    Loc: Shugborough Hall, Stafford.

267. A 'China Case' in the Chinese taste carved with blind and open-fret ornamentation, and perhaps inspired by designs in the *Director* (probably slightly cut-down).
    Loc: Private Collection.

268. A 'China Case' with rather more restrained ornamentation than the previous example, but very much in the *Director* style.
    Loc: Private Collection.

269. A cabinet-on-stand in the Chinese taste, the doors veneered with amboyna wood and enclosing a hundred drawers, each veneered with a different kind of wood.
    Lit: *D.E.F.*, I, p. 182, fig. 35, pl. V, p. 181.
    Exhib: The Royal Academy of Arts, 1955–56, *English Taste in the Eighteenth Century*, Cat. No. 248.
    Loc: On loan to the Lady Lever Art Gallery, Cheshire.

270. A mahogany cabinet-on-stand in the Chinese taste, the simulated lacquer door mounted with soapstone carvings — from Langley Park, Norfolk, where Chippendale is thought to have been employed (see p. 114).
    Lit: *D.E.F.*, I, fig. 51, p. 190.
            F. J. B. Watson, 'A Princely Collection of English furniture', *Apollo*, June 1964.
    Exhib: *Op. cit.*, Cat. No. 259.
    Loc: Private Collection.

271. A mahogany display-cabinet in the Chinese taste with lattice-work doors in the *Director* style.
    Loc: Private Collection.

272. A mahogany secretaire-cabinet of rare shape, the fretted ornamentation of mixed Gothic and Chinese form, presumably inspired by designs in the *Director*.
    Lit: *D.E.F.*, I, p. 150, fig. 56.
            Yvonne Hackenbroch (Ed.), *English furniture in the Collection of Irwin Untermyer*, London, 1958, figs. 293–4, pls. 252–3.
            R. W. Symonds, 'The China Case and China Closet', *Connoisseur*, June 1952.
    Loc: The Irwin Untermyer Collection, New York.

273. The interior of the japanned 'pagoda' cabinet illustrated in Colour Plate A: note the inset Florentine *pietre dure* panels and the ivory portrait medallions. The cabinet was ordered by Sir Mathew Fetherstonhaugh, Bt., for his house, Uppark, Sussex.
    Lit: Anthony Coleridge, 'Georgian Cabinet-Makers at Uppark, Sussex — II', *Connoisseur*, November, 1967.
    Loc: Uppark, Sussex.

274. A carved mahogany wardrobe, or 'Commode Cloths Press', based on pl. 131 in the first edition of the *Director*. A similar example was in the Mülliner collection.
    Lit: *D.E.F.*, II, 1924, p. 183, fig. 18.
            G.C-M., p. 169, pl. 94.
            Oliver Bracket, *Thomas Chippendale*, London, 1930, pl. 25.
    Exhib: Temple Newsam House, Leeds, 1951, *Thomas Chippendale*, Cat. No. 132.
    Loc: Temple Newsam House, Yorkshire.

275. A mahogany wardrobe of Transitional design of about 1770 at Nostell Priory. The serpentine-shaped base and doors above with neo-classical carved enrichments: almost certainly supplied by Chippendale's firm. The broken front is a curious feature more reminiscent of German

than English furniture. The outward spiralling scrolls at the top of the canted corners are forms frequently found on furniture attributed to Chippendale (see Pl. 239). A commode resembling the lower section of this is at Saltram House, Devon.

> Loc: Nostell Priory, Yorkshire.

276. A wardrobe which was invoiced by Chippendale as 'a large mahogany cloaths press with folding doors, fine wood, sliding shelves lined with marble paper and baize aprons . . .': he charged Ninian Home, of Paxton House, Berwick-on-Tweed, £12. 12. 0. for it in 1774.

> Lit: Anthony Coleridge, 'Chippendale, Interior-Decorator and House-Furnisher', *Apollo*, April 1963.
> Loc: Paxton House, Berwick-on-Tweed.

277. A set of mahogany hanging-shelves, or 'Shelfs for Books', and 'Shelves for China', as they are called in the *Director* — third edition, pls. 138–41 — this example has satinwood veneers and tulipwood bandings.

> Loc: Private Collection.

278. Plate 139 from the third edition of the *Director*, showing what are there called 'Hanging Shelves': they are usually found in pairs.

279. One of a pair of mahogany hanging-shelves at Nostell Priory of Chinese design with a Baron's coronet as finial, which were probably supplied by Chippendale's firm.

> Lit: *D.E.F.*, III, p. 118, fig. 10.
> *G.C-M.*, p. 200, pl. 154.
> Exhib: Temple Newsam House, Leeds, 1951, *Thomas Chippendale*, Cat. No. 24.
> Loc: Nostell Priory, Yorkshire.

280. One of a pair of mahogany 'Shelfs for Books' which were supplied by Chippendale to Ninian Home for Paxton House, Berwick-on-Tweed, in 1774, at a cost of 15s. each. Cf. the *Director*, pl. 192, third edition, for similar designs to their fretted ends.

> Lit: Coleridge, 'Chippendale, Interior-Decorator', *loc. cit.*
> Loc: Paxton House, Berwick-on-Tweed.

281. One of a pair of japanned standing-shelves of Chinese design from Badminton House, Gloucestershire — it is thought that Chippendale was employed there (see p. 107).

> Lit: *D.E.F.*, III, p. 118, fig. 7.
> P. Macquoid, *English furniture, Tapestries and Needlework . . . in the Lady Lever Art Gallery*, London, 1928, No. 168, pl. 52.
> Exhib: Royal Academy of Arts, 1955–56, *English Taste in the Eighteenth Century*, Cat. No. 241.
> Loc: The Lady Lever Art Gallery, Cheshire. One is on loan to the Victoria and Albert Museum.

282. A set of standing-shelves of similar design to that shown in Pl. 281 but with a door in the middle section.

> Exhib: Royal Academy, *English Taste in the Eighteenth Century*, Cat. No. 265.
> B.F.A.C., Winter 1935, Cat. No. 34a.
> Loc: Private Collection.

283. Another set with unusual pagoda cornice: (cf. design for 'Shelves for China' — the *Director*, third edition, pl. 141).

> Lit: *D.E.F.*, III, pp. 117–18, fig. 5.
> Exhib: *Op. cit.*, *English Taste in the Eighteenth Century*, Cat. No. 235.
> B.F.A.C., *loc. cit.*, Cat. No. 23.
> Loc: Kedleston Hall, Derbyshire.

284. A mahogany 'China Shelf' based on pl. 143 in the third edition of the *Director*.

> Loc: Private Collection.

285. A mahogany three-tier what-not with open-fret sides — designs for these are not included in the *Director*, but examples were made in the full *Director* tradition.
  Loc: Private Collection.

286. A rare form of what-not with open-fret decoration and drawers below.
  Loc: Private Collection.

287. Plate 144 from the third edition of the *Director*, showing what are there called 'Candle Stands'.

288. One of a pair of 'Candle Stands', or *torchères*, supplied by Chippendale to the second Duke of Atholl, in 1758, for Blair Castle, Perthshire: his account reads, 'A pair of large candlestands neatly carved and painted white . . . £7. 7. 0.' They are now gilded.
  Lit: Anthony Coleridge, 'Chippendale, The Director, and some Cabinet-Makers at Blair Castle', *Connoisseur*, December 1960.
  Exhib: *Treasures from Scottish Houses*, 21st Edinburgh International Festival, Royal Scottish Museum, Edinburgh, 1967, cat. nos. 248/9.
  Loc: Blair Castle, Perthshire.

289. A candlestand, one of a pair, originally in the collection of Marquis Curzon of Kedleston.
  Lit: Francis Lenygon, *English Furniture, 1660–1760*, p. 190.
  Loc: Private Collection.

290. A candlestand probably based on the designs in the *Director* but of less attenuated proportions than Chippendale's compositions.
  Exhib: Victoria and Albert Museum, 1962, *International Art Treasures Exhibition*, Cat. No. 112.
  Loc: Private Collection.

291. One of a pair of unusual black and gold japanned candlestands, perhaps decorated at a later date.
  Loc: Private Collection.

292. A carved mahogany candlestand with fretted hexagonal top, its design based on pl. 120 in the first edition of the *Director*.
  Loc: Private Collection.

293. One of a pair of mahogany candlestands which Chippendale supplied to Ninian Home for Paxton House, Berwick-on-Tweed, in 1774 at a cost of £3. 6. 0. the pair.
  Lit: Anthony Coleridge, 'Chippendale, Interior-Decorator and House-Furnisher', *Apollo*, April 1963.
  Loc: Paxton House, Berwick-on-Tweed.

294. One of a pair of mahogany candlestands of 'transitional' design with marble tops — at Wilton House and probably supplied by Chippendale to the Earl of Pembroke.
  Lit: Anthony Coleridge, 'Chippendale at Wilton', *Apollo*, July 1964.
  Loc: Wilton House, Wiltshire.

295. A gilt-bronze 'Lanthorn for a Hall or Staircase', as the designs in the third edition of the *Director* (cf. pl. 153) are called — from St. Dunstan's House, Regent's Park, London.
  Lit: *D.E.F.*, II, p. 284, fig. 9.
    G.C-M., p. 179, pl. 112.
    Antiques, Vol. XLIV, September 1943, p. 130.
  Loc: The Philadelphia Museum of Art.

296. One of a pair of carved mahogany lanterns with mirror backs and platforms: cf. pl. 153 in the third edition of the *Director*. The design for a lantern of similar form is in the Lock drawings in the Victoria and Albert Museum (No. 62), which must date from about 1755.
  Lit: *D.E.F.*, Vol. II, p. 283, fig. 6.
    H. A. Tipping, 'English Furniture of the Cabriole Period', *Burlington*, Vol. XXXVI, 1920, pl. 21D, pp. 78–83, and pl. XXXII, fig. 2.

Yvonne Hackenbroch (Ed.), *English Furniture in the Collection of Irwin Untermyer*, fig. 184, pl. 153.
Loc: The Irwin Untermyer Collection, New York.

297. A carved giltwood chandelier of rococo design — pls. 154 and 155 in the third edition of the *Director* illustrate designs for 'Chandeliers for Halls . . .'.
Loc: Private Collection.

298. Another of rather more ponderous design.
Loc: The Metropolitan Museum of Art.

299. Another, carved with satyr masks and an eagle, which is still hanging in the dining-room at St. Giles's House, Dorset — Lady Shaftesbury was a subscriber to the first edition of the *Director*.
Lit: *D.E.F.*, I, fig. 20, p. 335.
Charles Lines, 'My House at St. Giles's', *Connoisseur*, October 1959.
R. W. Symonds, 'Rococo at St. Giles's House', *Antique Collector*, December 1955.
Loc: St. Giles's House, Dorset.

300. A carved mahogany tripod 'Fire Screen' related to a design in the third edition of the *Director* (pl. 156): The panel is filled with tapestry.
Exhib: The Royal Academy of Arts, 1955–56, *English Taste in the Eighteenth Century*, Cat. No. 183.
Loc: Private Collection.

301. A fire-screen at St. Giles's House for which Chippendale may well have supplied furniture. The tapestry panel perhaps from the Fulham or Exeter workshops.
Exhib: *op. cit.*, *English Taste in the Eighteenth Century*, Cat. No. 220.
Loc: St. Giles's House, Dorset.

302. A fire-screen, the carved mahogany tripod support being similar to one shown on pl. 156, left, in the third edition of the *Director*. The screen probably once had a panel of needlework or tapestry.
Loc: Private Collection.

303. A carved mahogany 'Horse Fire-Screen' based on a design in the first edition of the *Director*, pl. 127. The needlework panel is contemporary. Previously in the collection of Cora, Countess of Strafford.
Lit: *D.E.F.*, III, p. 64, pl. 11.
Oliver Bracket, *Thomas Chippendale*, London, 1930, pl. 40.
Ralph Edwards, *Georgian Furniture*, London, 1951, fig. 127.
Loc: The Victoria and Albert Museum.

304. A mahogany framed, folding fire-screen with Chinese paper panels of unusually fine quality painted in colours. Based on a design on pl. 157, right, in the third edition of the *Director*.
Loc: The Victoria and Albert Museum.

305. A pair of giltwood 'Brackets for Bustos' as such pieces are called by Chippendale (cf. pl. 161 in the third edition of the *Director*, bottom right design). Originally at Langley Park, Norfolk (see p. 114) where Chippendale is supposed to have been employed.
Lit: *D.E.F.*, I, p. 117, fig. 5.
G.C-M., p. 191, pls. 136–7.
Oliver Bracket, *Thomas Chippendale*, London, 1930, pl. 41.
Ralph Edwards, *Georgian Furniture*, London, 1951, figs. 113–14.
Loc: The Victoria and Albert Museum.

306. One, from a pair, in mahogany carved with rococo motives, in the *Director* style.
Lit: *D.E.F.*, I, p. 118, fig. 10.
Loc: Private Collection.

307. A mahogany longcase-clock, with enrichments similar to those shown in designs for 'Clock Cases' in the third edition of the *Director*, pls. 163–4. The movement of this example was made by John Holmes, a celebrated maker of the period.
    Loc: The Philadelphia Museum of Art.

308. Plate 177 from the third edition of the *Director* showing five alternate designs for 'Gerandoles'.

309. A pair of carved giltwood-framed 'Gerandoles' in the Chinese taste with mirror-panelled backs, possibly inspired by designs in the *Director*.
    Loc: Private Collection.

310. A pair of girandoles of exaggerated rococo design, in the *Director* taste.
    Loc: Private Collection.

311. One, from a pair, originally at Woodcote Park, Epsom, Surrey — based on a design in the first edition of the *Director*.
    Loc: The Museum of Fine Arts, Boston.

312. A pair of girandoles carved with Gothic summer-houses, in the *Director* style. Note the chased metal-gilt nozzles and drip-pans.
    Loc: Private Collection.

313. Another, one of a pair, based on the bottom left design in pl. 177 (see Pl. 308) in the third edition of the *Director*.
    Loc: Private Collection.

314. One of a pair of girandoles at St. Giles's House, Dorset (see note to 299 above). The general design is influenced by Thomas Johnson's published work.
    Lit: R. W. Symonds, 'Rococo at St. Giles's House', *Antique Collector*, December 1955 and 'St. Giles's House', *Antique Collector*, August 1762.
    Loc: St. Giles's House, Dorset.

315. One of a pair of girandoles which was probably supplied by Chippendale to Edwin Lascelles for Harewood House, Leeds; one of the few examples at Harewood House in the full *Director* style.
    Loc: Harewood House, Yorkshire.

316. One of a pair of giltwood 'Pier Glass Frames', based on pl. 143 in the first edition of the *Director*: it is thought, on stylistic grounds, that Chippendale may have been employed at Crichel, Dorset; however, documentary evidence is lacking (see p. 111).
    Lit: *D.E.F.*, II, pp. 341–2, fig. 79.
            G.C-M., p. 182, pl. 120.
    Exhib: Royal Academy of Arts, 1955–56, *English Taste in the Eighteenth Century*, Cat. No. 244.
    Loc: Crichel, Dorset.

317. One of a pair from St. Giles's House, Dorset — see notes on 299 and 314 above.
    Lit: R. W. Symonds, 'St. Giles's House', *Antique Collector*, August 1962.
    Loc: St. Giles's House, Dorset.

318. One of a set of four pier-glasses, surmounted by a shield carved with the cross of St. George: these were moved from Kensington Palace to Buckingham Palace in the eighteenth century, and were then taken to Windsor in 1902.
    Lit: *D.E.F.*, II, fig. 76, p. 340.
            G. F. Laking, *The Furniture of Windsor Castle*, London, N.D., pl. 19.
    Loc: The Royal Collection.

319. A giltwood-framed pier-glass, based on pl. 141 in the first edition of the *Director*. It was ordered from London in 1765 as a wedding present for a girl in the Marblehead family. Some aspects of the design and carved detail, especially the sheep, are reminiscent of the style of Thomas Johnson.
    Loc: The Museum of Fine Arts, Boston.

320. One of a pair of carved oval pier-glasses of typical restrained rococo design, showing the influence of the *Director* style, and of Thomas Johnson's publications.
    Loc: Private Collection.

321. A giltwood-framed overmantel, or chimney-glass, carved with naturalistic foliage and with typical tripartite divided plate in the *Director* style.
    Loc: Private Collection.

322. One of a pair of giltwood-framed pier-glasses, its swan-neck pediment carved with the Pembroke Wyvern: perhaps designed by Chippendale to harmonise with the existing Kentian style furniture in the Double Cube Room at Wilton House.
    Lit: Anthony Coleridge, 'Chippendale at Wilton', *Apollo*, July 1964.
    Loc: Wilton House, Wiltshire.

323. A giltwood-framed overmantel glass in Chippendale's *Director* tradition — from Stone Easton House, near Bath, Wiltshire: its design is also influenced by the published work of Thomas Johnson.
    Loc: Private Collection.

324. An overmantel and mantelpiece of carved pine in the Chinese taste and in the *Director* tradition — from Eltham Lodge, Kent: the influence of Thomas Johnson's published designs can also be traced.
    Lit: H. Clifford-Smith, *Buckingham Palace*, London, 1930, pl. 90.
    Loc: The Royal Collection.

325. A white marble mantelpiece inspired by the same source as pl. 184 in the third edition of the *Director* — from Linton Park, Maidstone, Kent.
    Loc: Private Collection.

326. Plate 184 from the third edition of the *Director*, dated 1761 (cf. Pl. 325).

327. One of a pair of Chinese paintings on mirror glass, in English giltwood frames of *Director* design, and showing the influence of Thomas Johnson.
    Lit: L. G. G. Ramsey, 'Chinoiserie in the Western Isles', *Connoisseur*, June 1958.
    Loc: Private Collection.

328. A looking-glass painted in China with exotic birds in an unusual and naturalistically carved frame.
    Loc: Private Collection.

329. A looking-glass, one of a pair, painted with Chinese ladies minding sheep of a breed that looks European.
    Loc: Private Collection.

330. A Chinese painted glass-picture with a finely carved giltwood frame in the *Director* idiom — some of the carved detail, e.g. the swan, in the manner of Thomas Johnson.
    Lit: M. Jourdain and R. Soame Jenyns, *Chinese Export Art*, London, 1950, frontis.
           L. G. G. Ramsey, 'Chinoiserie in the Western Isles', *Connoisseur*, June 1958.
    Loc: Private Collection.

331. A Chinese mirror-picture, from a pair, painted with figures on a terrace, in a frame in the tradition of the first edition of the *Director*.
    Lit: Ramsey, 'Chinoiserie in the Western Isles', *loc. cit.*
    Loc: Private Collection.

332. A japanned commode from the Chinese bedroom at Badminton House, Gloucestershire, which was probably supplied by Chippendale to the fourth Duke of Beaufort, who was a subscriber to the first edition of the *Director* (see p. 107).
    Loc: The Victoria and Albert Museum.

333. A japanned commode, also from the Chinese bedroom at Badminton House, the top drawer in this case being fitted as a dressing-table as in Pl. 332.
    Loc: Private Collection.

NOTES TO THE ILLUSTRATIONS

334. A commode, the doors faced with panels of so-called 'coromandel' lacquer, the borders of English japanned work, the angles and borders mounted in chased ormolu.
    Loc: Private Collection.

335. A commode of similar design and in a similar technique to that shown in Pl. 334.
    Loc: Private Collection.

336. A commode, one of a pair, at St. Giles's House, Dorset — see note to 299 above.
    Lit: *D.E.F.*, II, p. 114, fig. 12; p. 110.
    Exhib: Royal Academy of Arts, 1955–56, *English Taste in the Eighteenth Century*, Cat. No. 245.
    Loc: St. Giles's House, Dorset.

337. One of a set of four japanned and lacquered commodes which were probably ordered by Sir Mathew Fetherstonhaugh, Bt., for his house, Uppark, Sussex (see colour plate B).
    Lit: Anthony Coleridge, 'Georgian Cabinet-Makers at Uppark, Sussex — Part I', *Connoisseur*, October, 1967.
    Loc: Uppark, Sussex.

338. One of a set of twelve mahogany stools supplied by Chippendale for the Library at Christ Church, Oxford, in 1764, at a cost of £38. 15. 0. for the set.
    Lit: *G.C-M.*, p. 72.
    W. G. Hiscock, 'Christ Church. Furniture, II', *Country Life*, 5 January 1945.
    Loc: Christ Church Library, Oxford.

339. A mahogany *bonheur-du-jour* from Coombe Abbey, Warwickshire, where Chippendale is thought to have been employed (see p. 110) — Designs for such pieces of furniture are not included in the *Director*, but are discussed here as they were a popular type during the period under discussion.
    Loc: Private Collection.

340. A mahogany desk with filing-cabinet in the *Director* tradition.
    Loc: Private Collection.

341. A carved mahogany-framed open-armchair from Corsham Court, Wiltshire. See Pl. 204 and the relevant note about this and the set to which it belongs.
    Loc: Corsham Court, Wiltshire.

342. One of a pair of green japanned bedside-cupboards, probably supplied by Chippendale to Edwin Lascelles for Harewood House, Yorkshire — cf. the similarly decorated furniture at Nostell Priory, Pls. 349–51.
    Loc: Harewood House, Yorkshire.

343. One of a set of eight painted open-armchairs, probably supplied by Chippendale for Harewood House — they represent the 'transitional' phase between the rococo and the neo-classical. A similar set of 4 armchairs from Cliveden, Bucks., were sold at Christie's 6 July, 1967, lot 44.
    Lit: *G.C-M.*, p. 198, pl. 149.
    Exhib: Temple Newsam House, Leeds, 1951, *Thomas Chippendale*, Cat. No. 20.
    Loc: Harewood House, Yorkshire.

344. A painted open-armchair from a set which was probably supplied by Chippendale for Harewood House.
    Loc: Harewood House, Yorkshire.

345. One of a set of mahogany-framed side-chairs, probably supplied by Chippendale to Sir Rowland Winn, Bart., for Nostell Priory, near Wakefield, Yorkshire, about 1766–70.
    Loc: Nostell Priory, Yorkshire.

346. A tulipwood barometer, inlaid with ebony, and described by Chippendale in the Nostell Priory accounts for 1769 as 'To a very neat case for a barometer made of fine tulip and other woods and very rich carvd ornaments Gilt in Burnish gold and plate Glass in the doors . . . £25.': In 1770 another entry reads, 'Altering the ornaments of the Barometer frame and Gilding in Burnish Gold . . . £1. 3. 0.' In another letter of 4 October 1769, Chippendale

writes, 'Mr. Vullime says that the barometer is to stay in town but it is intirely finished . . .' Mr. Vullime was almost certainly the celebrated clock-maker Justin Vulliamy (fl. about 1730–90) who worked for the Crown. He must have supplied the movement.

> Lit : *G.C-M.*, p. 178, fig. 109.
> Nicholas Goodison, 'Clockmaker and Cabinet-maker', *Journal of the Furniture History Society*, Vol. II, 1966.
> Exhib : Temple Newsam House, Leeds, 1951, *Thomas Chippendale*, Cat. No. 28.
> Loc : Nostell Priory, Yorkshire.

347. A barometer, in a mahogany case carved with rococo motives, the dial inscribed 'Whitehurst, Derby 1760' — John Whitehurst, F.R.S., originally of Derby and afterwards of London, was established in Bolt Court, Fleet Street, and is said to have ordered cases for his instruments from Chippendale : the movement is identical to that of the Nostell example shown in Pl. 346.

> Loc : Private Collection.

348. Another, of Torricellian stick form, carved with rococo motives and with a giltwood sunburst terminal : the barometer and thermometer by James Ayscough, 'at the sign of Great Golden Spectacles, Ludgate Street'.

> Lit : *D.E.F.*, I, p. 33, fig. 22.
> Loc : The Victoria and Albert Museum.

349. A knee-hole dressing-table with top drawer retaining the original fittings, e.g. a hair-brush. The green japanned ground is decorated with Chinoiseries in gold and silver. Probably supplied by Chippendale's firm to Sir Rowland Winn, Bart., for Nostell Priory in about 1770. A second table was made to match at some later date.

> Loc : Nostell Priory, Yorkshire.

350. A green japanned wardrobe that was probably supplied by Chippendale for Nostell Priory (see Pl. 349).

> Lit : *D.E.F.*, II, p. 167, fig. 27.
> *G.C-M.*, p. 189, pl. 132.
> O. Bracket, *Thomas Chippendale*, London, 1930, p. 275, pl. 58.
> Loc : Nostell Priory, Yorkshire.

351. A green japanned break-front commode, the canted angles enriched by pendant husks — probably supplied by Chippendale for Nostell Priory. The outward turned volutes forming capitals at the corners and the vase-shaped legs are features often found in what is believed to be Chippendale's work (cf. 238, 247, 249, 256).

> Lit : *D.E.F.*, II, p. 116, fig. 16.
> *G.C-M.*, p. 190, pl. 134.
> Loc : Nostell Priory, Yorkshire.

352. A mahogany commode, veneered with satinwood, banded with rosewood and inlaid with various woods — the interior veneered with stained oak, and mounted in ormolu : supplied by Chippendale for Nostell Priory, and probably the one invoiced to Sir Rowland Winn in 1770 as 'a large antique commode very curiously inlaid with various fine woods. With folding doors and drawers within and very rich chasd brass ornaments complete . . . £40.'

> Exhib : Temple Newsam House, Leeds, 1951, *Thomas Chippendale*, Cat. No. 22.
> Loc : Nostell Priory, Yorkshire.

353. A commode, also at Nostell Priory, in mahogany, veneered with satinwood and inlaid with various woods — mounted in cast and chased ormolu. Like the commode shown in Pl. 352, this may also have been supplied by Chippendale and it should be noted that the entry in the account, suggested as perhaps relating to 352 above, could equally be applied to this example. A commode in the private apartments at Hatfield House, Hertfordshire, has identical mounts to this example (ill. *Burlington*, see Lit. below).

Lit: *G.C-M.*, p. 191, pl. 135.
O. Brackett, *Thomas Chippendale*, London, 1930.
Anthony Coleridge, 'English Furniture and Cabinet-Makers at Hatfield House, Part II', *Burlington*, March 1967.
Loc: Nostell Priory, Yorkshire.

354. A tulipwood veneered lady's writing-table with fitted side drawer, baize-lined slide and adjustable fire-screen invoiced by Chippendale to Sir Rowland Winn on 23 June 1766, as 'A Lady's commode writing table made of tulip and rosewood with a slider covered with green cloth . . . £5. 14. 0.'
Loc: Nostell Prior, Yorkshire.

355. A mahogany pembroke table, banded in rosewood, the divided drawer inlaid with a back-gammon board and retaining the original ebony and ivory *men* (cf. Pl. 363).
Loc: Nostell Priory, Yorkshire.

356. One of a set of mahogany-framed open-armchairs at Nostell Priory — covered in leather and illustrating Chippendale's 'transitional' style between the rococo and the neo-classical; this was probably supplied by his firm.
Loc: Nostell Priory, Yorkshire.

357. A portrait of Sir Rowland and Lady Winn standing by the library table, supplied by Chippendale in 1767 (cf. 249), in the library at Nostell Priory — the attribution of the picture to Mercier, who died in 1760, is untenable.
Lit: M. W. Brockwell, *The Nostell Collection*, London, 1915, No. 45.
Exhib: Royal Academy of Arts, *English Taste in the Eighteenth Century*, 1955–56, Cat. No. 405.
Temple Newsam House, Leeds, 1951, *Thomas Chippendale*, Cat. No. 34.
Loc: Nostell Priory, Yorkshire.

358. A pair of carved giltwood *torchères* probably supplied by Chippendale to Sir Rowland Winn for Nostell Priory — they are good examples of his work in the neo-classical taste.
Exhib: Temple Newsam, *Thomas Chippendale*, Cat. No. 27.
Loc: Nostell Priory, Yorkshire.

359. One of a pair of carved mahogany serving-tables at Nostell Priory — probably supplied by Chippendale.
Lit: *G.C-M.*, p. 177, pl. 105.
Exhib: Temple Newsam, *Thomas Chippendale*, Cat. No. 25.
Loc: Nostell Priory, Yorkshire.

360. A carved mahogany medal-cabinet fitted into the wall, behind a door, at Nostell Priory: invoiced by Chippendale to Sir Rowland Winn on 30 June 1767, as 'a very neat mahogany Cabinet with drawers and a medall case, with a glass door to ditto elegantly ornamented with carved work and made to fit into the recess of a blanck door . . . £38. 10. 0.'.
Loc: Nostell Priory, Yorkshire.

361. A mahogany, tray-top bedside-commode with tambour shutter, which Chippendale's firm supplied to Ninian Home, of Paxton House, Berwick-on-Tweed, in 1774 at a cost of £2. 12. 6.; it was invoiced as 'a mahogany night table and stool with sliding door and stone pan'. It is curious to note that 'four spare close stool pans' are also invoiced at 12s. This rather suggests that the pans were often broken.
Lit: Anthony Coleridge, 'Chippendale, Interior-Decorator and House-Furnisher', *Apollo*, April 1963.
Loc: Paxton House, Berwick-on-Tweed.

362. One of the examples of mahogany chests extant at Paxton House; these were supplied by Chippendale in 1774 and might be related to the account entry 'a mahogany commode chest of drawers . . . £6. 16. 4.'.

Lit :   Coleridge, 'Chippendale, Interior-Decorator', *loc. cit.*
Loc :   Paxton House, Berwick-on-Tweed.

363. An ebony and ivory games-box with mosaic inlay which was invoiced in the Paxton House accounts as 'to a larger size ebony and ivory backgammon table with ivory men, boxes and dice compleat . . . £4. 16. 0.' : Chippendale probably called on a specialist to supply this piece.

Lit :   Coleridge, 'Chippendale, Interior-Decorator', *loc. cit.*
Loc :   Paxton House, Berwick-on-Tweed.

364. A mahogany side-table, the frieze pierced and carved with rococo motives, originating from Raynham Hall, Norfolk — it is traditionally held that Chippendale's firm supplied furniture to Captain Townshend, M.P., of Raynham, during the 1750's.

Loc :   Private Collection.

365. A carved giltwood pier-table with veined *rouge* marble slab banded in green marble : perhaps supplied by Chippendale's firm to the fourth Earl of Shaftesbury and his first wife — the Countess being a subscriber to the first edition of the *Director* (cf. Pl. 317). The general design, however, is influenced by Thomas Johnson's published work (see Helena Hayward, *Thomas Johnson and English Rococo*, 1964, figs. 65, 153/4, 172/3).

Lit :   'St. Giles's House', *Antique Collector*, August 1962, p. 150.
Loc :   St. Giles's House, Dorset.

366. One of a set of six single and two open-arm hall-chairs in padoukwood, probably supplied by Chippendale's firm for St. Giles's House, Dorset : cf. the design in pl. 17 right in the third edition of the *Director*.

Lit :   R. C. Lines, 'My House at St. Giles's', *Connoisseur*, October 1959, p. 77, pl. 11.
Loc :   St. Giles's House, Dorset.

367. A giltwood-framed open-armchair from a suite which originally comprised ten chairs and three sofas : designed by Adam in 1764 for Sir Lawrence Dundas, Bart., for his house at 19 Arlington Street : it was made by Chippendale in 1764/5 and he charged the high price of £20 for each chair and £54 for each sofa. They were invoiced as follows :

'to 8 large Arm Chairs exceeding Richly Carv'd in the Antick Manner & Gilt in Oil Gold stuff'd and cover'd with your own damask — and strong castors on the feet . . . £160. 4 large sofas exceeding Rich to match the Chairs . . . £216.'

They have previously been attributed to Samuel Norman.

Lit :   the chair : *D.E.F.*, I, fig. 200, p. 289.
           G.C-M., pl. 83.
           Eileen Harris, *The Furniture of Robert Adam*, p. 91, no. 102.
           Clifford Musgrave, *Adam and Hepplewhite*, 1966, pl. 57.
           P. Macquoid, *The Age of Mahogany*, 1906, p. 218, fig. 198.
           A. T. Bolton, *The Architecture of Robert James Adam*, Vol. 1, pp. 291–3.
           Anthony Coleridge, 'Sir Lawrence Dundas and Chippendale', *Apollo*, September 1967.
Exhib : *The Loan Exhibition of English Decorative Art*, Lansdowne House, 1929.
Sales : Christie's, 26 April 1934, Lot 73 (part of the suite).
           Sotheby's, 6 June 1947, Lot 154 (part of the suite).
           Sotheby's, 5 July 1963, Lot 171 (part of the suite).
Loc :   The Victoria and Albert Museum — (one chair). The major portion of the suite is at Aske Hall, near Richmond, Yorkshire.

368. A mahogany table-press which can probably be related to an entry in the *Holkham Departmental Accounts*, 11 June 1757, for work supplied by Benjamin Goodison, which reads :

'Mr. Goodison for a mahog. table press carv'd and Gilt with wire doors for ye Gallery . . . £4. 16. 0.'

    Lit: Anthony Coleridge, 'Some Mid-Georgian Cabinet-Maker's at Holkham', *Apollo*, February 1964.

    Loc: Holkham, Norfolk.

369. A detail of a side of the press shown in Pl. 368.

    Lit: Coleridge, 'Holkham', *loc. cit.*

    Loc: Holkham, Norfolk.

370. A mahogany knee-hole writing or dressing-table, similar in design and execution to the press shown in Pl. 368.

    Lit: Coleridge, 'Holkham', *loc. cit.*

    Loc: Holkham, Norfolk.

371. One of a pair of card-tables of unusual design: William Vile used similar decoration on the toes of Queen Charlotte's work-table, cf. Pl. 17 — Benjamin Goodison charged £12. 10. for '2 card table for ye Gallery at Holkham' in March 1756 — he invoiced these as 'two mahogany card tables with white Frett workt borders round the tops and frames and ye feet ornamented with carveing and gilding. . .'. It is probable that these are the tables concerned.

    Lit: Coleridge, 'Holkham', *loc. cit.*

    Loc: Holkham, Norfolk.

372. A scarlet and gold japanned side-chair bearing the trade label of Giles Grendey, of about 1730. Part of a suite of seat-furniture consisting of a day-bed, six armchairs and twenty single chairs, purchased in 1935 from the Duke of Infantado, Castle of Lazcano, Spain, whither it was probably exported when new.

    Lit: The day-bed from the suite is in the Victoria and Albert Museum.
            Ill. *G.C-M.*, p. 48, pl. 47.
            The chair, *London Furniture Makers*, Fig. 22.

    Loc: The Metropolitan Museum, New York.

373. A mahogany clothes-press attributed to Giles Grendey, of about 1740. The double serpentine-shaped panels on the doors are typical of his style.

    Lit: *D.E.F.*, II, p. 164, fig. 18.
            G.C-M., pl. 49.
            London Furniture Makers, Fig. 28.
            R. W. Symonds, 'In Search of Giles Grendey', *Country Life*, 30 November, 1951, p. 1794, pl. 7.

    Loc: The Victoria and Albert Museum.

374. A mahogany bureau-cabinet in the tradition of Giles Grendey (cf. Pl. 373).

    Loc: The Museum of Fine Arts, Boston.

375. A scarlet and gilt japanned bureau-cabinet bearing the trade label of Giles Grendey, about 1745.

    Lit: *G.C-M.*, p. 145, fig. 50.

    Loc: The Victoria and Albert Museum.

376. A mahogany-framed open-armchair, one of a set at Longford Castle, attributed to Giles Grendey: these are probably the chairs bought for Longford Castle, by the first Lord Folkestone, from '*Greenday* [Grendey], *chair-maker*', who was paid £68 in 1739 — *Longford Castle Archives*.

    Lit: *D.E.F.*, 1927, I, p. 265, fig. 123, p. 268.
            G.C-M., p. 47, pl. 48.

    Exhib: Royal Academy of Arts, *English Taste in the Eighteenth Century*, 1955–56, Cat. No. 74.

    Loc: Longford Castle, Wiltshire.

377. A mahogany centre-table in the same tradition, about 1740 — also perhaps by Giles Grendey.

    Loc: Private Collection.

378. One of a set of six armchairs and two settees made by Paul Saunders in 1757 for Holkham: The original entry in *The Holkham Departmental Accounts*, for the week ending 11 June 1757, reads:

'Mr. Saunders for 10 Elbow chairs with carved and gilt frames and
covd. cut blue Turkey leather . . .   £74. 0. 4.
Do for 2 large sophas ditto . . .   41. 18. 0.'

    Lit: Anthony Coleridge, 'Some Mid-Georgian Cabinet-Makers at Holkham', *Apollo*, February 1964.
    Loc: Holkham, Norfolk.

379. One of a set of nine single-chairs probably made by Paul Saunders for Holkham in 1757. They differ slightly in design and detail from the armchairs illustrated in Pl. 378 above but can probably be related to an entry in *The Holkham Departmental Accounts* for 11 June 1757, reading:

'12 chairs, mahog. frames Gilt and Stuffed . . . £39. 10. 3.'

    Lit: Coleridge, 'Holkham', *loc. cit.*
    Loc: Holkham, Norfolk.

380. One of a set of 23 armchairs, 9 settees and 4 stools in carved giltwood — the contemporary crimson cut Genoa velvet and carved seat-frames probably supplied by Benjamin Goodison in *c.* 1735–40.

    Lit: A settee ill. D.E.F. III, fig. 51, p. 93.
    Loc: Holkham, Norfolk.

381. One of a pair of pier-glasses made for the State Apartments at Holkham. Mathew Brettingham, Jr., in *The Plans, Elevations and Sections of Holkham House in Norfolk* (1773), refers to one of them as 'a magnificent pier-glass the frame by Whittle'. (James Whittle was in partnership with Samuel Norman.)

    Lit: C. W. James, *Chief Justice Coke, His Family and Descendants at Holkham*, 1929.
            Coleridge, 'Holkham', *loc. cit.*
    Loc: Holkham, Norfolk.

382. Three of a set of four pier-glasses and console-tables in the Saloon at Holkham which were perhaps, like that illustrated in Pl. 381, made by Whittle and Norman.

    Lit: Coleridge, 'Holkham', *loc. cit.*
    Loc: Holkham, Norfolk.

383. A fine mahogany commode in the *Director* tradition which may well have been supplied by Norman for Aske Hall, near Richmond in Yorkshire. His account to Sir Lawrence Dundas, between 1763–66, included, amongst entries for Aske Hall, '2 very large & neat Mahogany Commodes extra fine Wood Best Lox Large lifting handles at the Ends Complete'.

    Lit: Anthony Coleridge, 'Sir Lawrence Dundas and Chippendale', *Apollo*, September, 1967.
    Loc: Aske Hall, near Richmond, Yorkshire.

384. One of a pair of gilt-framed pier-glasses which were delivered to Woburn Abbey, Bedfordshire, for the Duke of Bedford by Messrs. Norman and Whittle, in 1760, at a cost of £412. 5. 0.

    Lit: G. Scott-Thomson, *Family Background*, 1949, pp. 67–8, 74–8.
            Ralph Edwards, 'Patrons of Taste and Sensibility, English Furniture of the Eighteenth Century, Woburn Abbey', *Apollo*, December 1965.
    Loc: Woburn Abbey, Bedfordshire.

385. A giltwood-framed pier-glass sometimes attributed to Samuel Norman.
    Loc: The Victoria and Albert Museum.

386. A settee from a large suite of giltwood-framed seat furniture, originally consisting of two settees, two window-seats, two stools, four fire-screens and ten armchairs. It is covered in contemporary Gobelins tapestry woven in Jacques Neilson's atelier between 1765 and 1769. Made for the Tapestry Room at Moor Park by Samuel Fell and William Turton, in 1771, at

a cost of £25. (cf. the Ince and Mayhew suite in the Metropolitan Museum, New York, from the Croome Court Tapestry Room, Pl. 117).

> Lit: Clifford Musgrave, *Adam and Hepplewhite Furniture*, 1966, pl. 82.
> Eileen Harris, 'Robert Adam and the Gobelins', *Apollo*, April 1962.
> Eileen Harris, 'The Moor Park Tapestries', *Apollo*, September, 1967.
> *G.C-M.*, p. 61, pl. 86.
> N.B. A window-seat from the suite is discussed and illustrated by Eileen Harris in *The Furniture of Robert Adam*, 1963, p. 92, No. 105.
>
> Sale: Christie's, 26 April 1934, Lots 80–5 : Sotheby's, 26 May 1967.
> Exhib: A firescreen from the suite at *The Loan Exhibition of English Decorative Art, Lansdowne House, 1929*.
> Loc: The Philadelphia Museum of Art.

387. 'A neat mahogany secretary' supplied to the Princess Royal, then aged eight, by John Bradburn in 1774 : It cost £20 and was for her apartments at Buckingham House.

> Lit: H. Clifford-Smith, *Buckingham Palace*, 1931, p. 232, pl. 71.
> *G.C-M.*, p. 62, pl. 88.
> Loc: The Royal Collection.

388. 'A mahogany press for linen', or low cabinet, supplied to Buckingham House by John Bradburn in 1770. It cost £84.

> Lit: H. Clifford-Smith, *Buckingham Palace*, p. 279, pl. 65.
> Loc: The Royal Collection.

389. A mahogany low cabinet in the same tradition as that illustrated in Pl. 388.

> Loc: Private Collection.

390. A mahogany chair from a large set of seat-furniture, consisting of five settees, six open-armchairs and seven single chairs, supplied by France and Bradburn to the Vyne : their account to John Chute for work carried out at the Vyne is dated March 1765 to January 1767 : '8 armed chairs with mahoy feet and brackets on castors' cost £36. 0. 0.

> Lit: Anthony Coleridge, '18th Century Furniture at The Vyne', *Country Life*, 25 July 1963.
> Loc: The Vyne, Hampshire.

391. One of a pair of mahogany side-tables supplied by France and Bradburn to the Vyne between 1765 and 1767. They cost £11 the pair and are invoiced as 'for 2 mahoy half circle sidebord tables with gadroon edges and carved fronts'.

> Lit: Coleridge, 'The Vyne', *loc. cit.*
> Loc: The Vyne, Hampshire.

392. A large mahogany reading-stand supplied by William France's firm to the Earl of Mansfield for the Library at Kenwood, Hampstead, in 1770 : it cost £6. 14. 0. and its tripod support and scrolled feet are similar to a design by Ince and Mayhew, pl. 26, in *The Universal System of Household Furniture*, 1759–62.

> Lit: *D.E.F.*, III, p. 187, fig. 7.
> *G.C-M.*, p. 82, pl. 181.
> *Georgian Furniture, Victoria and Albert Museum*, pl. 16.
> Exhib: The Iveagh Bequest, Kenwood, *The Adam Style in Furniture*, 1964, Cat. No. 10.
> Loc: The Victoria and Albert Museum, London.

393. One of a pair of carved giltwood console-tables made by France and Bradburn for Sir Lawrence Dundas, Bart., in January and December 1765 at a cost of £37. 10. 0. each. They were made from a design of Robert Adam's, dated 1765 (*Soane*, Vol. 17, no. 5), for which he charged £5. 5. 0. on 18 July 1765 (*Bolton*, II, p. 345).

> Lit: *D.E.F.*, Vol. III, p. 296, fig. 63.
> A. T. Bolton, *Architecture of Robert and James Adam*, 1922, Vol. II, pp. 291, 345.

Eileen Harris, *The Furniture of Robert Adam*, 1963, p. 65, pl. 8.

Clifford Musgrave, *Adam and Hepplewhite*, 1966, pl. 21.

Anthony Coleridge, 'Dundas and some Rococo Cabinet-Makers', *Apollo*, September, 1967.

Sale: Christie's, 26 April 1934, Lot 77.

Loc: Unknown.

394. A mahogany break-front bookcase by Gillows of Lancaster about 1765. It is of the highest quality. Its fretted swan-neck pediment is, in many ways, similar to that on a bureau-bookcase illustrated in *G.C-M.*, pl. 191, which is also by Gillow and Co.

Lit: Anthony Coleridge, 'The Firm of Gillow and Co. at Blair Castle', *Connoisseur*, October 1964.

Loc: Ugbrooke Park, Devon.

395. The first of William Masters' twenty extant accounts at Blair Castle, p. 1. Note the Sign of the Golden Fleece in its rococo cartouche.

Lit: Anthony Coleridge, 'William Masters and Some Early 18th Century Furniture at Blair Castle', *Connoisseur*, October 1963, pl. 3.

Loc: Blair Castle, Perthshire.

396. A mahogany hall-table with granite slab, for which William Masters charged the second Duke of Atholl £2. 15. 0. in 1749.

Lit: Coleridge, 'William Masters . . . at Blair Castle', *loc. cit.*, pl. 4.

Loc: Blair Castle, Perthshire.

397. One of a set of twelve oak chairs delivered by William Masters in 1751. In the following year Sam Cobb charged 7s. 6d. each for painting them with 'crests, coronetts, garters and stars'.

Lit: Coleridge, 'William Masters . . . at Blair Castle', *loc. cit.*, pl. 5.

Loc: Blair Castle, Perthshire.

398. An octagonal mahogany tea-table supplied by William Masters in 1755: it has an unusual open tripod support.

Lit: *G.C-M.*, fig. 220.

Coleridge, 'William Masters . . . at Blair Castle', *loc. cit.*, pl. 6.

Loc: Blair Castle, Perthshire.

399. A pair of mahogany *torchères* by William Masters: he charged £3. 0. 0. for them in 1756 and invoiced them as '2 mahogany candlestands with openwork tops and fluted pillows ribb'd'.

Lit: *G.C-M.*, fig. 221.

Coleridge, 'William Masters . . . at Blair Castle', *loc. cit.*, pl. 8.

Anthony Coleridge, 'Chippendale, Interior-Decorator and House Furnisher, at Paxton House, Berwick-on-Tweed', *Apollo*, October 1963, pl. 5.

Loc: Blair Castle, Perthshire.

400. One of a pair of mahogany dumb-waiters in the State Dining-Room at Blair Castle, for which William Masters charged £2. 2. 0. each in 1753.

Lit: Coleridge, 'William Masters . . . at Blair Castle', *loc. cit.*, pl. 10.

Anthony Coleridge, 'John Hodson and Some Cabinet-Makers at Blair Castle', *Connoisseur*, April 1963, pl. 3.

Loc: Blair Castle, Perthshire.

401. A mahogany side-table which Masters delivered to the Duke of Atholl in 1753 at a cost of £10. 10. 0. It was invoiced as 'A large mahogany sideboard table, the top full 2 inches thick, 6'6" long and 2'9" broad in one piece of fine wood, key work round the frame and Gothick brackets . . .'. Cf. the third edition of the *Director*, 1762, No. 58.

Lit: Coleridge, 'William Masters . . . at Blair Castle', *loc. cit.*, pl. 11.

Loc: Blair Castle, Perthshire.

402. One of a set of four mahogany chests of drawers which can perhaps be related to Masters' account of February 1756. He charged £8. 10. 0. for the chest described in the account.

Lit: Coleridge, 'William Masters . . . at Blair Castle', *loc. cit.*, pl. 13.
Loc: Blair Castle, Perthshire.

403. A portrait of George Sandeman of Perth, cabinet-maker, 1724–1803, who 'was at the head of his trade and was a most industrious cabinet-maker'.
Lit: Anthony Coleridge, 'George Sandeman of Perth, Cabinet-Maker', *Connoisseur*, March 1960, pl. 1.
Loc: Blair Castle, Perthshire.

404. A bureau-bookcase veneered with broomwood: this was made by George Sandeman of Perth in 1758 for 'The Hon. John Murray Esquire' at a cost of £19. 10. 8. It is endorsed on the outer face of the bill 'A Plantaginet Cabinet'. This is a pun on *planta genista*, the Latin name for broom, which was not only the badge of the House of Plantagenet, but also that of the House of Murray.
Lit: Coleridge, 'Sandeman', *loc. cit.*, pl. 5.
Loc: Blair Castle, Perthshire.

405. An interior of the bureau section of 404 above showing a 'secret', built-in medal cabinet. The interior is lined with mahogany and the pigeon holes are centred by a mirror glass panel painted with flowers which is *en suite* with two others hanging elsewhere in the Castle.
Lit: Coleridge, 'Sandeman', *loc. cit.*, pl. 7.
Loc: Blair Castle, Perthshire.

406. A medal-cabinet, veneered with broomwood, which is attributed to Sandeman on stylistic grounds. Like the bureau-bookcase ill. in Pl. 404 it is also at Blair Castle, Perthshire. The ivory statuettes on the pediment were perhaps taken from a seventeenth-century cabinet. It was probably also made for John Murray who must have had a large collection of medals and coins.
Lit: Coleridge, 'Sandeman', *loc. cit.*, pl. 8.
Loc: Blair Castle, Perthshire.

407. One of a pair of giltwood-framed girandoles which were probably supplied in 1755 by James Cullen for 'The New Dining Roome' at Hopetoun House — described in Cullen's memo of 1 February 1755.
Lit: Anthony Coleridge, 'James Cullen, Cabinet-Maker at Hopetoun House', *Connoisseur*, November and December 1966.
Loc: Hopetoun House, West Lothian.

408. A detail of one of the pair of pier-tables, standing below the girandoles shown in Pl. 407, supplied as a result of recommendations made by James Cullen in 1755.
Lit: Coleridge, 'James Cullen', *loc. cit.*
Loc: Hopetoun House, West Lothian.

409. One of a pair of mahogany-framed sofas, probably supplied by Cullen for the Red Drawing-Room — a pair is listed in 'Mr. Cullen's Memo of Furniture to be made, 1758, for the appartments'.
Lit: Coleridge, 'James Cullen', *loc. cit.*
Loc: Hopetoun House, West Lothian.

410. An armchair and a single-chair from the same large set of seat-furniture as the sofa shown in Pl. 409.
Lit: Coleridge, 'James Cullen', *loc. cit.*
Loc: Hopetoun House, West Lothian.

411. One of a set of four pier-glasses in the Red Drawing-Room which were probably provided by Cullen in 1766, after designs by Matthias Lock, and carved and gilded by Samuel Norman.
Lit: Coleridge, 'James Cullen', *loc. cit.*
Loc: Hopetoun House, West Lothian.

412. One of a set of four console-tables which may perhaps have been originally provided by Cullen for the pier-glasses shown in Pl. 411 — but now, no longer, standing under them.

Lit: Coleridge, 'James Cullen', *loc. cit.*
Loc: Hopetoun House, West Lothian.

413. The giltwood-framed State Bedstead which Cullen purchased for the Earl of Hopetoun through Samuel Norman in 1768 for £230.
Lit: Coleridge, 'James Cullen', *loc. cit.*
Loc: Hopetoun House, West Lothian.

414. A detail from the bedstead above, showing the headboard and dome. Cullen, on 18 January 1768, sent Lord Hopetoun a letter enclosing two sketches of the bedstead, one of which, as he wrote, 'shows the Ornaments and drapery where the inside head Vallens commonly are, and a Section of the inside of Doom with the coves and gilt Embellishments'. The silk damask hangings are original.
Lit: Coleridge, 'James Cullen', *loc. cit.*
Loc: Hopetoun House, West Lothian.

415. One of two designs for a pair of commodes sent by James Cullen to the Earl of Hopetoun in 1768 — the other design, which was probably returned to Cullen, was the one, in fact, chosen. Cullen, in a letter of 25 February 1768, wrote, 'I have made some very fine ones of this kind for Ld Walgrave . . .'.
Lit: Coleridge, 'James Cullen', *loc. cit.*
Loc: Hopetoun House, West Lothian.

416. One of a pair of most unusual commodes supplied by James Cullen in 1768 — cf. the design shown in Pl. 415. The metal-gilt escutcheons, mounts and handles are highly distinctive in form and execution, and Cullen, in his letter, wrote, 'Herewith are the designs for the Commodes in the Grand Bedch^r one of which is intended to introduce different collour'd woods which with good brasses has an Effect that is generally approved here . . .'. Mr. Peter Thornton has pointed out to me that the bifurcated scrolled toes and angle mounts and the shape of the front and back angles are reminiscent of the work of Pierre Langlois (cf. Pls. 50, 51 and 55).
Lit: Coleridge, 'James Cullen', *loc. cit.*
Loc: Hopetoun House, West Lothian.

417. A design for a most unusual pier-glass, dated 1767 — probably sent to the Earl of Hopetoun by James Cullen.
Lit: Coleridge, 'James Cullen', *loc. cit.*
Loc: Hopetoun House, West Lothian.

418. An impressive giltwood-framed pier-glass at Hopetoun House. The plates of mirror glass in the border are engraved, a feature perhaps owing its inspiration to some Venetian prototype.
Lit: Coleridge, 'James Cullen', *loc. cit.*
Loc: Hopetoun House, West Lothian.

419. A fine pier-glass at Hopetoun House, the giltwood frame of highly distinctive form and carved with dolphins and entwined serpents.
Lit: Coleridge, 'James Cullen', *loc. cit.*
Loc: Hopetoun House, West Lothian.

420. A fine part gilt 'pagoda cabinet', its design based on plates 105 to 111 in the first edition of the *Director*, 1754.
Loc: Originally at Kinure Park, Co. Dublin. Messrs. Mallett and Son Ltd.

Select Bibliography

Adam (R. and J.), *The Works in Architecture*, facsimile edition, Tiranti, London, 1959.

Avrey Tipping (H.), *English Homes*, Country Life, London, 1926, 9 vols.
    English Furniture of the Cabriole Period, London, 1922.

Bolton (A. T.), '*The Architecture of Robert and James Adam (1758–94)*', Country Life, London, 1922, 2 vols.

Bracket (O.), *Encyclopaedia of English Furniture*, London, 1927.
    Thomas Chippendale, London, 1930.

Bracket (O.) and Clifford-Smith (H.), *English Furniture Illustrated*, London, 1950.

Brockwell (M. W.), *The Nostell Collection*, London, 1915.

Cescinsky (H.), *English Furniture of the Eighteenth Century*, London, 1909, 3 vols.

Clifford-Smith (H.), *Buckingham Palace*, Country Life, London, 1931.

Clouston (R. S.), *English Furniture and Furniture-Makers of the Eighteenth Century*, London, 1906.

Edwards (R.), *English Chairs*, V.A.M. Publications, H.M.S.O., London, 1951.
    Georgian Furniture, V.A.M. Publications, H.M.S.O., London, 1958.
    The Dictionary of English Furniture, Country Life, London, 1954, 3 vols.
    The Shorter Dictionary of English Furniture, Country Life, London, 1964.

Edwards (R.), foreword by, *The Universal System of Household Furniture, 1762*, published by Alec Tiranti, London, 1960.

Edwards (R.) and Jourdain (M.), *Georgian Cabinet-Makers*, Country Life, London, 1946; Revised Edition, 1955.

Fastnedge (R.), *English Furniture Styles*, Penguin Books, 1955; Reprinted, 1961.
    Sheraton Furniture, Faber and Faber, London, 1962.

FitzGerald (B.), Ed., *Correspondence of Emily Duchess of Leinster*, Irish MSS. Commission, Vol. 1, Dublin, 1949.

Hackenbroch (Y.) (Ed.), *English Furniture in the Collection of Irwin Untermyer*, Thames and Hudson, London, 1958.

Harris (E.), *The Furniture of Robert Adam*, Tiranti, London, 1964.

Harris (J.), *Sir William Chambers*, Zwemmer, London, 1968.

Hayward (H.), *Thomas Johnson and English Rococo*, Tiranti, London, 1964.
    (Ed.), *World Furniture*, Paul Hamlyn, London, 1965.

Heal (Sir A.), *The London Furniture Makers (1660–1840)*, Batsford, London, 1953.

James (C. W.), *Chief Justice Coke, His Family and Descendants at Holkham*, London, 1929.

Jourdain (M.), *The Work of William Kent*, Country Life, London, 1948.
    English Decoration and Furniture of the later Eighteenth Century, London, 1922.

Jourdain (M.) and Rose (F.), *English Furniture, The Georgian Period*, Batsford, London, 1953.

Jourdain (M.) and Soame Jenyns (R.), *Chinese Export Art*, Country Life, London, 1950.

Kimball (F.), *Creation of the Rococo*, Philadelphia, 1943.

Laking (G. F.), *Windsor Castle Furniture*, London, N.D.

Layton (E. J.), *Thomas Chippendale*, London, 1928.

Macquoid (P.), *English Furniture, Tapestry and Needlework . . . in the Lady Lever Art Gallery, Port Sunlight*, Batsford, London, 1928.
    History of English Furniture, London, 1904–8, 4 vols.

SELECT BIBLIOGRAPHY

Macquoid (P.) and Edwards (R.), *The Dictionary of English Furniture*, Country Life, London, 1924–7, 3 vols.

Mülliner (H. H.), *Decorative Arts in England (1660–1780)*, London, N.D.

Musgrave (C.), *Adam and Hepplewhite and other Neo-Classical Furniture*, Faber and Faber, London, 1966.

Phillips (H.), *Mid-Georgian London*, Collins, London, 1964.

Pyne (W. H.), *The History of the Royal Residences*, London, 1819.

Salverte (Comte de), *Les Ebénistes du XVIIIᵉ Siècle*, Paris, 1953.

Scott-Thomson (G.), *Family Background*, London, 1949.

Simon (C.), *English Furniture Designers of the Eighteenth Century*, Batsford, London, 1907.

Strange (T. A.), *English Furniture, Woodwork, Decoration etc.*, London, N.D.

Symonds (R. W.), *Furniture-making in 17th and 18th Century England*, London, 1955.
   The Present State of Old English Furniture, London, 1921.

Thornton (P.), *Baroque and Rococo Silks*, Faber and Faber, London, 1965.

Ward-Jackson (P.), *English Furniture Designs of the Eighteenth Century*, H.M.S.O., 1958.

Watson (F. J. B.), *Louis XVI Furniture*, Tiranti, London, 1960.

Wills (G.), *English Looking Glasses*, Country Life, London, 1965.

NOTE: *The eighteenth-century design and pattern books cited in the text are* NOT *included in the above list.*

PUBLISHED ARTICLES CITED IN THIS BOOK

Avrey Tipping (H.), 'English Furniture of the Cabriole Period', *Burlington*, Vol. XXXVI, 1920.

Boynton (L.), 'An Ince and Mayhew Correspondence', *Journal of the Furniture History Society*, Vol. II, 1966.

Bracket (O.), 'Documented Furniture at Corsham', *Country Life*, 28 November 1963.

Clifford-Smith (H.), 'Attributions to William Vile', letter to *Country Life*, 4 November 1954.
   'Some Georgian Furniture from the Royal Collections', *Apollo*, May 1935.
   'Two hundred years of the Mansion House, London, and Some of its Furniture', *Connoisseur*, December 1952.

Coleridge (A.), 'A Reappraisal of William Hallett', *Journal of the Furniture History Society*, Vol. i, 1965.
   'Chippendale, The *Director*, and Some Cabinet-Makers at Blair Castle', *Connoisseur*, December 1960.
   'Chippendale, Interior Decorator and House-Furnisher', *Apollo*, April 1963.
   'Chippendale at Wilton', *Apollo*, July 1964.
   'Dundas and Some Rococo Cabinet-Makers', *Apollo*, September, 1967.
   'Eighteenth Century Furniture at The Vyne', *Country Life*, 25 July 1963.
   'English Furniture in the Duke of Argyll's Collection', *Connoisseur*, March 1965.
   'English Furniture and Cabinet-Makers at Hatfield House, Part II, — The First Marquess's English Furniture', *Burlington*, March 1967.
   'Furniture in the Collection of Viscount and Viscountess Lewisham', *Connoisseur*, November 1962.
   'Georgian Cabinet-Makers at Uppark (Parts I and II)', *Connoisseur*, October and November, 1967.
   'George Sandeman of Perth, Cabinet-Maker', *Connoisseur*, March 1960.
   'James Cullen, Cabinet-Maker, at Hopetoun House', *Connoisseur*, November and December 1966.

PUBLISHED ARTICLES CITED IN THIS BOOK

'John Hodson and Some Cabinet-Makers at Blair Castle', *Connoisseur*, April 1963.

'John Vardy and the Hackwood Suite', *Connoisseur*, January 1962.

'Pierre Langlois, His Oeuvre and some Recent Discoveries', *Gazette des Beaux-Arts*, September 1967.

'Sir Lawrence Dundas and Chippendale', *Apollo*, September, 1967.

'Some Mid-Georgian Cabinet-Makers at Holkham', *Apollo*, February 1964.

'Some Furniture in the Collection of the Earl of Mansfield', *Connoisseur*, April 1966.

'The Firm of Gillow and Co. at Blair Castle', *Connoisseur*, October 1964.

'William Masters and Some Early Eighteenth Century Furniture at Blair Castle', *Connoisseur*, October 1963.

Edwards (R.), 'Attributions to William Vile', *Country Life*, 7 October 1954.

'A Bill from Vile and Cobb', *Country Life*, 7 June 1956.

'A great Georgian Cabinet-Maker', *Country Life*, 21 October 1933.

'Patrons of Taste and Sensibility, English Furniture of the Eighteenth Century, Woburn Abbey', *Apollo*, December 1965.

'Two Commodes by John Cobb', *Country Life*, 22 May 1937.

Fastnedge (R.), 'A Chippendale Gothic bookcase in the Lady Lever Art Gallery', *Apollo*, October 1960.

'An unpublished Commode attributed to Pierre Langlois', *Journal of the Furniture History Society*, Vol. III, 1967.

Girouard (M.), 'Curraghmore, County Waterford', *Country Life*, 26 December 1963.

'Stedcombe House, Devon', *Country Life*, Vol. CXXXIII, p. 370.

Goodison (N.), 'Clockmaker and Cabinet-Maker', *Journal of the Furniture History Society*, Vol. II, 1966.

Harris (E.), 'Robert Adam and the Gobelins', *Apollo*, April 1962.

'The Moor Park Tapestries', *Apollo*, September, 1967.

Hayward (H.), 'Thomas Johnson and Rococo Carving', *Connoisseur Year Book*, 1964.

Hayward (J.), 'A China Case attributed to Thomas Chippendale', *Connoisseur*, June 1962.

'English Brass-inlaid Furniture', *Victoria and Albert Museum Bulletin*, Vol. 1, No. 1, January 1965.

'Furniture designed and carved by Matthias Lock for Hinton House, Somerset', *Connoisseur*, December 1960.

'The Channon family of Exeter and London, Chair and Cabinet-Makers', *Victoria and Albert Museum Bulletin*, Vol. II, No. 2, April 1966.

Heal (Sir A.), 'The Firm of Seddon', *Country Life*, 20 January 1934.

Hiscock (W. G.), 'Christ Church, Furniture (Part II)', *Country Life*, 5 January 1954.

Hussey (C.), 'Ashburnham Place (Part II)', *Country Life*, 23 April 1959.

Jourdain (M.), 'A pair of Royal Medal-Cabinets', *Country Life*, 29 April 1949.

'Furniture at Hagley Hall', *Apollo*, January 1950.

Joy (E. T.), 'Chippendale in Trouble', *Country Life*, 24 August 1951.

Kimball (F.) and Donnell (E.), 'The Creators of the Chippendale Style', *Metropolitan Museum Studies*, 1 May 1929.

'Chippendale Designs in the Book of the Society of Upholsterers', *Metropolitan Museum Studies*, 11 November 1929.

Lines (R. C.), 'My House at St. Giles's', *Connoisseur*, October 1959.

Luff (R. W.), 'Two Chippendale Bookcases', *Antique Collector*, August 1962.

Molesworth (D.), 'Problem Pieces in Furniture', Lecture at The Victoria and Albert Museum, 3 March 1965.

Oswald (A.), 'Okeover Hall, Staffordshire (Part II)', *Country Life*, 30 January 1964.

Parker (J.), 'Croome Court, The Architecture and Furniture', *Metropolitan Museum of Art Bulletin*, November 1959.

PUBLISHED ARTICLES CITED IN THIS BOOK

'Rococo and formal order in English Furniture', *Metropolitan Museum of Art Bulletin*, January 1957.

Pinto (E. H.), 'The furniture of William Vile and John Cobb', *Antiques*, January 1959.

Ramsey (L. G. G.), 'Chinoiserie in the Western Isles', *Connoisseur*, June 1958.

Shaw (B.), 'Gillows of Lancaster', *Country Life*, Vol. CII, p. 430, 1947.

Shrub (D.), 'The Vile Problem', *Victoria and Albert Museum Bulletin*, Vol. 1, No. 4, October 1965.

Standen (E. A.), 'Croome Court, The Tapestries', *Metropolitan Museum of Art Bulletin*, Vol. XVII, No. 3, November 1959.

Symonds (R. W.), 'A George II Writing Cabinet', *Country Life*, 13 January 1950.

'A Magnificent Dressing-Table', *Country Life*, 16 February 1956.

'An English Commode of rare design and quality', *Leeds Art Calendar*, Vol. 12, No. 39, Spring 1938.

'Furniture of the Nobility', *Country Life*, 7 May 1948.

'In Search of Giles Grendey', *Country Life*, 30 November 1951.

'Rediscovering Old Furniture', *Country Life*, 18 October 1956.

'Rococo at St. Giles' House', *Antique Collector*, December 1955.

'The China Case and China Closet', *Connoisseur*, June 1952.

Thornton (P.) and FitzGerald (D.), 'Abraham Roentgen "Englische Kabinettmacher" and some further reflections on the work of John Channon', *Victoria and Albert Museum Bulletin*, October 1966, Vol. 11, No. 4.

Watson (F.), 'A Princely Collection of English Furniture', *Apollo*, June 1964.

Wills (G.), 'Furniture-Smuggling in Eighteenth Century London', *Apollo*, August 1965.

Index

Abercorn, Duke of, 161, 169
Adam and Hepplewhite Furniture by Clifford Musgrave, 18, 55, 112, 133
Adam, Robert, 23, 33, 55, 56, 66, 67, 68, 78, 79, 94, 111, 112, 113, 121, 122, 142, 147, 149, 150, 161 : *Plates 119, 393*
Adam, William, 161
Admiralty Office, 137
Aesop's Fables, 59, 62 : *Plates 99, 113*
Agar, Samuel, 82
Age of Mahogany by Percy Macquoid, 112, 131
Alkin, Sefferin, 33
Alnwick Castle, Northumberland, 21, 81, 106
Althorp, Northants, 50, 51, 101 : *Plates 76, 81, 82, 83, 84, 85*
Ambulator, The, or a Pocket Companion in a Tour Round London, 43
Ampton Hall, Suffolk, 106
Ancaster, Duke and Duchess of, 69, 191
Annual Register for 1768, 153
Anti-Gallican Association, 64
Arbury, 88
Architecture in the Gothic, Chinese and Modern Taste by Charles Over (1758), 88
Argyll, Duke of, *Plate 209*
Arniston, Lady, 93, 113 : *Plate 165*
Arts, Society of, 77, 95
Arundel Castle, Sussex, 96, 106 : *Plate 167*
Ashburnham Place, Kent, 21, 173 : *Plate 3*
Ashmolean Museum, Oxford, *Plate 159*
Aske Hall, Yorks, 36, 122, 144, 169, 173 : *Plates 51, 257, 383*
Assembly Rooms, York, 62 : *Plate 103*
Atholl, Jean, Duchess of, 182
Atholl, Dukes of, 51, 57, 58, 60, 103, 108, 155, 156, 160 : *Plates 86, 87, 100, 101, 102, 288, 395–406*
Atholl House : *see under* Blair Castle
Audley End, Essex, 38 : *Plates 59, 152*
Austin, W., 58

Badminton House, Glos, 83, 98, 107 : *Plates 206, 281, 332, 333*
Bardwell, Thomas, *Plate 159*
Barker, Robert, 83
Barlow, Francis (illustrator), 59, 62

Barn Elms, 136, 150
Barrett, Thomas, 189
Beard, Geoffrey, 29n, 33, 44n
Beauchamp-Proctor, Sir William, Bt., 100
Beaufort, Duke of, 83, 98, 107, 205 : *Plates 206, 332*
Beaumont, William, 20, 33
Becket, T., 91, 93
Beckwith, Samuel, 20, 149, 150
Bedford, Duke of, 36, 56, 141, 164
Bentley, Richard, 43, 87, 189
Bérain, Jean, 47, 92
Berlindis, Baron, 32, 160
Birmingham, City of, Art Gallery, *Plate 237*
Bladwell, John, 82
Blair Castle, Perthshire, 51, 58, 60, 103, 108, 156, 157, 158, 160 : *Plates 86, 87, 97, 100, 101, 102, 268, 395, 396, 397, 398, 399, 400, 401, 402, 403, 404, 405, 406*
Blakeney, Lord, 59
Blathwayt, W., of Dyrham, 69
Bolton, Dukes of, 50
  arms of, *Plates 77, 78, 79, 80*
Bolton Hall, Yorks, 50n : *Plate 77*
Bonfoy, Mrs., 33
Book of tables, candle stands, pedestals by M. Lock (1768), 53
Boscowen, Admiral, 107
Boughton, Northants, 36
Boulton and Fothergill, Soho, Birmingham, 68
Boulton, Matthew, 99
Bowood House, Wilts, 66
Boynton, Dr. Lindsay, 68
Brabourne, Lord, 126, 127
Bracken, 139
Bracket, Oliver, 83, 109, 114, 117, 118, 129, 185, 191, 192, 194, 197, 198, 200, 203, 207
Bradburn (Bradbourne), John, 19, 20, 31, 145–8, 169 : *Plates 387–93*
Bradshaw, George Smith, 137
Bradshaw, Mr., 54, 55, 62, 81
Bradshaw, William, 137
Bramcote, Warwick, 108
Bramshill, Hants, 188
Braxted Park, Essex, 27
Brettingham, Matthew, Jun., 140

Brettingham, Matthew, Sen., 100, 114
Brinkburn Priory, Northumberland, 62 : *Plate 111*
Bristol, Earl of, 137
Bristol City Art Gallery, *Plate 66*
British Architect or the Builder's Treasury of Stair-cases by Abraham Swan (1745), 52
British Chronicle, 64, 90, 93, 94
British Museum, 24, 25, 44 : *Plates 74, 75*
Bromwich, Thomas, 42
Bruce, Sir William, 161
Brunetti, Gaetano, 48 : *Plate 73*
Buckingham Palace (also Buckingham House, Queen's House), 23, 24, 26, 27, 28, 29, 31, 145, 148, 174, 212 : *Plates 24, 387*
Building Society Offices, Otley, Yorks, 79
Buller, James, 108
Burdett, Sir Robert, 108
Burges, Robert, 76
Burlington, Lord, 21, 48, 49, 50, 140, 173
Burney, Fanny, 109*n*
Buscot Park, Berks, 62

Cabinet and Chairmakers Real Friend, The, by Robert Manwaring (1765), 70, 188, 189 : *Plates 133, 136, 137, 139, 142, 144*
Cabinet-Maker, The (1923), 74
Cabinet Makers and Upholsterers Drawing Book by Thomas Sheraton (1791), 84
Cadogan, Lord, 69
Calthorpe, James, 106
Cambridge, Richard, 42
Came House, Dorset, 22, 27, 44
Cannon Hall, Yorks, *Plate 38*
Canons Park, Middlesex, 43
Cardigan, 4th Earl of, 42, 134, 137, 140
Carlisle House, Soho Square, 109, 161
Carpenters Companion for Chinese Railings and Gates by J. H. Morris and John Crunden (1765), 87
Carpenter's Compleat Guide, The by Robert Manwaring (1765), 70
Carr, John, 112
Cartwright, Capt. C. A., R. N., 24
Castle Mona, Isle of Man, 57, 155
Cathcart, Mary, 32
Chair-Maker's Guide, The, by Robert Manwaring (1766), 70, 71, 95, 188
Chair-Maker's Real Friend and Companion, The, 71
Chambers, Sir William, 52, 79, 115 : *Plate 185*
Chandos, Duke of, 43, 69
Channon, John, 19, 23, 40, 74 : *Plates 60–6*
Charlemont House, Dublin, 30
Charlotte, Queen, 22, 24, 25, 26, 30, 174, 210 : *Plates 12, 13, 14, 17*
Chatelin, 48

Chatsworth House, Derby, *Plate 1*
Chauncey, Richard, 24, 28, 178 : *Plate 29*
Chesterfield, Earl of, 43, 83
Chesterfield House, Mayfair, 84
Chevening, Kent, 137
Chewton House, Somerset, *Plate 49*
Child, Mr., 68 : *Plate 128*
Chinese and Gothic Architecture by William Halfpenny (1752), 88
Chippendale, Edward, 74, 75
Chippendale, John, 73, 74
Chippendale, Thomas, 20, 21, 23, 26, 33, 35, 40, 43, 47, 52, 54, 55, 56, 60, 62, 63, 66, 68, 70, 71, 72, 144, 150, 152, 155 : *Plates 164–205, 208–11, 219–23, 229–60, 264–8, 277–94, 307–15, 324–6, 338, 342–63, 365–6, 367*
his life, 73–132
Chippendale, Thomas by Edwin Layton (1928), 73
Chippendale, Thomas by Oliver Bracket (1924): *see under* Bracket, Oliver
Chippendale, William, 73
Chippindall, Col. W. H., 73
Chiswick House, Middlesex, 21, 49, 173 : *Plate 1*
Christ Church Library, Oxford, 108, 109 : *Plate 338*
Christian, John, 155
Chrysler, Walter P., 21, 22
Chute, Anthony, 29, 37, 44, 45, 88, 176, 189 : *Plates 27, 28*
Chute, John, 27, 148 : *Plate 54*
Cipriani, 65
City and Country Builders and Workmans Treasury of Designs by Batty Langley, engraved by Thomas Langley (1740), 51–2, 183
Clemapon, G., 152
Clifford, Lord, 155
Clifford-Smith, H., 23*n*, 24, 174, 175 : *Plates 12, 13, 14, 15, 16, 17*
Clive, Lord, of India, 192
Clouston, R. S., 63
Clowes, B., 91
Cobb, Sir George, Bt., 34*n*
Cobb, John, 19–46, 59, 76, 80, 91, 98, 110, 160 : *Plates 12, 23, 27, 28, 38–44: see also* Vile
Cobb, Mary, 31
Cobb, Samuel, 157
Coke, Thomas, 44 : *see also* Leicester, Earl of
Coldbrook, Mon, 28, 46
Collection of Designs by Thomas Johnson (1758), 61, 62, 184, 185
Collins, J., 48
Cook, Robinson, 83
Cooke, Robert, 118
Coombe Abbey, Warwick, 100, 110
Copland, H., 20, 53, 55, 58, 65, 72, 94, 95
Cornelys, Teresa, 80, 109, 161

INDEX

Corsham House (now Court), Wilts, *33, 34, 59*, 60, 61, 98, 99, 110, 184 : *Plates 39, 40, 104, 105, 106, 204, 207, 216, 341*

Cottrell, Sir Charles, 118

Cour, de la, 48

Coventry, Earl of, *33*, 65, 66, 186 : *Plates 38, 55, 117, 118, 119*

Craven, William, 5th Baron, 100, 110

Creators of the Chippendale Style, The by F. Kimball and E. Donnell (1929), *55, 94, 184, 185*

Crichel, Dorset, 105, 111 : *Plate 316*

Croome Court, Worcs, *33, 37, 38*, 65, 66 : *Plates 38, 55, 117, 118, 119*

Croome Court Tapestry Room, Metropolitan Museum, New York, *65, 66*

Crunden, John, 87

Cullen, James, *33, 54, 80, 109n, 159, 160–9* : *Plates 407–19*

Cumberland, Duke of, 69

Curraghmore, Co. Waterford, *59, 61*

Curwen, Samuel, *109n*

Curzon, Sir Nathaniel (created Baron Scarsdale 1761), 69

Cuvilliés, François, 47, 69 : *Plate 127*

Damer, Hon. John, 22, 27, 33, 44

Dance, Sir Nathaniel, 31

Darly, Matthew, 52, 55, 64, 72, 75, 84, 88, 89, 91 : *Plates 132–45*

Dartmouth, Earl of, 58, 59 : *Plates 93, 94, 99*

David, L., Collection, Copenhagen, 102 : *Plate 265*

Davis, Elizabeth, *74, 79*

Deene Park, Northants, 134

Deffand, Mme. du, 41

Derby, Earl of, 155

Designs of Chinese Buildings, Furniture, by Sir William Chambers (1757), 52

Devis, Arthur, 88 : *Plate 151*

Dictionary of Artists by Samuel Redgrave (1874), 73

Dictionary of English Furniture, ed. Ralph Edwards, 62, 107, 150, 172 (also ref. to *D.E.F.* throughout)

Director, The, by Thomas Chippendale, 17, 23, 35, 40, 52, 54, 55, 59, 62, 63, 65, 66, 67, 70, 75, 77, 78, 80–105, 106, 107, 108, 110, 111, 112, 113, 114, 115, 117, 118, 119, 120, 149, 153, 155, 161, 167 : *Plates 164–205, 208–10, 219–23, 229–60, 264–8, 277–94, 307–15, 324–6, 420*

   Preface, 123–4

   Title-page, 125

Ditchley Park House, Oxon, 42, 58

Donegall, Marquess of, 69

Donnell, Edna, *55n, 70n, 94, 104, 185*

Dormer, Lieut-Gen. James, 118

Dover House, London, 134

Downes, Devon, 108

Drake, Mary, 74

Drake, William, 69, 151, 152

Dulwich College Chapel, 101

Dumfries and Morton, Earls of, *93, 111*

Dumfries House, Ayrshire, *93, 111*

Duncan, Jane, 157

Dundas, Lady Charlotte, 123

Dundas, Sir Lawrence, Bt., 36, 121, 130, 142, 144, 147, 169, 170 : *Plates 51, 393*

Dundas Suite, 18

Dunkeld House, Perthshire, 60, 155

Dupplin, Perthshire, 158

Dutton, G. M., *Plate 57*

Edgecote House, Northants, 24, 28 : *Plate 29*

Edwards, 52, 86

Edwards, Ralph, 20, 36, 101n, 106, 172, 185, 187, 190, 191, 203

Eltham Lodge, Kent, 205

Elvaston Castle, Derby, 133

Elward, Christopher, 73

English Furniture Designs of the 18th Century, 87n, 172, 183, 186, 187, 188, 189, 190

English Furniture in the Collection of Irwin Untermyer by Yvonne Hackenbroch (1958), 190, 192, 196, 200, 203

English Furniture of the 18th Century by H. Cescinsky (1916), 183

English Looking Glasses, 53

Faraquer, Captain, 57

Faringdon, Lord, 62

Farnley Hall, Yorks, 74, 155

Farrer, Richard, 83

Fawkes, Mr., of Farnley Hall, 155

Fell and Turton, 121, 143 : *Plate 386*

Fermor, Lady Louisa, 65

Ferry, Mr., 62

Fetherstonhaugh, Sir Matthew, Bt., *33, 42, 44*, 102

Fielding, Henry, 168

First Book of Ornament, 48

FitzGerald, Mrs. Derek, 123 : *Plate 109*

Fitzwilliam Museum, Cambridge, 29, 36, 176 : *Plate 32*

Fletcher, John, 73

Foley, Lord, 54, 84

Folkestone, Viscount, 22, 28, 41, 44, 133, 136, 176, 177, 210 : *Plate 30*

Fontaine, 49

Foster, W., 91

France, Edward, 147, 149

France, William, 20, 57, 148–50, 170 : *Plates 387–93*

Furniture History Society Bulletin, The, 68

Galliers-Pratt, K., 67

Garrick, David, 113

Gates, William, 135, 149

General Advertiser, 44

General Evening Post, 140

General System of Useful and Ornamental Furniture by Ince and Mayhew (1759), 63

Gentleman and Cabinet-Maker's Director, The, by Thomas Chippendale (1754), 17, 47n, 82, 90, 93 : *see also under Director*

Gentleman's Magazine, The, 44, 63, 77, 82, 89

Gentlemen's or Builder's Companion, The, by William Jones (1739), 51, 183

George III, 22, 25, 26, 99, 148, 176 : *Plate 21*

George IV, 25

Georgian Cabinet-Makers by R. Edwards and M. Jourdain, 21, 22, 27, 30, 101, 111, 134, 152, 155, 172 (also ref. to *G.C-M.* throughout)

Georgian Furniture by Ralph Edwards (1947), 199, 203

Gillow, James, 155

Gillow, Richard, 82, 154–6

Gillow, Robert, Jun., 154–6

Gillow, Robert, Sen., 57, 154, 155 : *Plate 394*

Glazier, P., 48

Goodison, Benjamin, Jun., 23, 28, 135

Goodison, Benjamin, Sen., 49, 133–5, 174 : *Plates 368–71*

Goodwood House, Sussex, 21, 173 : *Plate 7*

Gordon, John, 51, 182 : *Plates 84–87*

Gordon, William, 51, 82n, 182 : *Plates 82, 84, 85*

Gordon and Taitt, 51, 182 : *Plate 183*

Gori, Lambertus Christianus, 179

Gothic Architecture Improved by Batty Langley (1742), 87

Gower, Earl, 22

Grafton, Duke of, 69

Graham, John, 20, 31, 41

Graham and Litchfield, 41

Grendey, Giles, 135–37 : *Plates 372–7*

Grimthorpe Castle, Lincs, *Plate 182*

Guiness, Mr. Desmond, 37

Guisachan House, Inverness, 178

Hackenbroch, Miss Yvonne, 190, 192, 193, 196, 200, 203

Hackwood Park, Hants, 50, 182 : *Plates 79, 80*

Haddington, Earl of, 69

Haddock, E., 49

Hagley Hall, Worcs, 61, 87, 185 : *Plates 107, 108, 109, 110*

Haig, Thomas, 79, 109, 110, 112, 113, 114, 115, 116, 119, 120, 194

Hakerborn, J., 90

Halfpenny, William, 87, 88

Hall, Patrick, 41

Hallett, William, 19, 20, 30, 31, 41–4, 49, 76 : *Plates 67–72, 147*

Halswell Park, Somerset, 43, 61

Hambro, Olaf R., *Plate 45*

Hamilton, Duke of, 83

Hamilton, Miss Mary, 196

Hamilton, 'Single-Speech', 88, 100 : *Plate 245*

Hamilton and Balfour, 89, 90

Hamilton Palace, Lanarkshire, 58, 83 : *Plate 96*

Hampton Court Palace, 133, 134

Hanbury-Williams, Sir Charles, Bt., 28, 33, 44

Harewood, Earl of, 111 : *Plates 342, 343, 344*

Harewood House, Yorks, 18, 22n, 74, 104, 111–2, 174 : *Plates 315, 342, 343*

Harper, Samuel, 73

Harrington, Earl of, 133

Harris, Eileen, 112

Harris, Mrs., 142, 144

Harris, Mr. and Mrs. John, 121, 143n

Harrowby, Nathaniel Ryder, First Baron, 29, 119, 152

Hartwell, 151

Hayward, Mrs. Helena, 47n, 59n, 60, 62, 90, 92, 119, 184 : *Plate 103*

Hayward, John, 39, 40, 48, 181 : *Plates 65, 66*

Heal, Sir Ambrose, 29n, 35n, 41n, 44

Heathfield Park, Sussex, 185

Heckell, A., 48

Hertford, Countess of, 21

Hinton House, Somerset, 55, 56, 58 : *Plates 90, 91, 94*

Hiorn, William, 88, 189 : *Plate 151*

Hoare, Sir Richard, Bt., 136, 150

Hodson, John, 184, 213

Hogarth, 48

Hoghton, Sir Henry, 155

Holdernest, Lord, 54, 55, 81

Holkham, Norfolk, 27, 29, 42, 44, 49, 134, 137, 140, 141 : *Plates 67, 368, 369, 370, 371, 378, 379, 380, 381, 382, 383*

Holland House, Kensington, 34

Holland, Lady, 37

Holmes, John, 204

Holt Castle, Cambs, 84

Holyrood Palace, 24, 175 : *Plate 18*

Home, Ninian, 116 : *Plates 220, 276, 280, 293, 361*

Hondt, de, P. A., 91, 93

Hope, John, 161

Hopetoun House, West Lothian, 54, 160: *Plates 407, 408, 409, 410, 411, 412, 413, 414, 415, 416, 417, 418, 419*

Hopetoun, the Earl of, 54, 161, 165, 166

Hopson, Nathaniel, 75

Horlick, Sir James, 173: *Plate 8*

Houghton, Norfolk, 49

House of Lords, 192

Household Furniture for the Year 1763, 70

Household Furniture in Genteel Taste by a Society of Upholsterers (1760), 67, 69, 70, 91

Hughes, G. Bernard, 75*n*, 76

Hutchinson, T., 117

Hyde, Robert, 142

Ilchester, Earl of, 34

Ince, William, 23, 26, 59, 63, 65, 66, 67, 68, 69, 70, 71, 82, 90, 93, 135, 140, 144, 149

Ince and Mayhew, 23, 26, 60, 64–68, 70, 90, 136, 140: *Plates 115–26*

Infantado, Duke of, 136, 210

Inveraray Castle, Argyll, 209

Irwin, Arthur Ingram, 6th Viscount, 62

Irwin, 9th Viscount, 119

Iveagh Bequest, 66

Jenkins, John, 20, 31, 41

Johnson, Stewart, 92

Johnson, Thomas, 48, 58–62, 68, 70, 90, 105, 119: *Plates 99–114*

Johnson, Thomas, and English Rococo by Helena Hayward, 184, 185, 186

Joiners Company, 136, 154: *Plate 155*

Jones, Inigo, 51

Jones, William, 51: *Plate 89*

Jourdain, Margaret, 49*n*, 101*n*, 106

Joy, Edward, 79

Kedleston House, Derby, 69: *Plate 283*

Kensington Palace, 23, 26, 29, 134, 204

Kent, William, 21, 42, 48, 49–51, 173: *Plates 69, 72*

Kenwood House, Middlesex, 56, 66, 113, 187: *Plate 119*

Kew Palace, 25, 147

Kimball Fiske, 55*n*, 70*n*, 94, 104, 185

Kimbolton Castle, Hunts, 93, 113, 190

Kingston, Duke of, 48

Kinure Park, Co. Dublin, *Plate 420*

Kirkington Park, 190

Knatchbull, Sir Edward, Bt., 57, 114, 126, 127

Kroms, Mrs., 146

Ladies Amusement or Whole Art of Japanning made easy (1760), 86

Lady Lever Art Gallery, 101, 107, 113: *Plates 113, 165, 196, 197, 218, 254, 269, 281*

Laking, G. F., 204

Lambe, John, 120

Lamerie, Paul de, 48

Lane family crest, 71

Langley, Batty, 51, 52, 87: *Plate 89*

Langley, Thomas, 51, 65: *Plate 89*

Langley Park, Norfolk, 100, 114: *Plates 270, 305*

Langlois, Daniel, *Plate 50*

Langlois, Pierre E., 19, 35, 172: *Plates 49–59*

Lansdowne House (formerly Shelburne House), 65, 66, 67, 114

Lascelles, Edwin, First Lord Harewood, 111: *Plates 315, 342*

Lascelles, Henry, 74, 95

Lauch, Johann Friedrich, 52

Lauderdale, Mr., 161

Layton, E. J., 73

Lazcano Castle, Spain, 136

Lea, Sir William, 151

Leareth, John, 120

Lee Priory, Littlebourne, Kent, 88: *Plate 150*

Leeds, Duke of, 26

Leicester, Earl and Countess of, 27

Leicester Square, 43

Lesage, Augustus, 109, 161

Leven and Melville, Earl of, 22

Lewis, A. G., 23, 84, 89

Lichfield, Earl of, 69, 102

Linnell, John, 62, 68, 150–2: *Plates 127–31*

Linnell, Mary, 151

Linnell, William, 62, 68, 150–2

Linton Park, Kent, 105: *Plates 45, 325*

Lisburne, Earl of, 69

Lock, George, 54, 94

Lock, Matthias or Matthew, 20, 53, 54, 55, 56, 58, 60, 65, 68, 69, 81, 86, 90, 94, 95, 145, 164: *Plates 90–8, 113*

Loman, 56

Londinium Redivivum, 153

London Chronicle, 91

London County Council, 77

London Directories, 19, 68, 137, 140, 161

London Furniture Makers, 44

London Gazette, 109, 137

London House, Aldersgate St., 153

London Polling Lists, 145

Longford Castle, Wilts, 22, 27, 28, 29, 30, 41, 44, 101, 133, 136, 176: *Plates 26, 30, 31, 351, 376*

Longford Hall, Salop, 41

Luton Hoo, 55

Lyttleton, George, 87

McInnes, John, 160
Macquoid, Percy, 122, 172
Madeley Manor, Staffs, 196
Malton, Thomas, 83
Manchester, Duke and Duchess of, 68, 93, 190
Mansfield, Earl of, 30, 56, 71, 113, 149, 212
Mansion House, London, 24, 175 : *Plate 19*
Manwaring, Robert, 70–72, 95 : *Plates 132–45*
Marblehead family, 204
Marchmont, Third Earl of, 137
Marlborough, Sarah, Duchess of, 134
Marlborough, Duke of, 63
Marot, 92
Masters, Charles, 156
Masters, William, 156–7 : *Plates 395–402*
Mathew, Mr. and Mrs. Robert, 58
Mayhew, John, 23, 26, 59, 60, 62, 64–71, 90, 93,
    136, 138, 140, 145, 149
Mayhew, Thomas, 144
Meissonnier, J. A., 47, 48, 68
Melbourne, Lord, 79, 115
Melville, Viscount, 93, 190
Mercier, 208
Mersham-le-Hatch, Kent, 57, 110, 114, 126–8
Methuen, Lord, 98
Methuen, Paul, 33, 60, 61, 98, 110, 177, 178, 184 :
    Plates 39, 40, 106
Metropolitan Museum, New York, 22, 25, 34, 35,
    54, 58, 65, 66, 67, 70, 71, 94, 136, 175, 178,
    184, 188, 212 : *Plates 10, 11, 43, 48, 55, 96,
    117, 118, 122, 132, 175, 192, 205, 298, 372*
Middlesex, Lord, 48
Middlesex Register, 75
Miller, Sanderson, 87, 88, 100, 190, 198
Molesworth, Delves, 25
Mona, Castle, Isle of Man, 57, 155
Mondon, Jean, 47
Montagu, Duke of, 36, 140
Montagu, Mrs., 69, 151
Montford, Lord, 84
Moor Park, Middlesex, 121, 143, 147, 169, 171 :
    Plate 386
Morris, Hemerick, 91
Morris, J. H., 87
Mortimer, Thomas, 29, 35, 140, 151, 165
Morval, Cornwall, 108
Müller, T. and J. S., 86, 91
Murray family, 159
Murray, Hon. John, 159, 214
Murray, James, Lord, 159
Museum of Decorative Arts, Copenhagen, 67,
    187 : *Plate 120*
Museum of Fine Arts, Boston, Mass., 136 : *Plates
    180, 311*
Musgrave, Clifford, 17, 18, 55, 112, 133, 152

Napier, Sir William, 105, 111
Neilson, Jacques, 65, 143, 186 : *Plate 386*
New Book of Chinese Designs by Matthew Darly and
    Edwards (1754), 52, 86
New Book of Chinese, Gothic and Modern Chairs by
    Matthew Darly (1751), 52, 88, 188
*New Book of Foliage for Instruction of Young
    Artists* by M. Lock (1769), 53, 55
New Book of Ornaments by Thomas Johnson
    (1760), 59, 61
New Book of Ornaments for Looking-Glass Frames
    by M. Lock, 53
*New Book of Ornaments . . . of Chimneys, sconces,
    tables . . .* by M. Lock and H. Copland (1752),
    53, 55, 95
*New Book of Ornaments consisting of Tables,
    Chimnies, sconces, spandles, clock cases . . .* by
    M. Lock and H. Copland (1769), 53
New Book of Pier Frames, Ovals, Gerandoles by
    M. Lock (1769), 53, 55
New Designs for Chinese Temples by William
    Halfpenny (1750), 87
New Drawing Book . . . printed for Robert Sayer
    by M. Lock, 53
New Drawing Book of Ornaments, Shields . . . by
    M. Lock (1740), 53
Newburgh Priory, Yorks, 62
Newcastle, Duke of, 135
Newdigate, Lady, 190 : *Plate 154*
Newdigate, Sir Roger, 88, 190 : *Plate 151*
Newman, Edward, 155
Nollekens and his Times by J. T. Smith, 31
Norfolk, Duke of, 83, 96, 106, 197 : *Plates 167, 234*
Norfolk House, London, 107, 197 : *Plate 234*
Norman, Samuel, 57, 63, 121, 140, 162, 165, 169 :
    Plates 381–5
Norman, William, 57
Northumberland, Earl of, 54, 55, 75, 81, 83, 91,
    106
Northumberland House, 75, 81
Norton, Eardley, 146
Nostell Priory, Yorks, 18, 55, 74, 92, 93, 94, 96,
    101, 102, 112, 115, 116, 117, 129 : *Plates
    146, 176, 177, 235, 249, 253, 261, 262, 275,
    279, 345, 346, 349, 350, 351, 352, 353, 354,
    355, 356, 357, 358, 359, 360*
Notes and Queries, 73
Nouveaux Desseins de Pieds de Table by Nicolas
    Pineau, 183

Oeben, Jean-François, 38
Okeover Hall, Staffs, 42
Okeover, Leak, 42
Old English and French Ornaments (1835–1858),
    60

One Hundred and Fifty New Designs by Thomas Johnson (1761), 58, 59*n*, 61, 90, 185
Original Designs by M. Lock (1740–1765), 54
Original Designs for Furniture by Ince and Mayhew (1760), 64
Ornamental Architecture by Charles Over (1768), 72
Ornamental Architecture or Young Artists Instructor by M. Darly (1770), 55
Osborne, T., Bookseller, 89
Osterley Park, Middlesex, 69, 142, 187 : *Plate 128*
Oswald, Arthur, 42*n*
Otley, Yorks, 73
Over, Charles, 72, 88

Parke-Bernet Galleries, New York, 34 : *Plates 4, 44, 88, 125, 186*
Parker (Stalker and Parker), 86
Parran, Benjamin, 82, 135
Patshall House, Staffs, 59, 61, 184
Paxton House, Berwickshire, 99, 103, 116 : *Plates 220, 221, 276, 280, 293, 361, 362, 363*
Pembroke, Earl and Countess of, 26, 42, 69, 77, 93, 96, 97, 98, 103, 120, 175 : *Plate 23*
Penny's Traditions of Perth, 158
Percier, 49
Pervil, 78
Philadelphia Museum of Art, 61, 62, 69*n* : *Plates 107, 108, 131, 236, 295, 307, 386*
Piers, H., Bookseller, 89
Piffetti, Pietro, *36n*
Pignatelli, Count, 32, 160
Pillement, Jean, 86
Pineau, Nicolas 47, 51 : *Plate 89*
Pinto, E. H., 22*n*, 33
Piozzi, Mrs., 155
Pococke, Dr., 83, 98, 107
Poke, Frederick, 103
Polebarn House, Wilts, 199
Pomfret, Earl of, 88, 100 : *Plate 159*
Portland, Duke of, 77, 83, 117
Poulett, Earl, 56, 69 : *Plates 90, 93, 94*
Powderham Court, Exeter, 40 : *Plate 65*
Powerscourt House, Wexford, 59
Pranker, Robert, 70
Prince of Wales, Frederick, 30; George, 22, 26, 28, 30, 34
Princess of Wales, 29
Princess Royal, 146 : *Plate 387*
Principles of Ornament by M. Lock, 54
'Pugh', 141
Public Advertiser, 62, 78, 140, 151
Public Ledger, The (1760), 90
Pwllywrack, Glamorgan, 68
Pyne, W. H., *The History of Royal Residences*, 23, 26

Queen's House : *see under* Buckingham Palace
Queensberry, Duke of, 69

Rackstrow, Benjamin, 57
Radnor, Earl of, 101
Rannie, James, 76, 77, 78, 82, 90, 91, 108, 111, 121
Raynham Hall, Norfolk, 99, 118, 194 : *Plates 203, 236*
Redgrave, Samuel, 73
Redshaw, Catherine, 74
Reynolds, Sir Joshua, 107
Riley and Walls, 32
Robinson, Sir Thomas, 21, 77, 173
Roche, Sophie von la, 153
Rockley, Lord, 30 : *Plate 34*
Rococo defined, 17
Rokeby Hall, Yorks, 21, 173 : *Plate 2*
Rotch, Claude, 30
Rousham, Oxon, 118
Royal Collection, 22, 30, 38, 105, 173, 174, 175 : *Plates 12, 13, 14, 15, 16, 17, 56, 57, 58, 318, 324, 387, 388*
Royal Institute of British Architects, 50, 182 : *Plates 77, 78*
Royal Residences by W. H. Pyne, 23, 26
Russell, John, 135

St. Andre, Mrs., 29
St. Dunstan's House, Regents Park, 202
St. Giles' House, Dorset, 21, 29, 30, 35, 84, 98, 104, 105, 107, 119, 174, 198 : *Plates 9, 32, 48, 299, 301, 314, 336, 365, 366*
St. James's Palace, 23, 24, 26, 29, 134
St. Martin's Lane, 19, 20, 49, 74
St. Peter's Church, Winchcombe, Glos, 101
Salisbury, James, Earl of, 76
Saltram House, Devon, 118 : *Plate 275*
Salverte, Comte de, 25
Sandeman, David George, 158
Sandeman, George, 157–60 : *Plates 403–6*
Sandeman, Katherine, 158
Sandon Hall, Stafford, 119
Saunders, Paul, 137–40 : *Plates 378, 379*
Sayer, Anthony, 120
Sayer, Robert, Bookseller, 54, 64*n*, 70, 71, 90, 91
Scarsdale, Lord (formerly Sir N. Curzon), 69
Schübler, Johann Jakob, 52
Scone Palace, Perthshire, 30, 71 : *Plates 36, 137, 211, 246*
Seddon, George, 74, 82, 152–4
Seddon, John, 152
Seddon, Miss, 153
Seddon, Thomas, 153, 154
Shackleton, 154

Shaftesbury, Earl and Countess of, 22, 35, 84, 98, 104, 119, 174

Shardeloes, Bucks, 69, 151

Shelburne, Earl and Countess of, 65, 67, 114, 123

Shelburne (now Lansdowne) House, 65 : *see also* Lansdowne House

Sheraton, Thomas, 68, 84, 149, 196

Shrub, Derek, 25

Shugborough Hall, Staffs, 102 : *Plate 266*

Singleton, Henry, 27, 176

Sion House, Isleworth, 81 : *see also* Syon House

Six Sconces by M. Lock (1744), 53, 183 : *Plate 92*

Six Tables by M. Lock (1746), 53, 55

Sixty Different Sorts of Ornaments by G. Brunetti (1736), 48, 181

Smith, Charles, 30, 62, 142n

Smith, John, Bookseller, 89

Smith, J. T., 31

Smithson, Lady Elizabeth (later Duchess of Northumberland), 21

Soane Museum, 68

Society of Upholsterers, 69, 91

Some Designs of Mr. Inigo Jones and Mr. William Kent by John Vardy (1744), 49

Spencer House, 49, 50, 51 : *Plates 74, 76, 81, 82, 83, 84, 85*

Spencer, Samuel, 109, 161

Stalker (Stalker and Parker), 86

Stanhope, Earl, 137

Stanstead (House), 81

Stanwick House, 21

Stedcombe House, Devon, 58

Stephanoff, 23

Stone Easton, Somerset, 105 : *Plate 323*

Stonor Park, Oxon, *Plate 153*

Stourhead House, Wilts, 140

Stowe House, Bucks, 188 : *Plate 71*

Strafford, Cora, Countess of, 203

Strafford, Earl of, 155

Stratfield Saye House, Hants, 25, 175

Strawberry Hill, Twickenham, 29, 37, 44, 87, 189

Streatham Park, 155

Strickland, 20, 41

Stroud, Miss D., 36

Strype, 75

Stuart, James (Athenian), 50, 78

Sun Insurance Company, 77

Swan, Abraham, 52

Swan, J., Bookseller, 89

Symonds, R. W., 39, 95n, 136, 180

Syon House, Isleworth, 38, 81

Taitt (Gordon and Taitt), 51

Tatham, C. H., 68

Taylor, I., 91

Temple Newsam House, Leeds, 41, 56, 58, 61, 62, 99, 102, 119 : *Plates 98, 111, 114, 134, 230, 245, 263, 274*

Thornton, Mr. Peter, 38, 92, 93, 118

Thorpe Underwood Hall, Yorks, 183

Thrale, Mrs., 34

Toro, Bernard, 47, 92

Tottenham Court Road, 35

Townshend, Capt., M. P., 118, 194, 197, 209

Townshend, the Marquis of, 99

Treasury of Designs by Langley, 65

Treatise of Japanning by Stalker and Parker (1688), 86

Trotter, John, 82

Tweedmouth, Lord, 34, 177 : *Plate 41*

Twelve Gerondoles by Thomas Johnson (1755), 58, 62, 184, 186

Tyrone House, Dublin, 59

Ugbrooke Park, Devon, 155 : *Plate 394*

Underwood, Hugh, 83

Universal Director by Mortimer (1763), 29, 140, 151

Universal System of Household Furniture by Ince and Mayhew (1762), 63–70, 90, 149, 172, 186, 187

Untermyer, Judge Irwin, 25, 104n : *Plates 22, 163, 182, 183, 232, 272, 295*

Upholsterers and Cabinet-Makers, 19

Upholsterers, Society of, 69, 70, 90

Uppark, Sussex, 33, 42, 44, 102, 107, 172 : *Plates 68, 273, 337*

Vardy, John, 49–51 : *Plates 74–83*

Vardy, Thomas, 50, 76

Verulam, Earl of, 150

Victoria and Albert Museum, 25, 30, 34, 39, 51, 54, 55, 56, 61, 62, 68, 69, 70, 71, 83n, 94, 98, 99, 101, 107, 113, 117, 123, 136, 142, 173, 175 : *Plates 9, 20, 21, 33, 35, 60, 61, 89, 90, 91, 92, 93, 95, 127, 128, 129, 130, 142, 144, 150, 155, 157, 162, 179, 181, 194, 197, 198, 206, 217, 222, 223, 260, 303, 304, 305, 332, 348, 367, 373, 375, 385, 392*

Vile, Sarah, 30

Vile, William, 17, 19–31, 33, 35, 44, 45, 46, 60, 76, 92, 110, 134, 145, 155 : *Plates 1–37, 147*

Vyne, The, Hants, 19, 27, 29, 39, 44, 88, 148, 176 : *Plates 25, 27, 28, 54, 148, 149, 390, 391*

Walcot House, 192

Waldegrave, the Earl of, 161, 178

Walpole, Horace, 29, 37, 43, 44, 81, 87, 88, 148, 189

Wanstead House, Essex, 43

Ward-Jackson, Peter, 48, 65, 68, 69, 71, 87, 88, 92, 149n
Warkworth Castle, 81
Watson, Francis, 23
Weale, John, 60
Webley, H., 70
Welbeck Abbey, Notts, 117
Wellington, Duke of, 25, 175
Wentworth Castle, 155
West, Cabinet-Maker, 62n, 140
West, Gilbert, 151
West Wycombe Park, Bucks, 35, 46
Westminster Fire Office, 67
Wharton, Lord, 43
Whitehurst, John, F.R.S., 207
Whitmarsh Collection, 34
Whittle, James, 63, 140, 141, 142 : *Plates 381–5*
Whittle, Thomas, 82
Wicksted, 152
Wildsmith, John, 66 : *Plate 118*
Wills, Geoffrey, 32n, 33, 53, 161
William Henry, Prince, 91, 92
Williams, Iolo, 181

Wilton House, Wilts, 42, 49, 96, 97, 99, 100, 101, 103, 104, 105, 120 : *Plates 187, 188, 190, 199, 200, 201, 212, 215, 256, 258, 294, 322*
Winchcombe, St. Peter's Church, 101
Windsor Castle, 24, 38, 204
Winn, Sir Rowland, 92, 94, 95, 100, 102, 116, 131, 198 : *Plates 235, 249, 261, 262, 345, 349, 352, 354, 357, 358, 360*
Woburn Abbey, Beds, 36, 37, 56, 140 : *Plates 50, 52, 384*
Wood, Richard, 56, 83
Woodcote Park, Surrey, *Plate 311*
Woodin, Thomas, 141
Workington Hall, Cumberland, 155
World, The, 88
Wright, David, 24 : *Plate 20*
Wright, Thomas, Watchmaker, 32
Wrights Incorporation of Perth, 157
Wyatt, James, 88, 189

York, Duke and Duchess of, 27

Zetland, Marquess of, 36, 121, 143, 169
Zuccarelli, 65
Zucchi, 65

1. Library writing-table possibly designed by William Kent for Chiswick House, about 1730, and perhaps one of William Vile's earliest creations.
Trustees of the Chatsworth Settlement.

2. Library writing-table in the style of Vile from Rokeby Hall. *Reproduced by gracious permission of Her Majesty the Queen.*

3. Library writing-table in the style of Vile from Ashburnham Place.
Victoria and Albert Museum.

4. Writing-table with folding top.
Photograph Parke-Bernet Galleries Inc.

5. A commode of similar design to that shown in 4. *John Hayward Esq.*
Photograph J. A. Lewis and Son.

6. A metal and gilt escutcheon from the commode shown in 5.
Photograph J. A. Lewis and Son.

7. Commode in the style of Vile, at Goodwood House, Sussex.
His Grace the Duke of Richmond and Gordon.

8. Kneehole writing-table.
Photograph Parke-Bernet Galleries Inc.

9. Commode in the style of Vile from St. Giles's House. *The Claude Rotch Bequest, Victoria and Albert Museum. Photograph Frank Partridge Ltd.*

10. Commode in the manner of Vile. *The Metropolitan Museum of Art. Gift of Irwin Untermyer, 1955.*

11. Mahogany cabinet in the style of Vile. *The Metropolitan Museum of Art. Morris Loeb Gift, 1956.*

12. Queen Charlotte's jewel-cabinet by Vile and Cobb, 1761. *Reproduced by gracious permission of Her Majesty the Queen.*

13. Mahogany bureau-cabinet made by William Vile for
Queen Charlotte in 1761. *Reproduced by gracious permission
of Her Majesty the Queen.*

17. Worktable made by Vile for Queen Charlotte in 1763.
Reproduced by gracious permission of Her Majesty the Queen.

18. Kneehole writing-table in the style of Vile.
Reproduced by gracious permission of Her Majesty the Queen.

19. Kneehole writing-table in the style of Vile.
The Mansion House, The Corporation of London.

20. Kneehole writing-table inscribed *David Wright Lancaster 1751*, and made in a style derived from that of Vile. *Victoria and Albert Museum.*

21. One of a pair of medal-cabinets adapted, from a large cabinet, by William Vile for George III in 1761. *Victoria and Albert Museum. Photograph Phillips of Hitchin Ltd.*

22. Medal-cabinet in three sections. *Collection of Irwin Untermyer.*

23. *Bonheur-du-jour* in the French taste.
Photograph Leonard Knight Ltd.

24. Engraving of the marriage of the Duke and Duchess of York in
the Saloon at Buckingham House, showing the chandeliers which
were probably supplied by Vile in 1764.
Photograph courtesy of Country Life.

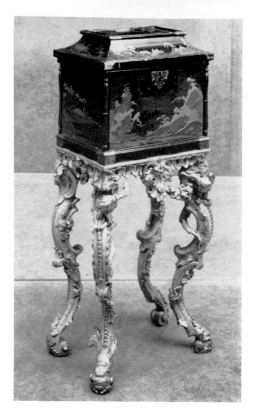

25. A giltwood cabinet-stand attributed to Vile and Cobb. *The National Trust, The Vyne, Hampshire.*

26. Oriental lacquer casket on carved giltwood stand. *Longford Castle, Wiltshire. The Earl of Radnor.*

27. Chair made by Vile and Cobb for the Vyne in 1753. *The National Trust, The Vyne, Hampshire. Photograph courtesy of* Country Life.

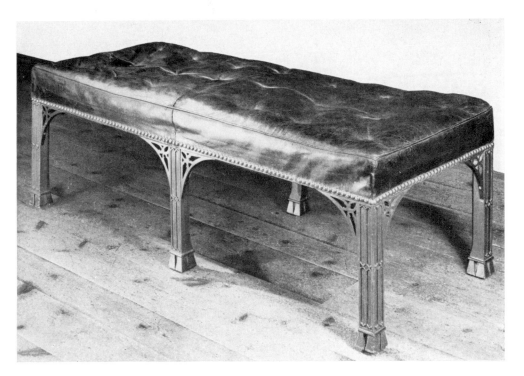

28. Stool made by Vile and Cobb for the Vyne in 1753.
The National Trust, The Vyne, Hampshire.

29. Chair-back settee thought to have been made by Vile for Edgecote.
Photograph Leonard Knight Ltd.

30. Carved and gilt chest probably made by Vile for the 1st Lord Folkestone. *Longford Castle, Wiltshire. The Earl of Radnor.*

31. Carved mahogany stand attributed to Vile. *Longford Castle, Wiltshire. The Earl of Radnor.*

32. Rosewood commode with carved and gilt enrichments from St. Giles's House, Dorset, possibly supplied by Vile. *The Fitzwilliam Museum, Cambridge.*

33. Bookcase in the style of Vile.
*Mrs. H. Scudamore. On loan to the
Victoria and Albert Museum.*

34. Bookcase in the style of Vile.
The Lord Rockley.

35. Bookcase in the style of
Vile. *Victoria and Albert Museum.
The Claude Rotch Bequest.*

36. Bureau-bookcase in the
manner of Vile. *Scone Palace,
Perthshire. The Earl of
Mansfield.
Photograph courtesy of* The
Connoisseur.

37. Goldfish-bowl on mahogany stand attributed to Vile. *Private collector. Photograph Phillips of Hitchin Ltd.*

38. Mahogany armchair made by Cobb for Croome Court in 1764, the splat carved by Sefferin Alken. *The Earl of Coventry, at Cannon Hall, Barnsley, Yorkshire.*

47. Commode with inlaid marble top.
Photograph Frank Partridge Ltd.

48. Inlaid commode from St. Giles's House, Dorset.
The Metropolitan Museum of Art, Morris Loeb Gift, 1955.

49. Inlaid *bureau-de-dame* bearing the arms of Walpole impaling Waldegrave.
The Earl Waldegrave.
Photograph Christie, Manson and Woods Ltd.

50. Inlaid commode made by Langlois for the Duke of Bedford in 1760.
Woburn Abbey, Bedfordshire. His Grace The Duke of Bedford and the Trustees.

51. One of a pair of similar commodes almost certainly made by Langlois for Sir
Lawrence Dundas. *The Marquess of Zetland. Aske, Yorkshire.*
Photograph courtesy of Apollo.

52. An inlaid commode with ormolu mounts, signed 'Daniel Langlois'.
The Fitzwilliam Museum, Cambridge.

53. The signature on the carcase of the top drawer of the
above. *The Fitzwilliam Museum, Cambridge.*

54. Inlaid commode attributed to Langlois which was made for John Chute.
The National Trust, The Vyne, Hampshire.

55. Inlaid commode made by Langlois in 1764 for the Earl of Coventry
for Croome Court. *The Metropolitan Museum of Art, Fletcher Fund, 1959.*

56. Inlaid commode in the style of Langlois.
Reproduced by gracious permission of Her Majesty the Queen.

57. Kingwood commode in the French taste.
Reproduced by gracious permission of Her Majesty the Queen.

58. Mahogany commode in the French taste.
Reproduced by gracious permission of Her Majesty the Queen.

59. Inlaid and giltwood table made by Gordon and Taitt in 1771.
The Hon. R. H. C. Neville, on loan to The Ministry of Works, Audley End, Essex.

60. An inlaid and mounted cabinet-on-stand, probably made in the workshop of John Channon. *The Victoria and Albert Museum. Photograph courtesy of J. A. Lewis and Son.*

61. A mahogany library-desk with fine gilt brass mounts, probably made in the workshop of John Channon. *The Victoria and Albert Museum.*

62. A detail of 61. *The Victoria and Albert Museum.*

63. A mahogany commode with cast, chased and gilt mounts, probably made in the workshops of John Channon. *The Fitzwilliam Museum. L. C. G. Clarke Bequest.*

64. An inlaid mahogany writing-cabinet with gilded brass mounts, probably made by John Channon of St. Martin's Lane.
Arthur Bull, Esq.

65. One of a pair of rosewood bookcases with gilded wood mounts and feet, made by John Channon in 1740 for Powderham Castle, Devon. *The Earl of Devon. Photograph courtesy of the Victoria and Albert Museum.*

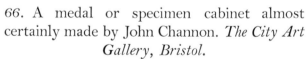

66. A medal or specimen cabinet almost certainly made by John Channon. *The City Art Gallery, Bristol.*

67. A mahogany open-armchair per-
haps provided by William Hallett, in
1737, for Holkham House, Norfolk.
The Earl of Leicester.
Photograph courtesy of Apollo, *and*
The National Buildings Record.

68. A mahogany cabinet perhaps provided
by Hallett, in 1754, for Uppark, Sussex.
Mrs. R. Meade-Fetherstonhaugh.
Photograph courtesy of The Connoisseur.

69. A mahogany cabinet in the Kentian tradition, signed by Hallett and
dated 1763. *Colonel Norman Colville.*
Photograph J. A. Lewis and Son.

70. Detail of 69 above.

71. The inscription in pencil on the carcase of the base of 69 above — 'William Hallett 1763 Long Acre'.

72. A mahogany bookcase of Kentian tradition and in the manner associated with Hallett's work. *Photograph Christie, Manson and Woods Ltd.*

73. A mahogany chair inspired by a design by Gaetano Brunetti. *John Hayward Esq.*

74. A drawing by John Vardy
for Spencer House, Green Park.
British Museum.

75. A similar drawing, signed by
John Vardy 1758.
British Museum.

76. A giltwood framed pier-glass probably designed for Spencer House by John Vardy, about 1758. *The Earl Spencer, Althorp, Northamptonshire.*

77. A design drawn by John Vardy in 1761 for the Duke of Bolton. *Royal Institute of British Architects' Library.*
Photograph by courtesy of The Connoisseur.

78. A design for a pier-glass and table drawn by John Vardy and made for the 3rd or 4th Duke of Bolton, cf. 79 and 80 below. *Royal Institute of British Architects' Library.*

79. One of a pair of giltwood pier-glasses and tables made for the 3rd or 4th Duke of Bolton at Hackwood Park, Basingstoke, after John Vardy's design (cf. 78). *Viscount Camrose, Hackwood Park, Hampshire.*

80. One of a pair of giltwood pier-glasses and tables made for the 3rd or 4th Duke of Bolton at Hackwood Park, Basingstoke, after John Vardy's design (cf. 78 above). *Viscount Camrose, Hackwood Park, Hampshire. Photographs for 78, 79 and 80 by courtesy of* The Connoisseur.

81. An hexagonal hall-lantern probably designed by John
Vardy for the hall of Spencer House.
The Earl Spencer, Althorp, Northamptonshire.

82. One of a set of mahogany single chairs — made for Spencer House, probably after designs by Vardy, and perhaps by William and John Gordon. *The Earl Spencer, Althorp, Northamptonshire.*

83. One of a set of twelve hall-chairs, the seatrails carved with bucrania, probably designed by Vardy in 1758. *The Earl Spencer, Althorp, Northamptonshire.*

84. A chair from a suite made for Spencer House, perhaps by William and John Gordon. *The Earl Spencer, Althorp, Northamptonshire.*

85. A chair from Spencer House attributed to William and John Gordon. *The Earl Spencer, Althorp, Northamptonshire.*

86. One of a set of six chairs and two settees which John Gordon made for The 2nd Duke of Atholl in 1753. *The Duke of Atholl, Blair Castle, Perthshire.*
Photograph courtesy of The Connoisseur.

87. One of a set of eight chairs which John Gordon made for the 2nd Duke of Atholl in 1756. *The Duke of Atholl, Blair Castle, Perthshire.*
Photograph courtesy of The Connoisseur.

88. Two mahogany chairs similar to those shown above.
Photograph courtesy of Parke-Bernet Galleries Inc.

89. A mahogany side-table after designs published by William Jones, and by Thomas and Batty Langley, plagiarised from Nicolas Pineau.
The Victoria and Albert Museum.

90. A sketch by Matthias Lock for a console-table bought by Earl Poulett for Hinton House, Somerset, in about 1745.
The Print Room, The Victoria and Albert Museum.

91. A pier-glass after a design by Matthias Lock, originally bought by Earl Poulett for Hinton House. *Victoria and Albert Museum.*

92. A design from Matthias Lock's *Six Sconces*, 1744. *The Print Room, The Victoria and Albert Museum.*

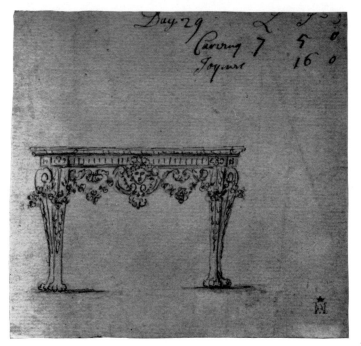

93. A sketch by Matthias Lock for a side-table — one example was bought by Earl Poulett, another is in the Earl of Dartmouth's collection. *The Print Room, The Victoria and Albert Museum.*

94. A carved giltwood side-table attributed to Matthias Lock after the design shown in 93. The mirror is earlier. *The Earl of Dartmouth. Photograph courtesy of* The Connoisseur.

95. A design for a side-table by Matthias Lock.
The Print Room, The Victoria and Albert Museum.

96. A painted and giltwood side-table, after the design 95
above, from Hamilton Palace, Lanarkshire.
The Metropolitan Museum of Art, Rogers Fund, 1926.

97. A painted side-table of similar design.
The Duke of Atholl, Blair Castle, Perthshire.
Photograph courtesy of The Connoisseur.

98. A giltwood pier-glass in the tradition of Matthias Lock. *In the collection of the City Art Gallery and Temple Newsam House, Leeds, Yorkshire.*

99. A giltwood console-table attributed to Thomas Johnson inspired by a design, in his *Twelve Gerondoles*, 1755.
Ex *the collection of the Earl of Dartmouth.*
Photograph courtesy of Sotheby and Co.

100. A pier-glass made for the Duke of Atholl in 1763. Provided by George Cole but probably designed and carved by Thomas Johnson. *The Duke of Atholl, Blair Castle, Perthshire. Photograph courtesy of* The Connoisseur.

101. Carved detail of the pier-glass, shown in 100. *The Duke of Atholl, Blair Castle, Perthshire. Photograph courtesy of* The Connoisseur.

102. Carved detail on the supports of one of three console-tables made by Cole *en suite* with the Blair Castle pier-glasses. *The Duke of Atholl, Blair Castle, Perthshire. Photograph courtesy of* The Connoisseur.

103. An overmantle-glass after a design by Thomas Johnson, 1758. *The Assembly Rooms, York. Photograph courtesy of Mrs. John Hayward.*

104. One of a pair of giltwood pier-glasses, sold to Paul Methuen for Corsham House. *Lord Methuen, Corsham Court, Wiltshire.*

105. A design by Thomas Johnson, 1761, from which the Corsham pier-glasses (104), were copied.

106. One of a pair of giltwood pier-glasses, also at Corsham Court, (cf. 104),
and also inspired by the design illustrated in 105.
Lord Methuen, Corsham Court, Wiltshire.

107. A pair of candlestands, and a pair of girandoles made for Hagley Hall, Worcestershire, after designs by Thomas Johnson (cf. 108 and 110 below).
Philadelphia Museum of Art.

108. A design by Thomas Johnson, 1761, from which the Hagley Hall girandoles (107), were copied.

109. One of a pair of gilt-wood girandoles in Thomas Johnson's tradition — perhaps from Hagley Hall. *Private Collection.*
Photograph courtesy of Sotheby and Co.

125. A mahogany hall-seat, about 1760. Cf. the unusual design of the back with the tracery of the cupboards shown in 116.
Photograph courtesy of Parke-Bernet Galleries Inc.

126. A mahogany open armchair, stamped I.M; — the splat similar to one in an Ince and Mayhew design for four 'Parlour Chairs'.
Photograph courtesy of Messrs. Hotspur Ltd.

127. A design by John Linnell for a side-table: apparently derived from a composition for a table with dragons by François Cuvilliés.
The Print Room, The Victoria and Albert Museum.

128. A chimney-glass at Osterley Park, Middlesex, designed and carved in John Linnell's workshops for Mr. Child (cf. 129). *The Victoria and Albert Museum.*

129. The design by John Linnell for the chimney-glass shown in 128. *The Print Room, The Victoria and Albert Museum.*

130. A design by John Linnell for a console-table and pier-glass,
about 1760.
The Print Room, The Victoria and Albert Museum.

131. A giltwood framed sofa after designs by John Linnell and Robert Adam.
Philadelphia Museum of Art.

132. A carved mahogany armchair, the back similar to
a design of Robert Manwaring's (cf. 133). *The
Metropolitan Museum of Art, Gift of Marion E. Cohn,
1950.*

156. An unusual armchair of Gothic design.
Photograph Frank Partridge Ltd.

157. A 'Windsor-chair' of Gothic design.
The Victoria and Albert Museum.

158. A settee of Gothic design in oak from Kirtlington Park.
Courtesy of Museum of Fine Arts, Boston.

159. The Earl and Countess of Pomfret by Thomas Bardwell, in a frame of Gothic design.
The Ashmolean Museum, Oxford.

160. A giltwood and ebonised wall-glass in the Gothic and Chinese taste, with rococo details.
Photograph Mallett & Sons Ltd.

161. A mahogany aviary carved with Gothic motives. *Photograph courtesy of Parke-Bernet Galleries Inc.*

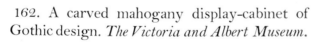

162. A carved mahogany display-cabinet of Gothic design. *The Victoria and Albert Museum.*

163. A mahogany clothes-press of Gothic design. *Collection of Irwin Untermyer.*

164. A dressing-table, probably by Thomas Chippendale, from Kimbolton Castle, Huntingdonshire. *Photograph courtesy of Leonard Knight Ltd.*

165. A rosewood dressing-table, probably also by Chippendale. *Lady Lever Art Gallery.*

166. 'A design for a dressing-table for a lady' from the 3rd edition of *The Director*.

167. A mahogany dining-chair
of *Director* design. *The Duke of
Norfolk, Arundel Castle, Sussex.*

168. A mahogany dining-chair of *Director*
design. *Mrs. C. A. Joll.*

169. A mahogany dining-chair, probably by Chippendale. *Lord St. Oswald, Nostell Priory, Yorkshire.*

170. A mahogany open-armchair of *Director* design. *Photograph courtesy of W. Waddingham, Esq.*

171. A mahogany single-chair of pre-*Director*
design, about 1745.
Photograph courtesy of W. Waddingham, Esq.

172. *The Director*, 1st Edit. pl. 16, cf. 173–177.

173. A mahogany 'ribband back chair'.
The Victoria and Albert Museum.

174. A mahogany 'ribband chair-back' settee.
The Victoria and Albert Museum.

175. A mahogany 'ribband back chair'. *The Metropolitan Museum of Art. Gift of Edwin C. Vogel, 1957.*

176. A mahogany 'ribband chair-back' settee, which can be converted into a day-bed (see 177). *Lord St. Oswald, Nostell Priory, Yorkshire.*

177. The settee shown in 176 converted to form a day-bed.

178. A plate showing 'French Chairs' in the third edition of *The Director*.

179. A mahogany 'French chair'. *The Victorian and Albert Museum.*

180. A mahogany 'French chair' covered in tapestry. *Courtesy, Museum of Fine Arts, Boston.*

181. A mahogany open-armchair of *Director* design, in the French taste. *The Victoria and Albert Museum.*
Photograph courtesy of Hotspur Ltd.

182. A mahogany chair in the French taste covered with Beauvais tapestry, made for Grimthorpe Castle, Lincolnshire about 1760.
Collection of Irwin Untermyer.

183. A mahogany 'French chair' covered with needlework.
Collection of Irwin Untermyer.

184. An open-armchair like that shown in
181 but of simpler form.
Photograph courtesy of W. Waddingham, Esq.

185. A pair of chairs in the French taste covered in tapestry.
Photograph courtesy of Parke-Bernet Galleries Inc.

186. A 'French chair' in Fulham tapestry:
originally in the House of Lords.
*Photograph courtesy of
Parke-Bernet Galleries Inc.*

187. A giltwood-framed 'French chair' at
Wilton House, probably supplied by
Chippendale. *The Earl of Pembroke, Wilton
House, Wiltshire.*
Photograph courtesy of Apollo.

188. A mahogany-framed chair at Wilton,
probably supplied by Chippendale. *The Earl
of Pembroke, Wilton House, Wiltshire.*
Photograph courtesy of Apollo.

189. A mahogany open-armchair of *Director*
design.
Photograph courtesy of W. Waddingham, Esq.

190. A mahogany hall-chair at Wilton House, having devices of the Pembroke family, probably supplied by Chippendale.
The Earl of Pembroke, Wilton House, Wiltshire.
Photograph courtesy of Apollo.

191. A pair of hall-chairs of unusual form, related to a design in *The Director*.
Photograph courtesy of W. Waddingham, Esq.

192. A mahogany armchair in the Chinese taste, based on a design in *The Director*. *The Metropolitan Museum of Art, Kennedy Fund, 1918.*

193. A mahogany chair-back settee in the Chinese-Gothic tradition. *Photograph courtesy of W. Waddingham, Esq.*

194. A mahogany single chair of *Director* design. *The Victoria and Albert Museum.*

195. A mahogany settee in the Chinese taste. *Mrs. David Gubbay.*

196. A mahogany single chair based on a *Director* design. *The Lady Lever Art Gallery, Cheshire.*

197. A mahogany chair carved with grotesque *chinoiserie* motives. *The Lady Lever Art Gallery.*

198. A mahogany stool based on a *Director* chair design.
The Victoria and Albert Museum.

199. A giltwood stool probably supplied by Chippendale for Wilton.
The Earl of Pembroke, Wilton House, Wiltshire.
Photograph courtesy of Apollo.

200. A giltwood settee in the Double Cube Room at Wilton, probably made by Chippendale. *The Earl of Pembroke, Wilton House, Wiltshire.*
Photograph courtesy of Apollo.

201. A giltwood settee at Wilton House showing signs of Neoclassicism, probably made by Chippendale. *The Earl of Pembroke, Wilton House, Wiltshire.*
Photograph courtesy of Apollo.

202. A mahogany settee of *Director* design from a large suite of seat furniture, most of which is still at St. Giles's House, Dorset.
Photograph courtesy of Leonard Knight, Ltd.

203. A mahogany chair similar to the settee in 202: from Raynham Hall, Norfolk.
Robert Cooke Esq., Athelhampton, Dorset.

204. A mahogany settee from a large suite of seat furniture at Corsham.
Lord Methuen, Corsham Court, Wiltshire.

205. A mahogany settee of *Director* design.
The Metropolitan Museum of Art, Dick Fund, 1957.

206. A mahogany bedstead with anthemion acroters, about 1765.
The Marquess of Zetland, Aske Hall, Richmond, Yorkshire.
Photograph courtesy of Apollo.

207. A mahogany bedstead with cluster
pillars of *Director* design. *Lord Methuen,
Corsham Court, Wiltshire.*

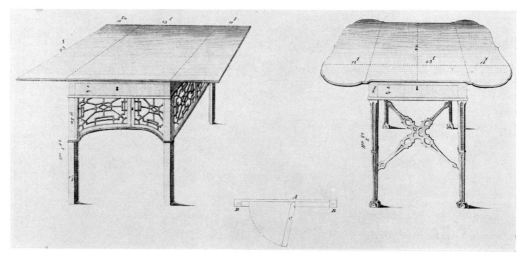

208. Plate 53, the third edition of *The Director*, (cf. 209–211).

209. A mahogany 'Breakfast Table' of *Director* design. *The Duke of Argyll, Inveraray Castle, Argyll.* *Photograph courtesy of* The Connoisseur.

210. A mahogany 'Breakfast Table' of *Director* design. *Photograph courtesy of Messrs. Ayer of Bath.*

211. A mahogany 'Breakfast Table' of *Director* design. *The Earl of Mansfield, Scone Palace, Perthshire.* *Photograph courtesy of* The Connoisseur.

212. A mahogany 'China Table' of *Director* design at Wilton, probably supplied by Chippendale. *The Earl of Pembroke, Wilton House, Wiltshire.* *Photograph courtesy of* Apollo.

213. A 'China Table' with unusual rustic border, in the *Director* style. *Photograph courtesy of Frank Partridge & Sons Ltd.*

214. A 'China Table' with a crossed stretcher and *Director* motifs. *Photograph courtesy of W. Waddingham Esq.*

215. A walnut 'Sideboard Table' of *Director* design at Wilton House, probably supplied by Chippendale. *The Earl of Pembroke, Wilton House, Wiltshire. Photograph courtesy of* Apollo.

216. A 'Sideboard Table' with inset porphyry top and ormolu border, at Corsham and possibly by Chippendale. *Lord Methuen, Corsham Court, Wiltshire.*

217. A 'Sideboard Table' of Gothic taste based on a *Director* design.
The Victoria and Albert Museum.

218. A 'Sideboard Table' with marble top in the *Director* style.
The Lady Lever Art Gallery, Cheshire.

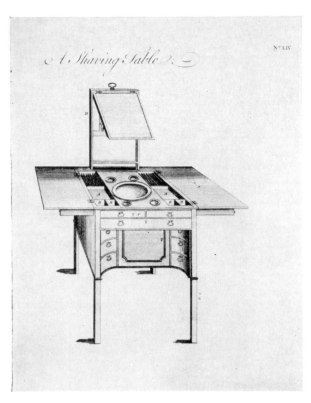

219. Plate 54, right, the third edition of *The Director* (cf. 220).

220. A mahogany shaving-table supplied by Chippendale to Ninian Home at Paxton House in 1774. *Mrs. Home-Robertson, Paxton House, Berwick-on-Tweed.*

221. A shaving-table shown open, also supplied by Chippendale for Paxton House. *Mrs. Home-Robertson, Paxton House, Berwick-on-Tweed.*
Photograph (also 220) courtesy of Apollo.

222. A mahogany 'Bason Stand'
of *Director* design.
The Victoria and Albert Museum.

223. A basin-stand in the
Director tradition.
*Photograph courtesy of
W. Waddingham Esq.*

224. A mahogany 'Teakettle Stand'
of *Director* design.
The Victoria and Albert Museum.

225. A carved mahogany tripod table.
Mrs. David Gubbay.

226. A tea-table with finely carved 'pie-crust' border.
Photograph courtesy of Phillips of Hitchin Ltd.

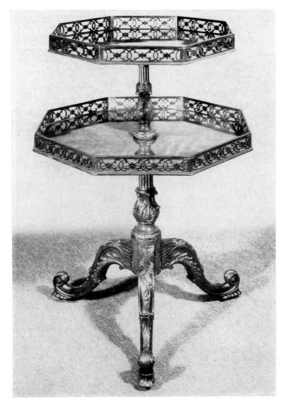

227. A mahogany dumb-waiter, with stand of *Director* form.
Photograph courtesy of Hotspur Ltd.

228. A dumb-waiter with parcel-gilt details, in the *Director* style.
Photograph courtesy of H. Blairman & Sons Ltd.

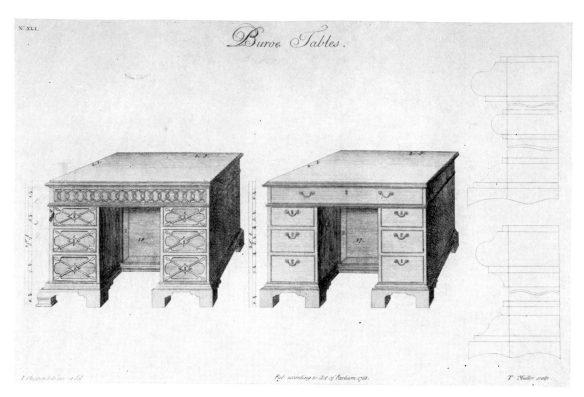

229. Plate 41, the first edition of *The Director* (cf. 230–232).

230. A mahogany 'Buroe Table' bearing the Crewe family crest, from Madeley Manor.
In the collection of the City Art Gallery and Temple Newsam House, Leeds.
Photograph courtesy of W. Waddingham Esq.

231. Another with unusual gilded enrichments. *J. Lyons, Esq.*
Photograph courtesy of H. Blairman & Sons Ltd.

232. Another in the Chinese taste with unusual coved, block-front
pedestals. *Collection of Irwin Untermyer.*

233. Plate 65, the third edition of *The Director* (cf. 234–238).

234. A mahogany commode with ormolu mounts from Norfolk House, London.
Photograph courtesy of Frank Partridge & Sons Ltd.

235. A commode at Nostell Priory, probably supplied by Chippendale to Sir Rowland Winn. *Lord St. Oswald, Nostell Priory, Yorkshire.*

236. A mahogany commode of *Director* design, perhaps made by Chippendale's firm for Captain Townshend of Raynham Hall, Norfolk. *Philadelphia Museum of Art.*

237. A commode similar to that shown in 236. *Trustees of the late A. C. J. Wall, on loan to the City of Birmingham Art Gallery.*

238. A commode of *Director* design, similar to those shown in 236 and 237.
Photograph courtesy of W. Waddingham Esq.

239. A detail of a commode of *Director* design, showing the carved angles with outward scrolled volutes, typical of much of Chippendale's furniture.

240. A mahogany 'Writing Table', or card-table, related to a *Director* pattern.
Photographs courtesy of Hotspur Ltd.

241. A 'Writing Table' of *Director* design, in the Gothic tradition and of serpentine form.
Photograph courtesy of W. Waddingham Esq.

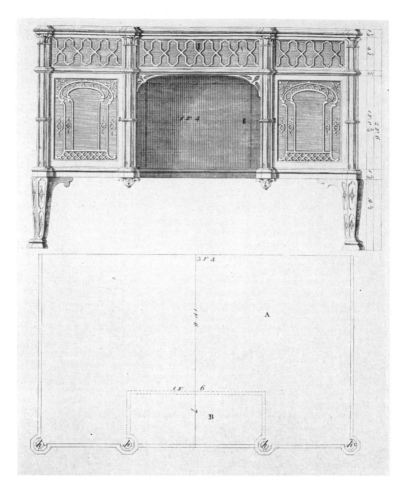

242. Plate 76, the third edition of *The Director* (cf. 243–244).

243. A mahogany 'Writing Table' after the *Director* design shown in 242. *Photograph courtesy of Leonard Knight Ltd.*

244. A mahogany writing-table of similar tradition. *Noel G. Terry Esq.*

245. A mahogany partner's desk of Gothic design, made for 'Single Speech Hamilton'.
In the collection of the City Art Gallery and Temple Newsam House, Leeds.

246. A mahogany pedestal-desk in two sections.
The Earl of Mansfield, Scone Palace, Perthshire.
Photograph courtesy of The Connoisseur.

252. A breakfront bookcase of similar design to that shown in 251.
Photograph courtesy of M. Harris & Son.

253. A breakfront bookcase at Nostell Priory, probably supplied by Chippendale. *Lord St. Oswald, Nostell Priory, Yorkshire.*

254. A bookcase based on the design shown in
255. *The Lady Lever Art Gallery, Cheshire*.

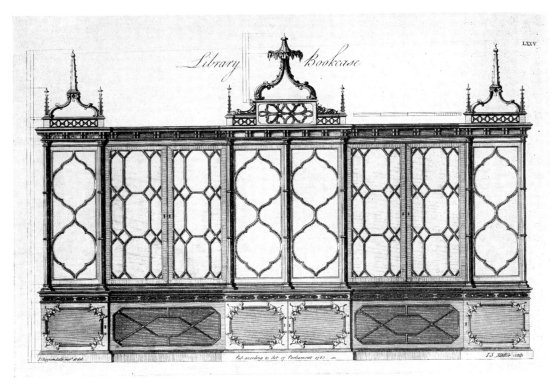

255. Plate 75, the first edition of *The Director*.

281. A set of japanned standing-shelves from Badminton House, thought to have been made by Chippendale's firm.
The Lady Lever Art Gallery.

282. A similar set with a door. *Alice, Countess of Gainsborough, on loan to Leicester Museum.*

283. A japanned set of 'Shelves for China' of *Director* design. *The Viscount Scarsdale, Kedleston Hall, Derbyshire.*

284. A set of mahogany China-shelves,
based on a design in *The Director*.
*Photograph courtesy of
Parke-Bernet Galleries Inc.*

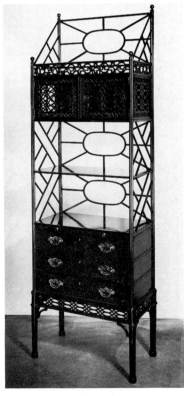

285. A mahogany what-
not with open-fret sides.
*Photograph courtesy of
Hotspur Ltd.*

286. A   what-not   with
drawers below.
*Photograph courtesy of
Phillips of Hitchin Ltd.*

287. *The Director,* 3rd Edit. Pl. 144.

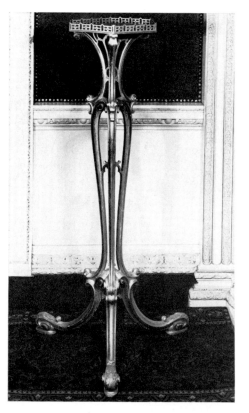

288. A giltwood 'Candle Stand' supplied by Chippendale to the Duke of Atholl in 1758. *The Duke of Atholl, Blair Castle, Perthshire. Photograph courtesy of* The Connoisseur.

289. Another of more elaborate design. *Photograph courtesy of H. Blairman and Sons Ltd.*

290. Another.
Photograph courtesy of A. Cook.

291. A pair of japanned candle-stands.
Photograph courtesy of Mallett & Son Ltd.

292. Another of *Director* design in mahogany.
Photograph courtesy of Hotspur Ltd.

293. Another supplied by Chippendale to Ninian Home in 1774. *Mrs. Home-Robertson, Paxton House, Berwick-on-Tweed.*
Photograph courtesy of Apollo.

294. Another probably supplied by Chippendale for Wilton. *The Earl of Pembroke, Wilton House, Wiltshire.*
Photograph courtesy of Apollo.

295. A giltbronze 'Lanthorn for a Hall or Staircase' of *Director* design. *Philadelphia Museum of Art.*

296. Another in mahogany. *Collection of Irwin Untermyer.*

297. A giltwood chandelier of rococo design. *Philip Blairman Esq.*

298. A giltwood chandelier in the *Director* tradition.
The Metropolitan Museum of Art, Gift of Irwin Untermyer, 1950.

299. A giltwood chandelier at St. Giles's House, Dorset.
Shaftesbury Estates Company.

300. A mahogany tripod 'Fire Screen', associated with a *Director* pattern.
Mrs. David Gubbay.

301. A fire-screen at St. Giles's House, perhaps by Chippendale.
Shaftesbury Estates Company.

302. A fire-screen of *Director* design.
Photograph courtesy of Hotspur Ltd.

303. A giltwood framed 'Horse Fire-Screen' of *Director* design.
The Victoria and Albert Museum.

316. A giltwood 'Pier Glass Frame' based on a *Director* design. *The Hon. Mrs. George Marten, Crichel, Dorset.*

317. A pier-glass at St. Giles's House, Dorset, in the *Director* style. *Shaftesbury Estates Company.*

318. One of a set of four pier-glasses surmounted by a shield with the cross of St. George. *Reproduced by gracious permission of Her Majesty the Queen.*

319. A pier-glass based on a *Director* design (cf. the sheep at the base with 317). *Courtesy Museum of Fine Arts, Boston*

320. A carved oval pier-glass of rococo design, showing the influence of the *Director* style. *Robert Cooke Esq., Athelhampton, Dorset.*

321. A giltwood overmantel glass in the *Director* style.
Photograph courtesy of Mallett & Son Ltd.

322. A giltwood pier-glass in the Kentian style but probably supplied by Chippendale for Wilton House.
The Earl of Pembroke, Wilton House, Wiltshire.
Photograph courtesy of Apollo.

323. An overmantel-glass in the *Director* tradition, from
Stone Easton House, near Bath.
Photograph courtesy of Mallett & Son Ltd.

324. An overmantel in the *Director* Chinese taste.
*Reproduced by gracious permission of
Her Majesty The Queen.*

325. A white marble mantelpiece
inspired by the same source as the
Director design shown in 326.
*Photograph courtesy of
Stanley J. Pratt Ltd.*

326. Plate 184, the third edition of
Director, dated 1761 (cf. 325).

327. A Chinese 'mirror picture' in a giltwood frame of *Director* design. *Sir James Horlick Bt., Isle of Gigha, Argyll.*

328. A Chinese painted looking-glass in a naturalistically carved frame.
Photograph H. Blairman and Sons Ltd.

329. A Chinese painted glass-picture with carved frame. *S. B. Page Esq.*

330. A Chinese painted glass-picture in a giltwood frame in the *Director* idiom. *Sir James Horlick Bt., Isle of Gigha, Argyll.*

331. A Chinese mirror-picture with a frame in the *Director* style. *Sir James Horlick Bt., Isle of Gigha, Argyll.*

332. A japanned commode from the Chinese bedroom at Badminton House, probably supplied by Chippendale.
The Victoria and Albert Museum.

333. A japanned commode, the top drawer fitted as a dressing-table, from Badminton House (see also 332).
Photograph courtesy of Hotspur Ltd.

334. A commode mounted with Chinese lacquer panels.
Photograph courtesy of Mallett & Son Ltd.

335. A commode similar to that shown in 334.
Photograph courtesy of Mallett & Son Ltd.

336. A commode at St. Giles's House, Dorset.
Shaftesbury Estates Company.

337. A commode, from a set of four, at Uppark.
Mrs. R. Meade-Fetherstonhaugh, Uppark, Sussex.
Photograph courtesy of The Connoisseur.

338. A mahogany stool supplied by Chippendale for Christ Church Library, Oxford, in 1764. *Christ Church Library, Oxford. Copyright*, Country Life

339. A mahogany *bonheur-du-jour* from Coombe Abbey, Warwickshire, possibly supplied by Chippendale.
Photograph courtesy of Leonard Knight Ltd.

340. A mahogany desk with filing-cabinet, in the *Director* tradition.
Photograph courtesy of W. Waddingham Esq.

341. A mahogany-framed armchair from a large set of seat furniture at Corsham Court (see also 204). *Lord Methuen, Corsham Court, Wiltshire.*

342. A green japanned bedside-cupboard, probably supplied by Chippendale for Harewood House. *The Earl of Harewood, Harewood House, Yorkshire.*

343. A painted open-armchair in the 'transitional style', at Harewood: probably supplied by Chippendale. *The Earl of Harewood, Harewood House, Yorkshire.*

344. A painted open-armchair, again probably supplied by Chippendale for Harewood House. *The Earl of Harewood, Harewood House, Yorkshire.*

345. A mahogany-framed side-chair probably supplied by Chippendale to Sir Rowland Winn for Nostell Priory. *Lord St. Oswald, Nostell Priory, Yorkshire.*

346. A tulipwood and ebony barometer supplied by Chippendale for Nostell Priory in 1769 for £25 — the movement by Justin Vulliamy. *Lord St. Oswald, Nostell Priory, Yorkshire.*

347. A barometer in a carved mahogany frame : with a movement by John Whitehurst, dated 1760.
Photograph courtesy of Parke-Bernet Galleries Inc.

348. A Toricellian barometer with a carved case in the *Director* style. *The Victoria and Albert Museum.*

349. A green ground japanned dressing-table, probably supplied by
Chippendale for Nostell Priory, about 1770.
Lord St. Oswald, Nostell Priory, Yorkshire.

350. A green japanned commode,
probably supplied by Chippendale for
Nostell Priory. *Lord St. Oswald,
Nostell Priory, Yorkshire.*

351. A green japanned breakfront commode, probably
supplied by Chippendale for Nostell Priory.
Lord St. Oswald, Nostell Priory, Yorkshire.

352. An inlaid commode in the French taste, probably the one supplied by
Chippendale for Nostell Priory in 1770 at a cost of £40.
Lord St. Oswald, Nostell Priory, Yorkshire.

353. A commode at Nostell Priory, perhaps also supplied by Chippendale.
Lord St. Oswald, Nostell Priory, Yorkshire.

354. A tulipwood veneered writing-table with attached firescreen, supplied by Chippendale for Nostell Priory in 1766 for £5 14 0.

355. A mahogany pembroke-table with 'backgammon board' drawer.

356. A mahogany-framed open-armchair of 'transitional form', probably supplied by Chippendale for Nostell Priory.

354, 355, 356. Lord St. Oswald, Nostell Priory, Yorkshire.

357. A portrait of Sir Rowland and Lady Winn standing by 'Chippendale's'
library-table (cf. 249).

358. A carved
giltwood *torchère*
at Nostell Priory
in the neoclassical
style : probably
made by Chippen-
dale's firm.

359. A mahogany side-table probably supplied by Chippendale for
Nostell Priory.

357, 358, 359. Lord St. Oswald, Nostell Priory, Yorkshire.

360. A mahogany 'wall' medal-cabinet supplied by Chippendale to Sir Rowland Winn in 1767 for £38 10 0. *Lord St. Oswald, Nostell Priory, Yorkshire.*

361. A mahogany bedside-commode supplied by Chippendale to Ninian Home for Paxton House in 1774 for £2 12 6.
Mrs. Home-Robertson, Paxton House, Berwick-on-Tweed.
Photograph courtesy of Apollo.

362. A mahogany chest at Paxton House, probably supplied by Chippendale in 1774. *Mrs. Home-Robertson, Paxton House, Berwick-on-Tweed.*
Photograph courtesy of Apollo.

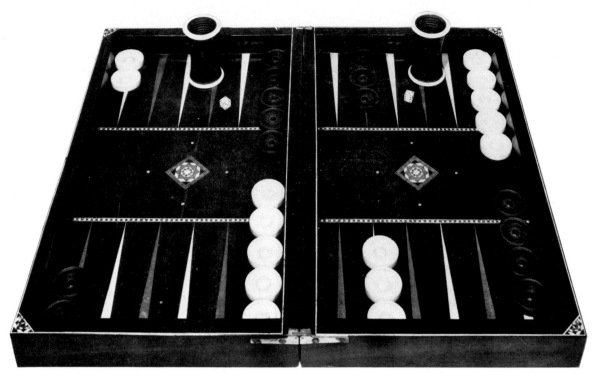

363. A games-box for which Chippendale charged Ninian Home £4 14 6.
Mrs. Home-Robertson, Paxton House, Berwick-on-Tweed.
Photograph courtesy of Apollo.

364. A detail of a mahogany side-table from Raynham Hall, Norfolk, where it is thought that Chippendale was employed.
Robert Cooke Esq., Athelhampton, Dorset.

365. A giltwood pier-table with marble top, perhaps supplied by Chippendale's firm. *Shaftesbury Estates Company, St. Giles's House, Dorset.*

366. One of a set of padouk-wood hall-chairs of *Director* design. *Shaftesbury Estates Company, St. Giles's House, Dorset.*

367. A giltwood chair, part of a suite, made by Chippendale in 1765 to a design of Robert Adam's for Sir Lawrence Dundas. *The Victoria and Albert Museum.*

368. A mahogany table-press at Holkham, perhaps by Benjamin Goodison, 1757.
The Earl of Leicester, Holkham, Norfolk.
Photograph courtesy of the National Buildings Record and Apollo.

369. A detail of the press shown in
368. *The Earl of Leicester, Holkham,*
Norfolk.
Photograph courtesy of the National
Buildings Record and Apollo.

370. A mahogany kneehole writing- or dressing-table perhaps also by Benjamin Goodison (cf. 368). *The Earl of Leicester, Holkham, Norfolk.*
Photograph courtesy of National Buildings Record and Apollo.

371. One of a pair of card-tables at Holkham — Benjamin Goodison charged £12 10 0 for 2 card tables 'for ye Gallery at Holkham' in 1757.
The Earl of Leicester, Holkham, Norfolk.
Photograph courtesy of the National Buildings Record and Apollo.

372. A scarlet and gold japanned side-chair bearing the trade label of Giles Grendey, about 1730. *The Metropolitan Museum of Art. Gift of Louis J. Boury, 1937.*

373. A mahogany clothes-press attributed to Giles Grendey, about 1740. *The Victoria and Albert Museum.*

374. A mahogany bureau-cabinet in the tradition of Giles Grendey, about 1740. *Courtesy Museum of Fine Arts, Boston.*

375. A scarlet and gilt japanned bureau-cabinet, bearing the trade label of Giles Grendey.
The Victoria and Albert Museum.

376. A mahogany framed open-armchair,
attributed to Giles Grendey.
The Earl of Radnor, Longford Castle, Wiltshire.

377. A carved mahogany centre-table, about 1740 — perhaps by Giles
Grendey.
Photograph M. Harris and Sons.

378. A mahogany armchair made by Paul Saunders in 1757 for Holkham. *The Earl of Leicester, Holkham, Norfolk.*

379. A mahogany single-chair probably made by Paul Saunders in 1757 for Holkham. *The Earl of Leicester, Holkham, Norfolk.*
Photographs courtesy of the National Buildings Record and Apollo.

380. A chair from a set of giltwood framed seat-furniture, covered in contemporary velvet, probably supplied by Benjamin Goodison for Holkham. *The Earl of Leicester, Holkham, Norfolk.*
Photograph courtesy of the National Buildings Record.

381. One of a pair of pier-glasses made for the State
Apartments at Holkham by James Whittle.
The Earl of Leicester, Holkham, Norfolk.
Photograph courtesy of the National Buildings Record and
Apollo.

382. Three pier-glasses and console-tables in the Saloon at Holkham, probably by Whittle and Norman. *The Earl of Leicester, Holkham, Norfolk. Photograph courtesy of the National Buildings Record and* Apollo.

383. A mahogany commode of *Director* design, probably supplied by Norman for Aske Hall. *The Marquess of Zetland, Aske, Yorkshire.*
Photograph courtesy of Apollo.

384. A gilt-framed pier-glass, one of a pair, which Samuel Norman delivered to Woburn Abbey in 1760. *His Grace the Duke of Bedford and the trustees, Woburn Abbey, Bedfordshire.*

385. A giltwood framed pier-glass sometimes attributed to Samuel Norman. *The Victoria and Albert Museum.*
Photograph courtesy of Frank Partridge & Sons Ltd.

386. A settee covered in contemporary Gobelins tapestry woven in Neilson's *atelier*, made by Fell and Turton in 1771 for the Tapestry Room at Moor Park, Middlesex. *Philadelphia Museum of Art*.

387. A 'mahogany secretary' supplied to the Princess Royal in 1774 by John Bradburn. *Reproduced by gracious permission of Her Majesty the Queen*.

388. A 'mahogany press for linen' supplied for Buckingham House in 1770 by John Bradburn. *Reproduced by gracious permission of Her Majesty the Queen.*

389. A mahogany cabinet in the same tradition as that shown in 388. *Photograph courtesy of Norman Adams Ltd.*

390. A mahogany chair supplied to John Chute
for The Vyne, by France and Bradburn, 1765–7.
The National Trust, The Vyne, Hampshire.

391. One of a pair of side-tables supplied by France and Bradburn
to The Vyne, 1765–7. *The National Trust, The Vyne, Hampshire.*

392. A large mahogany reading-stand supplied by William France's
firm to the Earl of Mansfield at Kenwood in 1770.
The Victoria and Albert Museum.

393. A giltwood console-table supplied by France and Bradburn to Sir Lawrence Dundas
in 1765, after a design by Robert Adam. *Formerly the Marquess of Zetland.*
Photograph courtesy of Christie, Manson and Woods Ltd.

394. A mahogany breakfront bookcase by Gillow's of Lancaster.
The Hon. L. H. Clifford, Ugbrooke Park, Devon.

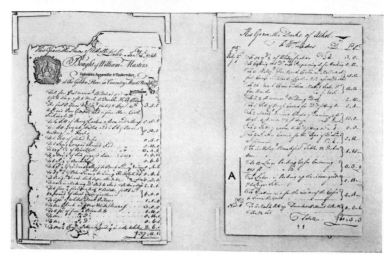

395. One of William Masters' accounts for furniture
delivered to Blair Castle.
The Duke of Atholl, Blair Castle, Perthshire.
Photograph courtesy of The Connoisseur.

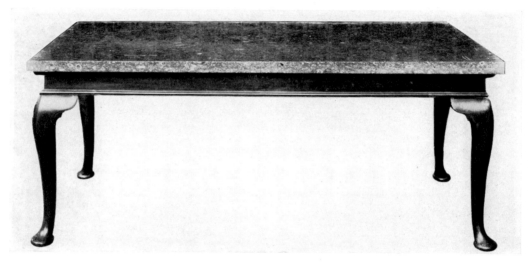

396. A mahogany hall table by William Masters, 1749.
The Duke of Atholl, Blair Castle, Perthshire.
Photograph courtesy of The Connoisseur.

397. One of twelve
oak hall-chairs by
William Masters,
1751. *The Duke of
Atholl, Blair Castle,
Perthshire.*
Photograph courtesy of
The Connoisseur.

398. A mahogany tea-table supplied by William Masters in 1755. *The Duke of Atholl, Blair Castle, Perthshire.*

399. A pair of mahogany *torchères* by William Masters, 1756. *The Duke of Atholl, Blair Castle, Perthshire.*

400. One of a pair of mahogany dumb-waiters supplied by William Masters in 1753. *The Duke of Atholl, Blair Castle, Perthshire.*

Photographs courtesy of The Connoisseur.

401. A mahogany side-table by William Masters, 1753. *The Duke of Atholl, Blair Castle, Perthshire.*
Photograph courtesy of The Connoisseur.

402. One of a set of four mahogany chests, probably by William Masters, 1756. *The Duke of Atholl, Blair Castle, Perthshire.*
Photograph courtesy of The Connoisseur.

403. A portrait of George
Sandeman of Perth, cabinet-
maker, 1724–1803.
*Photograph courtesy of
Robert Waterston, Esq.*

404. A bureau-bookcase veneered with broomwood,
supplied by George Sandeman to Blair Castle in 1758.
The Duke of Atholl, Blair Castle, Perthshire.
Photograph courtesy of The Connoisseur.

405. An interior of 404 above showing a 'secret' built-in medal-cabinet.
The Duke of Atholl, Blair Castle, Perthshire.
Photograph courtesy of The Connoisseur.

406. A medal-cabinet of broomwood fashioned as a temple, here attributed to George Sandeman. *The Duke of Atholl, Blair Castle, Perthshire.*
Photograph courtesy of The Connoisseur.

407. One of a pair of giltwood-framed girandoles at Hopetoun House, probably supplied in 1755 by James Cullen for 'The New Dining Room'. *The Marquess of Linlithgow, Hopetoun House, West Lothian.*

408. A detail of one of the pair of pier-tables, now standing below the girondoles (shown in 407).
The Marquess of Linlithgow, Hopetoun House, West Lothian.
Photographs courtesy of The Connoisseur.

409. One of a pair of mahogany framed sofas, probably supplied by Cullen for the Red Drawing Room. *The Marquess of Linlithgow, Hopetoun House, West Lothian. Photograph courtesy of* The Connoisseur.

410. An armchair and a single chair from the same large set of seat furniture (as the sofa in 409). *The Marquess of Linlithgow, Hopetoun House, West Lothian. Photograph courtesy of* The Connoisseur.

411. One of a set of four pier-glasses which were probably
provided by Cullen in 1766, after being designed by Matthias
Lock and carved and gilded by Samuel Norman.
The Marquess of Linlithgow, Hopetoun House, West Lothian.
Photograph courtesy of The Connoisseur.

412. One of a set of four console-tables which may have been originally provided by Cullen for the pier-glasses above.
The Marquess of Linlithgow, Hopetoun House, West Lothian.
Photograph courtesy of The Connoisseur.

413. The State Bedstead which Cullen purchased for the Earl of Hopetoun through Samuel Norman in 1768 for £230. *The Marquess of Linlithgow, Hopetoun House, West Lothian.*
Photograph courtesy of The Connoisseur.

414. A detail of the bedstead showing the headboard, dome and the original hangings. *The Marquess of Linlithgow, Hopetoun House, West Lothian.*
Photograph courtesy of
The Connoisseur.

415. One of two designs for a pair of commodes sent by James Cullen to the Earl in 1768 — the other design, which was probably returned to Cullen, was in fact chosen. *The Marquess of Linlithgow, Hopetoun House, West Lothian. Photograph courtesy of* The Connoisseur.

416. One of a most unusual pair of commodes supplied by Cullen in 1768 — cf. the design above. *The Marquess of Linlithgow, Hopetoun House, West Lothian. Photograph courtesy of* The Connoisseur.

417. A design for an unusual
pier-glass dated 1767 — prob-
ably sent to the Earl of
Hopetoun by Cullen.
*The Marquess of Linlithgow,
Hopetoun House, West Lothian.
Photograph courtesy of*
The Connoisseur.

418. An impressive pier-glass at Hopetoun
House. The plates of mirror glass in the
borders are engraved.
*The Marquess of Linlithgow, Hopetoun House,
West Lothian.
Photograph courtesy of* The Connoisseur.

419. A pier-glass at Hopetoun House, the giltwood frame carved with
dolphins and entwined serpents.
The Marquess of Linlithgow, Hopetoun House, West Lothian.
Photograph courtesy of The Connoisseur.

420. A part gilt 'pagoda cabinet' based on *Director* designs.
Photograph courtesy of Messrs. Mallett and Son Ltd.